Is America Safe?

Terrorism, Homeland Security, and Emergency Preparedness

Revised Edition

Robert T. Jordan and Don Philpott

GOVERNMENT INSTITUTES
An imprint of
THE SCARECROW PRESS, INC.
Lanham • Toronto • Plymouth, UK
2010

 **Government Institutes**

Published by Government Institutes
An imprint of The Scarecrow Press, Inc.
A wholly owned subsidary of The Rowman & Littlefield Publishing Group, Inc.
4501 Forbes Boulevard, Suite 200, Lanham, Maryland 20706
http://www.govinstpress.com

Estover Road, Plymouth PL6 7PY, United Kingdom

British Library Cataloguing in Publication Information Available

Library of Congress Cataloging-in-Publication Data

Jordan, Robert T.
   Is America safe? : terrorism, homeland security, and emergency preparedness / Robert T. Jordan and Don Philpott. — Rev. ed.
      p.   cm.
   Includes bibliographical references and index.
   ISBN 978-1-60590-649-2 (hardcover : alk. paper) — ISBN 978-1-60590-650-8 (pbk. : alk. paper) — ISBN 978-1-60590-651-5 (electronic)
   1. Terrorism—Government policy—United States. 2. Terrorism—United States—Prevention. 3. National security—United States. 4. Emergency management—United States. 5. United States—Politics and government. I. Philpott, Don, 1946– II. Title.
   HV6432.J67 2010
   363.325'15610973—dc22

                                                                2009029716

∞ ™ The paper used in this publication meets the minimum requirements of American National Standard for Information Sciences—Permanence of Paper for Printed Library Materials, ANSI/NISO Z39.48-1992.

Printed in the United States of America

Contents

Foreword

Is America Safe? is a much-needed, one-stop-shop "educational handbook" on what the average citizen should know and can do both in preparing for and responding to a terrorist attack on U.S. soil—an attack that most government officials who work in this field feel is inevitable.

Where and when the next attack will take place cannot be predicted; however, the facts are that the chances of a future terrorist attack are high and that a prime goal of most of these attacks is high civilian mortality rates. These facts obligate all of us to learn more about what actions we can take to help prevent, protect, or mitigate any such attempts.

Americans are, by nature, fighters when it comes to the endangering of our civil liberties. Americans are also aggressive. Sitting back and doing nothing, while terrorist organizations plot and attempt different ways to harm us, is not in our psyche.

Predictions of a hundred thousand or more innocent civilian casualties, particularly when they might include our own family and loved ones, is a silent call to arms and reason enough to do all we can to fight back. *Is America Safe?* mentally equips us with those skills.

The best way to prepare and to fight back is to first understand who the enemy is. This book provides the reader with well-researched and well-documented background and detail on terrorist organizations. It starts with defining terrorism and its origins and then goes on to describe present-day organizations, where they operate from, what their philosophies entail, and what their motivations and objectives are. It then addresses different terrorist tactics and techniques that are being contemplated and their desired effects, including individual descriptions of their destructive capabilities. A sampling of the book's extensive list includes terrorist weaponization of chemical, biological, and nuclear agents. Knowing how to prepare for

San Miguel, California, January 25, 2004. Damage to the historic Mission San Miguel was exacerbated by the 6.5 San Simeon Earthquake. Dane Golden/FEMA News Photo

and how to survive during any of these attacks is a big step toward marginalizing their intended high casualty rates, psychological impact, and propaganda value. The added value is that these same lifesaving skills may also be used in naturally occurring catastrophic events such as hurricanes, tornadoes, floods, or earthquakes.

Is America Safe? empowers the average citizen with the knowledge and skills to understand terrorist strategies—which, in turn, allows each of us to contribute to disrupting the terrorists' intended goals through observing and reporting suspicious activity, reducing target vulnerabilities, and minimizing casualties through education and preparation. The better the chances we have to reduce the effects of an attack, the better the chances we have to minimize the importance of the event, thereby denying terrorists the propaganda value they seek from surprise, shock, and fear on an unprepared and panicky public. Prevention and preparedness are also in step with and a part of our national strategy.

Although not a terrorist attack, the aftermath of Hurricane Katrina was a prime example of lack of preparation and response and an unrealistic expectation and reliance on outside authorities during the first twenty-four to forty-eight hours of a disaster. If any lesson is to be learned from Katrina, it is that the average citizen and local governments have to become more self-reliant. *You and I have to make plans that will allow us to help ourselves.*

Is America Safe? is intended to help us help ourselves. It is intended to reduce some of our fear by educating us and providing us with the confidence that comes with not feeling powerless. In essence, it gives us all a chance to do our part—not only to protect ourselves and our families, but also to fight back by denying the enemy any chance of even partial success.

The Department of Homeland Security is spending considerable amounts of money and time trying to educate the public on basic survival skills. A primary concern is that certain public communications systems may be temporarily out of order. Therefore public messaging, particularly on educating the public as to what type of method was used and how it acts, as well as what personal measures should be initiated to reduce casualties, may not get through to all of those in the impact area(s). Simple precautions and a little knowledge may be the difference between survival and death to large numbers of unsuspecting individuals, particularly in scenarios involving weapons of mass destruction—the terrorists' preferred method of attack.

Understanding the enemy, reporting suspicious activity, reducing vulnerabilities, knowing how to survive, and initiating preparatory actions are ways for each individual American to do his or her part in helping to win the war on terrorism.

Brigadier General Matthew E. Broderick, U.S. Marine Corps (retired)
Vice President for DHS and DoD, Abraxas Corporation
Former Director of Operations for Homeland Security

Introduction

We hold these truths to be self-evident, that all men are created equal, that they are endowed by their Creator with certain unalienable rights, that among these are life, liberty, and the pursuit of happiness. That to secure these rights, governments are instituted among men, deriving their just powers from the consent of the governed, that whenever any form of government becomes destructive to these ends, it is the right of the people to alter or to abolish it, and to institute new government, laying its foundation on such principles and organizing its powers in such form, as to them shall seem most likely to effect their safety and happiness.

—Thomas Jefferson, Declaration of Independence

Terror may strike anywhere . . . anytime . . . anyone.

When terror strikes, it is indifferent to who its victims may be.

Terrorists come in all ages, all religious persuasions, both sexes, all races, and all nationalities.

Terrorists' goals include intimidation, subjugation, and elimination of anyone who opposes their particular view of the world.

Terrorists' strategies include murder and mayhem, attacking our core values, and destroying our economy.

TERROR RETURNED TO PARADISE
THE EVENING OF OCTOBER 1, 2005

Amateur video captured a vision of one suspected bomber as he calmly sauntered through a crowded restaurant jammed with unsuspecting international tourists. About 8 p.m., explosions rocked a pair of popular steak and noodle restaurants, killing two dozen tourists and seriously wounding over a hundred others. Among the wounded were two Americans. The horror and carnage repeated scenes only days short of the third anniversary and only a short distance away from the Bali Marriott, where more than two hundred innocent souls were killed on October 12, 2002.

Indonesian and Western intelligence agencies warned repeatedly that they suspected Jemaah Islamiya of plotting more attacks despite a string of arrests. In August, President Susilo Bambang Yudhoyono had warned that he was especially worried the extremist network was about to strike.

Two fanatics chose to sacrifice their lives in order to kill, maim, intimidate, and horrify scores of innocent civilians whose only crime was coming from a different culture and not subscribing to the religious dictates of their assailants.

A few tourists raced to the airport to escape from Bali as fast as they could. Interestingly, a majority chose to remain, declaring that to leave would give the terrorists the victory that they wanted. They made a choice not to be intimidated—to accept the risk of repeated attacks, to sacrifice their personal safety and security for a principle.

Are you willing to sacrifice your freedoms for personal safety?

TERROR FROM THE SEA

Terror once more played out for the world to see on the evening of November 26, 2008, in India's centuries-old financial and entertainment capital, Mumbai. The city's luxury hotels and financial institutions stand in stark contrast to the poor slums and the poverty-afflicted citizens who subsist within them.

Business travelers and tourists strolled leisurely along the streets, taking in the cool air following dinner at the luxurious 565-room Taj Mahal Palace and Tower around 9 p.m.—oblivious of the horrendous scenes that would soon explode on television screens around the globe. Offshore, ten determined fanatics approached from the Arabian Sea in rubber boats, heavily armed with AK-47 automatic rifles and carrying backpacks stuffed with ammunition and explosives.

The terrorists' goal, according to the lone survivor, 21-year-old Azam Amir Kasab, was to kill five thousand people. He was quoted as saying that he was ordered to keep killing until he breathed his last breath. The group's target, according to U.K.'s *Daily Mail*, was mostly "whites, preferably Americans and British." In reality, the target was opulence, decadence, and luxury—which is why the primary target was the 105-year-old Taj hotel and its guests.

The two-man killing teams arrived on shore at 9:15 p.m. and then spread out to their assigned targets to launch their terror. Among the first to die were American Alan Scherr and his thirteen-year-old daughter, Naomi, from Faber, Virginia; they were shot while eating a snack at the Oberoi Hotel café before going to bed. Others would die at a nearby Jewish center and in the Chatrapathi Sivaji Terminal railway station.

How Could This Happen?

Investigators believe that the killing teams visited the area in 2007, posing as students. They reconnoitered their chosen targets and obtained layouts of the buildings. They even planned which rooms they would use for command and control of their bloody operations. Despite warnings of a possible attack days before, the Taj management said they doubted that they could have foiled the attack with the preparations they had had in place, but removed just a day before. The terrorists knew the hotel so well that they avoided the most likely entrances, choosing instead to enter through the back of the hotel. Once inside, they began to slaughter hotel guests and staff without mercy.

Could this scenario play out in New York City, Miami Beach, New Orleans, Galveston, San Francisco, Los Angeles, or Seattle?

One observer characterized the attackers as "mere boys." Another commented that they looked like they should be in college somewhere. But what they were was highly trained and determined young men on a mission to inflame the world—and they were so passionate about their cause that they were willing to die in accomplishing their mission.

The terrorist slaughter lasted for three days, claiming 166 victims. The U.S. State Department confirmed that six Americans died in the attacks and two others were wounded. Many others survived because they took the initiative to lock their doors and barricade themselves in their rooms or took evasive action to remove themselves from where the attacks were taking place.

What would your choice be in similar circumstances?

Do you feel safe?

How secure do you feel your family is today as we face attacks from international terrorists, carjackings and home invasions in our cities, and natural disasters of historical proportions wherever you look? Do you feel in control? Or do you feel helpless and unable to protect yourself or your loved ones? Are you among those who feel that it is the federal government's primary responsibility to ensure your safety and security? Or do you feel that there are times when you would forgo safety and security for the sake of freedom and liberty?

What were our founding fathers' intentions when they included the terms "safety and happiness" in the Declaration of Independence? Old Ben Franklin said, "The Constitution only guarantees the American people the right to pursue happiness. You have to catch it yourself."

It was also Franklin who insisted, "They that can give up essential liberty to obtain a little temporary safety deserve neither liberty nor safety." And yet we hear a loud vocal minority asking us to do just that in every generation, without regard to the ultimate cost.

To many of us, safety and security are interchangeable terms. And that's true to some degree. However, for our purposes in this book, we'd like you to think of safety in more personal terms, and security in terms of community and national interests.

Think about it. You can control much of what goes on in your own life: whether or not to smoke, whether or not to overindulge in food or alcohol, whether to swim in unknown waters or to take your family only to a guarded and protected beach. All of these things have to do with your own and your family's personal safety and health—and for the most part are within your personal choice and within your own control. But what about natural disasters like Hurricane Katrina, or terrorist acts such as the Beslan School massacre in Russia? What can you do about those if they threaten your neighborhood?

Regardless of what you think, *you have the power* to enhance our security by discouraging potential terrorist attacks and by mitigating the terrible effects inflicted on our communities by catastrophic natural or man-made disasters. Think about it—can you ever be truly "safe" if your nation or your community is at risk?

This book is dedicated to protecting Americans and securing our homeland. But we need your help.

IRRATIONAL FEAR . . . OR INFORMED DECISIONS?

Ignorance, prejudice, unfounded fear, and apathy compromise both our safety and our security. Each of us needs to be fully informed as to what threats we face, become engaged in educating and helping others, and become actively involved in viable solutions rather than being part of the problem.

For example, David Meyers pointed out in an article for the American Psychological Society *Observer* that many people refused to fly in commercial aircraft following the September 11 terrorist attacks in New York City, Pennsylvania, and Washington, D.C. In fact, so many people canceled flights that airlines, travel agencies, and hotels suffered economic losses for months to come. You and I became unsuspecting terrorist victims because of other people's fears and the negative economic fallout. As Meyers explained:

Indeed, the terrorists may still be killing us, in ways unnoticed. If we now fly 20 percent less and instead drive half those unflown miles, we will spend 2 percent more time in motor vehicles. This translates into 800 more people dying as passengers and pedestrians. So, in just the next year the terrorists may indirectly kill three times more people on our highways than died on those four fated planes.

Thus, irrational fear and ignorance sometimes kill more people than do bullets and bombs.

> Christopher Robin says to Pooh, "Promise me that you'll always remember: You're braver than you believe . . . and stronger than you seem . . . and smarter than you think."
>
> —A. A. Milne

Terrorists count on horror to intimidate their victims to the point that they become frozen by fear, immobilized like trapped animals incapable of response. As philosopher Edmund Burke said, "All that is necessary for evil to succeed is for good men to do nothing." Fortunately, that is not our history. We are a blend of the sons and daughters of the world of nations—stepbrothers and stepsisters, if you will—many of whom fled tyranny and share a common bond of loving freedom and liberty.

That doesn't mean, however, that all Americans understand the threats to our way of life, nor does it mean that all our citizens are motivated by "brotherly love" to assist one another in times of crisis. Attacks at home and abroad accentuate the sad fact that homegrown "domestic terrorists" may be of more concern than those who attack us from abroad—and reports of a few New Orleans policemen taking advantage of their fellow citizens by shoplifting and looting during recent hurricanes unfairly blacken the reputation of those gallant souls who continued to "protect and serve" despite the tragedies and hardships imposed by nature upon their own families and loved ones.

WHO SHOULD READ THIS BOOK?

Every taxpaying citizen should read this book. In 2006 the combined budgets for the Department of Defense, Homeland Security, and Veterans Affairs was $601 billion, of which over $200 billion was used to support the war on terror. The combined estimated budget for 2009 is $745 billion, and this figure is expected to rise again in 2010 to around $762 billion.

The cost for the post-Katrina cleanup and rebuilding bill for Louisiana, Mississippi, and Alabama—latest estimate $125 billion—by far exceeded the $70 billion spent to recover from the terrorist attacks of September 11, 2001.

Add to that another $11 billion for Hurricane Rita, which slammed into the Gulf Coast less than four weeks after Katrina, and you have the makings of a serious "beans or bullets" debate shaping up. Will you choose to (1) continue supporting the war on terror; (2) demand that more resources be devoted to domestic issues and infrastructure; or (3) insist that we "cut the political pork," tighten our belts, and try to do both?

Scholars are invited to use this book. We invite you to use it to spark debate, to enhance understanding of the choices that Americans face, and to act as background and a resource for serious students of the history and impact of terror upon international dynamics.

Similarly, we urge professional and volunteer first responders to read this book. It's important to note that experience shows that 95 percent of all first responders are either bystanders or the victims themselves. Unfortunately, many of these individuals have minimal to no training, and even fewer understand the nature of the danger that they face. We hope you'll find *Is America Safe?* not only a source of valuable information, but also an asset in determining what priorities you need to set within your scope of influence or service.

Once you've read it, put it in your library for future reference, and then send copies to others who you feel would benefit from what you've learned. We need you to volunteer to enlist in your local Neighborhood Watch. Then we need you to elevate your neighborhood's awareness to a point that no terrorist may operate there without raising suspicion. We need you to join your fellow Americans to win the war on terror.

I'm not afraid of storms, for I'm learning how to sail my ship.

—Louisa May Alcott

APPLYING LESSONS LEARNED

The sad story about Hurricane Katrina is that much of the tragedy was avoidable. Lessons learned from previous killer hurricanes and from a computer-generated training exercise, called Pam, offered New Orleans years of lead time to prepare for the worst.

In the aftermath, it is now apparent that the majority of the responsibility for failing to implement those lessons lay at the feet of New Orleans city and Louisiana state officials. But their lapses in planning and judgment also highlighted weaknesses in Homeland Security and identified a need for greater federal involvement much earlier in the planning and preparation phase whenever Level 3 through Level 5 hurricanes threaten heavily populated areas such as the Gulf Coast. But the biggest lesson of all is that you must never expect your government to provide your every need, nor to keep you safe and secure in every circumstance.

Unfortunately, one wonders if we are applying lessons learned in the wake of 9/11 any more effectively than we have applied the lessons drawn from these recent natural disasters. Of course, you probably don't work in a 110-story building like the World Trade Center. But what would you do differently today if you did?

- Do you work in a "lucrative target" for foreign or domestic terrorists? If not, is your workplace or home in close proximity to a prospective target?
- Do you understand what motivates terrorists to attack innocent civilians?
- What would you do if tomorrow you found yourself a hostage aboard a commercial aircraft?
- How would you react if terrorists stormed into the local school your children attend and threatened to blow it up if their terms weren't met?
- If you heard that a terrorist detonated a "dirty bomb" in an area of town where your family lives, would you know what to do?
- Do you have a plan for your family to survive destructive weather events?
- How should you go about assessing the natural and man-made dangers around you?
- What can you do to protect yourself, your family, or your business from terrorist attacks or natural disasters?
- What are the most likely types of weapons of mass destruction (WMDs) that a terrorist might use?

INFORMATION IS POWER

The goal of this book is to help you answer these and other questions and equip you to make intelligent decisions about how best to keep your loved ones, yourself, and your neighbors safe and secure.

Here's what we hope you'll understand once you complete reading *Is America Safe?*

- Terror in America is not a new phenomenon. Our forefathers endured it and, in some cases, perpetuated it. But terror's history is one of being ineffective except in the short term.
- Various forms of domestic terrorism continue to plague us even today, and no doubt will continue to frustrate us for years to come.
- International terrorism, once practiced by weak states against stronger states, is now "asymmetric"—transnational by design. No nation is immune.

- Our homeland is under constant threat. The fact that we have not been struck since 9/11 is a combination of preemptive strikes overseas, extra measures of diligence at home, and a whole lot of good luck.
- As potential targets such as military facilities, symbols of democracy, government buildings, and infrastructure are "hardened," terrorists will shift to softer targets such as churches, schools, malls, mass entertainment centers, high-rise apartments, transportation centers, and energy facilities. Their goal will be to disrupt or destroy our economy, impose fear and uncertainty, break our national will, and deflect our attention and support from the Middle East.
- Safety and security are nebulous concepts requiring eternal vigilance, intuitive thinking, intelligent planning, and personal involvement at every level.

It is not the intent of this book to exaggerate the threats to your safety and security. It is, rather, to equip our readers with information that empowers them not to overreact. Our hope is that you'll use this book as a resource to intelligently put things in proper perspective, so you and your loved ones may fully enjoy your birthright as Americans to pursue "safety and happiness," as is promised in the Declaration of Independence.

For example, in September 2005, Alan C. McMillan, secretariat of the Seventeenth World Congress and president and CEO of the National Safety Council, closed the World Congress in Orlando, Florida, with a vision statement: "Prevention: Today's Value for Tomorrow's World." McMillan pointed out that each year, an estimated 270 million occupational accidents and 160 million work-related illnesses are reported throughout the world. McMillan told an audience of more than three thousand attendees, from more than one hundred countries and six continents, that in many developing nations, occupational safety remains a largely reactive approach to injuries and illnesses sustained in the workplace:

> We heard throughout the week's sessions that making the world of work safer and healthier is as simple and as profoundly complex as these three things: securing top management's commitment to safety and health; involving employees in developing a safety culture; and integrating safety and health fully into normal business planning and operations.

A U.S. Bureau of Labor Statistics census found that a total of 5,488 fatal work injuries were recorded in the United States in 2007—a slight decrease over the number of fatal work injuries reported for 2006. The rate at which fatal work injuries occurred in 2007 was 3.7 per 100,000 workers, the lowest rate reported since the census started keeping these statistics in 1992. How-

Earthquakes strike suddenly and cause instant panic and confusion.

ever, the number of fatal falls was the highest ever recorded, and workplace homicides rose 13 percent in 2007 over 2006.

Anywhere you live is subject to some natural disaster, such as wildfires, earthquakes, and mudslides on the West Coast; tornadoes and flooding almost anywhere; and hurricanes along our coastal areas.

In 2002, Dr. Barbara Starfield of the Johns Hopkins School of Hygiene and Public Health reported that doctors' errors cause about 250,000 deaths per year, thus being the third-largest cause of death in the United States, following heart disease and cancer. Shockingly, a newer study now shows that figure rising to 783,936 at an annual cost of $282 billion, making medical errors the leading cause of death in America—and that figure could possibly soar to over 1 million!

Put that into perspective with the U.S. State Department's report that there were about 14,499 acts of international terrorism in 2007, which claimed 22,685 lives. There were 6,212 terrorist attacks in Iraq—up from 3,469 in 2005 but lower than in 2006, when 6,628 attacks were reported—and 1,127 attacks in Afghanistan—up from 491 in 2005 and 970 in 2006. Attacks in Iraq accounted for 43 percent of all attacks worldwide and 60 percent of fatalities.

As was the case in 2006, most 2007 attacks were perpetrated by terrorists applying conventional fighting methods such as bombs and weapons, including small arms. However, technology continues to empower terrorists, and effective methods of attack are offsetting countermeasures against terrorism. Terrorists continued their practice of coordinated attacks, including secondary attacks on first responders at attack sites with uniquely configured weapons and other materials to create improvised explosive devices (IEDs), including the introduction of chemical IEDs in 2007.

The State Department's report confirmed what analysts have been saying for months—that al-Qaeda as a worldwide network is getting weaker but the threat remains from small, loosely affiliated groups.

> This trend means there could be a larger number of smaller attacks, less meticulously planned, and local rather than transnational in scope. [As a result,] there should be stepped up global and regional cooperation to combat the increasing use by terrorists of the Internet and satellite communications for recruitment, training, intelligence and resource sharing.

However, these are exceptional times. In 2002, there were only 205 reported acts of terrorism worldwide, which claimed 725 lives. In 2003, 625 people were killed and 3,646 were wounded, a sharp increase from 2,013 wounded the year before. This increase reflected the numerous indiscriminate attacks on "soft targets," such as places of worship, hotels, and commercial districts, intended to produce mass casualties. But only 35 U.S. citizens died in international terrorist attacks in 2003. There has been a steady escalation in attacks and deaths each year since.

Though any death is regrettable, it's obvious that most of us have more to fear from our workplaces, our doctors, our homes, and natural disasters than we do from terrorists who are upset with our lifestyle. However, we must remain always mindful of the nearly three thousand souls killed and six thousand injured on September 11, 2001—and that in the space of only a few hours.

You should be aware that terrorists are patient. They don't operate on a predictable timeline. The attack in Bali on October 1, 2005, came within less than two weeks of the third anniversary of the day that terrorists struck near that same site. Witness, however, that it was nine years between the first bombing of the World Trade Center in 1993 and the devastating aerial attack that brought the Twin Towers down on September 11, 2001. Much planning and preparation went into those intervening years—with horrific results!

Knowledge will help you assess the level of risk that you may face. Awareness will minimize terrorists' ability to act. Involvement will ensure that we maximize our potential to protect those we love and to preserve the freedom that we enjoy. Smart choices will mitigate the potential damage that a terrorist attack may generate.

Part I

TERRORISM TODAY

Chapter One

Twenty-First-Century Threats to the Homeland

The number one threat to American national security during this long war is neither anthrax nor truck bombs . . . it is uncontrolled spending. We cannot afford to put guards on every bridge and at every critical node of our infrastructure. The outcome of this war will determine the type of nation our grandchild will know. I do not want that to be a nation that is bankrupt.

—Randall Larsen, Director, ANSER Institute for Homeland Security

The history of the United States is replete with examples of our citizens overcoming enormous challenges to form our democracy from the crucibles of conquest, exploitation, internal and external strife, pandemic disease, and global war.

Though we have emerged as one of the most powerful democracies the world has known, it was not without sacrifice. America has never been "safe," it is not presently safe, and the odds are that it will never be safe. But that doesn't mean that we need to live in constant fear. It means that we do need to be aware of what threats we face and make informed decisions as to how we as a nation, as communities, and as individuals respond to those threats.

What are your worst fears about your future?

Is it another 9/11 attack?

Is it being caught in an underwater tunnel when a terrorist explodes a truck bomb inside?

Is it being taken hostage at a large entertainment event?

What about your family and your children? Do you fear that terrorists will attack your children's school? Are you afraid that your home will be invaded and your loved ones threatened or killed?

Is it possible that you or your family will suffer from some natural or man-made disaster? Or . . . have you ever considered what you would do if the U.S. economy should be seriously affected by man-made or natural disasters?

You should be concerned about these and a myriad of other security and safety concerns. But you would do well to put them into a rational perspective. Some things you can control, others you can avoid, minimize, or mitigate—but there are some things over which you have little or no control. You also need to determine how likely certain things are to be a threat to you and which things should be of little concern.

Is America Safe? will help you to sort through the threats to the homeland that you and your family may face and then assist you in developing a plan to eliminate or minimize your exposure.

The federal government recognizes that the Constitution requires it to "provide for the common defense" and to "repel invasions." Many would interpret those requirements to justify homeland security and related counterterrorism activities as inherently governmental obligations. However, they point out that the vast majority of the targets that require protection are those owned by the private sector—information systems, port facilities, railroads, airports, ground transportation systems, and critical infrastructure such as water and power sources. This amplifies the need for a coalition to be formed among industry, the private sector, and government to address overarching homeland security issues.

How do you see your role in defending against terrorist threats or preparing for natural disasters?

The Department of Homeland Security (DHS) incorporates several initiatives in its strategic planning that we, as individuals should also use:

1. *Awareness.* Identify and understand threats, assess vulnerabilities, determine potential impacts, and disseminate timely information to our community leaders, to law enforcement, to our neighbors, and to our families.
2. *Prevention.* Detect, deter, and mitigate threats to our nation, our community, our family, and ourselves.
3. *Protection.* Safeguard our fellow citizens and their freedoms, and defend our critical infrastructure, our public and private property, and the economy of our nation from acts of terrorism, natural disasters, or other threats.
4. *Response.* Work with our community leaders, first responders, law enforcement, volunteer agencies, our churches, our schools, and each other to learn how to properly prepare for and respond to acts of terrorism, natural disasters, or other emergencies.

5. *Recovery.* Support national, state, local, and private sector efforts to restore services and rebuild our communities after acts of terrorism, natural disasters, or other emergencies.

VULNERABILITY AUDIT

The first step to prepare your defense against attack, injury, or disease is to enhance your *awareness* of potential threats. That's what this book is all about. It's impossible to defend yourself against anything until you know:

- The nature of the threat
- The probability that the threat may be directed toward you, your family, your community, or your nation
- The means at your disposal to address the threat to either avoid it, mitigate it, or defend against it

President George W. Bush succinctly defined the individual's role in homeland security when he said:

> Defending our nation against its enemies is the first and fundamental commitment of the federal government. Today, that task has changed dramatically. Enemies in the past needed great armies and great industrial capabilities to endanger America. *Now, shadowy networks of individuals can bring great chaos and suffering to our shores for less than it costs to purchase a single tank.*

It will also be individual citizens' collective awareness of and response to these threats that will ultimately defeat the asymmetrical threat from global terrorism. Each and every one of us has a role to play in combating terror; in responding to human needs in the aftermath of disaster; and in recovering from adversity, destruction, and disease.

HOW DO OTHERS RESPOND?

During our travels around the globe, one human characteristic stands out: *resiliency.* Whether innocent victims of war in Vietnam, terror in Beirut or Iraq and Afghanistan, or tsunamis in Southeast Asia, the human instinct to survive is amazing.

In 1968, I (RTJ) recall seeing a little Vietnamese girl who looked to be about eight or nine years of age who was terrified as the night sky lit up with explosions of artillery barrages raining down on her little village as our Marine column drove forward to force North Vietnamese army regulars entrenched within to surrender, withdraw, or be killed. Tears streamed down her cherubic face as she watched her father, a suspected Viet Cong guerrilla, being interrogated. It was obvious that she was traumatized, yet the next day, after the Marines had driven the enemy soldiers out and set up a perimeter defense, there she was—prancing up the hill to our command post offering the Marines ice-cold Coca-Colas for a dollar each.

Beirut, Lebanon, was little different in 1983, as various militias contested with each other and constant artillery barrages and .50 caliber machine-gun fire lit up the night skies. Hotels, recreation areas, businesses, and homes were constantly being damaged or destroyed. Periodic cease-fires resulted in people quickly responding to repair the damage, and Beirut's citizens would respond to the respite from war to visit the beautiful Mediterranean beaches and recreation centers. During one period when the electricity was knocked out, I witnessed appliance dealers who normally sold refrigeration units quickly shifting to sell generators; soon business resumed as usual.

In Afghanistan and Iraq similar scenes are being repeated. Pockets of insurgency terrorize local residents, but a majority of these two countries' citizens are concentrating on rebuilding and establishing infrastructures of water, electricity, sewage treatment, schools, and hospitals that promise a future much brighter than they would have known under the Taliban or Saddam Hussein's rule.

It is the same in our own history. Some of our citizens may be briefly intimidated by terror or deterred and depressed by nature's wrath—but not for long. Our founders and each generation since demonstrate a will not only to survive but to overcome adversity and to thrive.

WHAT ARE THE THREATS?

First and foremost, we must be concerned with *economic threats*. Whether we are threatened by a terrorist or by a series of natural disasters, we must guard against economic chaos, both as a nation and as individuals.

Second, in terms of national concern, we must be aware of the threat of *weapons of mass destruction*, or WMDs. Technology is such that one or more dedicated fanatics could feasibly threaten us physically, economically, and psychologically with nuclear, biological, or chemical WMDs. The attack on 9/11 demonstrated that the homeland is vulnerable and that thousands may be slaughtered—and many more severely injured—by the willful acts of just a few zealots.

Third is the threat of *natural disasters* that range from horrific earthquakes, to monster storms and tornadoes, to the possibility of a pandemic outbreak of disease. As we witnessed during Hurricane Katrina, when destruction is so widespread and inclusive, it may become impossible to draw upon government, our friends and neighbors, or anyone else besides ourselves for sustenance, shelter, or anything else for days, weeks, and possibly months.

Then, finally, there are more *personal threats*, such as anarchy, murder, hostage taking, assault, carjacking, home invasion, robbery, accidents, and disease.

Economic Threats

The then DHS secretary Michael Chertoff, testifying before Congress in early March 2006, stated that he wanted his department to move from a population-based funding formula to a risk-based one, which depends on criteria such as the nature of critical infrastructure and proximity to borders. Chertoff pointed out that "the issue is not where state lines are drawn. The issue is where are the vulnerabilities, where are the consequences."

The president's FY 2006 budget request included a total of $41.1 billion for the DHS. This was an increase in total budgetary authority of 7 percent over the enacted FY 2005 funding, excluding Project BioShield, and clearly demonstrated the administration's continued commitment to making further improvements in the nation's homeland security. Among the operating entities with significant budgetary increases were Immigration and Customs Enforcement (a 13.5 percent increase) and the U.S. Coast Guard (an increase of more than 9 percent, adjusting for transferred programs). The budget also streamlined screening programs, increasing resources for these activities under a new screening office by 68 percent. This was on top of $35.6 billion authorized in FY 2004 and $38.6 billion funded in FY 2005.

The president requested and received $42.9 billion for DHS during FY 2007—an increase of 6 percent over the $41.1 billion Congress authorized in 2006 and double the $20 billion authorized for the twenty-two agencies that became DHS in 2001. The approved 2008 budget for DHS was $47 billion, and $50.5 billion has been earmarked for 2009. How much more can we afford to spend to keep our nation safe?

As Randall Larsen, director of the ANSER Institute for Homeland Security, said in 2001:

> We cannot afford to put guards on every bridge and at every critical node of our infrastructure. Nor can we afford a sophisticated chemical and biodetector in every government building. . . . America cannot afford a risk-free society in a

world of global terrorism. *The enemy's strategy is to destroy our economy.* We must not facilitate their efforts. America will need to spend considerable sums of money to ensure our security . . . but we must do it wisely. . . . There will be no money to waste on irrational fear and unconscionable pork. We must develop a strategic plan to guide our efforts. This must include federal, state, and local governments, plus the private sector. Since 9/11, more than 130 bills regarding homeland security have been introduced in the House of Representatives. This is not the example of spending based on a strategic plan.

Here we are years later and yet we see continuing reports of pork-barrel politics and inappropriate spending of the resources dedicated to protecting the homeland.

"How does that affect me?" you might ask.

Wasteful spending affects every American citizen. It raises our taxes, thus depriving us of personal choices as to how we might spend our income. It depresses the economy in critical areas where those tax dollars might better be applied. More importantly, it dilutes the security for you and me for which it was intended.

Taken to the extreme, the pork-barrel politicians and the greedy state, regional, and local representatives who misspend homeland security funds give aid and comfort to the fanatical enemy who is dedicated to destroying our infrastructure and bankrupting our society.

On a moral and humanitarian level, misuse of these funds restricts our capability and capacity to respond to both man-made and natural disasters, such as terrorist sabotage or attacks and hurricanes, tornadoes, flooding, and earthquakes.

Weapons of Mass Destruction

I'm not too sure that all our citizens know what WMDs really are. From the rhetoric being spouted in the media, it's apparent that most people only think of nuclear bombs or intercontinental missiles as weapons of mass destruction. Nuclear devices are high on the list of WMDs, but they are only part of the mix. Civil Defense categorizes WMDs as chemical, biological, radiological, nuclear, and explosive (CBRNE), defined as:

1. Any explosive, incendiary, poison gas, bomb, grenade, or rocket having a propellant charge of more than four ounces [113 g], missile having an explosive or incendiary charge of more than one-quarter ounce [7 g], or mine or device similar to the above.
2. Poison gas.
3. Any weapon involving a disease organism.

4. Any weapon that is designed to release radiation at a level dangerous to human life. (18 U.S.C. Section 2332a)

Among the most insidious of these are the biological weapons targeted toward inflicting hideous diseases upon thousands of innocent civilians who are unaware and unprotected. How would you protect yourself and your family from being a victim of a biological attack?

The media continues to present nightly reminders of how deadly and innovative our terrorist enemies can be in launching indiscriminate suicide attacks on hotels, hospitals, police stations, restaurants, open air markets, and any other target where people congregate in large numbers. Are you apt to run over an IED here in the United States? Well, it's relatively unlikely at present. However, it is not unthinkable that such a device might be employed in a theater, shopping center, school, apartment building, or sports arena.

High on the list of threats that the DHS is guarding against is the "dirty bomb," an explosive device. How would you respond if you were working on one side of town and a dirty bomb was exploded over another area of the town where your spouse and your children were threatened? What do you need to know to minimize danger to yourself and your loved ones from the radiated dust that such an attack would spread by air currents passing over your community?

You probably recall the anthrax scare that the United States experienced just a few years ago as the deadly chemical arrived in personal mail of various politicians and average citizens. A few deaths caused by the agent created waves of fear across the country, causing disruption of mail service and costing huge sums to detect and decontaminate.

Do you recall the symptoms? Do you know what to look for? Do you know who to call if you receive a suspicious piece of mail?

Natural Disasters

Hurricanes form at sea, gain strength in warm tropical waters, and then continue to travel along a certain course until either weather conditions and cooler water dissipate their power or they blow themselves out over land. June through November is hurricane season on the East Coast. These storms usually form in the Gulf and then move north, east, or west. But any point along the Eastern seaboard may experience their fury.

The 2005 hurricane season, setting a new season record of twenty-six named storms, fourteen of which became hurricanes, demonstrated that nature must remain one of our more serious concerns. The Atlantic and Gulf regions spawned more destructive hurricanes than we've seen in decades,

Hurricane Andrew, Florida, August 24, 1992. Many houses, businesses, and personal effects suffered extensive damage from one of the most destructive hurricanes ever recorded in America. Bob Epstein/FEMA News Photo

An aerial view of a gas leak located next to a house impacted by Hurricane Katrina. Jocelyn Augustino/FEMA Photo

causing more than $107 billion in damage (previous record 2004, $45 billion). That doesn't take into account the economic output that was lost from thousands of victims who remain without work and businesses that will fail for lack of customers.

One bright note: The loss of life in 2004 was minimal compared to other monster storms. It wasn't until 1953 that tropical storms received formal names. But as early as September 1775, we have reports about a huge hurricane called the "Hurricane of Independence," which spread destruction from North Carolina to Nova Scotia and killed an estimated 4,170 in the United States and Canada.

The "Galveston Hurricane" is considered the deadliest in U.S. history. On September 8, 1900, an estimated six to eight thousand people died in the hurricane and its subsequent tidal surge. A lack of any sophisticated storm monitoring and a series of faulty conclusions contributed to the huge loss of life and property.

The second most deadly hurricane caused 1,836 deaths September 6–20, 1928, as it made landfall in southeastern Florida at West Palm Beach, then plowed through the area of Lake Okeechobee. The barometer dropped to 27.57, which is believed to be the lowest reading ever recorded in the United States. Thousands were injured, fifteen thousand were made homeless, and property losses were estimated at $50 million to $75 million.

Approximately 90 percent of deaths attributed to hurricanes are caused by storm surge—the dome of water created by the low pressure center of a hurricane. This storm surge quickly floods low-lying coastal areas with anywhere from three feet for a Category 1 storm to more than nineteen feet for a Category 5 storm. As oceanfront properties attracted more dense populations, fatalities and physical damage increased.

By August 23, 1992, when a Category 5 storm named Andrew slammed ashore near South Miami, early warning systems that rely on weather satellites and computer models to detect hurricanes in advance were in use. That, combined with proactive evacuation plans, minimized human exposure so that only twenty-three deaths were directly attributed to the storm. But more than 135,000 single-family and mobile homes were destroyed or damaged, 160,000 people were left homeless, and 86,000 lost their jobs. Total damage caused by Hurricane Andrew was estimated near $25 billion.

Sadly, the 2005 hurricane season recorded over 2,000 deaths, with 1,071 dying in New Orleans alone as a result of Hurricane Katrina. As 2005 neared its end, bodies were still being discovered as New Orleans residents returned to the city.

So what can you expect for the future?

Unfortunately, experts say that nearly a third of all Floridians and nearly half of all Americans have no hurricane preparedness plan, according to a

The destruction from Hurricane Katrina. Jocelyn Augustino/FEMA Photo

The destruction from Hurricane Katrina. Jocelyn Augustino/FEMA Photo

The destruction from Hurricane Katrina. Marvin Nauman/FEMA Photo

The destruction from Hurricane Katrina. Jocelyn Augustino/FEMA Photo

recent survey. Forecasters hope that residents pay attention to news reports when storms brew, and that they follow advice to evacuate when necessary.

The experts attribute the high number of tropical storms and hurricanes to a cyclical pattern that is repeated over time. That cycle is not expected to end for several years to come.

Tornadoes are somewhat related to hurricanes in that they are cyclonic in nature. And though most of the one thousand tornadoes reported each year

Caruthersville, Missouri, April 9, 2006. A home damaged by the tornado that swept through the town of Caruthersville, and a resident holding an American flag. Patsy Lynch/FEMA Photo

occur in early spring and fall, tornadoes may appear almost anywhere and at any time throughout the year. They tend to form primarily in the southern and central regions of the United States. Although tornadoes cause billions in damage each year, only an average of about sixty result in death.

Earthquakes occur worldwide millions of times each year, as the earth's tectonic plates and fault lines shift and grind, releasing pent-up energy and then settling quietly for a period of time. About three thousand of these occur within the United States. The majority of earthquakes are rated between magnitudes 2.0 and 4.9—which are very minor in terms of potential damage. Still, four or five earthquakes occur each year in the United States that measure 6.0 or above on the seismograph—and these should be of some concern if they activate in any population center. The worst earthquake recorded in the United States was the 1906 San Francisco earthquake; three thousand souls perished as a result of the earthquake and from the extensive fires that erupted in its aftermath. On average, less than ten people are killed each year by earthquakes, with the toll periodically rising to sixty or seventy.

Tsunamis, the Japanese name for "harbor waves," are relatively rare but present the potential for massive destruction and death. The waves may travel in the open sea as fast as 450 miles per hour. As the big waves approach shallow waters along the coast, they grow to a great height and smash into the shore. They can be as high as one hundred feet. They can cause a lot of de-

A U.S. Navy helicopter arrives with food, water, and humanitarian supplies for tsunami survivors on Sumatra, Indonesia, on January 7, 2005.

Banda Aceh, January 6, 2005. The ruins of a once-thriving city. Mglaboh, Sumatra, Indonesia, is now trying to recover from the devastating tsunami that hit this region. Abraham Lincoln Carrier Strike Group joined operations in the Indian Ocean off the waters of Indonesia and Thailand. U.S. Navy photo by Photographer's Mate Airman Jordon R. Beesley

struction on the shore. They are sometimes mistakenly called "tidal waves," but tsunamis have nothing to do with the tides.

Hawaii is the state at greatest risk for tsunamis. They get about one a year, with a damaging tsunami happening about every seven years. In 1946, a tsunami with waves of twenty to thirty-two feet crashed into Hilo, Hawaii, flooding the downtown area. Alaska is also at high risk. California, Oregon, and Washington experience a damaging tsunami about every eighteen years. In 1964, an Alaskan earthquake generated a tsunami with waves that reached between ten and twenty feet high along parts of the California, Oregon, and Washington coasts.

More than 225,000 people were killed and 125,000 injured by the tsunami that struck following a massive seaquake of around 9 on the Richter scale, with an epicenter off the Indonesian island of Sumatra in South Asia on December 26, 2004. It displaced 1.5 million more people in coastal areas and caused enormous loss of property, livelihoods, and infrastructure. Over 47,000 victims in Indonesia's Aceh province share a mass grave and many victims remain missing. One year later progress moved slowly. Hundreds of thousands of survivors still live in temporary shelters of tents and shelters made of scrap materials. Government bureaucracy and ethnic divisions continue to hamper rebuilding efforts.

Experts say that it's not a matter of "if" but "when" and "where" a cataclysmic tsunami will hit the United States. Warning systems of delicate sensors lie on the ocean floor. These could offer Hawaii hours of advance warning time in which to evacuate. Unfortunately, the U.S. West Coast may only have the advantage of minutes instead of hours to react—but every minute can make a huge difference if you are prepared.

Floods. The National Safety Council (NSC) calculates that your chance of dying in a flood is about one in 32 million for any given year and about one in 414,000 throughout your lifetime. To put that into perspective, NSC sets your odds of drowning in your bathtub at one in 818,000 each year and one in 10,582 during your lifetime. So perhaps you should worry more about taking a bath than avoiding a flood? Not really. But the choices that you make and the lifestyle that you choose obviously impact for good or bad upon your chances of being killed or injured.

Pandemic Diseases. There is a historical record of influenza pandemics of varying severity at twenty-to-forty-year intervals. The "Spanish flu" began in August 1918 in three disparate locations: Brest, France; Boston, Massachusetts; and Freetown, Sierra Leone. The unusually severe and deadly strain of influenza spread worldwide, killing 25 million in the course of six months; some estimates put the total of those killed worldwide at over twice that number. An estimated 17 million died in India, 500,000 in the United States, and

200,000 in the U.K. It vanished within eighteen months. It was caused by the H1N1 type of flu virus, which has since been reconstructed at the CDC.

The "Asian flu," an H2N2 virus, caused about 70,000 deaths in the United States. First identified in China in late February 1957, the Asian flu rapidly spread throughout the United States by June 1957.

The "Hong Kong flu," an H3N2 virus, caused about 34,000 deaths in the United States. This virus was first detected in Hong Kong in early 1968 and spread to the United States later that year. H3N2 viruses still circulate today.

In 2003, avian influenza virus was detected in Vietnam, increasing fears of new variant strains emerging. After a lull, several new cases were reported in Egypt in April 2009—raising fears that the virus had mutated into a form that could more easily be transmitted from people to people. According to the World Health Organization (WHO), as of April 8, 2009, a total of 417 bird flu cases have been reported worldwide since the virus was first detected, resulting in 257 deaths. It's feared that if the avian influenza virus combines with a human influenza virus, the new subtype created could be both highly contagious and highly lethal in humans. Such a subtype could cause a global influenza pandemic similar to the Spanish flu or the lower-mortality pandemics such as the Asian flu and the Hong Kong flu.

Also in April 2009, the first cases of what was initially called "swine flu" were reported in Mexico. WHO spokesperson Peter Cordingley said the new virus (later identified as novel H1N1 virus) was spreading quickly in Mexico and the southern United States, raising fears of a global pandemic. As of April 26, the number of suspected H1N1 flu cases in Mexico had climbed to 1,614, including as many as 103 deaths, according to Health Secretary José Angel Córdova. The United States has confirmed at least 11 cases of H1N1 flu, and Canada 6 cases. It has also been reported in France, Spain, Brazil, and New Zealand. (See appendix for further information.)

What about the future?

Diseases that can attain pandemic proportions include Lassa fever, Rift Valley fever, Marburg virus, Ebola virus, and Bolivian hemorrhagic fever. However, emergence of these diseases into the human population in recent years has shown that their virulence is so high they dissipate in geographically confined areas. Thus their effect on humans is currently considered limited.

HIV. HIV, the virus that causes AIDS, may be considered a global pandemic, but it is currently most extensive in southern and eastern Africa. It is restricted to a small proportion of the population in other countries, and is only spreading slowly in those countries. If there were to be a true destruction-of-life pandemic it would be likely to be similar to HIV—that is, a constantly evolving disease.

Superbugs. There is a fear that antibiotic-resistant superbugs may also revive diseases previously regarded as conquered. This threat has come about in part by an insistence by patients that their doctors prescribe antibiotics for every sniffle, when in fact antibiotics are both inappropriate and ineffective for most viruses or colds.

Personal Threats

How safe are you in your own home? It may depend on where you live, what lifestyle you pursue, what circles you move within, what sex you are, and where you are on an economic scale.

Anarchy is indiscriminate. Unleashed by ineffective authority or absence of authority, individuals who would otherwise be law abiding and civil may deteriorate into a mob mentality, destroying public and private property, inflicting harm on others, and giving in to immoral and unlawful conduct of every type.

Murder. The Federal Bureau of Investigation (FBI) reported that there were 1,408,337 violent crimes reported nationwide in 2007 (the latest published figures). There were a reported 16,424 murders—a 0.6 decrease compared to 2006. The data showed that most murder victims (90.6 percent) were adults and most were males (77.6 percent). Of the male murder victims, 8.2 percent were juveniles (persons under the age of 18). Juvenile females comprised 13.5 percent of female murder victims nationwide. By race, 48.7 percent of murder victims were white, 48.5 percent were black. In 44.5 percent of murders, the relationship of the murder victim to the offender was unknown. Of the 55.5 percent of murders in which the victim-offender relationship was known, 77.6 percent of the victims knew their assailants. The FBI estimates that:

- Every 31.8 minutes someone is murdered.
- Every 5.8 minutes someone commits a forcible rape.
- Every 1.2 minutes someone is robbed.
- Every 36.8 seconds someone is the victim of an aggravated assault.
- Every 14.5 seconds someone commits a burglary.
- Every 4.8 seconds someone is the victim of larceny/theft.
- Every 28.8 seconds someone's automobile is stolen.

Carjacking is defined as completed or attempted robbery of a motor vehicle by a stranger to the victim. It differs from other motor vehicle theft because the victim is present and the offender uses or threatens to use force. Carjacking victimization rates are highest in urban areas, followed by suburban and rural areas. Ninety-three percent of carjackings occurred in cities or suburbs. A weapon was used in 74 percent of carjacking victimizations. Firearms were used in 45 percent of carjackings, knives in 11 percent, and other weapons in 18 percent of the crimes.

Home Invasion. Security consultant Chris E. McGoey describes home invasion as the residential equivalent of an automobile carjacking, and he says that it is on the rise. Like the crime of carjacking, most police agencies don't track home invasions as a separate crime. Most police agencies and the FBI statistically record the crime as a residential burglary or a robbery. Without the ability to track the specific crime of home invasion, little can be done to alert the public as to the frequency of its occurrence in their community or to devise a law enforcement plan of action to control it.

McGoey points out that home invasion robbers, in contrast to burglars, work more often at nights and on weekends when residences are more likely to be occupied. The home invaders will sometimes target the resident as well as the residence. The selection process may include a woman living alone, a senior citizen, or a known drug dealer, for example. It is not unheard of for a robber to follow you home based on the value of the car you are driving or the jewelry you are wearing.

Many home robbers have been in the home before as a delivery person, installer, or repair vendor. Home robbers rarely work alone and rely on an overwhelming physical confrontation to gain control and instill fear in their victims. The greatest violence usually occurs during the initial confrontation; home invaders often come prepared with handcuffs, rope, duct tape, and firearms. Some in-home robbers appear to enjoy the intimidation, domination, and violence, and some even claim it's a rush.

Though the FBI reports that most personal crime is on the decline, you must always evaluate your individual safety and security based upon your lifestyle, your environment, and the choices that you make. Chapter 9 addresses your alternatives and strategies in making the world in which you and your loved ones live a much safer place to be.

Chapter Two

Counterterrorism Tactics

[Terrorists] cannot go out and plan what they are getting ready to do and if it doesn't exactly work out today, they can disappear into the population and make it work tomorrow. Guerrillas can do that forever. But terrorists cannot do that. That is why they are ultimately going to be destroyed, because they are isolated within the community or area in which they operate. The other factor that relates to it is that these terrorists are not natives to the region in which they are operating. The terrorists that attacked the United States were from foreign countries. They stand out like sore thumbs in our countries. Therefore they will always be open to be seen and to be reported and to be knocked out.

—Bevin Alexander

STRATEGY FOR VICTORY

President George W. Bush developed a multiple-approach strategy to defeating terrorists both at home and overseas, and this approach is being continued by President Barack Obama. Within the United States, law enforcement and intelligence agencies are tasked with protecting the homeland, although every citizen has a role to play. Overseas, the U.S. military and the CIA are working with foreign governments, their military, and their intelligence communities as part of the global war on terrorism.

On October 6, 2005, President Bush gave a speech in which he talked about the war on terror. The White House press release about his speech said:

In this new century freedom is once again under assault. In the four years since September 11, the United States and the world have been committed to winning the war on terror. The evil that came to our shores on September 11 has reappeared on other days and in other places. In cities across the world, we have seen images of destruction and suffering that can seem like random acts of madness but are part of a larger terrorist threat. To combat this evil, we must remember the calling of September 11—we will confront this mortal danger to all humanity and not tire or rest until the war on terror is won.

Bush insisted that Muslims are now playing a vital role in the war on terror:

Muslim leaders are denouncing terrorism, and the time has come for all responsible Islamic leaders to denounce an ideology that exploits Islam for political ends and defiles a noble faith. Many Muslims have joined the fight against extremism. The United States is proud to stand by those who stand up for the liberty, justice, and humanity of their own tradition.

Then senator Barack Obama, in a speech in the Senate on March 6, 2007, said:

We are here to do the work that ensures no other family members have to lose a loved one to a terrorist who turns a plane into a missile, a terrorist who straps a bomb around her waist and climbs aboard a bus, a terrorist who figures out how to set off a dirty bomb in one of our cities. This is why we are here: to make our country safer and make sure the nearly three thousand who were taken from us did not die in vain; that their legacy will be a more safe and secure Nation.

THE BUSH GOVERNMENT'S RATIONALE

In its news release about President Bush's October 6, 2005, speech, the White House said:

The Militant Threat and the Importance of Winning the War on Terror

The ideology known as Islamic radicalism, militant jihadism, or Islamo-fascism—different from the religion of Islam—exploits Islam to serve a violent political vision that calls for the murder of all those who do not share it. The followers of Islamic radicalism are bound together by their shared ideology, not by any centralized command structure. Although they fight on scattered battlefields, these terrorists share a similar ideology and vision for the world openly stated in videos, audiotapes, letters, declarations, and websites.

First, these extremists are determined to end American and Western influence in the Middle East. Because the United States is spreading democracy and peace, we stand in the way of their radical ambitions. Al-Qaeda's leader, Osama bin Laden, has called on Muslims to dedicate their "resources, sons, and money to driving the infidels out of their lands." To meet this goal, they hit us and expect us to run in the hope that we will repeat the sad history of Beirut in 1983 and Mogadishu in 1993—only this time on a larger scale and with greater consequences.

Second, the militant network wants to use the vacuum created by retreat to expand its power. As they once did in Afghanistan and are trying to do now in Iraq, they will seek to gain control of an entire country—a base from which to launch attacks and conduct their war against non-radical Muslim governments.

Third, from their new base, these militants will seek to establish a radical Islamic empire [a caliphate]. The militants believe that controlling one country will rally the Muslim masses, enabling them to overthrow moderate governments in the Middle East and establish a radical Islamic empire that spreads from Spain to Indonesia.

To accomplish their extremist agenda, the militants thrive on the suffering and frustrations of others. The radicals exploit local conflicts to build a culture of victimization, exploit resentful and disillusioned young men and women, and use modern technology to multiply their destructive power. . . .

They are sheltered and supported by authoritarian regimes—allies of convenience like Syria and Iran—that share the goal of hurting America and moderate Muslim governments, and that use terrorist propaganda to blame their own failures on the West, America, and Jews. They are strengthened by front operations—such as corrupted charities—and those who aggressively fund the spread of radical, intolerant versions of Islam. The militants are aided by elements of the Arab news media that incite hatred and anti-Semitism, feed conspiracy theories, and speak of a so-called American "war on Islam"—with seldom a word about American action to protect Muslims in Afghanistan, Bosnia, Somalia, Kosovo, Kuwait, and Iraq.

This extremism may not be given concessions, bribed, or appeased. We must never accept anything less than victory. To those who argue that extremism has been strengthened by the actions of our Coalition in Iraq, we must remember that we were not in Iraq on September 11, 2001. The radicals' hatred existed before Iraq was an issue, and it will exist after Iraq is an excuse. The government of Russia did not support Operation Iraqi Freedom, and yet the Islamic militants killed more than 180 Russian schoolchildren in Beslan.

Islamic Radicalism Is Another in a Line of Bankrupt Ideologies

The murderous ideology of the Islamic radicals is the great challenge of our century. Yet, in many ways, this fight resembles the struggle against communism in the last century.

Like communism, Islamic radicalism is led by an elitist self-appointed vanguard that presumes to speak for the Muslim masses. Bin Laden says his role is to tell Muslims "what is good for them and what is not." What this man who grew up in wealth and privilege considers good for poor Muslims is that they become killers and suicide bombers. He assures them that this is the road to paradise—though he never offers to go along for the ride.

Islamic radicals purposely target innocent individuals for a political vision. This explains their cold-blooded contempt for human life, seen in the murders of Daniel Pearl, Nicholas Berg, Margaret Hassan, and many others. These militants have shown themselves to be enemies of not only America and Iraq, but enemies of Islam and humanity. The world has witnessed this kind of cruelty before—the heartless zealotry that led to the gulags, the Cultural Revolution, and the killing fields.

Islamic radicals pursue totalitarian aims. Islamic radical leaders have endless ambitions of imperial domination, and they wish to make everyone powerless except themselves. While promising a future of justice and holiness, the terrorists are preparing a future of oppression and misery—banning dissent and books, brutalizing women, and controlling every aspect of life.

Islamic radicalism is dismissive of free peoples. Zarqawi has said that Americans are "the most cowardly of God's creatures." However, it is cowardice that kills children and the elderly with car bombs, cuts the throat of a bound captive, or targets worshipers leaving a mosque. It is courage that liberated 50 million people from tyranny, keeps an untiring vigil against the enemies of a rising democracy, and will once again destroy the enemies of freedom.

And like communism, Islamic radicalism contains inherent contradictions that doom it to failure. By fearing freedom, distrusting human creativity, punishing change, and limiting the contributions of half the population, this ideology declares war on the idea of progress itself. The only thing modern about the militants' vision is the weapons they seek to use. The outcome of this war is not in doubt—those who despise freedom and progress have condemned themselves to isolation, decline, and collapse. Because free people believe in the future, they will own the future.

The U.S. Strategy to Win

Defeating a broad and adaptive network requires patience, constant pressure, and strong partners. Working with these partners, the United States is disrupting militant conspiracies, destroying their ability to make war, and giving millions a hopeful alternative to resentment and violence.

First, we are preventing terrorist attacks before they occur. We are reorganizing government for a broad and coordinated homeland defense, reforming intelligence agencies for the difficult task of tracking enemy activity, and acting, along with governments from many countries, to destroy the terrorist networks and incapacitate their leaders. We have prevented terrorist plots and al-Qaeda efforts to case targets in the United States. Because of strikes against terrorist leaders and disruption of their plots, the enemy is wounded but still capable of deadly operations around the globe. Our commitment is clear: we must not relent until the organized international terror networks are exposed and broken and their leaders held to account for their acts of murder.

Second, we are denying weapons of mass destruction to outlaw regimes and their terrorist allies. Working with Great Britain, Pakistan, and other nations, we shut down A. Q. Khan's black-market operation in nuclear technology. Libya abandoned its chemical and nuclear weapons programs, as well as its long-range ballistic missiles. In the last year, America and our partners in the Proliferation Security Initiative have stopped more than a dozen shipments of suspect weapons technology—including equipment for Iran's ballistic missile programs. This progress has reduced the danger, but not removed it. Evil men still work to gain these weapons, and we are working urgently to keep them out of their hands.

Third, we are determined to deny radical groups the support and sanctuary of outlaw regimes. State sponsors like Syria and Iran have a long history of collaboration with terrorists—and they deserve no patience from the victims of terror. The United States makes no distinction between those who commit acts of terror and those who support and harbor terrorists, because they are equally guilty of murder.

Fourth, we are fighting to deny the militants control of any nation. The United States is fighting beside our Afghan partners against the remnants of the Taliban and its al-Qaeda allies. We are working with President Musharraf to isolate the militants in Pakistan. We are fighting the terrorists and regime remnants in Iraq who seek to overthrow a democracy, claim a strategic country as a haven of terror, destabilize the Middle East, and strike America and other free nations with ever increasing violence. Our goal is to defeat the terrorists and their allies at the heart of their power—and we are achieving this goal.

- With Iraqi forces, the Coalition is fighting the enemy with a comprehensive and specific military plan. We are improving the lives of Iraqi citizens by conducting offensive operations to clear out enemy forces and leave Iraqi units behind to prevent the enemy from returning. With our help, the Iraqi military is gaining new capabilities and new confidence with every passing month. At the time of our Fallujah operations 11 months ago, there were only a few Iraqi battalions in combat—today there are more than 80. The progress is not easy, but it is steady.
- Iraq is making incredible political progress. The extremists in Iraq are not patriots or resistance fighters but murderers at war with the Iraqi people. In contrast, the elected leaders of Iraq are proving to be strong and steadfast. In the space of two and a half years, Iraq has made incredible progress on the path to becoming a democracy. It is true that the seeds of freedom have only recently been planted, but we are confident that if our Coalition and the Iraqi people each does their part, Iraqi democracy will succeed.
- We must reject the dangerous illusion of those who claim that America would be better off by cutting our losses and leaving Iraq now. Having removed a dictator who hated free peoples, we will not stand by as a new set of killers seize control of Iraq. There is always a temptation, in the middle of a long struggle, to seek the quiet life, escape the duties and problems of the world,

and hope the enemy grows weary. However, this enemy is never tired and considers every retreat an invitation to greater violence. In Iraq, there is no peace without victory. We will keep our nerve and win that victory.

Fifth, we are denying the militants future recruits by advancing democracy and hope across the broader Middle East. If the region is left to grow in bitterness and misery, while radicals stir the resentments of millions, then that part of the world will be a source of endless conflict and mounting danger. However, the extremists will be marginalized and their violence ended if the peoples of that region are permitted to choose their own destiny and advance by their own energy and participation as free men and women. America is making this stand in practical ways. We are encouraging our friends in the Middle East, including Egypt and Saudi Arabia, to take the path of reform to strengthen their own societies in the fight against terror by respecting the rights of people. We are standing with dissidents and exiles against oppressive regimes, because we know that the dissidents of today will be the democratic leaders of tomorrow. We are making our case through public diplomacy—stating clearly and confidently our belief in self-determination, religious freedom, and equal rights for women. By standing for the hope and freedom of others, we will make our own freedom more secure.

U.S. COUNTERTERRORISM POLICY

1. Make no concessions to terrorists and strike no deals.
2. Bring terrorists to justice for their crimes.
3. Isolate and apply pressure on states that sponsor terrorism to force them to change their behavior.
4. Bolster the counterterrorism capabilities of those countries that work with the United States and require assistance.

U.S. GOVERNMENT PROGRAMS AND POLICY

In 2003, the U.S. Department of State released the following outline as appendix D to the report *Patterns of Global Terrorism* (www.globalsecurity .org/security/library/report/2004/pgt_2003/pgt_2003_31747pf.htm):

Anti-Terrorism Assistance Program

Congress authorized the Anti-Terrorism Assistance (ATA) Program in 1983 as part of a major initiative against international terrorism. Since that time, ATA has provided training for more than 36,000 students from 142 countries. The

ATA Program provides training and related assistance to law enforcement and security services of selected friendly foreign governments. Assistance to the qualified countries focuses on the following objectives:

- Enhancing the antiterrorism skills of friendly countries by providing training and equipment to deter and counter the threats of terrorism
- Strengthening the bilateral ties of the United States with friendly foreign governments by offering concrete assistance in areas of mutual concern
- Increasing respect for human rights by sharing with civilian authorities modern, humane, and effective antiterrorism techniques

ATA courses are developed and customized in response to terrorism trends and patterns. The training can be categorized into four functional areas: Crisis Prevention, Crisis Management, Crisis Resolution, and Investigation. Countries needing assistance are identified on the basis of the threat or actual level of terrorist activity they face.

Antiterrorism assistance and training may be conducted either in-country or within the United States. This arrangement provides flexibility to maximize the effectiveness of the program for countries of strategic importance in the global war on terrorism.

ATA programs may take the form of advisory assistance, such as police administration and management of police departments, how to train police instructors or develop a police academy, and modern interview and investigative techniques. This approach enables the program to provide a narrow focus to solutions for country-specific problems that are not resolved in the classroom-training environment. Equipment or explosive-detection trained dogs may also be included in the assistance package.

The ability of the United States to assist friendly governments to master the detection and prevention of terrorist activities will clearly enhance the mutual security of all the participating nations. Detecting and eliminating terrorist cells at the root before their violence can cross borders and oceans will ensure a safer world for all nations.

ATA continues its efforts to familiarize ambassadors, regional security officers, and other U.S. officials with the program offerings. The success of these efforts is evidenced by the fact that every frontline nation has requested antiterrorist assistance in some form. U.S. diplomats report that the ability of the United States to offer immediate, specific, and intensive training, along with technical tools and equipment, has succeeded in breaking down barriers and building trust.

ATA is responding to the growing demand for training and services not only by expanding course selection but also by pursuing development of the Center for Antiterrorism and Security Training. ATA is already offering training at a variety of venues, to include other government agencies and state and local facilities—both within and outside the Washington, D.C., metropolitan area.

Rewards for Justice Program

The Rewards for Justice Program is one of the most valuable U.S. Government assets in the fight against international terrorism. Established by the 1984 Act To Combat International Terrorism—Public Law 98-533—the Program is administered by the U.S. Department of State's Bureau of Diplomatic Security.

Under the Program, the Secretary of State may offer rewards of up to $5 million for information that prevents or favorably resolves acts of international terrorism against U.S. persons or property worldwide. Rewards may also be paid for information leading to the arrest or conviction of terrorists attempting, committing, and conspiring to commit—or aiding and abetting in the commission of—such acts.

The USA Patriot Act of 2001 authorizes the Secretary to offer or pay rewards of greater than $5 million if he determines that a greater amount is necessary to combat terrorism or to defend the United States against terrorist acts. Secretary Powell has authorized a reward of up to $25 million for the information leading to the capture of Osama bin Laden and other key al-Qaeda leaders.

In November 2002, the State and Treasury Departments announced a $5 million rewards program that will pay for information leading to the disruption of any terrorism financing operation.

Diplomatic Security has fully supported the efforts of the private business sector and citizens to establish a Rewards for Justice fund, a nongovernmental, nonprofit 501C(3) charitable organization administered by a group of private U.S. citizens. One hundred percent of all donated funds will be used to supplement reward payments only. Diplomatic Security has forged a strong relationship with the private business and U.S. citizen representatives of the Rewards for Justice Fund. Diplomatic Security has embarked on a much closer relationship with the U.S. public and private businesses in the U.S. Government's continuing efforts to bring those individuals responsible for the planning of the September 11 attacks to justice and to prevent future international terrorist attacks against the United States at home or abroad.

Since its inception, the Rewards for Justice Program has been very effective. In the past seven years, the Secretary of State has authorized payments for more than $52 million to 33 people who provided credible information that put terrorists behind bars or prevented acts of international terrorism worldwide. The program played a significant role in the arrest of international terrorist Ramzi Yousef, who was convicted in the 1993 bombing of the World Trade Center and most recently in the efforts to locate Uday and Qusay Hussein.

International Terrorism: U.S. Hostages and U.S. Government Policy

The U.S. Government will make no concessions to individuals or groups holding official or private U.S. citizens hostage. The United States will use every appropriate resource to gain the safe return of U.S. citizens who are held hostage.

Customs and Border Protection officers provide security for the USS Iwo Jima *in New Orleans during Katrina relief operations.*

At the same time, it is U.S. Government policy to deny hostage takers the benefits of ransom, prisoner releases, policy changes, or other acts of concession.

Basic Premises. It is internationally accepted that governments are responsible for the safety and welfare of persons within the borders of their nations. Aware of both the hostage threat and public security shortcomings in many parts of the world, the United States has developed enhanced physical and personal security programs for U.S. personnel and established cooperative arrangements with the U.S. private sector. It has also established bilateral assistance programs and close intelligence and law enforcement relationships with many nations to prevent hostage-taking incidents or resolve them in a manner that will deny the perpetrators benefits from their actions. The United States also seeks effective judicial prosecution and punishment for hostage takers victimizing the U.S. Government or its citizens and will use all legal methods to these ends, including extradition. U.S. policy and goals are clear, and the U.S. Government actively pursues them alone and in cooperation with other governments.

U.S. Government Responsibilities When Private U.S. Citizens Are Taken Hostage. On the basis of past experience, the U.S. Government concluded that making concessions that benefit hostage takers in exchange for the release of hostages increased the danger that others will be taken hostage. U.S. Government policy is, therefore, to deny hostage takers the benefits of ransom, prisoner releases, policy changes, or other acts of concession. At the same time, the U.S.

Government will make every effort—including contact with representatives of the captors—to obtain the release of hostages without making concessions to the hostage takers.

Consequently, the United States strongly urges U.S. companies and private citizens not to accede to hostage-taker demands. It believes that good security practices, relatively modest security expenditures, and continual close cooperation with Embassy and local authorities can lower the risk to U.S. citizens living in high-threat environments.

The U.S. Government is concerned for the welfare of its citizens but cannot support requests that host governments violate their own laws or abdicate their normal enforcement responsibilities.

If the employing organization or company works closely with local authorities and follows U.S. policy, U.S. Foreign Service posts can be involved actively in efforts to bring the incident to a safe conclusion. This includes providing reasonable administrative services and, if desired by local authorities and the U.S. entity, full participation in strategy sessions. Requests for U.S. Government technical assistance or expertise will be considered on a case-by-case basis. The full extent of U.S. Government participation must await an analysis of each specific set of circumstances.

The host government and the U.S. private organizations or citizen must understand that if they wish to follow a hostage-resolution path different from that of U.S. Government policy, they do so without U.S. Government approval. In the event a hostage-taking incident is resolved through concessions, U.S. policy remains steadfastly to pursue investigation leading to the apprehension and prosecution of hostage takers who victimize U.S. citizens.

Legal Caution. Under current U.S. law, 18 USC 1203 (Act for the Prevention and Punishment of the Crime of Hostage-Taking, enacted October 1984 in implementation of the UN convention on hostage taking), seizure of a U.S. citizen as a hostage anywhere in the world is a crime, as is any hostage-taking action in which the U.S. Government is a target or the hostage taker is a U.S. national. Such acts are, therefore, subject to investigation by the Federal Bureau of Investigation and to prosecution by U.S. authorities. Actions by private persons or entities that have the effect of aiding or abetting the hostage taking, concealing knowledge of it from the authorities, or obstructing its investigation may themselves be in violation of U.S. law.

U.S. Terrorism Lists: Prevention, Punishment, and Pressure

The U.S. Government has established four primary counterterrorism lists to serve as tools in the fight against terrorism: the State Sponsors of Terrorism, Foreign Terrorist Organizations (FTO), Executive Order 13224, and the Terrorist Exclusion List (TEL). Each list has its individual mechanisms, but they all serve to prevent terrorism, punish terrorists and their supporters, and pressure changes in the behavior of designated states and groups.

Because these lists are a means to fight terrorism rather than an end unto themselves, they are not designed or intended to be immutable. The U.S. Government encourages states and organizations to take the necessary actions to get out of the terrorism business. The bar for a state or group being removed from a terrorism list is and must be high—it must end all involvement in any facet of terrorism, including passive support, and satisfy all U.S. Government counterterrorism concerns.

State Sponsors of Terrorism. The Secretary of State is authorized to designate a government as a state sponsor of terrorism if that government "has repeatedly provided support for acts of international terrorism." U.S. law requires the imposition of various sanctions on a state so designated. A number of U.S. laws and sanctions affect countries whose governments have been designated as state sponsors of terrorism.

The four main categories of sanctions include a ban on arms-related exports and sales; restrictions on exports of dual use items; prohibitions on official U.S. Government economic assistance (except humanitarian assistance), including a requirement that the U.S. Government oppose multilateral bank assistance; and imposition of miscellaneous trade and other restrictions, including a prohibition on imports and liability in U.S. courts for officials of that country that engage in terrorist activity. Inclusion on the State Sponsors of Terrorism list also targets a country for other sanctions laws that penalize persons and countries engaging in certain trade with state sponsors. In 2003 there were seven countries on the list: Cuba, Iran, Iraq, Libya, North Korea, Sudan, and Syria. Iraq was removed from the list in October 2004, Libya in May 2006, and North Korea in October 2008.

Foreign Terrorist Organizations. The Secretary of State is authorized to designate as foreign terrorist organizations (FTOs) groups that conduct terrorism and threaten the interests of the United States. The designation allows the U.S. Government to block designees' assets in U.S. financial institutions, criminalize witting provision of material support to designated groups, and block visas for members of FTOs without having to show that the individual was involved in specific terrorist activities. FTO designation also sends a strong signal that any group that engages in terrorism—regardless of its purported goals—will be condemned and penalized for its actions.

Executive Order 13224: Terrorist Financing. President Bush signed Executive Order 13224 on 23 September 2001, giving the U.S. Government a strong tool for eliminating the financial supporters and networks of terrorism. E.O. 13224 enables the U.S. Government to block designees' assets in any financial institution in the United States or held by any U.S. person. It also expands government authority to permit the designation of individuals and organizations that provide support or financial or other services to, or associate with, designated terrorists. E.O. 13224 designations have allowed the USG, as well as Coalition partners acting in concert, to block tens of millions of dollars intended to bankroll the murderous activities of al-Qaeda and other terrorist groups.

Patriot USA Act: Terrorist Exclusion List

On 26 October 2001, President Bush signed into law a comprehensive coun-terterrorism bill (Public Law 107-56, also known as USA PATRIOT). The new law strengthened enforcement tools and made improvements to the last major terrorism bill, the Antiterrorism and Effective Death Penalty Act of 1996. The USA Patriot Act also created a Terrorist Exclusion List (TEL) with immigration consequences for groups named therein. Designation on the TEL allows the U.S. Government to exclude or deport aliens who provide material assistance to, or solicit it for, designated organizations, giving the Department of State and U.S. law enforcement agencies a critical tool for bolstering homeland security. [The Patriot Act was renewed on March 8, 2006, with minor modifications.]

TERRORISM AND IMMIGRATION IN EUROPE

Recent developments have seen a divergence in social and political responses to terrorism between the United States and western Europe. The September 11, 2001, attacks were carried out by foreigners who entered the United States to deliberately carry out terrorist attacks, on behalf of a foreign organization, operating from bases in a remote country. Western European countries, on the other hand, confront domestic terrorism based within a domestic religious minority—some recent immigrants, but many native-born citizens, as the July 2005 London suicide bombings illustrated.

Although Muslims are a relatively small minority in the United States, in some European cities they are approaching a majority. In many cases they are concentrated in areas of poor housing and low employment, which has led to increasing frustration and bitterness.

The 2005 rioting in France was concentrated in communities dominated by North African and Middle Eastern immigrants and with a high Muslim population. These areas have long been ignored by politicians and many have almost become no-go areas for the police, with gangs and drug dealers controlling the streets.

Following the 9/11, Madrid, and London bombings there was a backlash against the Muslim population. Many Muslims were assaulted and mosques attacked. Defusing potential backlash is now a standard item of European counterterrorism policy.

The direction of European responses to terrorism is indicated by new poli-cies, proposed by Tony Blair in August 2005 following the deadly London mass transit bombings, including:

• Deportation and exclusion on grounds of fostering hatred, advocating violence to further a person's beliefs, or justifying or validating such vio-lence

- Condoning or glorifying terrorism made a criminal offense
- Refusal of asylum to anyone with a connection to terrorism
- New pretrial procedures and extending detention precharge of terrorist suspects
- Extended use of control orders for those who are British nationals and who cannot be deported, with imprisonment for any breach of the order
- New power to order closure of a place of worship that is used as a "centre for fomenting extremism"

TARGET-HARDENING

Common targets of terrorists are areas of high population concentration, such as mass transit vehicles (metro, bus, and trains), aircraft, office buildings, and crowded restaurants. Whatever the target of terrorists, there are multiple ways of hardening the targets so as to prevent the terrorists from hitting their mark. Perhaps the single most effective of these is bag-searching for explosives, which is only effective if it is conducted before the search subjects enter an area of high population concentration.

Another method is to place concrete barriers a sufficient distance outside buildings to prevent truck bombing. Aircraft cockpits are kept locked during flights and have reinforced doors, which only the pilots in the cabin are capable of opening.

TELEWORK DISPERSAL

In 1999, the federal government authorized telework—working in your home, at a hotel, or other offsite location rather than at your office—as a means of reducing fuel consumption, improving employee quality of life by reducing commuting time and reducing the need for child care. Telework has now become an integral component of continuity of operations (COOP) planning. By equipping employees to work from home or other remote locations, the government reduces the number of people concentrated in one office facility, thus making that structure less attractive as a prospective terrorist target. It also enhances the government's capacity to maintain operations in the wake of man-made or natural disasters.

PREEMPTIVE NEUTRALIZATION

Some countries see preemptive attacks as a legitimate strategy. This includes capturing, killing, or disabling suspected terrorists before they can mount an attack. Israel, the United States, and Russia have taken this approach, while western European states are generally more cautious.

In July 2005, Brazilian Jean Charles de Menezes was shot dead by police at Stockwell tube station in London, because he was misidentified as a suspected suicide bomber, and police feared he had a bomb ready for detonation. The shooting led to public concern and diplomatic protest.

Another major method of preemptive neutralization is interrogation of known or suspected terrorists to obtain information about specific plots, targets, the identity of other terrorists, and whether the interrogation subject himself is guilty of terrorist involvement. Sometimes methods such as sleep deprivation or drugs are used to increase suggestibility. Human rights objections apart, such methods may lead captives to offer false information in an attempt to stop the treatment, or because of confusion brought on by it.

DOMESTIC INTELLIGENCE AND SURVEILLANCE

Most counterterrorism strategies involve an increase in standard police and domestic intelligence. The central activities are traditional: interception of communications and the tracing of persons. New technology has, however, expanded the range of such operations. Domestic intelligence is often directed at specific groups defined on the basis of origin or religion, which is a source of political controversy. Mass surveillance of an entire population raises objections on civil liberties grounds.

MILITARY INTERVENTION

Countries often use terrorism to justify military intervention in countries where terrorists are said to be based. That was the main stated justification for the U.S. invasion of Afghanistan and one reason for the 2003 invasion of Iraq. It was also a stated justification for the second Russian invasion of Chechnya.

GLOBAL TRENDS

Since 1968, the U.S. State Department has tallied deaths due to terrorism. In 1985, it counted 816 deaths, the highest annual toll until then. The deaths decreased since the late 1980s, then rose to 3,295 in 2001, mainly as a result of the 9/11 attacks. In 2003, more than 1,000 people died as a result of terrorist acts. Many of these deaths resulted from suicide bombings in Chechnya, Iraq, India, and Israel. It does not tally victims of state terrorism. Data from the Terrorism Knowledge Base showed a similar decline since the 1980s, especially in western Europe. On the other hand, Asia experienced an increase in international terrorist attacks. Other regions experienced less consistent patterns over time. From 1991 to 2003, there was a consistent increase in the number of casualties from international terrorist attacks in Asia, but few other consistent trends in casualties from international terrorist attacks.

A CALL TO ARMS

> How will we fight and win this war? We will direct every resource at our command—every means of diplomacy, every tool of intelligence, every instrument of law enforcement, every financial influence, and every necessary weapon of war—to the disruption and to the defeat of the global terror network.
>
> —President George W. Bush

The president's call to arms, presented in the U.S. Department of State's *Patterns of Global Terrorism 2001*, outlines a global campaign of unprecedented scale and complexity along multiple fronts:

Diplomatic

Diplomatic action for the campaign began within minutes of the attack [on September 11, 2001]. State Department officials immediately began working with foreign officials around the world to forge a coalition to support our response. The fruits of that labor have been assessed by President Bush as having resulted in the "greatest worldwide coalition in history."

Since September 11, the President has met with leaders from more than 50 nations, and Secretary Powell has met with even more foreign ministers and other representatives of our Coalition partners. Senior members of the Departments of State and Defense and the Central Intelligence Agency . . . have also met with numerous foreign officials in Washington and have traveled to every continent to help fashion the diplomatic framework needed to wage the campaign to combat terrorism with a global reach.

Diplomacy abroad is also the leading edge of every nation's homeland security, and the global Coalition against terrorism has required—and will continue to require—intensive and innovative effort in that arena. Since September 11, for instance, the Department of State has begun formal dialogues with China and Pakistan on terrorism, and Department officials have brought their expertise to numerous conferences around the world, such as the one hosted by Polish President Kwasniewski, designed to strengthen the capabilities of our global partners in defeating terrorism.

In addition, numerous multilateral fora such as the EU, OAS, NATO, G-7, G-8 and others have taken substantive steps to enhance information sharing, tighten border security, and combat terrorist financing. On 28 September the UN Security Council adopted Resolution 1373, which requires all states to prevent and suppress the financing of terrorist acts, including freezing funds and other financial assets. The resolution also obliges all states to improve border security, clamp down on the recruitment of terrorists, intensify information sharing and law enforcement cooperation in the international campaign against terrorism, and deny terrorists and their supporters any support or safehaven. This resolution augments the positive trend of Security Council resolutions 1267 and 1333 (passed in 1999 and 2000, respectively) which imposed targeted or "smart" sanctions against the Taliban in Afghanistan.

The existing 12 UN Conventions against terrorism represent a solid international foundation for nations to support this global struggle. In December, the United States ratified the two newest, the UN Convention for the Suppression of the Financing of Terrorism and the UN Convention for the Suppression of Terrorist Bombings. All nations should become parties to all 12 of these conventions so that terrorists can be more readily apprehended and prosecuted wherever they are located.

Public diplomacy has been an important aspect of our efforts as well. The Department of State has aggressively sought to counter distorted views of the United States overseas, to emphasize that the war on terrorism is not a war against Islam, and to underscore that terrorists are not martyrs but cowards and criminals. Senior U.S. officials have conveyed these messages in hundreds of media interviews, and ambassadors have organized thousands of outreach activities around the world to build and maintain an international Coalition. The United States maintains Coalition Information Centers in London and Islamabad. The Department of State has an active speakers' program to explain U.S. policies to foreign and domestic audiences. The Office of International Information Programs maintains an informative and frequently visited website featuring publications such as "The Network of Terrorism" and "Islam in the United States."

Intelligence

Cooperation among intelligence agencies around the world has expanded to unprecedented levels. Sharing of intelligence about terrorists, their movements, and their planned attacks is an absolute prerequisite for successful interdiction. Governments in every region of the world have been able to use this information to expose the criminal netherworld in which terrorists operate. Undoubtedly, planned attacks have been prevented, and lives have been saved.

Our military campaign in Afghanistan as well as law-enforcement and intelligence operations by Coalition members have yielded a wealth of intelligence that will require further exploitation for action. Such information will be extremely valuable in identifying and interdicting other terrorist cells around the world. Effective intelligence exchange allows countries to act preemptively to counter terrorists before they act. It closes an important seam that terrorists exploit to their advantage. There is room for continued improvement, but the initial results have been very encouraging.

Law Enforcement

The world's law enforcement professionals have launched a global dragnet to identify, arrest, and bring terrorists to justice. In the United States, the FBI has led the law-enforcement engagement, working with all federal, state, and local law-enforcement agencies. More than 7,000 FBI Agents and support personnel have worked diligently with their U.S. and foreign law-enforcement partners to unravel the planning leading to the execution of the 9/11 operation, as well as to interdict other al-Qaeda cells and operatives in the United States and around the world. Their enhanced law-enforcement efforts, and cooperative work by officials around the world, have resulted in the apprehension of more than 1,000 suspected terrorists and the breakup of al-Qaeda and other terrorist cells. . . .

During 2001 and through March 2002, Secretary Powell designated or redesignated 33 groups as foreign terrorist organizations under the Immigration and Nationality Act, as amended by the Antiterrorism and Effective Death Penalty Act of 1996. The designations make it a criminal offense to provide funds or other material support to such organizations; require U.S. financial institutions to block the funds of the groups; and make members of the groups ineligible for U.S. visas and, if they are aliens, deportable. . . .

The United States brought to conclusion the prosecution of four al-Qaeda members for the bombing of the U.S. Embassies in Kenya and Tanzania. In May, in a courtroom within sight of the World Trade Center, guilty verdicts were handed down on all 302 counts in the trial of the bombing suspects, and all were sentenced to life in prison.

Economic

Money is like oxygen to terrorists, and it must be choked off. When President Bush signed Executive Order 13224 on 23 September, he imposed dramatic penalties on those who provide financial support to terrorist organizations. The Order blocks the assets of designated organizations and individuals linked to global terrorism. It prohibits transactions with terrorist groups, leaders, and corporate and charitable fronts listed in the Order. It also establishes America's ability to block the U.S. assets of, and deny access to U.S. markets to, those foreign banks that refuse to freeze terrorist assets. As of March 2002, the Order contained the names of 189 groups, entities, and individuals. Accordingly, approximately 150 countries and independent law-enforcement jurisdictions (for example, Hong Kong, Taiwan) issued orders freezing the assets of suspected terrorists and organizations.

The U.S. Department of Treasury has been leading the war against terrorist financing and has worked with all relevant agencies and departments to identify terrorist financing networks and to find ways to disrupt their operations.

Many nations and independent law-enforcement jurisdictions have made changes in their laws, regulations, and practices in order to suppress terrorism financing more effectively. UNSCR 1373 mandates worldwide improvements, and we are working with the UN Counter Terrorism Committee (CTC) and others to help improve the capability of countries to meet their obligations under the resolution to combat terrorist financing.

The first step has been to deny terrorists access to the world's organized financial structures; simultaneously, we have been moving to prevent the abuse of informal money-transfer systems and charities. Both lines of attack have produced results.

- President Bush launched the first offensive in the war on terrorism on 23 September by signing Executive Order 13224, freezing the U.S.-based assets of those individuals and organizations involved with terrorism.
- All but a handful of the countries in the world have expressed their support for the financial war on terror.
- Approximately 150 countries and jurisdictions have issued orders freezing terrorist assets, and the international community was helping others improve their legal and regulatory systems so they can move effectively to block terrorist funds.
- At the end of 2001, the United States had designated 158 known terrorists, terrorist organizations, and terrorist financial networks, whose assets are now subject to freezing in the U.S. financial system.
- Between September 11 and 31 December 2001, the United States blocked more than $34 million in assets of terrorist organizations. Other nations also blocked more than $33 million. The funds captured only measure the money in the pipeline at the time the accounts were shut down, which is a small fraction of the total funds disrupted by the closing of the pipeline.
- On 7 November, the United States and its allies closed down operations of two major financial networks—al-Barakaat and al-Taqwa—both of which were used by al-Qaeda and Osama bin Laden in more than 40 nations as sources of income and mechanisms to transfer funds. As part of that action, the Office of Foreign Assets Control (OFAC) was able to freeze $1,100,000 domestically in al-Barakaat-related funds. Treasury also worked closely with key officials in the Middle East to facilitate blocking of al-Barakaat's assets at its financial center of operations.

- On 4 December, President Bush froze the assets of a U.S.-based foundation—The Holy Land Foundation for Relief and Development—that had been funneling money to the terrorist organization Hamas. In 2000, the foundation had raised $13 million.
- International organizations are key partners in the war on financial terrorism. Since 28 September, over 100 nations have submitted reports to the United Nations on the actions they have taken to block terrorist finances, as required under United Nations Security Council resolution 1373 which calls on all nations to keep their financial systems free of terrorist funds.
- The Financial Action Task Force—a 29-nation group promoting policies to combat money laundering—adopted strict new standards to deny terrorists access to the world financial system.
- The G-20 and IMF member countries have agreed to make public the list of terrorists whose assets are subject to freezing, and the amount of assets frozen.

For the first five months of this effort, the United States identified terrorists for blocking and then sought cooperation from our allies around the world. A new stage in international cooperation was reached on 28 December 2001, when the EU took the lead and designated 6 European-based terrorists for asset blocking, on which the United States followed suit. Nations around the world have different information and different leads, and it is crucial that each of our allies not only blocks the terrorist financiers we identify but also develops its own leads to broaden the effort to identify and take action against those who fund terrorism.

Military

The terrorist attacks of September 11 were acts of war against the United States and a grievous affront to all humanity. The international community has responded accordingly:

- On 12 September, the UN Security Council condemned the attacks and reiterated the inherent right of collective self defense in accordance with the UN Charter.
- On 21 September, Foreign Ministers of the OAS invoked the collective self-defense clause of the Inter-American Treaty of Reciprocal Assistance ("Rio Treaty").
- In Brussels on 5 October, NATO invoked Article 5 of the Washington Treaty, which states that an armed attack on one or more of the allies in Europe or North America shall be considered an attack against them all.
  - 136 countries offered a range of military assistance.
  - 89 countries granted overflight authority for U.S. military aircraft.
  - 76 countries granted landing rights for U.S. military aircraft.
  - 23 countries agreed to host U.S. and Coalition forces involved in military operations in Afghanistan.

THE OBAMA STRATEGY

Al-Qaeda is still a threat. We cannot pretend somehow that because Barack Hussein Obama got elected as president, suddenly everything is going to be OK.

—Barack Obama

I think it is important for Europe to understand that even though I am president and George Bush is not president, al-Qaeda is still a threat.

—Barack Obama

Before the 2008 election, the following strategy was posted on the campaign website change.gov:

The first responsibility of any president is to protect the American people. As president, Barack Obama will provide the leadership and strategies to strengthen our security at home.

Barack Obama and Joe Biden's strategy for securing the homeland against 21st century threats is focused on preventing terrorist attacks on our homeland, preparing and planning for emergencies, and investing in strong response and recovery capabilities. Obama and Biden will strengthen our homeland against all hazards—including natural or accidental disasters and terrorist threats—and ensure that the federal government works with states, localities, and the private sector as a true partner in prevention, mitigation, and response.

Defeat Terrorism Worldwide

- *Find, disrupt, and destroy al-Qaeda.* Responsibly end the war in Iraq and focus on the right battlefield in Afghanistan. Work with other nations to strengthen their capacity to eliminate shared enemies.
- *New capabilities to aggressively defeat terrorists.* Improve the American intelligence apparatus by investing in its capacity to collect and analyze information, share information with other agencies, and carry out operations to disrupt terrorist networks.
- *Prepare the military to meet 21st century threats.* Ensure that our military becomes more stealthy, agile, and lethal in its ability to capture or kill terrorists. Bolster our military's ability to speak different languages, navigate different cultures, and coordinate complex missions with our civilian agencies.
- *Win the battle of ideas.* Defeat al-Qaeda in the battle of ideas by returning to an American foreign policy consistent with America's traditional values, and work with moderates within the Islamic world to counter al-Qaeda propaganda. Establish a $2 billion Global Education Fund to work to eliminate the global education deficit and offer an alternative to extremist schools.

- *Restore American influence and restore our values.* Stop shuttering consulates and start opening them in the tough and hopeless corners of the world. Expand our foreign service and develop the capacity of our civilian aid workers to work alongside the military.

Prevent Nuclear Terrorism

Barack Obama and Joe Biden have a comprehensive strategy for nuclear security that will reduce the danger of nuclear terrorism, prevent the spread of nuclear weapons capabilities, and strengthen the nuclear nonproliferation regime. They will:

- *Secure nuclear weapons materials in four years and end nuclear smuggling.* Lead a global effort to secure all nuclear weapons materials at vulnerable sites within four years—the most effective way to prevent terrorists from acquiring a nuclear bomb. Fully implement the Lugar-Obama legislation to help our allies detect and stop the smuggling of weapons of mass destruction.
- *Strengthen policing and interdiction efforts.* Institutionalize the Proliferation Security Initiative (PSI), a global initiative aimed at stopping shipments of weapons of mass destruction, their delivery systems, and related materials worldwide.
- *Convene a summit on preventing nuclear terrorism.* Convene a summit in 2009 (and regularly thereafter) of leaders of Permanent Members of the UN Security Council and other key countries to agree on preventing nuclear terrorism.
- *Eliminate Iran's and North Korea's nuclear weapons programs through tough, direct diplomacy.* Use tough diplomacy—backed by real incentives and real pressures—to prevent Iran from acquiring nuclear weapons and to eliminate fully and verifiably North Korea's nuclear weapons program.
- *Strengthen the International Atomic Energy Agency (IAEA).* Seek to ensure that the Agency gets the authority, information, people, and technology it needs to do its job.
- *Control fissile materials.* Lead a global effort to negotiate a verifiable treaty ending the production of fissile materials for weapons purposes.
- *Prevent nuclear fuel from becoming nuclear bombs.* Work with other interested governments to establish a new international nuclear energy architecture—including an international nuclear fuel bank, international nuclear fuel cycle centers, and reliable fuel supply assurances—to meet growing demands for nuclear power without contributing to proliferation.
- *Set the goal of a nuclear-free world.* Show the world that America believes in its existing commitment under the Nuclear Nonproliferation Treaty to work to ultimately eliminate all nuclear weapons. America will not disarm unilaterally.
- *Seek real, verifiable reductions in nuclear stockpiles.* Seek deep, verifiable reductions in all U.S. and Russian nuclear weapons and work with other nuclear powers to reduce global stockpiles dramatically.

- *Work with Russia to increase warning and decision time.* Work with Russia to end dangerous Cold War policies like keeping nuclear weapons ready to launch on a moment's notice, in a mutual and verifiable manner.
- *Appoint White House coordinator for nuclear security.* Appoint a deputy national security advisor to be in charge of coordinating all U.S. programs aimed at reducing the risk of nuclear terrorism and weapons proliferation.
- *Strengthen nuclear risk reduction work at Defense, State, and Energy departments.* Expand our foreign service, and develop the capacity of our civilian aid workers to work alongside the military. Thwarting terrorist networks requires international partnerships in military, intelligence, law enforcement, financial transactions, border controls, and transportation security.

Strengthen American Biosecurity

Biological weapons pose a serious and increasing national security risk. Barack Obama and Joe Biden will work to prevent bioterror attacks and mitigate consequences. They will:

- *Prevent bioterror attacks.* Strengthen U.S. intelligence collection overseas to identify and interdict would-be bioterrorists before they strike.
- *Build capacity to mitigate the consequences of bioterror attacks.* Ensure that decision makers have the information and communication tools they need to manage disease outbreaks by linking health care providers, hospitals, and public health agencies. A well-planned, well-rehearsed, and rapidly executed epidemic response can dramatically diminish the consequences of biological attacks.
- *Accelerate the development of new medicines, vaccines, and production capabilities.* Build on America's unparalleled talent to create new drugs, vaccines, and diagnostic tests and to manufacture them more quickly and efficiently.
- *Lead an international effort to diminish impact of major infectious disease epidemics.* Promote international efforts to develop new diagnostics, vaccines, and medicines that will be available and affordable in all parts of the world.

Protect Our Information Networks

Barack Obama and Joe Biden—working with private industry, the research community, and our citizens—will lead an effort to build a trustworthy and accountable cyber infrastructure that is resilient, protects America's competitive advantage, and advances our national and homeland security. They will:

- *Strengthen federal leadership on cyber security.* Declare the cyber infrastructure a strategic asset and establish the position of national cyber advisor, who will report directly to the president and will be responsible for coordinating federal agency efforts and development of national cyber policy.

- *Initiate a safe computing R&D effort and harden our nation's cyber infrastructure.* Support an initiative to develop next-generation secure computers and networking for national security applications. Work with industry and academia to develop and deploy a new generation of secure hardware and software for our critical cyber infrastructure.
- *Protect the IT infrastructure that keeps America's economy safe.* Work with the private sector to establish tough new standards for cyber security and physical resilience.
- *Prevent corporate cyber espionage.* Work with industry to develop the systems necessary to protect our nation's trade secrets and our research and development. Innovations in software, engineering, pharmaceuticals, and other fields are being stolen online from U.S. businesses at an alarming rate.
- *Develop a cyber crime strategy to minimize the opportunities for criminal profit.* Shut down the mechanisms used to transmit criminal profits by shutting down untraceable Internet payment schemes. Initiate a grant and training program to provide federal, state, and local law enforcement agencies the tools they need to detect and prosecute cyber crime.
- *Mandate standards for securing personal data and require companies to disclose personal information data breaches.* Partner with industry and our citizens to secure personal data stored on government and private systems. Institute a common standard for securing such data across industries and protect the rights of individuals in the information age.

Improve Intelligence Capacity and Protect Civil Liberties

- *Improve information sharing and analysis.* Improve our intelligence system by creating a senior position to coordinate domestic intelligence gathering, establishing a grant program to support thousands more state and local level intelligence analysts, and increasing our capacity to share intelligence across all levels of government.
- *Give real authority to the Privacy and Civil Liberties Board.* Support efforts to strengthen the Privacy and Civil Liberties Board with subpoena powers and reporting responsibilities. Give the Board a robust mandate designed to protect American civil liberties and demand transparency from the Board to ensure accountability.
- *Strengthen institutions to fight terrorism.* Establish a Shared Security Partnership Program overseas to invest $5 billion over three years to improve cooperation between U.S. and foreign intelligence and law enforcement agencies.

Protect Americans from Terrorist Attacks and Natural Disasters

- *Allocate funds based on risk.* Allocate our precious homeland security dollars according to risk, not as pork-barrel spending or a form of general revenue sharing. Eliminate waste, fraud, and abuse that cost the nation billions of Department of Homeland Security dollars.

- *Prepare effective emergency response plans.* Further improve coordination between all levels of government, create better evacuation plan guidelines, ensure prompt federal assistance to emergency zones, and increase medical surge capacity.
- *Support first responders.* Increase federal resources and logistic support to local emergency planning efforts.
- *Improve interoperable communications systems.* Support efforts to provide greater technical assistance to local and state first responders and dramatically increase funding for reliable, interoperable communications systems. Appoint a National Chief Technology Officer to ensure that the current non-interoperable plans at the federal, state, and local levels are combined, funded, implemented, and effective.
- *Working with state and local governments and the private sector.* Make the federal government a better partner to states and localities, one that listens to local concerns and considers local priorities. Reach out to the private sector to leverage its expertise and assets to protect our homeland security.

Protect Critical Infrastructure

- *Create a national infrastructure protection plan.* Develop an effective critical infrastructure protection and resiliency plan for the nation and work with the private sector to ensure that targets are protected against all hazards.
- *Secure our chemical plants.* Work with all stakeholders to enact permanent federal chemical plant security regulations.
- *Improve airline security.* Redouble our efforts to adequately address the threats our nation continues to face from airplane-based terrorism.
- *Monitor our ports.* Redouble our efforts to develop technology that can detect radiation and work with the maritime transportation industry to deploy this technology to maximize security without causing economic disruption.
- *Safeguard public transportation.* Work to protect the public transportation systems Americans use to get to work, school, and beyond every day.
- *Improve border security.* Support the virtual and physical infrastructure and manpower necessary to secure our borders and keep our nation safe.

Modernize America's Aging Infrastructure

- *Build-in security.* Ensure that security is considered and built into the design of new infrastructure, so that our critical assets are protected from the start and more resilient to naturally occurring and deliberate threats throughout their life-cycle.
- *Create a national infrastructure reinvestment bank.* Address the infrastructure challenge by creating a National Infrastructure Reinvestment Bank of $60 billion over 10 years, to expand and enhance, not supplant, existing federal

New York, New York, September 21, 2001. The World Trade Center was completely destroyed by the terrorist attacks on September 11. Cleanup worked around the clock for months. Michael Rieger/FEMA News Photo

transportation investments. This independent entity will be directed to invest in our nation's most challenging transportation infrastructure needs, without the influence of special interests.

• *Invest in critical infrastructure projects.* Invest in our nation's most pressing short- and long-term infrastructure needs, including modernizing our electrical grid and upgrading our highway, rail, ports, water, and aviation infrastructure. Establish a Grid Modernization Commission to facilitate adoption of Smart Grid practices to improve efficiency and security of our electricity grid.

CITIZEN SUPPORT

What can you do? Devastating acts, such as the terrorist attacks on the World Trade Center and the Pentagon, have left many concerned about the possibility of future incidents in the United States and their potential impact. They raise uncertainty about what might happen next, which increases stress levels. Nevertheless, you can do many things to prepare for the unexpected that will reduce the stress that you may feel now—and later, should any emergency arise. Taking preparatory action can reassure you and your children so you may exert a measure of control even in the face of such terrible events.

For detailed information on emergency preparedness and what you can do to protect yourself and your loved ones, after you read the following chapter, go to part III, "Be Prepared."

Chapter Three

Are We Winning the War?

The war on terror has been a hugely costly one—in terms of lives lost and money spent. But has it made America and Americans safer? Before we look at what is happening at home, it is worth examining what is happening beyond our borders.

OVERSEAS

Overseas, democracies are being restored to some extent in Afghanistan and Iraq, although progress is painfully slow. While there are hundreds of "good news" stories occurring every day in both these countries, the overwhelming image in the minds of most Americans is of countries still fighting to win a permanent peace.

Afghanistan

In Afghanistan—officially the Islamic Republic of Afghanistan—the ousted Taliban is now a militia openly operating in areas of the country outside the control of the government in Kabul, especially in the south and east. In fact, the government only effectively controls the area in and around the capital. In the south and east, the Taliban is acting as a shadow government and in some areas has popular support because they have brought about some semblance of order. Remnants of the Taliban continue to launch attacks on government troops, police, and overseas workers and are increasingly focusing on soft targets.

In January 2006, following two suicide bomb attacks that killed twenty-six people and wounded fifty others, Afghan President Hamid Karzai said:

> We are in a joint struggle against terrorism, for us and for the international community. . . . If you don't defend yourself here, you will have to defend yourself back home, in European capitals and Americans' capitals. It will take many, many more years before we can defend ourselves with our own means, before we can feed ourselves or work for our development with our own means.

Afghanistan is desperate for foreign aid and overseas investment to help rebuild the country, where warlords still control vast tracts of land and the poppy fields. Today, opium accounts for over half of the nation's economic output, and more than 3.3 million Afghans are involved in producing opium and its derivatives, morphine and heroine.

According to the United Nations Office on Drugs and Crime, opium production has grown every year since the Taliban were ousted in 2001. Afghanistan now produces over 90 percent of the world's opium, most of which is smuggled to Europe.

In 2007 the United States extended tours of duty in Afghanistan for the military because of increased Taliban activity—the number of insurgent attacks was 300 percent higher than in the previous twelve months. President Obama announced in early 2009 that he plans to add twenty-one thousand U.S. soldiers and Marines to the thirty-eight thousand Americans already fighting across Afghanistan. His strategy calls for an increased focus on boosting the capabilities of Afghanistan's security forces and improving the effectiveness of the government in Kabul.

Iraq

Since the ousting of Saddam Hussein, much has been achieved in Iraq. There have been democratic elections, a constitution has been approved, and parliament meets regularly. There has also been a steady transfer of security from the international coalition to the Iraqi army and police. There has been considerable reconstruction in some parts of the country, and many provinces are relatively peaceful today. However, attacks on military and civilian personnel and targets continue—especially in and around the capital, Baghdad—and are likely to increase as the international coalition plans to pull out.

Although some 220,000 Iraqi security forces have been trained, the country is still unable to defend itself without its allies. President Bush often said, "As the Iraqi army stands up, we will stand down."

In 2007, President Bush ordered an additional 21,500 troops to Iraq. This "surge" in security activity led to significant reductions in overall violence, although on August 14, 2007, the deadliest single attack of the war took place: almost eight hundred civilians were killed in coordinated suicide bomb attacks in non-Muslim villages in the north of the country. Over the next year the number of attacks decreased, and U.S. troop deaths fell to their lowest level since 2003.

In February 2009, President Obama announced an eighteen-month withdrawal window for "combat forces," leaving behind thirty thousand to fifty thousand troops "to advise and train Iraqi security forces and to provide intelligence and surveillance."

Iraq continues to be the battleground for hundreds of foreign terrorists opposed to the Iraqi government and the presence of Coalition forces. These terrorists are able to cross into Iraq freely from Iran, Syria, Jordan, and Saudi Arabia. Both Iran and Syria are known to be supporting terrorists by providing training camps, safe refuge, arms, equipment, and funding. There is growing evidence that insurgents in Iraq are turning against these foreigners because they indiscriminately kill innocent Iraqis.

For the last five years Sunni Arab tribesmen have been fighting alongside insurgents and foreign terrorists. Now many have turned against the foreign fighters, while support for al-Qaeda in Iraq is falling away. Abu Musab al-Zarqawi, who founded al-Qaeda in Iraq, was killed in a U.S. bombing raid on June 7, 2006, while attending a meeting in a safe house north of Baqubah. Many foreign fighters have been killed by Sunnis, and others have been captured along with arms caches following tip-offs from locals about their hideouts.

The aim of the U.S. intervention was always to topple Saddam and replace him with a democratic government representing all factions within the country. However, sectarianism has split Iraq for hundreds of years and continues to do so. Many times the country has been perilously close to civil war and remains so, as warring sectarian factions continue the cycle of attacks and reprisals. Foreign terrorists clearly have a vested interest in instigating a civil war—it will discredit all the efforts of the Coalition and, in the chaos, may allow the insurgents to take control.

The Iraqi people themselves hold the key to their future. On several occasions over the past three years, they have been able to pull back from the brink and resume talking to each other. If peace and common sense prevail, Iraq has a future; if not, it could slip into sectarian warfare that could create divisions that will last for years.

The Rest of the World

The U.S. invasion of Afghanistan and Iraq was not responsible for creating the various terrorist groups. Most were active in the 1990s, but certainly the invasion of Iraq provided them—and especially the radical Islamic groups, with a tangible cause and a battleground on which to fight it. Terrorists flooded into the Middle East and then into Iraq and to a lesser extent, Afghanistan. Ironically, as the security forces have started to gain the upper hand in Iraq, many of the insurgents have moved to the porous Pakistan-Afghanistan border.

Terror groups, though, have become increasingly active around the world. The number of attacks increased in the past few years and the attacks became more deadly as the terrorists become more sophisticated with bomb-making and attack strategies.

The number of serious international terrorist incidents continues to increase. According to the U.S. government's figures, there were 1,130 terrorist attacks worldwide in 2000 resulting in 778 deaths. In 2004 there were 2,646 attacks with 5,068 deaths and in 2008 (the last year for which official figures are available) there were 11,770 attacks resulting in 15,765 deaths (see table 3.1).

Table 3.1.   Incidents of Terrorism Worldwide

	2005	2006	2007	2008
Attacks worldwide	11,157	14,545	14,506	11,770
Attacks resulting in death, injury, or kidnapping of at least one person	8,025	11,311	11,123	8,438
Attacks resulting in the death of at least one individual	5,127	7,428	7,255	5,067
Attacks resulting in the death of zero individuals	6,030	7,117	7,251	6,703
Attacks resulting in the death of only one individual	2,880	4,139	3,994	2,889
Attacks resulting in the death of at least ten individuals	226	293	353	235
Attacks resulting in the injury of at least one individual	3,842	5,796	6,256	4,888
Attacks resulting in the kidnapping of at least one individual	1,475	1,733	1,459	1,125
People killed, injured, or kidnapped as a result of terrorism	74,280	74,709	71,608	54,747
People killed worldwide as a result of terrorism	14,560	20,468	22,508	15,765
People injured worldwide as a result of terrorism	24,875	38,386	44,118	34,124
People kidnapped worldwide as a result of terrorism	34,845	15,855	4,982	4,858

Source: U.S. Department of State, Office of the Coordinator for Counterterrorism, *Country Reports on Terrorism 2008* (www.state.gov/s/ct/rls/crt/2008/122452.htm).

If the number of attacks doesn't present an accurate measure of success in the war on terrorism, which numbers do? The following facts are also important in the equation:

- Number of Taliban-style states created since 9/11: 0
- Number of countries that have recognized al-Qaeda: 0
- Number of nations that have adopted "state-sponsored" terrorism as an official policy: 0
- Number of states that have voluntarily given up WMD programs since 9/11: 1
- Number of transnational nuclear smuggling networks broken up since 9/11: 1
- Number of Middle Eastern states that have moved closer to democracy: 5

Terrorist attacks, however, continue to take place worldwide. In the Far East, radical Islamic terrorist groups are active in many countries. There is an increasing threat from radical Islamic groups in India and Pakistan, and despite efforts by the government of Pakistan, leaders of al-Qaeda, including bin Laden, are being harbored by sympathetic tribesmen in the mountainous border region between Pakistan and Afghanistan.

Russia's southern flanks are threatened by almost a dozen countries—all former Soviet territories—that now have large and militant Muslim populations. Ongoing attacks in Russia that were attributed to Chechen rebels are now believed to be the work of home-grown Muslim terrorists.

Terrorism is rife throughout the Middle East, with deadly attacks in Jordan, Egypt, Kuwait, Saudi Arabia, and elsewhere. Almost all these attacks have been carried out by Islamic extremists who want to topple the existing regimes and replace them with an Islamic caliphate that would encompass all of the Middle East.

Europe is embroiled with terrorism, from Basque separatists to Muslim terror cells in Britain. In 2005, France suffered weeks of rioting, arson, and destruction, when tens of thousands of young immigrants, almost all of them Muslim, vented their anger and frustration at being treated, as they saw it, as second-class citizens. That rioting spread to surrounding countries, especially Belgium, although it was quickly contained.

Deadly bombings in Madrid in 2004 brought down the Spanish government, and suicide bombings in London in 2005 killed and maimed hundreds. Both were carried out by Islamic extremists. The London bombings sent a shock wave through the Western world because the terrorists, all Muslim, were almost all British born and seemingly leading normal, respectable lives in their communities. The subsequent Euro-wide police hunt found that sleeper cells existed throughout Europe and North Africa. Intelligence agencies are convinced that similar sleeper cells exist in North America.

WAR ON TERROR NOT CONFINED TO AL-QAEDA, CENTCOM GENERAL SAYS

As reported on March 13, 2006, by Sgt. Sara Wood of the American Forces Press Service (www.defenselink.mil/news/newsarticle.aspx?id=15193, accessed July 22, 2009):

The enemy in the war on terror is not limited to al-Qaeda and its associated movements in Iraq and Afghanistan but includes a global network of extremist groups, a U.S. Central Command [CENTCOM] general said [in Tacoma, Washington] March 11.

"If we declared victory and walked away from Iraq and Afghanistan tomorrow, we would be fighting this fight for years and years," said Army Brig. Gen. Mark T. Kimmitt, CENTCOM's deputy director of plans and policy, speaking at the Pacific Northwest National Security Forum. "We are fighting an insurgency, a terrorist movement, that is represented by al-Qaeda, but it is far more than al-Qaeda."

The terrorist network the United States is facing in this war includes extremist groups around the world, and it is a network the nation has been fighting since before Sept. 11, 2001, Kimmitt said. The extremist groups are made up of primarily Sunni Muslims whose goal is to reclaim what they see as the holy lands in the Middle East and to remove Western influence, he added. Their ultimate goal is to establish a caliphate in the region, where Sharia, or Islamic law, rules, and the people are oppressed, he said.

To defeat this network, CENTCOM is pursuing an aggressive campaign to defeat terrorists where they are active and to prevent the spread of their ideology, Kimmitt said.

One of the important aspects of the CENTCOM strategy is that it will take a network to defeat the terrorist network, Kimmitt said. The global terror network uses people, the Internet, smuggling, nongovernmental organizations that are sympathetic to their cause, legitimate governments, front companies, and safe havens to achieve its goals, he said.

"If that's the way that the enemy is going to fight us, it is important to understand that it's going to take far more than the military to defeat this network," the general said. "Our network needs to be equally strong, and it can't simply rely on the military."

CENTCOM is developing a strong network that uses all elements of national power to defeat terrorists, Kimmitt said. This network will rely on federal and state law enforcement agencies, the State Department, and federal intelligence agencies, he said.

Another important aspect of CENTCOM's strategy is building the capacity of other nations to fight terrorism themselves, Kimmitt said. Leaders of the al-Qaeda movement have been very clear in stating that their goal is to rid the region of Western influence and then go after surrounding countries, which they call apostate or secular governments, he said. These clear declarations have made countries such as Saudi Arabia, Qatar, Jordan, and Kuwait more willing to work with the United States and prepare to fight terrorism on their own, he said.

"These countries get it; they understand that it's not simply a problem [Osama bin Laden] has with the West, it is simply a problem that bin Laden and these organizations have with anybody that does not believe in their extremist ideology," he said.

Most of the high-value target operations in these neighboring countries have been conducted by the countries' own national forces, Kimmitt said, and the United States will continue to work with them to help them prevent terrorist activity inside their borders.

Also important to CENTCOM's strategy is denying safe havens or sanctuaries to terrorists, Kimmitt said. The United States has to ensure that as al-Qaeda and its related organizations are pushed out of Iraq and Afghanistan, they don't just resettle somewhere else, he said.

Combined Joint Task Force Horn of Africa, with headquarters in Djibouti, is the model for this preventive strategy, he said. American and coalition forces there focus primarily on civil affairs and humanitarian missions to establish relationships with the people and foster cooperation, should terrorists try to move into the area.

"It's much easier to stop al-Qaeda and its associated movements as it tries to establish rather than once it's already established," he said.

To make sure a victory in the war on terror lasts, the United States is tailoring its post-conflict strategy for the area, Kimmitt said. It would be a mistake for the United States to garrison the Middle East like it did to western Europe after World War II, he explained. The correct strategy for the Middle East is to maintain a sufficient capability in the region to do necessary tasks, such as deterring adversaries, maintaining lines of communication, and maintaining access to strategic resources, but not have any more U.S. military presence than is needed, he said.

"We cannot be seen as occupiers; we cannot breed a cycle of dependency in the region," he said. "The force that we see five years from now, 10 years from now, in the Middle East is a fraction of the size the force is today."

The war on terror will be a long fight, perhaps lasting a generation, Kimmitt said, but it is one that must be fought, and the support of the American public is crucial.

"I, for one, remain confident that America gets it, and America, despite what our critics may say, is willing to pay in treasure and in blood to defeat this enemy in The Long War," he said.

INCREASING SOPHISTICATION

Another alarming trend is the increasing number of terrorist groups that are seeking WMDs, said the U.S. State Department in a report on global terrorism in 2004.

"Although al-Qaeda remains the primary concern regarding possible WMD threats, the number of groups expressing interest in such material is increasing, and WMD technology and know-how is proliferating in the jihadist community," the report said.

Terrorist groups use the Internet to communicate with each other. They post bomb-making information on websites and they use all the latest multimedia skills to get their message across.

AT HOME

Certainly there have been no serious terrorist attacks on U.S. soil since 9/11, and a number of potential terror attacks have been foiled. Law enforcement and intelligence agencies have not released the full details of some of these attacks, but the perpetrators were in most cases of Middle Eastern or North African origin and all Muslim. Some were born in this country and many were recruited while in prison. It is known that there are strong radical Muslim gangs in many of the nation's prisons, which are fertile recruiting grounds. Prisons not only make great places to recruit new members, they provide an environment without distractions where recruits can be taught their terrorism skills. And what they don't acquire inside, they can get from activists and the Web outside.

What the intelligence agencies do not know, however, is how many sleeper cells may exist in the United States.

An article titled "Urgent Action Needed to Curb Militant Islam in the U.S." (www.free-press-release.com/news/200509/1127923481.html, accessed July 22, 2009) said:

Islam is the fastest growing religion in the U.S. In Illinois, a growth of about 25 percent in the Muslim population was due to conversion, but immigration, mainly from southwest Asia, accounts for most of the growth. While the exact number of Muslims living in the U.S. is not known, estimates place the number at between 7 and 9 million, of which almost 80% are aged between 16 and 65.

"Typically, young males prone to be recruited by Islamist activists generally fall in the 16–45 age bracket. The younger ones—those in their teens and early twenties—are typically the most vulnerable," said Claude Salhani [UPI Interna-

tional Editor in Washington, in a white paper he wrote for www.isamericasafe
.com in 2005].

"Just as Muslims make up the majority of the incarcerated population of
Europe's jails, so too, do Muslims comprise the majority of inmates crowding
American prisons. Much of the conversion takes place inside jails and usually
by Imams espousing radical thinking. Often, moderate Muslims who enter jail
leave incarceration far more radicalized," he said.

A survey of British Muslims found that 6 percent—about 100,000 people—
believed the London bombings were justified, and 1 percent felt that "the deca-
dent and immoral" Western society should be brought to an end and by violence
if necessary.

"Using the figure of 7 million Muslims living in the U.S., one percent would
amount to 70,000. That is a staggering 70,000 potential people supporting
violence against their adopted homeland. Break that down even further to one
percent of one percent—and you have 700 probably extremists," he warned.

"The danger posed by sleeper cells, by al-Qaeda sympathizers and wannabe
jihadists is not to be underestimated. The threat is real," he said.

Post 9/11

There is no doubt that as a result of 9/11 we are as a nation better able to defend ourselves; slowly but surely, an infrastructure is being built that is better
able to identify threats and respond to them.

However, the PATRIOT Act and other anti-terrorism measures, such as the
domestic eavesdropping on the telephone calls of U.S. citizens, have eroded
some of the very freedoms we are fighting so hard to protect. Fighting wars
in Afghanistan and Iraq has put enormous strain on the military and their
families, especially members of the National Guard, many of whom never
expected to be deployed overseas.

The war on terror, being waged at home and overseas, has also placed a co-
lossal economic burden on the shoulders of the nation's taxpayers. While all
the government spending has not gone to homeland security and the military,
in eight years the United States has gone from a budget surplus to a massive
deficit. Apart from the cost of fighting tyranny and terrorism, the war on terror has impacted us in many ways.

Homeland Defense

The creation of the Department of the Homeland Security was the largest reorganization in federal government history. Not unexpectedly, when you try
to merge 180,000 people from twenty-two departments into four directorates
of one entity, you are going to have problems.

It was not simply a matter of merging the manpower and responsibilities of the different departments. Each department had its own computer system, its own software, and its own communications network. Billions are being spent trying to make all the systems compatible.

Travel

Most Americans have patiently endured the longer waits that have resulted from more stringent security checks at airports. Before 9/11 only 5 percent of passengers' bags were checked; now 1 billion bags are checked annually. Sky marshals travel on an undisclosed number of flights and a greater percentage of check-in luggage and air freight is screened. Cockpit doors have been strengthened and groups are not allowed to congregate in the aisles during flights.

Ports

Despite the furor over foreign companies taking over U.S. ports, there is concern that ports still represent a weak link in the nation's security. Every year, 16 million containers move through America's 361 ports. Only 2 percent are inspected—leaving what may be the biggest hole in the nation's terror shield. The Department of Homeland Security expects to have 100 percent screening of all containers by 2012. However, scanning is only one aspect of seaport security. Effective security also requires improvements in intelligence, cooperation with foreign ports, and tracking of containers while in transit.

Essential Infrastructure (Water, Nuclear, Food Chain)

Without doubt, much of our essential infrastructure remains vulnerable. However, our strategy of layered defenses aims to restrict access of potential terrorist threats by dealing with them at a distance. More cargo is now checked at ports of origin and manifests are screened for suspicious points of origin or dubious shippers. Ships' crews are screened and cargoes are tracked by satellite. Navy and Coast Guard ships stand ready to board ships far at sea to examine suspicious crew members and cargoes.

Our water supplies are very accessible. However, it would take huge volumes of pollutants or poison to be a threat to users after the water flows through our testing and treatment procedures.

Our nuclear power and chemical plants are in the process of hardening their sites. But many are still open to aerial attacks or a dedicated ground attack. Since most of these facilities are in remote areas, they probably rank lower on the terrorists' lucrative target list than one might think.

The same is true of our food supply. Small, isolated attacks are very feasible, but targeting mass casualties through our supply chain is less likely than other more spectacular and more effective terrorist alternatives.

WMD Attack

Could we cope? Most experts agree that WMDs should remain our primary concern from either foreign or domestic terrorist threats. Such attacks may be launched with minimal resources and by very few individuals. WMD attacks present all the attributes that terrorists seek to achieve: fear, confusion, mass casualties, and notoriety. But most WMDs are difficult to reliably employ. Delivery systems, wind direction, weather conditions—all must be just right to target huge groups of people in a contained situation, such as a meeting place or sporting event.

Mass Evacuation

The U.K. government's plan to evacuate London might be able to get 1 million people out of the capital in twenty-four hours, assuming the railways were still operating. The rest of the capital's population—about 7 million people—would have to fend for themselves. Could we do any better in evacuating a major U.S. city? Hurricane Katrina demonstrated how difficult it is to evacuate cities like New Orleans and Houston.

Tolerance

Are we more tolerant as a nation than we were before 9/11? Are we more sympathetic or more suspicious of our Muslim neighbors?

SUMMARY

The war on terror is high on most Americans' list of concerns. It promises to be with us for at least another generation. We are relatively safe from terror within our borders—now. But experts agree that it's not *if*, but *when* we may be attacked in the future. Much more needs to be done in many areas, such as protecting our borders, screening foreign visitors, and getting the public more involved in neighborhood watch programs on land and at sea.

Anchorage, Alaska, March 3, 2006. Petty Officer Brady Osborne stands over the Cape Orlando *(T-AKR-2044) at the Port of Anchorage in seven-degree weather. Osborne was part of a Coast Guard team tasked with providing security for the vessel while in port. The Army handled the offload of equipment, including CH-47 Chinook helicopters returning to Fort Wainwright from service in Iraq, Kuwait, and Afghanistan. USCG photo by PA3 Sara Francis*

For most of us, however, medical malpractice, smoking, disease, automobile accidents, and deaths and injuries in the home should be of greater concern—and they are within greater control of individual actions.

Man-made and natural disasters are also a greater threat to most of us than terrorism—and cost U.S. taxpayers and victims dearly. Still, there is much that we may do to minimize exposure to such threats and to mitigate the damage done to our loved ones and our property if we are caught in one of these disasters.

Of primary concern should be the billions that we are spending to keep America safe. We must realize that no amount of money will keep us perfectly safe. The nature of our free society makes us vulnerable . . . and a target for those who hate freedom. But we must charge our leadership to be good stewards of the money that we send them. There must be a balance between what we spend our tax dollars on and what we get in return in terms of safety, security, and quality of life.

Is America safe? What do you think?

New York City, New York, September 11, 2002. "Bruised, But Not Broken." People from all over the world came to New York for an observance ceremony for the one-year anniversary of 9/11. Andrea Booher/FEMA News Photo

Chapter Four

Terrorist Groups: Major Terrorist Organizations

Note: Unless otherwise noted, material in this chapter is drawn from two documents by the U.S. Department of State, Office of the Coordinator for Counterterrorism: "Terrorist Organizations: U.S. Government Designated Foreign Terrorist Organizations," in *Country Reports on Terrorism 2008*, chapter 6 (www.state.gov/s/ct/rls/crt/2008/122449.htm) and "Terrorist Organizations: Other Groups of Concern," in *Country Reports on Terrorism 2006*, chapter 6 (www.state.gov/s/ct/rls/crt/2006/82738.htm).

ABU NIDAL ORGANIZATION (ANO)

a.k.a. Arab Revolutionary Brigades; Arab Revolutionary Council; Black September; Fatah Revolutionary Council; Revolutionary Organization of Socialist Muslims

Description

The Abu Nidal Organization (ANO) was designated as a Foreign Terrorist Organization on October 8, 1997. The ANO, an international terrorist organization, was founded by Sabri al-Banna (a.k.a. Abu Nidal) after splitting from the Palestine Liberation Organization (PLO) in 1974. The group's previous known structure consisted of various functional committees, including political, military, and financial. In August 2002, Abu Nidal died in Baghdad, probably at the hands of Iraqi security officials. Present leadership of the organization remains unclear.

Activities

The ANO has carried out terrorist attacks in 20 countries, killing or injuring almost 900 persons. The group has not staged a major attack against Western targets since the late 1980s. Major attacks included the Rome and Vienna airports in 1985, the Neve Shalom synagogue in Istanbul, the hijacking of Pan Am Flight 73 in Karachi in 1986, and the City of Poros day-excursion ship attack in Greece in 1988. The ANO is suspected of assassinating PLO Deputy Chief Abu Iyad and PLO Security Chief Abu Hul in Tunis in 1991. In 2008, a Jordanian official reported the apprehension of an ANO member who planned to carry out attacks in Jordan. The ANO did not successfully carry out attacks in 2008.

Strength

Current strength is unknown.

Location/Area of Operation

The group is largely considered inactive, although former and possibly current ANO associates might be in Iraq and Lebanon.

External Aid

The ANO's current access to resources is unclear, but it is likely that the decline in state support has had a severe impact on its capabilities.

ABU SAYYAF GROUP (ASG)

a.k.a. al Harakat al Islamiyya

Description

The Abu Sayyaf Group (ASG) was designated as a Foreign Terrorist Organization on October 8, 1997. The ASG is a terrorist group operating in the southern Philippines. Some ASG leaders allegedly fought in Afghanistan during the Soviet invasion and are students and proponents of radical Islamic teachings. The group split from the much larger Moro National Liberation Front in the early 1990s under the leadership of Abdurajak Abubakar Janjalani, who was killed in a clash with Philippine police in December 1998. His younger brother, Khadaffy Janjalani, replaced him as the nominal leader of the group. In September 2006, Janjalani was killed in a gun battle with the Armed Forces of the Philippines. Radullah Sahiron is assumed to be the new ASG leader.

Activities

The ASG engages in kidnappings for ransom, bombings, beheadings, assassinations, and extortion. The group's stated goal is to promote an independent

Islamic state in western Mindanao and the Sulu Archipelago, areas in the southern Philippines heavily populated by Muslims, but the ASG primarily has used terrorism for financial profit. Recent bombings may herald a return to a more radical, politicized agenda, at least among certain factions. In 2006, the Armed Forces of the Philippines began "Operation Ultimatum," a sustained campaign that disrupted ASG forces in safe havens on Jolo Island in the Sulu archipelago, and resulted in the killing of ASG leader Khadaffy Janjalani in September 2006 and his deputy, Abu Solaiman, in January 2007. In July 2007, the ASG and Moro Islamic Liberation Front (MILF) engaged a force of Philippine marines on Basilan Island, killing fourteen, ten of which were beheaded.

The group's first large-scale action was a raid on the town of Ipil in Mindanao in April 1995. In April 2000, an ASG faction kidnapped 21 persons, including ten Western tourists, from a resort in Malaysia. In May 2001, the ASG kidnapped three U.S. citizens and 17 Filipinos from a tourist resort in Palawan, Philippines. Several of the hostages, including U.S. citizen Guillermo Sobero, were murdered. A Philippine military hostage rescue operation in June 2002 freed U.S. hostage Gracia Burnham, but her husband Martin Burnham, also a U.S. national, and Filipina Deborah Yap were killed.

U.S. and Philippine authorities blamed the ASG for a bomb near a Philippine military base in Zamboanga in October 2002 that killed a U.S. serviceman. In February 2004, Khadaffy Janjalani's faction bombed SuperFerry 14 in Manila Bay, killing 132. In March 2004, Philippine authorities arrested an ASG cell whose bombing targets included the U.S. Embassy in Manila. The ASG also claimed responsibility for the 2005 Valentine's Day bombings in Manila, Davao City, and General Santos City, which killed eight and injured more than 150. In November 2007, a motorcycle bomb exploded outside the Philippines Congress, killing a congressman and three staff members. While there was no definitive claim of responsibility, three suspected ASG members were arrested during a subsequent raid on a safe house.

Strength

ASG is estimated to have 200 to 500 members.

Location/Area of Operation

The ASG was founded in Basilan Province and operates primarily in the provinces of the Sulu Archipelago, namely Basilan, Sulu, and Tawi-Tawi. The group also operates on the Zamboanga peninsula, and members occasionally travel to Manila. In mid-2003, the group started operating in Mindanao's city of Cotobato and on the provincial coast of Sultan Kudarat, Mindanao. The ASG was expelled from Mindanao proper by the Moro Islamic Liberation Front in mid-2005. The group expanded its operational reach to Malaysia in 2000 with the abduction of foreigners from a tourist resort there.

External Aid

The ASG is funded through acts of ransom and extortion, and receives funding from both regional terrorist groups such as Jemaah Islamiya (JI), which is based mainly in Indonesia, and Middle Eastern Islamic extremists. In October 2007, the ASG appealed for funds and recruits on *YouTube* by featuring a video of the Janjalani brothers before they were killed.

AL-AQSA MARTYRS BRIGADE

a.k.a. al-Aqsa Martyrs Battalion

Description

The al-Aqsa Martyrs Brigade was designated as a Foreign Terrorist Organization on March 27, 2002. The al-Aqsa Martyrs Brigade consists of loose cells of Palestinian militants loyal to, but not under the direct control of, the secular-nationalist Fatah movement. Al-Aqsa emerged at the outset of the 2000 Palestinian al-Aqsa intifada as a militant offshoot of the Fatah party, attacking Israeli military targets and settlers with the aim of driving Israel from the West Bank and Gaza and establishing a Palestinian state. Al-Aqsa has no central leadership; the cells operate with autonomy, although they remained ideologically loyal to Palestinian Authority (PA) President and Fatah party head Yassir Arafat until his death in November 2004.

Activities

Al-Aqsa initially focused on small arms attacks against Israeli military personnel and settlers in the West Bank. In 2002, however, the group began to conduct suicide bombings against Israeli civilians. Al-Aqsa suspended most anti-Israel attacks as part of the broader unilateral Palestinian cease-fire agreement during 2004 but resumed them following Hamas's January 2006 victory in Palestinian Legislative Council elections. Al-Aqsa members continued the anti-Israeli and intra-Palestinian violence that contributed to the overall chaotic security environment in the Palestinian territories. In 2008, the majority of al-Aqsa attacks were rocket and mortar attacks into southern Israel from Hamas-ruled Gaza. Israel agreed to extend a conditional pardon to 300 West Bank al-Aqsa members, but did not expand the program to the rest of the organization. Al-Aqsa has not targeted U.S. interests as a policy, although its anti-Israeli attacks have killed some dual U.S.-Israeli citizens.

Strength

Current strength is unknown, but most likely numbers a few hundred.

Location/Area of Operation

Al-Aqsa operates mainly in the West Bank and Gaza Strip and has conducted attacks inside Israel and Gaza. The group also has members in Palestinian refugee camps in Lebanon.

External Aid

Iran has exploited al-Aqsa's lack of resources and formal leadership by providing funds and other aid, mostly through Hezbollah facilitators.

AL-BADHR MUJAHEDIN (AL-BADR)

Description

The al-Badhr Mujahedin split from Hizbul-Mujahedin (HM) in 1998. It traces its origins to 1971, when a group named al-Badr attacked Bengalis in East Pakistan. The group later operated as part of Gulbuddin Hekmatyar's Hizb-I Islami (HIG) in Afghanistan and, from 1990, as a unit of HM in Kashmir. The group was relatively inactive until 2000. Since then, it has increasingly claimed responsibility for attacks against Indian military targets. Since the late 1990s, al-Badhr leader Bakht Zamin repeatedly has expressed his support for Osama bin Laden and the Taliban, and in 2002 declared jihad against U.S. forces in Afghanistan.

Activities

The organization has conducted a number of operations against Indian military targets in Jammu and Kashmir. Since late 2001, al-Badr members have reportedly targeted Coalition Forces in Afghanistan.

Strength

Perhaps several hundred.

Location/Area of Operation

Jammu and Kashmir, Pakistan, and Afghanistan.

External Aid

Unknown.

AL-ITTIHAD AL-ISLAMI (AIAI)

Description

AIAI, a Somali extremist group that was formed in the 1980s and reached its peak in the early 1990s, failed to obtain its objective of establishing a Salafist emirate in Somalia and steadily declined following the downfall of the Siad Barre regime in 1991 and Somalia's subsequent collapse into anarchy. AIAI was not internally cohesive, lacked central leadership, and suffered divisions between factions. AIAI was militarily defeated by Ethiopian forces in 1997. In recent years, the existence of a coherent entity operating as AIAI has become difficult to prove. After the downfall of the Somali Council of Islamic Courts in late 2006, AIAI has re-emerged. Former elements of AIAI continue to pursue a variety of agendas ranging from social services and education to insurgency activities in the Ogaden region of eastern Ethiopia. Some sheikhs formerly associated with AIAI espouse a fundamentalist version of Islam, with particular emphasis on a strict adherence to Sharia (Islamic law), a view often at odds with Somalis' emphasis on clan identity. A small group of former AIAI members embrace global jihad and support al-Qaeda members in East Africa. The UN 1267 al-Qaida/Taliban/Usama bin Laden Sanctions Committee has listed AIAI for its associations with al-Qaeda.

Activities

Individuals formerly associated with AIAI may have been responsible for several kidnappings and murders of relief workers in Somalia and Somaliland since 2003 and in the late 1990s. Prior to its destruction in 1997, factions of AIAI also may have been responsible for a series of bomb attacks in public places in Addis Ababa in 1996 and 1997. Most AIAI factions in recent years have concentrated on broadening their religious base, renewed an emphasis on building businesses, and undertaken "hearts and minds" actions, such as sponsoring orphanages and schools and providing security that uses an Islamic legal structure in the areas where it is active.

Strength

The actual membership strength is unknown.

Location/Area of Operation

Primarily in Somalia, with a presence in the Ogaden region of Ethiopia, Kenya, and possibly Djibouti.

External Aid

Receives funds from Middle East financiers and Somali diaspora communities in Europe, North America, and the Arabian Peninsula.

ALEX BONCAYAO BRIGADE (ABB)

Description

The ABB, the breakaway urban hit squad of the Communist Party of the Philippines/New People's Army, was formed in the mid-1980s. The ABB was added to the Terrorist Exclusion list in December 2001.

Activities

Responsible for more than 100 murders, including the murder in 1989 of U.S. Army Col. James Rowe in the Philippines. In March 1997, the group announced it had formed an alliance with another armed group, the Revolutionary Proletarian Army (RPA). In March 2000, the group claimed credit for a rifle grenade attack against the Department of Energy building in Manila and strafed Shell Oil offices in the central Philippines to protest rising oil prices. The group has not been active/conducted attacks in recent years.

Strength

Unknown, but believed to number below 500.

Location/Area of Operation

The largest RPA/ABB groups are on the Philippine islands of Luzon, Negros, and the Visayas.

External Aid

Unknown.

AL-SHABAAB

a.k.a. the Harakat Shabaab al-Mujahidin; al-Shabab; Shabaab; the Youth; Mujahidin al-Shabaab Movement; Mujahideen Youth Movement; Mujahidin Youth Movement

Description

Al-Shabaab was designated as a Foreign Terrorist Organization on February 29, 2008. Al-Shabaab is the militant wing of the former Somali Islamic Courts Council that took over most of southern Somalia in the second half of 2006. In December 2006 and January 2007, Somali government and Ethiopian forces routed the Islamic Court militias in a two-week war. Since the end of 2006, al-Shabaab and disparate clan militias led a violent insurgency, using guerrilla warfare and terrorist tactics against the Ethiopian presence in Somalia and the Transitional Federal Government of Somalia, and the African Union Mission in Somalia (AMISOM) peacekeepers.

Activities

Al-Shabaab has used intimidation and violence to undermine the Somali government and regularly kills activists working to bring about peace through political dialogue and reconciliation. The group has claimed responsibility for several high profile bombings and shootings in Mogadishu targeting Ethiopian troops and Somali government officials. It has been responsible for the assassination of numerous civil society figures, government officials, and journalists. Al-Shabaab fighters or those who have claimed allegiance to the group have also conducted violent attacks and targeted assassinations against international aid workers and nongovernmental aid organizations.

Location/Area of Operation

The majority of Ethiopian troops left Somalia in late January and the subsequent security vacuum in parts of central and southern Somalia has led divergent factions to oppose al-Shabaab and its extremist ideology. However, hardcore al-Shabaab fighters and allied militias continue to conduct brazen attacks in Mogadishu and outlying environs, primarily in lower-Somalia. After al-Shabaab's leaders publicly ordered their fighters to attack African Union (AU) peace-keeping troops based in Mogadishu, a suicide vehicle bomber detonated near an AU base in the capital on January 24, 2008, killing an estimated 13 people.

Strength

Precise numbers are unknown; however some of al-Shabaab's senior leaders are affiliated with al-Qaeda operatives, and it is believed that specific al-Shabaab members have previously trained and fought with al-Qaeda in Afghanistan. Al-Shabaab has issued statements praising Osama bin Laden and linking Somalia jihadists to al-Qaeda's global ideology.

External Aid

Al-Shabaab receives significant donations from the global Somali diaspora. It also raises funds in Somalia.

ANSAR AL-ISLAM (AI)

a.k.a. Ansar al-Sunna; Ansar al-Sunna Army; Devotees of Islam; Followers of Islam in Kurdistan; Helpers of Islam; Jaish Ansar al-Sunna; Jund al-Islam; Kurdish Taliban; Kurdistan Supporters of Islam; Partisans of Islam; Soldiers of God; Soldiers of Islam; Supporters of Islam in Kurdistan

Description

Ansar al-Islam (AI) is a Salafi terrorist group whose goals include expelling the U.S.-led Coalition from Iraq and establishing an independent Iraqi state based on Sharia law. AI was established in 2001 in Iraqi Kurdistan with the merger of two Kurdish extremist factions that traced their roots to the Islamic Movement of Kurdistan. In a probable effort to appeal to the broader Sunni jihad and expand its support base, AI changed its name to Ansar al-Sunna in 2003, in a bid to unite Iraq-based extremists under the new name. In December 2007, it changed its name back to Ansar al-Islam. AI has ties to the al-Qaeda central leadership and to al-Qaeda in Iraq (AQI). Although AI did not join the AQI-dominated "Islamic State of Iraq," relations between AI and AQI have greatly improved and efforts to merge the groups are ongoing. Some members of AI trained in al-Qaeda camps in Afghanistan, and the group provided safe haven to affiliated terrorists before Operation Iraqi Freedom (OIF). Since OIF, AI has become the second-most prominent group engaged in anti-Coalition attacks in Iraq behind AQI and has maintained a strong propaganda campaign.

Activities

AI continued to conduct attacks against a wide range of targets including Coalition Forces, the Iraqi government and security forces, and Kurdish and Shia figures. AI has claimed responsibility for many high profile attacks in 2007, including the execution-style killing of nearly two dozen Yazidi civilians in Mosul in reprisal for the stoning death of a Muslim convert in April, the car-bombing of a police convoy in Kirkuk in July, the suicide bombing of Kurdistan Democratic Party offices in Khursbat in October, and numerous kidnappings, executions, and assassinations.

Strength

Precise numbers are unknown. AI is one of the largest Sunni terrorist groups in Iraq.

Location/Area of Operation

Primarily northern Iraq, but maintains a presence in western and central Iraq.

External Aid

AI receives assistance from a loose network of associates in Europe and the Middle East.

ANTI-IMPERIALIST TERRITORIAL NUCLEI FOR THE CONSTRUCTION OF THE COMMUNIST COMBATANT PARTY (NTA-PCC)

a.k.a. Anti-Imperialist Territorial Units

Description

The NTA-PCC is a clandestine leftist extremist group that first appeared in Italy's Friuli region in 1995. It adopted the class struggle ideology of the Red Brigades of the 1970s and 1980s, and a similar logo—an encircled five-point star—for its declarations. It seeks the formation of an "anti-imperialist fighting front" with other Italian leftist terrorist groups, including Revolutionary Proletarian Initiative Nuclei and the New Red Brigades. The group opposes what it perceives as U.S. and NATO imperialism, and condemns Italy's foreign and labor policies. In a leaflet dated January 2002, NTA-PCC identified experts in four Italian government sectors—federalism, privatizations, justice reform, and jobs and pensions—as potential targets.

Activities

To date, NTA-PCC has conducted attacks only against property. During the NATO intervention in Kosovo in 1999, NTA-PCC members threw gasoline bombs at the Venice and Rome headquarters of the then-ruling party, Democrats of the Left. NTA-PCC claimed responsibility for a bomb attack in September 2000 against the Central European Initiative office in Trieste and a bomb attack in August 2001 against the Venice Tribunal building. In January 2002, police thwarted an attempt by four NTA-PCC members to enter the Rivolto military air base. In 2003, NTA-PCC claimed responsibility for the arson attacks against three vehicles belonging to U.S. troops serving at the Ederle and Aviano bases in Italy. There has been no reported activity by the group since the arrest in January 2004 of NTA-PCC's founder and leader.

Strength

Accounts vary from one to approximately 20 members.

Location/Area of Operation

Primarily northeastern Italy and U.S. military installations in northern Italy.

External Aid

None evident.

ARMED ISLAMIC GROUP

a.k.a. GIA; al-Jama'ah al-Islamiyah al-Musallah; Groupement Islamique Armé

Description

The Armed Islamic Group (GIA) aims to overthrow the Algerian regime and re-place it with a state governed by Sharia law. The GIA began its violent activity in 1992 after the military government suspended legislative elections in antici-pation of an overwhelming victory by the Islamic Salvation Front, the largest Algerian Islamic opposition party.

Activities

The GIA engaged in attacks against civilians and government workers. The group began conducting a terrorist campaign of civilian massacres in 1992, sometimes wiping out entire villages and killing tens of thousands of Algerians, alienating it-self from the Algerian populace. Since announcing its campaign against foreign-ers living in Algeria in 1992, the GIA killed more than 100 expatriate men and women, mostly Europeans, in the country. Almost all of the GIA's members have now joined other Islamist groups or have been killed or captured by the Algerian government. The Algerian government's September 2005 reconciliation program led to an increase in the number of GIA terrorist suspects who surrendered to security forces. Algerian press continues to report attacks local people attribute to the GIA, but the most recent significant attacks known to be perpetrated by the GIA occurred in August 2001. After the arrest of the GIA's last known emir and subsequent counterterrorism operations, the Algerian government declared that the GIA network was almost entirely broken up.

Strength

Precise numbers are unknown, but the group continues to decline.

Location/Area of Operation

Algeria.

External Aid

Unknown.

ASBAT AL-ANSAR

Description

Asbat al-Ansar was designated as a Foreign Terrorist Organization on March 27, 2002. Asbat al-Ansar is a Lebanon-based Sunni extremist group composed primarily of Palestinians with links to the al-Qaeda organization and other Sunni extremist groups. Some of the group's goals include thwarting perceived anti-Islamic and pro-Western influences in the country.

Activities

Asbat al-Ansar maintains close ties with the al-Qaeda network. Its base of operations is located in the Ain al-Hilwah Palestinian refugee camp near Sidon. Asbat al-Ansar has recently been reluctant to involve itself in operations in Lebanon due in part to concerns over losing its safe haven in Ain al-Hilwah. Various extremist web forums criticized Asbat al-Ansar for its failure to support fellow Sunni extremist group Fatah al-Islam (FAI) during the Lebanese Armed Forces campaign in summer 2007. That campaign forced FAI out of Nahr al-Barid refugee camp in northern Lebanon, and severely damaged the group.

Members of Asbat al-Ansar were believed responsible for a Katyusha rocket attack on the Galilee region of Israel in December 2005. Asbat al-Ansar operatives have been involved in fighting Coalition Forces in Iraq since at least 2005 and several members of the group have been killed in anti-Coalition operations. Al-Sa'di was working in cooperation with Abu Muhammad al-Masri, the head of al-Qaeda at the Ain al-Hilwah refugee camp, where fighting has occurred between Asbat al-Ansar and Fatah elements. In 2007, Asbat al-Ansar remained focused on supporting jihad in Iraq and planning attacks against UNIFIL, Lebanese security forces, and U.S. and Western interests. Asbat al-Ansar–associated elements were implicated in the June 17, 2007 Katyusha rocket attack against northern Israel.

Asbat al-Ansar first emerged in the early 1990s. In the mid-1990s the group assassinated Lebanese religious leaders and bombed nightclubs, theaters, and liquor stores. It was involved in clashes in northern Lebanon in December 1999, and carried out a rocket-propelled grenade attack on the Russian Embassy in Beirut in January 2000. Asbat al-Ansar's leader, Ahmad Abd al-Karim al-Sa'di, a.k.a. Abu Muhjin, remains at large despite being sentenced to death in absentia for the 1994 murder of a Muslim cleric. In September 2004, operatives with links to the group were allegedly involved in planning terrorist operations targeting the Italian Embassy, the Ukrainian Consulate General, and Lebanese government offices. In October 2004, Mahir al-Sa'di, a member of Asbat al-Ansar, was sentenced in absentia to life imprisonment for his 2000 plot to assassinate then U.S. Ambassador to Lebanon, David Satterfield.

Strength

The group commands between 100 and 300 fighters in Lebanon. Its named leader is Ahmad Abd al-Karim al-Sa'di.

Location/Area of Operation

The group's primary base of operations is the Ain al-Hilwah Palestinian refugee camp near Sidon in southern Lebanon.

External Aid

It is likely the group receives money through international Sunni extremist networks.

AUM SHINRIKYO (AUM)

a.k.a. A.I.C. Comprehensive Research Institute; A.I.C. Sogo Kenkyusho; Aleph; Aum Supreme Truth

Description

Aum Shinrikyo was designated as a Foreign Terrorist Organization on October 8, 1997. Shoko Asahara established Aum Shinrikyo (Aum) in 1987, and the cult received legal status as a religious entity in 1989. Initially, Aum aimed to take over Japan and then the world, but over time it began to emphasize the imminence of the end of the world. Asahara predicted 1996, and 1999 to 2003, as likely dates and said that the United States would initiate Armageddon by starting World War III with Japan. The Japanese government revoked its recognition of Aum as a religious organization following Aum's deadly sarin gas attack in Tokyo in March 1995. In 1997, however, a government panel decided not to invoke the Operations Control Law to outlaw the group. A 1999 law authorized the Japanese government to maintain police surveillance over the group because of concerns that Aum might launch future terrorist attacks. In January 2000, under the leadership of Fumihiro Joyu, the chief of Aum's once thriving Moscow operation, Aum changed its name to Aleph and tried to distance itself from the violent and apocalyptic teachings of its founder. In late 2003, however, Joyu stepped down under pressure from members who wanted to return fully to the worship of Asahara. A growing divide between members supporting Joyu and Asahara emerged. In 2007, Joyu officially split and in May established a splinter group called Hikari No Wa, which is translated as 'Circle of Light' or 'Ring of Light.' Japanese authorities continued to monitor both Aum (now called Aleph) and Hikari No Wa.

Activities

On March 20, 1995, Aum members simultaneously released the chemical nerve agent sarin on several Tokyo subway trains, killing 12 persons and causing up to 6,000 to seek medical treatment. Subsequent investigations by the Japanese government revealed the group was responsible for other mysterious chemical incidents in Japan in 1994, including a sarin gas attack on a residential neighborhood in Matsumoto that killed seven and hospitalized approximately 500. Japanese police arrested Asahara in May 1995, and in February 2004 authorities sentenced him to death for his role in the 1995 attacks. In September 2006, Asahara lost his final appeal against the death penalty.

Since 1997, the cult has recruited new members, engaged in commercial enterprises, and acquired property, although it scaled back these activities significantly in 2001 in response to a public outcry. In July 2001, Russian authorities arrested a group of Russian Aum followers who had planned to set off bombs near the Imperial Palace in Tokyo as part of an operation to free Asahara from jail and smuggle him to Russia.

Although Aum has not conducted a terrorist attack since 1995, concerns remain regarding their continued adherence to the violent teachings of founder Asahara that led them to perpetrate the sarin gas attack in Tokyo.

Strength

According to a study by the Japanese government issued in December 2008, current Aum Shinrikyo/Aleph membership in Japan is approximately 1,500 as well as approximately 200 in Russia, in addition to maintaining 30 facilities in 15 Prefectures, to include Tokyo and a few in Russia. At the time of the Tokyo subway attack, the group claimed to have as many as 40,000 members worldwide, including 9,000 in Japan and 30,000 members in Russia.

Location/Area of Operation

Aum's principal membership is located in Japan while a residual branch of about 300 followers live in Russia.

External Aid

None.

BASQUE FATHERLAND AND LIBERTY (ETA)

a.k.a. ETA, Askatasuna; Batasuna; Ekin; Euskal Herritarrok; Euzkadi Ta Askata-suna; Herri Batasuna; Jarrai-Haika-Segi; K.A.S.; XAKI

Description

Basque Fatherland and Liberty (ETA) was designated as a Foreign Terrorist Organization on October 8, 1997. Basque Fatherland and Liberty (ETA) was founded in 1959 with the aim of establishing an independent homeland based on Marxist principles encompassing the Spanish Basque provinces of Vizcaya, Guipuzcoa, and Alava, the autonomous region of Navarra, and the southwest-ern French territories of Labourd, Basse-Navarre, and Soule. Spain and the EU both have listed ETA as a terrorist organization; in 2002 the Spanish Parliament banned the political party Batasuna, ETA's political wing, charging its members with providing material support to the terrorist group. In September 2008, Span-ish courts in September also banned two other Basque independence parties with reported links to Batasuna.

Spanish and French prisons together are estimated to hold a total of more than 750 ETA members. In March 2006, days after claiming responsibility for a spate of roadside blasts in northern Spain that caused no injuries, ETA announced that it would implement a "permanent" cease-fire. On December 30, 2006, however, ETA exploded a massive car bomb that destroyed much of the covered parking garage outside the new Terminal Four of Madrid's Barajas International Airport. Two individuals killed in the blast became ETA's first fatalities in more than three years. The Spanish Government suspended talks with ETA and government officials later said political negotiations with the group had ended.

Activities

ETA primarily conducts bombings and assassinations. Targets are typically Span-ish government officials, security and military forces, politicians, and judicial figures, but the group also has targeted journalists and tourist areas. The group is responsible for killing more than 800 and injuring thousands more since it began its lethal attacks in the late 1960s. Security service scrutiny and a public outcry after the Islamic extremist train bombings in Madrid in March 2004 have limited ETA's capability and willingness to inflict casualties. In February 2005, ETA detonated a car bomb in Madrid at a convention center where Spanish King Juan Carlos and then Mexican President Vicente Fox were scheduled to appear, wounding more than 20 people. ETA also detonated an explosive device at a stadium constructed as part of Madrid's bid to host the 2012 Olympic Games. There were no injuries in that attack. ETA's late 2006 attack at Madrid's airport was the group's first fatal attack since March 2003.

ETA formally renounced its "permanent" cease-fire in June 2007 and three months later threatened a wave of attacks throughout Spain. By mid-2007, there were indications that the group may have expanded its logistical operations, such as renting vehicles, into Portugal. In October 2007, Spain and Portugal agreed to intensify their cooperation against ETA by establishing a joint counterterrorism team based in Lisbon.

In 2008, ETA continued to perpetrate attacks which resulted in casualties. In March 2008, just days before the national election, ETA fatally shot a former Spanish politician, Isaias Carrasco, outside his home in northern Spain. In May, a car bomb exploded outside a Civil Guard barracks in Legutiano, killing one policeman and wounding four others. In July, ETA was responsible for five bomb explosions in northern Spain, including four at popular seaside resorts. In September, an ETA car bomb killed an army officer and injured several other people in the northern town of Santona. In October, ETA members conducted a car bomb attack at a university in Pamplona that injured more than one dozen people. The group also claimed responsibility for the December killing of Ignacio Uria, a leading Basque businessman, for failing to pay extortion money to ETA and for his construction company's involvement in the building of high-speed train links in the Basque Country, which ETA opposes.

In 2008, French authorities apprehended ETA's top three leaders, beginning in May with the arrest of Francisco Javier Lopez Pena (a.k.a. Thierry). In November, French police arrested Garikoitz Aspiazu (a.k.a. Txeroki), who is suspected of ordering a December 2006 car bombing at the Madrid airport. One month later, French police captured his alleged replacement, Aitzol Iriondo Yarza (a.k.a. Gurbitz).

Strength

ETA's current strength is unknown as a result of the arrest of 365 ETA members in 2007 and 2008.

Location/Area of Operation

ETA operates primarily in the Basque autonomous regions of northern Spain and southwestern France, but has attacked Spanish and French interests elsewhere.

External Aid

ETA finances its activities primarily through bribery and extortion of Basque businesses. It has received training at various times in the past in Libya, Lebanon, and Nicaragua. Some ETA members have allegedly fled to Cuba and Mexico, while others reside in South America. ETA members have operated and been arrested in other European countries, including France, Belgium, the Netherlands, the UK, Germany, and Portugal.

CAMBODIAN FREEDOM FIGHTERS (CFF)

a.k.a. Cholana; Kangtoap Serei Cheat; Kampouchea

Description

The Cambodian Freedom Fighters (CFF) emerged in November 1998 in the wake of political violence that saw many influential Cambodian leaders flee and the Cambodian People's Party assume power. With an avowed aim of overthrowing the government, the U.S.-based group is led by a Cambodian-American, a former member of the opposition Sam Rainsy Party. The CFF's membership reportedly includes Cambodian-Americans based in Thailand and the United States, and former soldiers from the Khmer Rouge, Royal Cambodian Armed Forces, and various political factions.

Activities

Alleged CFF leader Chhun Yasith was arrested in June in the United States on charges of conspiracy to kill in a foreign country, conspiracy to damage or destroy property in a foreign country, and engaging in a military expedition against a nation with which the United States is at peace. If convicted, Yasith faces life imprisonment without parole for each of the charges. Meanwhile, a Cambodian court in October dropped charges against five alleged CFF members arrested in April 2004 in connection with a bombing at a ferry, which slightly injured three persons. In 2003, the Cambodian government arrested seven CFF members who were reportedly planning an unspecified terrorist attack in southwestern Cambodia. Cambodian courts in February and March 2002 prosecuted 38 CFF members suspected of staging an attack in Cambodia in 2000. The courts convicted 19 members, including one U.S. citizen, of "terrorism" and/or "membership in an armed group," and sentenced them to terms of five years to life imprisonment. A Cambodian court later judged that the three-year sentences of six other members were too light and decided in December 2005 to extend them to 6 to 10 years. The group had claimed responsibility for an attack in late November 2000 on several government installations that killed at least eight persons and wounded more than a dozen. In April 1999, five CFF members also were arrested for plotting to blow up a fuel depot outside Phnom Penh with anti-tank weapons.

Strength

Exact strength is unknown, but totals probably never have exceeded 100 armed fighters.

Location/Area of Operation

Northeastern Cambodia near the Thai border, and the United States.

External Aid

U.S.-based leadership collects funds from the Cambodian-American community.

COMMUNIST PARTY OF INDIA (MAOIST)

a.k.a. Maoist Communist Center of India (MCCI) and People's War (PW)

Description

The Indian groups known as the Maoist Communist Center of India and People's War (a.k.a. People's War Group) joined in September 2004 to form the Communist Party of India (Maoist), or CPI (Maoist). The MCCI was originally formed in the early 1970s, while People's War (PW) was founded in 1975. Both groups are referred to as Naxalites, after the West Bengal village where a revolutionary radical Left movement originated in 1967. The new organization continues to employ violence to achieve its goals of peasant revolution, abolition of class hierarchies, and expansion of Maoist-controlled "liberated zones," eventually leading to the creation of an independent "Maoist" state. The CPI (Maoist) reportedly has a significant cadre of women. Important leaders include Ganapati (the PW leader from Andhra Pradesh), Pramod Mishra, Uma Shankar, and P.N.G. (alias Nathuni Mistry, arrested by Jharkhand police in 2002).

Activities

Prior to its consolidation with the PW, the MCCI ran a virtual parallel government in remote areas, where it collected a "tax" from villagers and, in turn, provided infrastructure improvements such as building hospitals, schools, and irrigation projects. It ran a parallel court system wherein allegedly corrupt block development officials and landlords—frequent MCCI targets—were punished by amputation and even death. People's War conducted a low-intensity insurgency that included attempted political assassination, theft of weapons from police stations, kidnapping police officers, assaulting civilians, extorting money from construction firms, and vandalizing the property of multinational corporations. Together the two groups were reportedly responsible for the deaths of up to 170 civilians and police a year.

The group conducted two major attacks in 2005. In June, some 500 members attacked a village in Uttar Pradesh, killing several local policemen, destroying buildings, and seizing weapons. In November, an estimated 300 members attacked a prison in Bihar, killing two people, freeing more than 300 inmates, and abducting 30 landowners belonging to a group opposed to the Naxalites.

Strength

Although difficult to assess with any accuracy, media reports and local authorities suggest the CPI's (Maoist) membership may be as high as 31,000, including both hard-core militants and dedicated sympathizers.

Location/Area of Operation

The CPI (Maoist), which is believed to be enlarging the scope of its influence, operates in the Indian states of Andhra Pradesh, Orissa, Jharkhand, Bihar, Chhattisgarh, and parts of West Bengal. It also has a presence on the Bihar-Nepal border.

External Aid

The CPI (Maoist) has loose links to other Maoist groups in the region, including the Communist Party of Nepal (Maoist), but does not appear dependent on outside sources of support. The MCCI was a founding member of the Coordination Committee of Maoist Parties and Organizations of South Asia (CCOMPOSA).

COMMUNIST PARTY OF NEPAL (MAOIST) (CPN/M)

Description

The Communist Party of Nepal (Maoist) insurgency grew out of the radicalization and fragmentation of left-wing parties following Nepal's transition to democracy in 1990. The United People's Front, a coalition of left-wing parties, participated in the elections of 1991, but the Maoist wing failed to win the required minimum number of votes, leading to its exclusion from voter lists in the elections of 1994 and prompting the group to launch the insurgency in 1996. The CPN/M's ultimate objective is the overthrow of the Nepalese government and the establishment of a Maoist state. On October 31, 2003, the United States designated Nepal's Maoists under E.O. 13224 for terrorist activity.

Activities

The Maoists have used traditional guerrilla warfare tactics and engage in murder, torture, arson, sabotage, extortion, child conscription, kidnapping, bombings, and assassinations to intimidate and coerce the populace. In 2002, Maoists claimed responsibility for assassinating two Nepalese U.S. Embassy guards, citing anti-Maoist spying, and in a press statement threatened foreign embassies, including the U.S. Mission, to deter foreign support for the Nepalese government. Maoists are suspected in the September 2004 bombing at the American Cultural Center in Kathmandu. The attack, which caused no injuries and only minor damage, marked the first time the Maoists had damaged U.S. Government property. The Maoists entered into peace talks with the government in 2001 and 2003, but negotiations failed after a few months. In 2005, the group announced a unilateral cease-fire in September, and entered into an alliance with the seven-party alliance of opposition political parties in November.

Strength

Approximately several thousand full-time members.

Location/Area of Operation

Operations are conducted throughout Nepal. Press reports indicate some Nepalese Maoist leaders reside in India.

External Aid

None.

COMMUNIST PARTY OF PHILIPPINES/NEW PEOPLE'S ARMY

a.k.a. CPP/NPA; Communist Party of the Philippines; the CPP; New People's Army; the NPA

Description

The Communist Party of the Philippines (CPP/NPA) was designated as a Foreign Terrorist Organization on August 9, 2002. The military wing of the Communist Party of the Philippines (CPP), the New People's Army (NPA), is a Maoist group formed in March 1969 with the aim of overthrowing the government through protracted guerrilla warfare. Jose Maria Sison, the chairman of the CPP's Central Committee and the NPA's founder, reportedly directs CPP and NPA activity from the Netherlands, where he lives in self-imposed exile. Luis Jalandoni, a fellow Central Committee member and director of the CPP's overt political wing, the National Democratic Front (NDF), also lives in the Netherlands and has become a Dutch citizen. Although primarily a rural-based guerrilla group, the NPA has an active urban infrastructure to support its terrorist activities and at times uses city-based assassination squads.

In September 2007, Sison was briefly arrested in the Netherlands, but was released on a judge's order a few days later. In November 2007, the Armed Forces of the Philippines announced the capture of Elizabeth Principe, a suspected member of the Central Committee of the Communist Party of the Philippines.

Activities

The NPA primarily targets Philippine security forces, government officials, local infrastructure, and businesses that refuse to pay extortion, or "revolutionary taxes." The NPA charges politicians running for office in NPA-influenced areas for "campaign permits." The group opposes any U.S. military presence in the Philippines and has attacked U.S. military interests; it killed several U.S. service personnel before the U.S. base closures in 1992. The NPA claimed responsibility for the assassination of two congressmen, one from Quezon in May 2001 and one from Cagayan in June 2001, among other killings. Periodic peace talks with the Philippine government stalled after these incidents. In December 2005, the NPA publicly expressed its intent to target U.S. personnel if they were discovered in NPA operating areas.

Strength

Estimated at less than 9,000, a number significantly lower than its peak strength of approximately 25,000 in the 1980s.

Location/Area of Operation

The NPA operates in rural Luzon, Visayas, and parts of northern and eastern Mindanao. There are cells in Manila and other metropolitan centers.

External Aid

Unknown.

CONTINUITY IRISH REPUBLICAN ARMY (CIRA)

a.k.a. Continuity Army Council; Continuity IRA; Republican Sinn Fein

Description

The Continuity Irish Republican Army (CIRA) was designated as a Foreign Terrorist Organization on July 13, 2004. CIRA is a terrorist splinter group formed in 1994 as the clandestine armed wing of Republican Sinn Fein, which split from Sinn Fein in 1986. "Continuity" refers to the group's belief that it is carrying on the original Irish Republican Army's (IRA) goal of forcing the British out of Northern Ireland. CIRA's aliases, Continuity Army Council and Republican Sinn Fein, are included in its FTO designation. CIRA cooperates with the larger Real IRA (RIRA).

Activities

CIRA has been active in Belfast and the border areas of Northern Ireland, where it has carried out bombings, assassinations, kidnappings, hijackings, extortion, and robberies. On occasion, it has provided advance warning to police of its attacks. Targets have included the British military, Northern Ireland security forces, and Loyalist paramilitary groups. CIRA did not join the Provisional IRA in the September 2005 decommissioning and remains capable of effective, if sporadic, terrorist attacks. In early 2006, the Independent Monitoring Commission reported that two splinter organizations, Óglaigh na hÉireann and Saoirse na hÉireann, were formed as a result of internal disputes within CIRA. In late 2006, CIRA members issued a list of up to 20 individuals they were targeting for paramilitary attacks, several of whom were wounded in subsequent shootings. Around the same time, CIRA claimed the firebomb attacks of B&Q home-supply stores, although RIRA also claimed such attacks. CIRA activity has largely decreased from previous levels seen in 2005.

By 2007, the group had become increasingly active in criminal activity in Northern Ireland and Ireland. In April 2007, following the discovery of an improvised mortar (direct-fire mode) adjacent to the railway line in Lurgan, three CIRA members were arrested and charged with conspiracy to murder, possession of explosives with intent to endanger life, and possession of articles for use in terrorism. The Independent Monitoring Commission, which was established to oversee the peace process, assessed that CIRA was responsible for both the June 2008 command detonated explosive device against a police patrol car and an August 2008 attempted rocket attack in Lisnaskea. In November 2008, CIRA publicly threatened to murder any Belfast Catholic community workers found to be cooperating with the police. In March 2009, it claimed responsibility for the murder of a police officer in Craigavon, County Armagh.

Strength

Membership is small, with possibly fewer than 50 hard-core activists. Police counterterrorist operations have reduced the group's strength.

Location/Area of Operation

Northern Ireland and the Irish Republic. CIRA does not have an established presence in Great Britain.

External Aid

Suspected of receiving funds and arms from sympathizers in the United States. CIRA may have acquired arms and materiel from the Balkans, in cooperation with the Real IRA.

DEMOCRATIC FORCES FOR THE
LIBERATION OF RWANDA (FDLR)

a.k.a. Army for the Liberation of Rwanda (ALIR); FAR/Interahamwe

Description

In 2001, the Democratic Forces for the Liberation of Rwanda (FDLR) supplanted the Army for the Liberation of Rwanda (ALIR), the armed branch of the Party for the Liberation of Rwanda (PALIR). ALIR was formed from the merger of the Armed Forces of Rwanda (FAR), the army of the ethnic Hutu-dominated Rwandan regime that orchestrated the genocide of over 500,000 Tutsis and regime opponents in 1994, and Interahamwe, the civilian militia force that carried out much of the killing. This occurred after the two groups were forced from Rwanda into the Democratic Republic of the Congo (DRC, then Zaire) that year. Though directly tied to those who organized and carried out the genocide, identified ALIR/FDLR leaders are not thought to have played a role in the killing. They have worked to build bridges to other opponents of the Kigali regime, including ethnic Tutsis.

Activities

ALIR sought to topple Rwanda's Tutsi-dominated government, reinstitute Hutu domination, and, possibly, complete the genocide. In 1996, a message—allegedly from the ALIR—threatened to kill the U.S. Ambassador to Rwanda and other U.S. citizens. In 1999, ALIR guerrillas critical of U.S.-UK support for the Rwandan regime kidnapped and killed eight foreign tourists, including two U.S. citizens, in a game park on the DRC-Uganda border. Three suspects in the attack are in U.S. custody awaiting trial. In the 1998–2002 Congolese war, the ALIR/FDLR was allied with Kinshasa against the Rwandan invaders. ALIR/FDLR's political wing mainly has sought to topple the Kigali regime via an alliance with Tutsi regime opponents. It established the ADRN Igihango alliance in 2002, but this has not resonated politically in Rwanda. In March 2005, FDLR representatives announced a willingness to cease military actions and return to Rwanda. FDLR denounced the genocide, committed to a political struggle rather than a military one, and indicated it would voluntarily demobilize and repatriate. No large-scale FDLR repatriation to Rwanda has occurred, however, owing to FDLR concerns about security and the "political space" it would be allowed in Rwanda.

Strength

Exact strength is unknown, but an estimated 8,000 to 10,000 FDLR guerrillas operate in the eastern DRC close to the Rwandan border. In 2003, the United Nations, with Rwandan assistance, repatriated close to 1,500 FDLR combatants from the DRC. A senior FDLR military commander returned to Rwanda in November 2003 and has been working with Kigali to encourage the return of his comrades.

Location/Area of Operation

Mostly in the eastern Democratic Republic of the Congo.

External Aid

The Government of the Democratic Republic of the Congo provided training, arms, and supplies to ALIR forces to combat Rwandan armed forces that invaded the DRC in 1998. Kinshasa halted that support in 2002, though allegations persist of continued support from several local Congolese warlords and militias, including the Mai Mai.

EAST TURKISTAN ISLAMIC MOVEMENT (ETIM)

Description

The East Turkistan Islamic Movement (ETIM) is a small Islamic extremist group linked to al-Qaeda and the international jihadist movement. It is the most militant of the ethnic Uighur separatist groups pursuing an independent "Eastern Turkistan," an area that would include Turkey, Kazakhstan, Kyrgyzstan, Uzbekistan, Pakistan, Afghanistan, and western China's Xinjiang Uighur Autonomous Region. On September 12, 2002, the group was designated under E.O. 13224 for its terrorist activity. ETIM is also listed by the UN 1267 al-Qaida/Taliban/ Usama bin Laden Sanctions Committee for its associations with al-Qaeda.

Activities

ETIM militants fought alongside al-Qaeda and Taliban forces in Afghanistan during Operation Enduring Freedom. In October 2003, Pakistani soldiers killed ETIM leader Hassan Makhsum during raids on al-Qaeda-associated compounds in western Pakistan. U.S. and Chinese government information suggests that

ETIM is responsible for various terrorist acts inside and outside China. In May 2002, two ETIM members were deported to China from Kyrgyzstan for plotting to attack the U.S. Embassy in Kyrgyzstan as well as other U.S. interests abroad.

Strength

Unknown. Only a small minority of ethnic Uighurs supports the Xinjiang independence movement or the formation of an Eastern Turkistan.

Location/Area of Operation

Afghanistan, China, Kyrgyzstan, and Pakistan.

External Aid

ETIM has received training and financial assistance from al-Qaeda.

FIRST OF OCTOBER ANTIFASCIST RESISTANCE GROUP (GRAPO); GRUPO DE RESISTENCIA ANTI-FASCISTA PRIMERO DE OCTUBRE

Description

GRAPO was formed in 1975 as the armed wing of the illegal Communist Party of Spain during the Franco era. It advocates the overthrow of the Spanish government and its replacement with a Marxist-Leninist regime. GRAPO is vehemently anti-American, seeks the removal of all U.S. military forces from Spanish territory, and has conducted and attempted several attacks against U.S. targets since 1977. The group issued a communiqué following the September 11, 2001, attacks in the United States, expressing its satisfaction that "symbols of imperialist power" were decimated and affirming that "the war" has only just begun. Spanish authorities believed they had nearly eradicated GRAPO, but a joint Spanish, French, and Italian police operation in October 2005 that resulted in the arrest of two GRAPO members led observers to speculate that the group may be reconstituting itself. GRAPO in a November 2006 internal publication announced that it was trying to find new members and resources but admitted it was having difficulty reorganizing because of sporadic arrests that continued well into 2006. The group was designated under E.O. 13224 in December 2001.

Activities

GRAPO suffered setbacks in 2004, with several members and sympathizers arrested and sentences upheld or handed down in the appellate case for GRAPO militants arrested in Paris in 2000. Press reports indicate that as of mid-2006, about 30 people connected with the terrorist group were in prison. The group's operations traditionally have been designed to cause material damage and gain publicity rather than inflict casualties, but the terrorists have conducted lethal bombings and close-range assassinations; GRAPO has killed more than 90 persons and injured more than 200 since its formation. GRAPO claimed responsibility for the murder in Zaragoza on 6 February 2006 of a Spanish businesswoman. Members of the group also have been charged with engaging in extortion and for carrying out a series of bank robberies in recent years.

Strength

Fewer than two-dozen activists remain. Police have made periodic large-scale arrests of GRAPO members, crippling the organization and forcing it into lengthy rebuilding periods. In 2002, Spanish and French authorities arrested 22 suspected members, including some of the group's reconstituted leadership. More members have been arrested in the past three years [2003–2005].

Location/Area of Operation

Spain.

External Aid

None.

GAMA'A AL-ISLAMIYYA (IG)

a.k.a. al-Gama'at; Egyptian al-Gama'at al-Islamiyya; GI, Islamic Gama'at, IG; Islamic Group; Egyptian Islamic Group

Description

Gama'a al-Islamiyya (IG) was designated as a Foreign Terrorist Organization on October 8, 1997. Gama'a al-Islamiyya, once Egypt's largest militant group, was active in the late 1970s, but is now a loosely organized network. Many of its members have renounced terrorism, although some have begun to work with or have joined al-Qaeda. The external wing, composed of mainly exiled members in several countries, maintains that its primary goal is to overthrow the Egyptian government and replace it with an Islamic state, though most of the group's leadership have renounced violence as a means to do so. The IG announced a cease-fire in 1997 that led to a split into two factions: one, led by Mustafa Hamza, supported the cease-fire; the other, led by Rifa'i Taha Musa, called for a return to armed operations. The IG announced another cease-fire in March 1999, but its spiritual leader, Sheik Umar Abd al-Rahman, sentenced to life in prison in January 1996 for his involvement in the 1993 World Trade Center bombing and incarcerated in the United States, rescinded his support for the cease-fire in June 2000. IG has not conducted an attack inside Egypt since the 1997 Luxor attack, which killed 58 tourists and four Egyptians, and wounded dozens more. In February 1998, a senior member signed Osama bin Laden's fatwa call for attacks against the United States.

In early 2001, Taha Musa published a book in which he attempted to justify terrorist attacks that cause mass casualties. Musa disappeared several months afterward and the United States has no information about his whereabouts. In March 2002, members of the group's historic leadership in Egypt declared the use of violence misguided and renounced its future use, prompting denunciations from much of the leadership abroad. The Egyptian government continued to release IG members from prison; approximately 900 were released in 2003 and most of the 700 persons released in 2004 at the end of the Muslim holy month of Ramadan were IG members. In August 2006, Ayman al-Zawahiri announced that IG had merged with al-Qaeda, but the group's Egypt-based leadership quickly denied this claim which ran counter to their reconciliation efforts.

Activities

Before the 1997 cease-fire, IG conducted armed attacks against Egyptian security and other government officials, Coptic Christians, and Egyptian opponents of Islamic extremism. After the cease-fire, the faction led by Taha Musa launched attacks on tourists in Egypt, most notably the 1997 Luxor attack. IG claimed responsibility for the June 1995 assassination attempt on Egyptian President Hosni Mubarak in Addis Ababa, Ethiopia. IG was dormant in 2008.

Strength

At its peak, IG probably commanded several thousand hardcore members and a similar number of supporters. Security crackdowns following the 1997 attack in Luxor, the 1999 cease-fire, and post–September 11 security measures and defections to al-Qaeda have probably resulted in a substantial decrease in what is left of an organized group and its ability to conduct attacks.

Location/Area of Operation

The IG maintains an external presence in Afghanistan, Yemen, Iran, the United Kingdom, Germany, and France. IG terrorist presence in Egypt is minimal due to the reconciliation efforts of former local members.

External Aid

Al-Qaeda and Afghan militant groups provide support to members of the organization to carry out support on behalf of al-Qaeda. IG also may obtain some funding through various Islamic non-governmental organizations.

HAMAS

Acronym for the Islamic Resistance Movement, Harakat al-Muqawama al-Islamiya

a.k.a. Izz al-Din al Qassam Battalions; Izz al-Din al Qassam Brigades; Izz al-Din al Qassam Forces; Students of Ayyash; Student of the Engineer; Yahya Ayyash Units; Izz al-Din al-Qassim Brigades; Izz al-Din al-Qassim Forces; Izz al-Din al-Qassim Battalions

Description

Hamas was designated as a Foreign Terrorist Organization on October 8, 1997. Hamas includes military and political wings and was formed in late 1987 at the onset of the first Palestinian uprising, or Intifada, as an outgrowth of the Palestinian branch of the Muslim Brotherhood. The armed element, called the Izz al-Din al-Qassam Brigades, conducts anti-Israeli attacks, including suicide bombings against civilian targets inside Israel. Hamas also manages a broad, mostly Gaza-based network of "Dawa" or ministry activities that include charities, schools, clinics, youth camps, fundraising, and political activities. A Shura council based in Damascus, Syria, sets overall policy. After winning Palestinian Legislative Council elections in January 2006, Hamas seized control of significant Palestinian Authority (PA) ministries, including the Ministry of Interior. Hamas subsequently formed an expanded, overt militia called the Executive Force, subordinate to the Ministry. This force and other Hamas cadres took control of Gaza in a military-style coup in June 2007, forcing Fatah forces to either leave Gaza or go underground.

Activities

Prior to 2005, Hamas conducted numerous anti-Israeli attacks, including suicide bombings, rocket launches, improvised explosive device (IED) attacks, and shootings. Hamas has not directly targeted U.S. interests, though the group makes little or no effort to avoid soft targets frequented by foreigners. The group curtailed terrorist attacks in February 2005 after agreeing to a temporary period of calm brokered by the PA, and ceased most violence after winning control of the PA legislature and cabinet in January 2006. After Hamas staged a June 2006 attack on IDF soldiers near Kerem Shalom that resulted in two deaths and the abduction of Corporal Gilad Shalit, Israel took steps that severely limited the operation of the Rafah crossing. In June 2007, Hamas took control of Gaza from the PA and Fatah in a military-style coup, leading to an international boycott and closure of Gaza borders. Hamas has since dedicated the majority of its activity in Gaza to solidifying its control, hardening its defenses, tightening security, and conducting limited operations against Israeli military forces.

Hamas fired rockets from Gaza into Israel in 2008 but focused more on mortar attacks targeting Israeli incursions. Additionally, other terrorist groups in Gaza fired rockets into Israel, most, presumably, with Hamas support or acquiescence. Following the June 2007 takeover of the Gaza Strip the majority of Hamas activity has been directed at solidifying its control, including providing security and enforcing law and order. In June 2008, Hamas agreed to a six-month cease-fire with Israel and temporarily halted all rocket attacks emanating from the Gaza Strip by arresting Palestinian militants and violators of the agreement. Hamas fought a 23-day war with Israel from late December 2008 to January 2009, in an effort to break an international blockade on the Gaza Strip and force the openings of the international crossings. Hamas's failure to end its international isolation and open the borders could lead to future violent actions, but Hamas appears, for now, to be focusing on a diplomatic solution.

Strength

Hamas probably has several thousand operatives with varying degrees of skills in its armed wing, the al-Qassam Brigades, along with its reported 9,000-man Executive Force and tens of thousands of supporters and sympathizers.

Location/Area of Operation

Hamas has an operational presence in every major city in the Palestinian territories and currently focuses its anti-Israeli attacks on targets in the West Bank and within Israel. Hamas could potentially activate operations in Lebanon or resume terrorist operations in Israel. The group retains a cadre of leaders and facilitators that conducts diplomatic, fundraising, and arms-smuggling activities in Lebanon, Syria, and other states. Hamas is also increasing its presence in the Palestinian refugee camps in Lebanon, probably with the mid-term goal of eclipsing Fatah's long-time dominance of the camps and long-term goal of seizing control of the Palestinian Liberation Organization.

External Aid

Hamas receives some funding, weapons, and training from Iran. In addition, fundraising takes place in the Persian Gulf countries, but the group also receives donations from Palestinian expatriates around the world and private benefactors in Arab states. Some fundraising and propaganda activity takes place in western Europe and North America.

HARAKAT UL-JIHAD-I-ISLAMI (HUJI)

a.k.a. Movement of Islamic Holy War

Description

HUJI, a Sunni extremist group that follows the Deobandi tradition of Islam, was founded in 1980 in Afghanistan to fight in the jihad against the Soviets. It also is affiliated with the Jamiat Ulema-i-Islam's Fazlur Rehman faction (JUI-F) of the extremist religious party Jamiat Ulema-i-Islam (JUI). The group, led by Qari Saifullah Akhtar and chief commander Amin Rabbani, is made up primarily of Pakistanis and foreign Islamists who are fighting for the liberation of Jammu and Kashmir and its accession to Pakistan.

Activities

The group has conducted a number of operations against Indian military targets in Jammu and Kashmir. It is linked to the Kashmiri militant group al-Faran that kidnapped five Western tourists in Jammu and Kashmir in July 1995; one was killed in August 1995, and the other four reportedly were killed in December of the same year.

Strength

Exact numbers are unknown, but there may be several hundred members in Kashmir.

Location/Area of Operation

Pakistan and Kashmir. Trained members in Afghanistan until autumn of 2001.

External Aid

Specific sources of external aid are unknown.

HARAKAT UL-JIHAD-I-ISLAMI/BANGLADESH (HUJI-B)

a.k.a. Harakat ul Jihad e Islami Bangladesh; Harkatul Jihad al Islam; Harkatul Jihad; Harakat ul Jihad al Islami; Harkat ul Jihad al Islami; Harkat-ul-Jehad-al-Islami; Harakat ul Jihad Islami Bangladesh; Islami Dawat-e-Kafela; IDEK

Description

Harakat ul-Jihad-i-Islami/Bangladesh (HUJI-B) was designated as a Foreign Terrorist Organization on March 5, 2008. HUJI-B was formed in April 1992 by a group of former Bangladeshi Afghan veterans to establish an Islamic social system based on the "Medina Charter." The group was banned by Bangladeshi authorities in October 2005. In May 2008, HUJI-B members formed a new organization, the Islamic Democratic Party (IDP). In November, government authorities rejected their application for registering as a party that could participate in elections. HUJI-B has connections to the Pakistani militant groups Harakat ul-Jihad-Islami (HUJI) and Harakat ul-Mujahedin (HUM), which advocate similar objectives in Pakistan, Jammu, and Kashmir. The leaders of HUJI-B and HUM both signed the February 1998 fatwa sponsored by Osama bin Laden that declared American civilians to be legitimate targets for attack.

Activities

HUJI-B may be responsible for numerous terrorist attacks in India, including an October 2008 attack in a shopping area in Agartala, Tripura. that killed three and wounded over 100 people. The Agartala attack may have been conducted jointly with a local Indian separatist group. HUJI-B has trained and fielded operatives in Burma to fight on behalf of the Rohingya, an Islamic minority group. Three HUJI-B members were convicted in December 2008 for the grenade attack on the British High Commissioner in May 2004 in Sylhet, Bangladesh. Bangladeshi courts issued warrants in December 2008 for the arrest of eight HUJI-B members for the bombing at a festival in April 2001 that killed 10 and injured scores of people. In May, Indian police arrested HUJI-B militant Mohammad Iqbal, a.k.a. Abdur Rehman, who was charged with plotting attacks in Delhi, India. HUJI-B and its detained leader, Mufti Hannan, are also suspected in a 2000 assassination attempt on Bangladeshi Prime Minister Sheikh Hasina.

Strength

HUJI-B leaders have claimed up to 400 members are Afghan war veterans, but its total membership is unknown.

Location/Area of Operation

The group operates primarily in Bangladesh, India, and Burma. HUJI-B has a network of madrassas and conducts trainings in Bangladesh.

External Aid

HUJI-B funding comes from a variety of sources. Several international Islamic NGOs such as the South African-based Servants of Suffering Humanity may have funneled money to HUJI-B and other Bangladeshi militant groups. HUJI-B also can draw funding from local militant madrassa leaders and teachers.

HARAKAT UL-MUJAHIDIN (HUM)

a.k.a. Harakat ul-Ansar; HUA; Jamiat ul-Ansar

Description

Harakat ul-Mujahideen (HUM) was designated as a Foreign Terrorist Organization on October 8, 1997. HUM, an Islamic militant group based in Pakistan, is politically aligned with the political party Jamiat Ulema-i-Islam's Fazlur Rehman faction (JUI-F), and operates primarily in Kashmir. Reportedly under pressure from the Government of Pakistan, HUM's long-time leader Fazlur Rehman Khalil stepped down and was replaced by Dr. Badr Munir as the head of HUM in January 2005. Khalil has been linked to Osama bin Laden, and his signature was found on bin Laden's fatwa in February 1998, calling for attacks on U.S. and Western interests. HUM operated terrorist training camps in eastern Afghanistan until Coalition air strikes destroyed them in autumn 2001. Khalil was detained by Pakistani authorities in mid-2004 and subsequently released in late December of the same year. In 2003, HUM began using the name Jamiat ul-Ansar (JUA). Pakistan banned JUA in November 2003.

Activities

HUM has conducted a number of operations against Indian troops and civilian targets in Kashmir. It is linked to the Kashmiri militant group al-Faran that kidnapped five Western tourists in Kashmir in July 1995; the five reportedly were killed later that year. HUM was responsible for the hijacking of an Indian airliner in December 1999 that resulted in the release of Masood Azhar, an important leader in the former Harakat ul-Ansar, who was imprisoned by India in 1994 and then founded Jaish-e-Mohammed (JEM) after his release. Ahmed Omar Sheik also was released in 1999 and was later convicted of the abduction and murder in 2002 of U.S. journalist Daniel Pearl.

Strength

HUM has several hundred armed supporters located in Azad Kashmir, Pakistan; India's southern Kashmir and Doda regions; and in the Kashmir valley. Supporters are mostly Pakistanis and Kashmiris, but also include Afghans and Arab veterans of the Afghan war. HUM uses light and heavy machine guns, assault rifles, mortars, explosives, and rockets. When JEM was founded in 2000, HUM lost a significant share of its membership in defections to the JEM.

Location/Area of Operation

Based in Muzaffarabad, Rawalpindi, and several other cities in Pakistan, HUM conducts insurgent and terrorist operations primarily in Kashmir, but members have also been found operating in Afghanistan. HUM trains its militants in Afghanistan and Pakistan.

External Aid

HUM collects donations from both wealthy and grassroots donors in Pakistan, Kashmir, Saudi Arabia, and other Gulf and Islamic states. HUM's financial collection methods include soliciting donations in magazine ads and pamphlets. The sources and amount of HUM's military funding are unknown. Its overt fundraising in Pakistan has been constrained since the government clampdown on extremist groups and the freezing of terrorist assets.

HEZBOLLAH

a.k.a. the Party of God; Islamic Jihad; Islamic Jihad Organization; Revolutionary Justice Organization; Organization of the Oppressed on Earth; Islamic Jihad for the Liberation of Palestine; Organization of Right against Wrong; Ansar Allah; Followers of the Prophet Muhammed

Description

Hezbollah was designated as a Foreign Terrorist Organization on October 8, 1997. Formed in 1982, in response to the Israeli invasion of Lebanon, this Lebanese-based radical Shia group takes its ideological inspiration from the Iranian revolution and the teachings of the late Ayatollah Khomeini. The group generally follows the religious guidance of Khomeini's successor, Iranian Supreme Leader Ali Khamenei. Hezbollah is closely allied with Iran and often acts at its behest, though it also acts independently. Although Hezbollah does not share the Syrian regime's secular orientation, the group has helped Syria advance its political objectives in the region. The Majlis al-Shura, or Consultative Council, is the group's highest governing body and has been led by Secretary General Hasan Nasrallah since 1992. Hezbollah remains the most technically-capable terrorist group in the world. It has strong influence in Lebanon's Shia community, which comprises about one-third of Lebanon's population. The Lebanese government and the majority of the Arab world, still recognize Hezbollah as a legitimate "resistance group" and political party. Hezbollah has 14 elected officials in the 128-seat Lebanese National Assembly and is represented in the Cabinet by the Labor Minister, Mohammed Fneish. After the group's May 2008 armed takeover of West Beirut, which resulted in over 60 deaths, the

Hezbollah-led opposition negotiated to obtain sufficient representation in the cabinet providing it veto power over government decisions.

Hezbollah has reduced its overt military presence in southern Lebanon in accordance with UNSCR 1701, although it likely maintains weapons caches in the area patrolled by the UN Interim Force in Lebanon, in contravention of UN-SCR 1701. It justifies its continued armed status by claiming to defend Lebanon against acts of Israeli aggression and citing unresolved territorial claims, such as the Sheba'a farms, which is legally considered part of the Israeli-occupied Syrian Golan Heights. Hezbollah provides support to several Palestinian terrorist organizations, as well as a number of local Christian and Muslim militias in Lebanon. This support includes the covert provision of weapons, explosives, training, funding, and guidance, as well as overt political support.

After the February 2008 killing in Damascus of Imad Mughniyah, the Hezbollah terrorist and military chief suspected of involvement in many of these attacks, senior Hezbollah officials have repeatedly made public statements blaming Israel for the killing and vowing retaliation.

Activities

Hezbollah is known to have been involved in numerous anti-U.S. and anti-Israeli terrorist attacks; prior to September 11, 2001, it was responsible for more American deaths than any other terrorist group. In July 2006, Hezbollah attacked an Israeli Army patrol, kidnapping two soldiers and killing three, starting a conflict with Israel that lasted into August. Since at least 2004, Hezbollah has provided training to select Iraqi Shia militants, including the construction and use of shaped charge IEDs that can penetrate heavily-armored vehicles, which it developed in southern Lebanon in the late 1990s. A senior Hezbollah operative, Ali Mussa Daqduq, was captured in Iraq in 2007 while facilitating Hezbollah training of Iraqi Shia militants.

Hezbollah's terrorist attacks have included the suicide truck bombings of the U.S. Embassy and U.S. Marine barracks in Beirut in 1983, and the U.S. Embassy annex in Beirut in 1984, and the 1985 hijacking of TWA flight 847, during which a U.S. Navy diver was murdered. Elements of the group were responsible for the kidnapping, detention, and murder of Americans and other Westerners in Lebanon in the 1980s. Hezbollah also was implicated in the attacks on the Israeli Embassy in Argentina in 1992 and the Argentine-Israeli Mutual Association in Buenos Aires in 1994. In 2000, Hezbollah operatives captured three Israeli soldiers in the Sheba'a Farms area and kidnapped an Israeli non-combatant.

Strength

Thousands of supporters, several thousand members, and a few hundred terrorist operatives.

Location/Area of Operation

Operates in the southern suburbs of Beirut, the Bekaa Valley, and southern Lebanon. Receives support from Lebanese Shia communities in Europe, Africa, South America, North America, and Asia. Much of the support from these communities is fundraising, although Hezbollah can expect to receive logistic support if needed.

External Aid

Receives training, weapons, and explosives, as well as political, diplomatic, and organizational aid from Iran, and diplomatic, political, and logistical support from Syria. Hezbollah also receives funding from private donations and profits from legal and illegal businesses.

HIZB-I ISLAMI GULBUDDIN (HIG)

Description

Gulbuddin Hikmatyar founded Hizb-I Islami Gulbuddin (HIG) as a faction of the Hizb-I Islami party in 1977, and it was one of the major mujahedin groups in the jihad against the Soviet occupation of Afghanistan. Hikmatyar has long-established links with Osama bin Laden. In the early 1990s, Hikmatyar ran several terrorist training camps in Afghanistan and was a pioneer in sending mercenary fighters to other Islamic conflicts. Hikmatyar offered to shelter bin Laden after the latter fled Sudan in 1996 and has consistently offered public support for him since the 9/11 attacks. Hikmatyar has issued regular statements on the need for Afghans to reject the international community's presence in their country. In 2005, he responded to protests against Danish cartoons of the prophet Mohammad with a new call for the expulsion of international troops from Afghanistan.

Activities

HIG has staged small attacks in its attempt to force the international community to withdraw from Afghanistan, overthrow the Afghan government, and establish an Islamic state. U.S. troops have encountered regular violence in Konar, the area of Afghanistan in which HIG is most active, which has occasionally led to U.S. casualties, and it is likely that HIG is responsible for at least some of this violence.

Strength

Unknown, but possibly could have hundreds of veteran fighters on which to call.

Location/Area of Operation

Eastern Afghanistan, particularly Konar and Nurestan Provinces, and adjacent areas of Pakistan's tribal areas.

External Aid

Unknown.

HIZBUL-MUJAHEDIN (HM)

Description

Hizbul-Mujahedin (HM) is the largest Kashmiri militant group, and was founded in 1989. It officially supports the liberation of Jammu and Kashmir and its accession to Pakistan, although some members favor independence. The group is the militant wing of Pakistan's largest Islamic political party, the Jamaat-i-Islami, and targets Indian security forces and politicians in Jammu and Kashmir. It reportedly operated in Afghanistan in the mid-1990s and trained with the Afghan Hizb-I Islami Gulbuddin (HIG) in Afghanistan until the Taliban takeover. The group, led by Syed Salahuddin, is composed primarily of ethnic Kashmiris.

Activities

HM has conducted a number of operations against Indian military targets in Jammu and Kashmir. The group also occasionally strikes at civilian targets, but has not engaged in terrorist acts outside India. HM claimed responsibility for numerous attacks within Kashmir in 2006.

Strength

Exact numbers are unknown, but estimates range from several hundred to possibly as many as 1,000 members.

Location/Area of Operation

Jammu, Kashmir, and Pakistan.

External Aid

Specific sources of external aid are unknown.

IRISH NATIONAL LIBERATION ARMY (INLA)

Description

The INLA is a terrorist group formed in 1975 as the military wing of the Irish Republican Socialist Party (IRSP), which split from the Official IRA (OIRA) because of OIRA's cease-fire in 1972. The group's primary aim is to end British rule in Northern Ireland, force British troops out of the province, and unite Ireland's 32 counties into a Marxist-Leninist revolutionary state. It is responsible for some of the most notorious killings of "The Troubles," including the bombing of a Ballykelly pub that killed 17 people in 1982. Bloody internal feuding has repeatedly torn the INLA. The INLA announced a cease-fire in August 1998 but continues to carry out occasional attacks and punishment beatings.

Activities

The INLA has been active in Belfast and the border areas of Northern Ireland, where it has conducted bombings, assassinations, kidnappings, hijackings, extortion, and robberies. It is also involved in drug trafficking. On occasion, it has provided advance warning to police of its attacks. Targets include the British military, Northern Ireland security forces, and Loyalist paramilitary groups. The INLA did not join the IRA's September 2005 weapons decommissioning, but continues to observe a cease-fire because, in the words of its leadership in 2003, a return to armed struggle is "not a viable option at this time." However, the group continues to recruit members and was responsible for a 2005 arson attack against the home of a local official.

Strength

Unclear, but probably fewer than 50 hard-core activists. Police counterterrorist operations and internal feuding have reduced the group's strength and capabilities.

Location/Area of Operation

Northern Ireland and the Irish Republic. Does not have a significant established presence on the UK mainland.

External Aid

Suspected in the past of receiving funds and arms from sympathizers in the United States.

IRISH REPUBLICAN ARMY (IRA)

a.k.a. Provisional Irish Republican Army (PIRA); the Provos

Description

Formed in 1969 as the clandestine armed wing of the political movement Sinn Fein, the IRA is devoted both to removing British forces from Northern Ireland and to unifying Ireland. The IRA conducted attacks until its cease-fire in 1997 and agreed to disarm as part of the 1998 Belfast Agreement, which established the basis for peace in Northern Ireland. Dissension within the IRA over support for the Northern Ireland peace process resulted in the formation of two more radical splinter groups: Continuity IRA (CIRA) in 1995, and the Real IRA (RIRA) in 1997. The IRA, sometimes referred to as the PIRA to distinguish it from RIRA and CIRA, is organized into small, tightly-knit cells under the leadership of the Army Council.

Activities

Traditional IRA activities have included bombings, assassinations, kidnappings, punishment beatings, extortion, smuggling, and robberies. Before the cease-fire in 1997, the group had conducted bombing campaigns on various targets in Northern Ireland and Great Britain, including senior British government officials, civilians, police, and British military targets. In August 2002, three suspected IRA members were arrested in Colombia on charges of helping the Revolutionary Armed Forces of Colombia (FARC) improve its explosives capabilities; the men subsequently escaped from prison and appeared in Ireland in 2005. Irish police have questioned the men but have filed no charges. Colombia has requested their extradition, which is unlikely, since Ireland has no extradition treaty with Colombia.

In July 2005, a spokesperson for the IRA made a statement calling for an end to all forms of IRA illegal activity. This statement was confirmed in September 2005 by the Independent International Commission on Decommissioning's announcement that the IRA had met its commitments to put all arms beyond use. The Independent Monitoring Commission (IMC) also reported that since the September decommissioning the IRA has shown no evidence of training and recruiting terrorists or an intent to return to violence. There have been indications of IRA members using violence in 2006; however, the IMC reports that these incidents were not sanctioned by IRA leadership. The IRA has yet to abandon its extensive criminal activities, which reportedly provide the IRA and the political party Sinn Fein with millions of dollars each year.

Strength

Several hundred members and several thousand sympathizers, despite the defection of some members to RIRA and CIRA.

Location/Area of Operation

Northern Ireland, Irish Republic, Great Britain, and Europe.

External Aid

In the past, the IRA has received aid from a variety of groups and countries, and considerable training and arms from Libya and the PLO. It is suspected of receiving funds, arms, and other terrorist-related materiel from sympathizers in the United States. In addition to the apparent contact with the FARC, similarities in operations suggest the IRA has links to the ETA.

ISLAMIC ARMY OF ADEN (IAA)

a.k.a. Aden-Abyan Islamic Army (AAIA)

Description

The Islamic Army of Aden (IAA) emerged publicly in mid-1998 when the group released a series of communiqués that expressed support for Osama bin Laden and called for the overthrow of the Yemeni government and for operations against U.S. and other Western interests in Yemen. IAA was first designated under E.O. 13224 in September 2001.

Activities

The IAA, a group with established connections to al-Qaeda and whose membership includes veteran fighters from the Soviet-Afghan war, in the past has engaged in small-scale operations such as bombings, kidnappings, and small arms attacks to further its agenda. In June 2003, the group reportedly was behind an attack against a medical convoy in the Abyan Governorate. Yemeni authorities responded with a raid on a suspected IAA facility that killed several individuals and captured others, including Khalid al-Nabi al-Yazidi, the group's leader. The IAA's previous involvement in terrorist attacks includes the throwing of a grenade into the British Embassy compound in Sanaa in October 2000. In 2001, Yemeni authorities found an IAA member and three associates responsible for that attack. In December 1998, the group kidnapped 16 British, American, and Australian tourists near Mudiyah in southern Yemen. The group's involvement in a 2003 attack against the medical convoy and reports that its leader was released from prison in October 2003 suggest that the IAA, or at least elements of the group, may remain active. However, Yemeni officials previously have claimed that IAA is operationally defunct, and the group has not claimed any attacks since 2003.

Strength

Not known.

Location/Area of Operation

Operates in the southern governorates of Yemen, primarily Aden and Abyan.

External Aid

Not known.

ISLAMIC GREAT EASTERN RAIDERS—FRONT (IBDA-C)

Description

The Islamic Great Eastern Raiders—Front (IBDA-C) is a Sunni Salafist group that supports Islamic rule in Turkey, is sympathetic to al-Qaeda, and believes that Turkey's present secular leadership is "illegal." It has been known to cooperate with various opposition elements in Turkey in attempts to destabilize the country's political structure. The group supports the establishment of a "pure Islamic" state to replace the present "corrupt" Turkish regime that is cooperating with the West. Its primary goal is the establishment of the Federative Islamic State, a goal backed by armed terrorist attacks primarily against civilian targets. It has been active since the mid-1970s.

Activities

IBDA-C has engaged in activities that minimize personal risk, such as bombings, throwing Molotov cocktails, and sabotage. The group has announced its actions and targets in publications to its members, who are free to launch independent attacks. IBDA-C typically has attacked civilian targets, including churches, charities, minority-affiliated targets, television transmitters, newspapers, pro-secular journalists, Ataturk statues, taverns, banks, clubs, and tobacco shops. One of IBDA-C's more renowned attacks was the killing of 37 people in a firebomb attack in July 1993 on a hotel in Sivas. In May 2004, Turkish police indicted seven members of the group for the assassination of retired Colonel

Ihsan Guven, including the alleged leader of the "Dost" (Friend) sect, and his wife. Turkish police believe that IBDA-C has also claimed responsibility for attacks carried out by other groups in order to elevate its image. Turkish government crackdowns continued into 2006. In a May operation, the government arrested 18 members.

Strength

Unknown.

Location/Area of Operation

Turkey.

External Aid

Unknown.

ISLAMIC INTERNATIONAL PEACEKEEPING BRIGADE (IIPB)

Description

The IIPB is a terrorist group affiliated with the Chechen separatist movement demanding a single Islamic state in the North Caucasus. In 1998 Chechen extremist leader Shamil Basayev established the IIPB, consisting of Chechens, Arabs, and other foreign fighters, which he led with Saudi-born mujahedin leader Ibn al-Khattab until the latter's death in March 2002. In July 2006, Basayev himself was killed by Russian forces. The IIPB was one of three groups affiliated with Chechen guerrillas that seized Moscow's Dubrovka Theater and took more than 700 hostages in October 2002. While this group has not been identified by the mujahedin media as conducting attacks since its designation three years ago, those Arab mujahedin still operating in Chechnya now fall under the command of Abu Hafs al-Urduni, who assumed the IIPB leadership in April 2004 after the death of Khattab's successor, Abu al-Walid. IIPB was designated under E.O. 13224 in February 2003 and listed by the UN al-Qaeda/Taliban Sanctions Committee for its associations with al-Qaeda.

Activities

The IIPB has engaged in terrorist and guerrilla operations against Russian forces, pro-Russian Chechen forces, and Chechen non-combatants.

Strength

At its peak, up to 400 fighters, including as many as 100 Arabs and other foreign fighters, but almost certainly has suffered significant attrition.

Location/Area of Operation

Primarily in Russia and adjacent areas of the North Caucasus, particularly in the mountainous south of Chechnya, with major logistical activities in Georgia, Azerbaijan, and Turkey.

External Aid

The IIPB and its Arab leaders appear to be a primary conduit for Islamic funding of the Chechen guerrillas, in part through links to al-Qaeda-related financiers on the Arabian Peninsula.

ISLAMIC JIHAD UNION (IJU)

a.k.a. Islomiy Jihod Ittihodi; formerly known as Islamic Jihad Group (IJG); al-Djihad al-Islami; Dzhamaat Modzhakhedov; Islamic Jihad Group of Uzbekistan; Jamiat al-Jihad al-Islami; Jamiyat; the Jamaat Mojahedin; the Kazakh Jama'at; the Libyan Society

Description

The Islamic Jihad Union (IJU) was designated as a Foreign Terrorist Organization on June 17, 2005. The IJU is a Sunni extremist organization that splintered from the Islamic Movement of Uzbekistan (IMU). They oppose secular rule in Uzbekistan and seek to replace it with a government based on Islamic law. They adhere to a radical Sunni extremist agenda.

Activities

IJU has claimed responsibility for attacks targeting Coalition Forces in Afghanistan in 2008, including a March 2008 suicide attack against a U.S. military post purportedly carried out by a German-born Turk. In September 2007, German authorities disrupted an IJU plot by detaining three IJU operatives involved in the operation. Two of the three had attended IJU-run terrorist training camps in Pakistan and maintained communications with their Pakistani contacts after returning to Germany. The operatives had acquired large amounts of hydrogen peroxide and an explosives precursor that they stockpiled in a garage in southern Germany. The group had acquired large amounts of hydrogen peroxide for possible use in multiple car bomb attacks. The IJU subsequently claimed responsibility for the foiled attacks.

The IJU issued a statement in May 2005, fully supporting the armed attacks on Uzbek police and military personnel in Andijon, Uzbekistan, and called for the overthrow of the regime in Uzbekistan. The group first conducted attacks in March and April 2004 targeting police at several roadway checkpoints and a popular bazaar. These attacks killed approximately 47 people, including 33 terrorists, some of whom were suicide bombers. The IJU's claim of responsibility, which was posted to multiple militant Islamic websites, denounced the leadership of Uzbekistan. These attacks marked the first use of suicide bombers in Central Asia.

In July 2004, the group carried out near-simultaneous suicide bombings in Tashkent of the Uzbekistani Prosecutor General's office and the U.S. and Israeli Embassies. The IJU again claimed responsibility via an Islamic website and stated that martyrdom operations by the group would continue. The statement also indicated that the attacks were done in support of IJU's Palestinian, Iraqi, and Afghan brothers in the global insurgency. The date of the July attack corresponded with the trial of individuals arrested for their alleged participation in the March and April attacks.

Strength

Unknown.

Location/Area of Operation

IJU members are scattered throughout Central Asia, South Asia, and Europe.

External Aid

Unknown.

ISLAMIC MOVEMENT OF UZBEKISTAN (IMU)

Description

The Islamic Movement of Uzbekistan (IMU) was designated as a Foreign Terrorist Organization on September 9, 2000. The IMU is a group of Islamic militants from Uzbekistan, other Central Asian states, and Europe. The IMU's goal is to overthrow the Uzbekistani regime and to establish an Islamic state in Uzbekistan. The IMU, under the leadership of Tohir Yoldashev, has embraced Osama bin Laden's anti-Western ideology.

Activities

Since the beginning of Operation Enduring Freedom, the IMU has been predominantly occupied with attacks on U.S. and Coalition soldiers in Afghanistan, and has also been active in terrorist operations in Central Asia. Government authorities in Tajikistan arrested several IMU members in 2005. In November 2004, the IMU was blamed for an explosion in the southern Kyrgyz city of Osh that killed one police officer and one terrorist. In May 2003, Kyrgyz security forces disrupted an IMU cell that was seeking to bomb the U.S. Embassy and a nearby hotel in Bishkek, Kyrgyzstan. The IMU was responsible for explosions in Bishkek in December 2002 and Osh in May 2003 that killed eight people. The IMU primarily targeted Uzbekistani interests before October 2001 and is believed to have been responsible for several explosions in Tashkent in February 1999. In August 1999, IMU militants took four Japanese geologists and eight Kyrgyz soldiers hostage, and in August 2000, they took four U.S. mountain climbers hostage.

Strength

Approximately 500 members.

Location/Area of Operation

IMU militants are located in South Asia, Central Asia, and Iran. Their area of operation includes Afghanistan, Iran, Kyrgyzstan, Pakistan, Tajikistan, Kazakhstan, and Uzbekistan.

External Aid

The IMU receives support from a large Uzbek Diaspora, Islamic extremist groups, and patrons in the Middle East, Central Asia, and South Asia.

JAISH-E-MOHAMMED (JEM)

a.k.a. the Army of Mohammed; Mohammed's Army; Tehrik ul-Furqaan; Khuddam-ul-Islam; Khudamul Islam; Kuddam e Islami

Description

Jaish-e-Mohammed (JEM) was designated as a Foreign Terrorist Organization on December 26, 2001. JEM is an Islamic extremist group based in Pakistan that was founded in early 2000 by Masood Azhar, a former senior leader of Harakat ul-Ansar, upon his release from prison in India. The group's aim is to unite

Kashmir with Pakistan and it has openly declared war against the United States. It is politically aligned with the radical political party Jamiat Ulema-i-Islam's Fazlur Rehman faction (JUI-F). Pakistan outlawed JEM in 2002. By 2003, JEM had splintered into Khuddam ul-Islam (KUI), headed by Azhar, and Jamaat ul-Furqan (JUF), led by Abdul Jabbar, who was released from Pakistani custody in August 2004. Pakistan banned KUI and JUF in November 2003.

Activities

JEM continued to operate openly in parts of Pakistan despite then President Musharraf's 2002 ban on its activities. The group was well-funded and was said to have tens of thousands of followers who supported attacks against Indian targets, the Pakistani government, and sectarian minorities. Since Masood Azhar's 1999 release from Indian custody in exchange for 155 hijacked Indian Airlines hostages, JEM has conducted many fatal terrorist attacks in the area.

JEM continued to claim responsibility for several suicide car bombings in Kashmir, including an October 2001 suicide attack on the Jammu and Kashmir legislative assembly building in Srinagar that killed more than 30 people. The Indian government has publicly implicated JEM, along with Lashkar e-Tayyiba (LT), for the December 2001 attack on the Indian Parliament that killed nine and injured 18. Pakistani authorities suspect that JEM members may have been involved in the 2002 anti-Christian attacks in Islamabad, Murree, and Taxila that killed two Americans. In December 2003, Pakistan implicated elements of JEM in the two assassination attempts against President Musharraf. In July 2004, Pakistani authorities arrested a JEM member wanted in connection with the 2002 abduction and murder of U.S. journalist Daniel Pearl. In 2006, JEM claimed responsibility for a number of attacks, including the killing of several Indian police officials in the Indian-administered Kashmir capital of Srinagar.

Strength

JEM has at least several hundred armed supporters, including a large cadre of former HUM members, located in Pakistan, in India's southern Kashmir and Doda regions, and in the Kashmir Valley. Supporters are mostly Pakistanis and Kashmiris, but also include Afghans and Arab veterans of the Afghan war. The group uses light and heavy machine guns, assault rifles, mortars, improvised explosive devices, and rocket-propelled grenades.

Location/Area of Operation

Pakistan and Kashmir. Prior to autumn 2001, JEM maintained training camps in Afghanistan.

External Aid

Most of JEM's cadre and material resources have been drawn from the Pakistani militant groups Harakat ul-Jihad-i-Islami (HUJI-B) and the Harakat ul-Mujahadin (HUM). In anticipation of asset seizures by the Pakistani government, JEM withdrew funds from bank accounts and invested in legal businesses, such as commodity trading, real estate, and production of consumer goods. In addition, JEM collects funds through donation requests in magazines and pamphlets, and allegedly from al-Qaeda.

JAMAATUL-MUJAHEDIN BANGLADESH (JMB)

Description

JMB is a Bangladeshi Islamic extremist group dedicated to the use of violence to achieve its objective of a state based on Islamic law. JMB, which emerged in the late 1990s, has been associated with several bombings during the past several years. The Bangladeshi government banned the group in February 2005.

Activities

On August 17, 2005, JMB claimed responsibility for nearly 500 simultaneous explosions throughout Bangladesh. Subsequent bombings, possibly involving suicide bombers, targeted judges, police, government offices, traditional folk festivals and cultural groups, and local non-governmental organizations. The Bangladeshi government has captured several of the group's most important leaders.

Strength

Estimates range as high as 11,000.

Location/Area of Operation

Bangladesh.

External Aid

JMB probably also receives some support from persons of Bangladeshi origin living in Europe and the Middle East.

JAMIAT UL-MUJAHEDIN (JUM)

Description

The JUM is a small pro-Pakistan militant group formed in Jammu and Kashmir in 1990 that seeks to unite Jammu and Kashmir with Pakistan. Followers are mostly Kashmiris, but the group includes some Pakistanis.

Activities

Has conducted a number of operations against Indian military and political targets in Jammu and Kashmir, including two grenade attacks in 2004.

Strength

Unknown.

Location/Area of Operation

Jammu, Kashmir, and Pakistan.

External Aid

Unknown.

JAPANESE RED ARMY (JRA)

a.k.a. Anti-Imperialist International Brigade (AIIB)

Description

The JRA is an international terrorist group formed around 1970 after breaking away from the Japanese Communist League—Red Army Faction. The JRA's historical goal has been to overthrow the Japanese government and monarchy and to help foment world revolution. The JRA's leader, Fusako Shigenobu, claimed that the forefront of the battle against international imperialism was in Palestine, and in the early 1970s she led her small group to the Middle East. After her arrest in November 2000, Shigenobu announced she intended to pursue her goals using a legitimate political party rather than revolutionary violence, and the group apparently disbanded in April 2001.

Activities

During the 1970s, the JRA carried out a series of attacks around the world, including the 1972 massacre at Lod Airport in Israel, two Japanese airliner hijackings, an attempted takeover of the U.S. Embassy in Kuala Lumpur, and the 1974 seizure of the French Embassy in The Hague, in which the ambassador was among the hostages. During the late 1980s, the JRA began to single out American targets and used car bombs and rockets in attempted attacks on U.S. Embassies in Jakarta, Rome, and Madrid. In April 1988, JRA operative Yu Kikumura was arrested with explosives on the New Jersey Turnpike, apparently planning an attack to coincide with the bombing of a USO club in Naples, a suspected JRA operation that killed five, including a U.S. servicewoman. Kikimura was convicted of the charges and is serving a lengthy prison sentence in the United States. JRA operative Tsutomu Shirosaki, captured in 1996, is also jailed in the United States. In 2000, Lebanon deported four members it arrested in 1997 to Japan, but granted a fifth operative, Kozo Okamoto, political asylum. Longtime leader Shigenobu was arrested in November 2000 and faced charges of terrorism and passport fraud. In February 2006, Shingenobu was sentenced to 20 years in prison for coordinating the 1974 French embassy siege. Four JRA members remain in North Korea following their involvement in an airline hijacking in 1970; five of their family members returned to Japan in 2004.

Strength

At its peak, the group claimed to have 30 to 40 members.

Location/Area of Operation

Possibly in Asia.

External Aid

Unknown.

JEMAAH ISLAMIYA ORGANIZATION (JI)

Description

Jemaah Islamiya (JI) was designated as a Foreign Terrorist Organization on October 23, 2002. Southeast Asia–based JI is a terrorist group that seeks the establishment of an Islamic caliphate spanning Indonesia, Malaysia, southern Thailand, Singapore, Brunei, and the southern Philippines. More than 300 JI operatives, including operations chief Hambali, have been captured since 2002, although many of these were subsequently released after serving short sentences, including former JI emir Abu Bakar Bashir. Abu Bakar was released from prison in 2006 after serving a 25-month sentence for his involvement in the 2002 Bali bombings. Indonesia's Supreme Court later that year acquitted him of the charges. The death of top JI bomb maker Azahari bin Husin in 2005 and a series of high-profile arrests between 2005 and 2008, in combination with additional efforts by the Government of Indonesia, likely disrupted JI's anti-Western attacks—that occurred annually from 2002–2005. These included the 2006 arrests of several close associates of senior JI operative Noordin Mat Top, the 2007 arrests of former acting JI emir Muhammad Naim (a.k.a. Zarkasih) and JI military commander Abu Dujana, the 2008 arrests of two senior JI operatives in Malaysia, and the mid-2008 arrest of a JI-linked cell in Sumatra.

Activities

The group's most recent high-profile attack occurred in Bali on October 1, 2005, which left 25 persons dead, including the three suicide bombers. Other major JI attacks included the September 2004 bombing outside the Australian Embassy in Jakarta, the August 2003 bombing of the J. W. Marriott Hotel in Jakarta, and the October 2002 Bali bombing. The 2002 Bali attack, which killed more than 200, was one of the deadliest terrorist attacks since 9/11. In December 2001, Singaporean authorities uncovered a JI plot to attack the U.S. and Israeli Embassies, and British and Australian diplomatic buildings in Singapore. In December 2000, JI coordinated bombings of numerous Christian churches in Indonesia and was involved in the bombings of several targets in Manila. In February 2004, JI facilitated attacks in Manila, Davao, and General Santos City. JI associates in the Philippines provide operational support and training for indigenous Philippine Muslim violent extremists.

Strength

Exact numbers currently are unknown. Estimates of total JI members vary from the hundreds to one thousand.

Location/Area of Operation

JI is based in Indonesia and is believed to have cells in Indonesia, Malaysia, and the Philippines.

External Aid

Investigations indicate that JI is fully capable of its own fundraising, although it also has received financial, ideological, and logistical support from Middle Eastern contacts and non-governmental organizations.

AL-JIHAD (AJ)

a.k.a. Egyptian Islamic Jihad; Egyptian al-Jihad; New Jihad; Jihad Group

Description

In 2001, this Egyptian Islamic extremist group merged with al-Qaeda. Osama bin Laden's deputy, Ayman al-Zawahiri, was the former head of Al-Jihad (AJ). Active since the 1970s, AJ's primary goal has been the overthrow of the Egyptian government and the establishment of an Islamic state. The group's targets, historically, have been high-level Egyptian government officials as well as U.S. and Israeli interests in Egypt and abroad. Regular Egyptian crackdowns on extremists and Cairo's deradicalization measures, such as its very successful reconciliation program aimed at imprisoned AJ members, have greatly reduced AJ's capabilities in Egypt.

Activities

The original AJ was responsible for the 1981 assassination of Egyptian President Anwar Sadat. It claimed responsibility for the attempted assassinations in 1993 of Interior Minister Hassan al-Alfi and Prime Minister Atef Sedky. AJ has not conducted an attack inside Egypt since 1993 and has never successfully targeted foreign tourists there. The group was responsible for the Egyptian Embassy bombing in Islamabad in 1995 and a disrupted plot against the U.S. Embassy in Albania in 1998. AJ has not committed independent acts of terrorism since its merger with al-Qaeda in 2001.

Strength

Believed to have an indeterminate number of hard-core members outside Egypt.

Location/Area of Operation

Most AJ members today are outside Egypt in countries such as Afghanistan, Pakistan, Lebanon, the United Kingdom, and Yemen. AJ activities have been centered outside Egypt for several years under the auspices of al-Qaeda.

KAHANE CHAI (KACH)

a.k.a. American Friends of the United Yeshiva; American Friends of Yeshivat Rav Meir; Committee for the Safety of the Roads; Dikuy Bogdim; DOV; Forefront of the Idea; Friends of the Jewish Idea Yeshiva; Jewish Legion; Judea Police; Judean Congress; Kach; Kahane; Kahane Lives; Kahane Tzadak; Kahane. org; Kahanetzadak.com; Kfar Tapuah Fund; Koach; Meir's Youth; New Kach Movement; Newkach.org; No'ar Meir; Repression of Traitors; State of Judea; Sword of David; the Committee against Racism and Discrimination (CARD); the Hatikva Jewish Identity Center; the International Kahane Movement; the Jewish Idea Yeshiva; the Judean Legion; the Judean Voice; the Qomemiyut Movement;

the Rabbi Meir David Kahane Memorial Fund; the Voice of Judea; the Way of
the Torah; the Yeshiva of the Jewish Idea; Yeshivat Harav Meir

Description

Kahane Chai's (Kach) stated goal was to restore the biblical state of Israel. Kach
was founded by radical Israeli-American rabbi Meir Kahane. Its offshoot, Kahane
Chai (translation: "Kahane Lives"), was founded by Meir Kahane's son Binyamin
following his father's 1990 assassination in the United States. Both Kach and
Kahane Chai were declared terrorist organizations in 1994 by the Israeli Cabinet
under its 1948 Terrorism Law. This designation followed the groups' statements
in support of Dr. Baruch Goldstein's attack in February 1994 on the Ibrahimi
Mosque and their verbal attacks on the Israeli government. Palestinian gunmen
killed Binyamin Kahane and his wife in a drive-by shooting in December 2000
in the West Bank. The group has attempted to gain seats in the Israeli Knesset
over the past several decades, but has won only one seat, in 1984.

Activities

Kach has harassed and threatened Arabs, Palestinians, and Israeli government
officials, and has vowed revenge for the death of Binyamin Kahane and his wife.
Kach is suspected of involvement in a number of low-level attacks since the start
of the al-Aqsa Intifada in 2000.

Strength

Unknown.

Location/Area of Operation

Israel and West Bank settlements, particularly Qiryat Arba' in Hebron.

External Aid

Receives support from sympathizers in the United States and Europe.

KUMPULAN MUJAHEDIN MALAYSIA (KMM)

a.k.a. Kumpulan Militan Malaysia

Description

Kumpulan Mujahedin Malaysia (KMM) favors the overthrow of the Malaysian
government and the creation of an Islamic state comprising Malaysia, Indone-

sia, and the southern Philippines (and Southern Thailand). Malaysian authorities believe an extremist wing of the KMM has engaged in terrorist acts and has close ties to the regional terrorist organization Jemaah Islamiya (JI). Key JI leaders, including the group's spiritual head, Abu Bakar Bashir, and JI operational leader Hambali, reportedly had great influence over KMM members. The Government of Singapore asserts that a Singaporean JI member assisted the KMM in buying a boat to support jihad activities in Indonesia.

Activities

Malaysia continues to hold a number of KMM members under the Internal Security Act for activities deemed threatening to Malaysia's national security, including planning to wage jihad, possession of weaponry, bombings, robberies, the murder of a former state assembly member, and planning attacks on foreigners, including U.S. citizens. A number of those detained also are believed to be members of Jemaah Islamiya. Several of the arrested KMM militants reportedly have undergone military training in Afghanistan, and some fought with the Afghan mujahedin during the war against the former Soviet Union. Some members allegedly have ties to Islamic extremist organizations in Indonesia and the Philippines. One alleged KMM member was sentenced to 10 years in prison for unlawful possession of firearms, explosives, and ammunition; eight other alleged members in detention since 2001 were later released in July and November 2004; three others were freed in November 2005. In March 2004, alleged KMM leader Nik Adli Nik Abdul Aziz and other suspected KMM members went on a hunger strike as part of an unsuccessful bid for freedom, but the Malaysian court in September 2004 rejected their applications for a writ of habeas corpus. In September 2005, detention orders for Aziz and eight other alleged KMM members were extended for another two years. The Malaysian government is confident that the arrests of KMM leaders have crippled the organization and rendered it incapable of engaging in militant activities. In May 2004, Malaysian officials denied Thailand's charge that the KMM was involved in the Muslim separatist movement in southern Thailand.

Strength

KMM's current membership is unknown.

Location/Area of Operation

The KMM is reported to have networks in the Malaysian states of Perak, Johor, Kedah, Selangor, Terengganu, and Kelantan. They also operate in Kuala Lumpur. The KMM has ties to radical Indonesian Islamic groups.

External Aid

Largely unknown, probably self-financing.

KURDISTAN WORKERS' PARTY (PKK)

a.k.a. the Kurdistan Freedom and Democracy Congress; the Freedom and De-
mocracy Congress of Kurdistan; KADEK; the Kurdistan Workers' Party; Partiya
Karkeran Kurdistan; the People's Defense Force; Halu Mesru Savunma Kuvveti
(HSK); Kurdistan People's Congress (KHK); People's Congress of Kurdistan;
KONGRA-GEL

Description

The Kurdistan Workers' Party (PKK) was designated as a Foreign Terrorist Organization on October 8, 1997. The PKK was founded by Abdullah Ocalan
in 1978 as a Marxist-Leninist separatist organization. The group, composed
primarily of Turkish Kurds, launched a campaign of violence in 1984. The PKK
aspired to establish an independent Kurdish state in southeastern Turkey, but in
recent years has spoken more often about autonomy within a Turkish state that
guaranteed Kurdish cultural and linguistic rights.

In the early 1990s, the PKK moved beyond rural-based insurgent activities to include urban terrorism. In the 1990s, southeastern Anatolia was the
scene of significant violence; some estimates place casualties at approximately
30,000 persons. Following his capture in 1999, Ocalan announced a "peace
initiative," ordering members to refrain from violence and requesting dialogue
with Ankara on Kurdish issues. Ocalan's death-sentence was commuted to life-
imprisonment; he remains the symbolic leader of the group. The group fore-
swore violence until June 2004, when the group's hard-line militant wing took
control and renounced the self-imposed cease-fire of the previous five years.
Striking over the border from bases within Iraq, the PKK engaged in terrorist
attacks in eastern and western Turkey.

Activities

Primary targets have been Turkish government security forces, local Turkish officials, and villagers who oppose the organization in Turkey. The PKK's reputed
military wing, the People's Defense Force (HPG), has been responsible mainly
for attacks against military and paramilitary targets in the southeastern area of
Turkey. The PKK's reported urban terrorist arm, the Kurdistan Freedom Hawks
(TAK), has attacked primarily tourist areas in western Turkey, and in late February 2008, announced a new wave of terrorist actions against Turkey.

In an attempt to damage Turkey's tourist industry, the PKK has bombed
tourist sites and hotels and kidnapped foreign tourists. In July, PKK operatives
kidnapped three German tourists on Mount Ararat in eastern Turkey in retaliation for Germany's tough stance against the group. On October 3, PKK militants
killed 15 Turkish soldiers at the Aktutun outpost on the Turkish-Iraqi border, and

five days later the group killed several police officers and wounded 19 in an attack in the southeastern province of Diyarbakir.

Strength

Approximately 4,000 to 5,000; 3,000 to 3,500 are located in northern Iraq.

Location/Area of Operation

Operates primarily in Turkey, Iraq, Europe, and the Middle East.

External Aid

In the past, the PKK received safe haven and modest aid from Syria, Iraq, and Iran. Since 1999, Syria and Iran have cooperated in a limited fashion with Turkey against the PKK. In 2008, Turkey and Iraq began cooperating to fight the PKK. The group maintains a large extortion, fundraising, and propaganda network in Europe.

LASHKAR E-TAYYIBA (LT)

a.k.a. al Mansooreen; Al Mansoorian; Army of the Pure; Army of the Pure and Righteous; Army of the Righteous; Lashkar e-Toiba; Lashkar-i-Taiba; Paasban-e-Ahle-Hadis; Paasban-e-Kashmir; Paasban-i-Ahle-Hadith; Pasban-e-Ahle-Hadith; Pasban-e-Kashmir; Jamaat-ud-Dawa, JUD; Jama'at al-Dawa; Jamaat ud-Daawa; Jamaat ul-Dawah; Jamaat-ul-Dawa; Jama'at-i-Dawat; Jamaiat-ud-Dawa; Jama'at-ud-Da'awah; Jama'at-ud-Da'awa; Jamaati-ud-Dawa; Idara Khidmat-e-Khalq

Description

Lashkar e-Tayyiba (LT) was designated as a Foreign Terrorist Organization on December 26, 2001. The group remains the prime suspect for the November 26, 2008, Mumbai attacks. LT is one of the largest and most proficient of the traditionally Kashmiri-focused militant groups. LT formed in the late 1980s or early 1990s as the militant wing of the Islamic extremist organization Markaz Dawa ul-Irshad (MDI), a Pakistan-based Islamic fundamentalist mission organization and charity founded to oppose the Soviet presence in Afghanistan. LT, which is not connected to any political party, is led by Hafiz Muhammad Saeed. Shortly after LT was designated as an FTO, Saeed changed the name to Jamaat-ud-Dawa (JUD) and began humanitarian projects to avoid restrictions. LT functions and disseminates its message through JUD's media outlets. Elements of LT and Jaish-e-Muhammad (JEM) combined with other groups to mount attacks as "The Save Kashmir Movement." The Pakistani government banned the group and froze its assets in January 2002. LT and its leader, Hafiz Muhammad Saeed, continued to spread ideology advocating terrorism, as well as virulent rhetoric condemning the United States, India, Israel, and other perceived enemies.

Activities

LT has conducted a number of operations against Indian troops and civilian targets in Jammu and Kashmir since 1993, as well as several high-profile attacks inside India itself. LT claimed responsibility for numerous attacks in 2001, including an attack in January on Srinagar airport that killed five Indians; an attack on a police station in Srinagar that killed at least eight officers and wounded several others; and an attack in April 2007 against Indian border security forces that left at least four dead. The Indian government publicly implicated LT, along with JEM, for the December 2001 attack on the Indian Parliament building, although concrete evidence was lacking. LT is also suspected of involvement in the May 2002 attack on an Indian Army base in Kaluchak that left 36 dead. India blamed LT for an October 2005 attack in New Delhi and a December 2005 Bangalore attack. Senior al-Qaeda lieutenant Abu Zubaydah was captured at an LT safe house in Faisalabad in March 2002, which suggested that some members were facilitating the movement of al-Qaeda members in Pakistan. Indian governmental officials hold LT responsible for the July 11, 2006 train attack in Mumbai and several attacks since then in Hyderabad. In 2008, the Indian government assessed that LT was behind the November 26–28 [2008] attacks in Mumbai against luxury hotels, a Jewish center, a prominent train station, and a popular café that killed at least 183, including 22 foreigners, and injured over 300.

Strength

The actual size of the group is unknown but LT has several thousand members in Azad Kashmir, Pakistan, in the southern Jammu and Kashmir and Doda regions, and in the Kashmir Valley. Most LT members are Pakistanis or Afghanis and/or veterans of the Afghan wars, though the group is alleged to augment its strength through collaboration with terrorist groups comprised of non-Pakistanis. The group uses assault rifles, light and heavy machine guns, mortars, explosives, and rocket-propelled grenades.

Location/Area of Operation

Based in Muridke (near Lahore) and Muzaffarabad, Pakistan; maintains a number of facilities, including training camps, schools, and medical clinics.

External Aid

Collects donations from the Pakistani expatriate communities in the Middle East and the United Kingdom, Islamic NGOs, and Pakistani and other Kashmiri business people. LT coordinates its charitable activities through its front organization Jamaat ud-Daawa (JUD), which spearheaded humanitarian relief to the victims of the October 2005 earthquake in Kashmir. The precise amount of LT funding is unknown.

LASHKAR I JHANGVI (LJ)

Description

Lashkar I Jhangvi (LJ) was designated as a Foreign Terrorist Organization on January 30, 2003. LJ is the militant offshoot of the Sunni Deobandi sectarian group Sipah-i-Sahaba Pakistan. LJ focuses primarily on anti-Shia attacks and was banned by then Pakistani President Musharraf in August 2001 as part of an effort to rein in sectarian violence. Many of its members then sought refuge in Afghanistan with the Taliban, with whom they had existing ties. After the collapse of the Taliban, LJ members became active in aiding other terrorists with safe houses, false identities, and protection in Pakistani cities, including Karachi, Peshawar, and Rawalpindi.

Activities

LJ specializes in armed attacks and bombings and has admitted responsibility for numerous killings of Shia religious and community leaders in Pakistan. In January, the Interior Ministry ordered the arrest of three LJ militants suspected of being involved in a suicide bombing at a Shia religious procession in Peshawar that killed 15 people. In February, police arrested 20 LJ militants wanted for various terrorism attacks in the Punjab and Sindh provinces. In June, Sindh authorities issued a statement attributing the April 2006 Mishtar Parking bombing in Karachi to a militant with ties to LJ. The Government of Pakistan claimed that the group was involved in the April 2006 assassination attempt and the July 2006 assassination of Allama Turabi, an influential Shia leader. In October 2008, Afghan security forces claimed to have arrested four Pakistani suicide bombers in Kandahar who asserted that they belonged to LJ.

In May 2006, Pakistani police arrested two LJ militants suspected of involvement in the March bombing outside the U.S. Consulate in Karachi that killed one U.S. official. Pakistani authorities have publicly linked LJ members to the 2002 abduction and murder of U.S. journalist Daniel Pearl. Media reports linked LJ to attacks on Christian targets in Pakistan, including a March 2002 grenade assault on the Protestant International Church in Islamabad that killed two U.S. citizens, but no formal charges were filed. Pakistani authorities believe LJ was responsible for the July 2003 bombing of a Shia mosque in Quetta, Pakistan. Authorities also implicated LJ in several sectarian incidents in 2004, including the May and June bombings of two Shia mosques in Karachi that killed more than 40 people. In January 1999, the group attempted to assassinate former Prime Minister Nawaz Sharif and his brother Shabaz Sharif, Chief Minister of Punjab Province.

Strength

Probably fewer than 100.

Location/Area of Operation

LJ is active primarily in Punjab and Karachi. Some members travel between Pakistan and Afghanistan.

External Aid

Unknown.

LIBERATION TIGERS OF TAMIL EELAM (LTTE)

a.k.a. Ellalan Force; Tamil Tigers

Description

The Liberation Tigers of Tamil Eelam (LTTE) was designated as a Foreign Terrorist Organization on October 8, 1997. Founded in 1976, the LTTE is a powerful Tamil secessionist group in Sri Lanka. The LTTE wants to establish an independent Tamil state in the island's north and east. Since the beginning of its insurgency against the Sri Lankan government in 1983, it has evolved its capability from terrorist and guerrilla tactics to conventional warfare. Although the LTTE nominally committed to a 2002 cease-fire agreement with the Sri Lankan government, it continued terrorist attacks against government leaders and dissident Tamils.

Activities

LTTE has integrated a battlefield insurgent strategy with a terrorist program that targets key personnel in the countryside and senior Sri Lankan political and military leaders in Colombo and other urban centers. It has conducted a sustained campaign targeting rival Tamil groups and figures, and assassinated Prime Minister Rajiv Gandhi of India in 1991, and President Ranasinghe Premadasa of Sri Lanka in 1993. Although most notorious for its cadre of suicide bombers, the Black Tigers, the organization also features an amphibious force, the Sea Tigers; and a nascent air wing, the Air Tigers. Fighting between the LTTE and the Sri Lanka government escalated in 2006 and continued through 2008. Open source reporting asserts the LTTE is believed to have detonated a claymore mine on a crowded bus near Colombo on June 6, 2008, killing 22 civilians and wounding more than 50 others. Political assassinations and bombings were commonplace tactics prior to the cease-fire and have increased again since mid-2005. Most LTTE attacks targeted Sri Lankan military and official personnel but, as illustrated by the June 6, 2008 bombing, the LTTE appears to continue to target civilians on occasion.

In January 2009, Sri Lanka President Mahinda Rajapaksa announced that the Tamil Tigers had been driven out of the city of Kilinochchi which they had used as their administrative base for more than 10 years. Several hundred insurgents were killed. They are now hiding out in the jungles of Mullaitvu, their last main base, and are expected to launch guerrilla raids from there.

Strength

Exact strength is unknown, but LTTE is estimated to have 8,000 to 10,000 armed combatants in Sri Lanka, with an elite cadre of 5,000 to 7,000. LTTE also has a significant overseas support structure for fundraising, weapons procurement, and propaganda activities.

Location/Area of Operation

In June 2008, Sri Lankan government forces increased military operations against the LTTE capturing the Jaffna Peninsula and Kilinochchi, LTTE's administrative center of operations, reducing LTTE's control in Sri Lanka to a region around the northeastern town of Mullaitvu.

External Aid

The LTTE uses its international contacts and the large Tamil Diaspora in North America, Europe, and Asia to procure weapons, communications, funding, and other needed supplies. The group employs charities as fronts to collect and divert funds for their activities.

LIBYAN ISLAMIC FIGHTING GROUP (LIFG)

Description

The Libyan Islamic Fighting Group (LIFG) was designated as a Foreign Terrorist Organization on December 17, 2004. In the early 1990s, LIFG emerged from the group of Libyans who had fought Soviet forces in Afghanistan and the Qadhafi regime in Libya, and declared Libyan President Muammar Qadhafi un-Islamic and pledged to overthrow him. In the years following, some members maintained a strictly anti-Qadhafi focus and targeted Libyan government interests. Others, such as Abu al-Faraj al-Libi, who in 2005 was arrested in Pakistan, aligned with Osama bin Laden, and are believed to be part of the al-Qaeda leadership structure or active in the international terrorist network. On November 3, 2007, senior al-Qaeda leaders announced that LIFG had officially joined al-Qaeda.

Activities

Libyans associated with LIFG are part of the broader international terrorist movement. LIFG is one of the groups believed to have planned the Casablanca suicide bombings in May 2003. LIFG continued to target Libyan interests, and attempted to assassinate Qadhafi four times; the last attempt was in 1998. The LIFG engaged Libyan security forces in armed clashes during the 1990s. However, the LIFG has been largely operationally inactive in Libya since the late 1990s when members fled predominately to Europe and the Middle East because of tightened Libyan security measures. To date, the November 3, 2007, merger with al-Qaeda has not resulted in a significant increase in LIFG activities within Libya.

Strength

The LIFG probably has several hundred active members or supporters, mostly in the Middle East or Europe.

Location/Area of Operation

Since the late 1990s, many members have fled to various Asian, Arabian Gulf, African, and European countries, particularly the UK. It is likely that LIFG maintains a limited presence in eastern Libya.

External Aid

Unknown. The LIFG has used Islamic charitable organizations as cover for fundraising and transferring money and documents; it may have also financed operations with criminal activity.

LORD'S RESISTANCE ARMY (LRA)

Description

The LRA, founded in 1987, succeeded the ethnic Acholi-dominated Holy Spirit Movement and other insurgent groups. LRA leader Joseph Kony has called for the overthrow of the Ugandan government and its replacement with a regime run on the basis of the Ten Commandments. More frequently, however, he has spoken of the liberation and honor of the Acholi people, whom he sees as oppressed by the "foreign" government of Ugandan President Museveni. Kony is the LRA's undisputed leader. He claims to have supernatural powers and to receive messages from spirits, which he uses to formulate the LRA's strategy.

Activities

Since the early 1990s, the LRA has kidnapped some 20,000 Ugandan children, mostly ethnic Acholi, to replenish its ranks. Kony despises Acholi elders for having given up the fight against Museveni and relies on abducted children who can be brutally indoctrinated to fight for the LRA. The LRA kidnaps children and adult civilians to become soldiers, porters, and "wives" for LRA leaders. The LRA prefers to attack camps for internally displaced persons and other civilian targets, avoiding direct engagement with the Ugandan military. The LRA stepped up its activities from 2002 to 2004 after the Ugandan army, with the Sudanese government's permission, attacked LRA positions inside Sudan. By late 2003, the number of internally displaced persons had doubled to 1.4 million, and the LRA had pushed deep into non-Acholi areas where it had never previously operated. During 2004, a combination of military pressure, offers of amnesty, and several rounds of negotiation markedly degraded LRA capabilities due to death, desertion, and defection of senior commanders. In October 2005, the International Criminal Court (ICC) issued arrest warrants for Kony and four other top LRA leaders. Since February 2006, the Government of Southern Sudan has been holding peace talks between the LRA and the Ugandan government.

Strength

Estimated at 500 to 700 fighters.

Location/Area of Operation

Northern Uganda, southern Sudan, and northeast Democratic Republic of the Congo.

External Aid

Although the LRA has been supported by the Government of Sudan in the past, the Sudanese now appear to be cooperating with the Government of Uganda in a campaign to eliminate LRA sanctuaries in Sudan.

LOYALIST VOLUNTEER FORCE (LVF)

Description

An extreme Loyalist group formed in 1996 as a faction of the Ulster Volunteer Force (UVF), the LVF did not emerge publicly until 1997. It is composed largely of UVF hardliners who have sought to prevent a political settlement with Irish nationalists in Northern Ireland by attacking Catholic politicians, civilians, and Protestant politicians who endorse the Northern Ireland peace process. LVF occasionally uses the Red Hand Defenders as a cover name for its actions but has also called for the group's disbandment. In October 2001, the British government ruled the LVF had broken the cease-fire it declared in 1998 after linking the group to the murder of a journalist. According to the Independent International Commission on Decommissioning, the LVF decommissioned a small amount of weapons in December 1998, but it has not repeated this gesture. The LVF was designated under E.O. 13224 in December 2001.

Activities

The group conducts bombings, kidnappings, and close-quarter shooting attacks. It finances its activities with drug money and other criminal activities. LVF attacks have been particularly vicious; the group has murdered numerous Catholic civilians with no political or paramilitary affiliations, including an 18-year-old Catholic girl in July 1997 because she had a Protestant boyfriend. LVF terrorists also have conducted successful attacks against Irish targets in Irish border towns. From 2000 to August 2005, the LVF engaged in a violent feud with other Loyalists, which left several men dead. In October 2005, the group said that it would stand down its "military units," but the Independent Monitoring Commission has no evidence of the LVF disbanding.

Strength

Small, perhaps dozens of active members.

Location/Area of Operation

Northern Ireland and Ireland.

External Aid

None.

MOROCCAN ISLAMIC COMBATANT GROUP (GICM)

a.k.a. Groupe Islamique Combattant Marocain (GICM)

Description

The Moroccan Islamic Combatant Group (GICM) was designated as a Foreign Terrorist Organization on September 11, 2005. The GICM is a clandestine transnational terrorist group centered in the Moroccan Diaspora communities of western Europe. Its goals include establishing an Islamic state in Morocco and supporting al-Qaeda's war against the West by assisting in the assimilation of al-Qaeda operatives into Moroccan and European society. The group emerged in the 1990s and is composed of Moroccan recruits who trained in armed camps in Afghanistan, including some who fought in the Soviet Afghan war. GICM members interact with other North African extremists, particularly in Europe.

Activities

GICM members were among those responsible for the 2004 Madrid bombing, and Moroccans associated with the GICM are part of the broader international terrorist movement. GICM members were implicated in the recruitment network of individuals for Iraq, and at least one GICM member carried out a suicide attack against Coalition Forces in Iraq. GICM individuals are believed to have been involved in the 2003 Casablanca attacks.

Strength

Much of the GICM's leadership in Morocco and Europe has been killed, imprisoned, or are awaiting trial. Alleged leader Mohamed al-Guerbouzi was convicted in absentia by the Moroccan government for his role in the Casablanca attacks but remains free in exile in the UK.

Location/Area of Operation

Morocco, western Europe, Afghanistan, and Canada.

External Aid

The GICM has been involved in narcotics trafficking in North Africa and Europe to fund its operations. Moroccan security officials believe money from drug trafficking largely financed the 2003 Casablanca attacks. The Madrid attacks were financed mainly by the narcotics trafficking of Moroccan terrorist Jamal Ahmidan.

MUJAHEDIN-E KHALQ ORGANIZATION

a.k.a. MEK; MKO; Mujahedin-e Khalq (Iranian government name for group); Muslim Iranian Students' Society; National Council of Resistance; NCR; Organization of the People's Holy Warriors of Iran; the National Liberation Army of Iran; NLA; People's Mujahedin Organization of Iran; PMOI; National Council of Resistance of Iran; NCRI; Sazeman-e Mujahedin-e Khalq-e Iran

Description

The Mujahedin-e Khalq Organization (MEK) advocates the violent overthrow of the Iranian government and was responsible for the assassination of several U.S. military personnel and civilians in the 1970s. The MEK's armed wing is known as the National Liberation Army of Iran (NLA). In December 2008, the European Court of First Instance annulled the European Union's designation of the MEK as a terrorist organization.

The MEK emerged in the 1960s as one of the more violent political movements opposed to the Pahlavi dynasty and its close relationship with the United States. MEK ideology has gone through several iterations and blends elements of Marxism, Islam, and feminism. The group has planned and executed terrorist operations against the Iranian government for nearly three decades from its European and Iraqi bases of operations. Additionally, it has expanded its fundraising base, further developed its paramilitary skills, and aggressively worked to expand its European ranks. In addition to its terrorist credentials, the MEK has also displayed cult-like characteristics.

Upon entry into the group, new members are indoctrinated in MEK ideology and revisionist Iranian history. Members are also required to undertake a vow of "eternal divorce" and participate in weekly "ideological cleansings." Additionally, children are reportedly separated from parents at a young age. MEK leader Maryam Rajavi has established a "cult of personality." She claims to emulate the Prophet Muhammad and is viewed by members as the "Iranian President in exile."

Activities

The group's worldwide campaign against the Iranian government uses propaganda and terrorism to achieve its objectives and has been supported by reprehensible regimes, including that of Saddam Hussein. During the 1970s, the MEK assassinated several U.S. military personnel and U.S. civilians working on defense projects in Tehran and supported the violent takeover in 1979 of the U.S. Embassy in Tehran.

In 1981, MEK leadership attempted to overthrow the newly installed Islamic regime; Iranian security forces subsequently initiated a crackdown on the group. The MEK instigated a bombing campaign, including an attack against the head office of the Islamic Republic Party and the Prime Minister's office, which killed some 70 high-ranking Iranian officials, including Chief Justice Ayatollah Mohammad Beheshti, President Mohammad-Ali Rajaei, and Prime Minister Mohammad-Javad Bahonar. These attacks resulted in a popular uprising against the MEK and an expanded Iranian government crackdown which forced MEK leaders to flee to France. For five years, the MEK continued to wage its terrorist campaign from its Paris headquarters. Expelled by France in 1986, MEK leaders turned to Saddam Hussein's regime for basing, financial support, and training. Near the end of the 1980–1988 Iran-Iraq War, Baghdad armed the MEK with heavy military equipment and deployed thousands of MEK fighters in suicidal, mass wave attacks against Iranian forces.

The MEK's relationship with the former Iraqi regime continued through the 1990s. In 1991, the group reportedly assisted the Iraqi Republican Guard's bloody crackdown on Iraqi Shia and Kurds who rose up against Saddam Hussein's regime. In April 1992, the MEK conducted near-simultaneous attacks on Iranian embassies and installations in 13 countries, demonstrating the group's ability to mount large-scale operations overseas. In April 1999, the MEK targeted key Iranian military officers and assassinated the deputy chief of the Iranian Armed Forces General Staff, Brigadier General Ali Sayyaad Shirazi.

In April 2000, the MEK attempted to assassinate the commander of the Nasr Headquarters, Tehran's interagency board responsible for coordinating policies on Iraq. The pace of anti-Iranian operations increased during "Operation Great Bahman" in February 2000, when the group launched a dozen attacks against Iran. One attack included a mortar attack against a major Iranian leadership complex in Tehran that housed the offices of the Supreme Leader and the President. In 2000 and 2001, the MEK was involved in regular mortar attacks and hit-and-run raids against Iranian military and law enforcement personnel, as well as government buildings near the Iran-Iraq border. Also in 2001, the FBI arrested seven Iranians in the United States who funneled $400,000 to an MEK-affiliated organization in the UAE, which used the funds to purchase weapons. Following an initial Coalition bombardment of the MEK's facilities in Iraq at the outset of Operation Iraqi Freedom, MEK leadership negotiated a cease-fire with Coalition Forces and voluntarily surrendered their heavy-arms to Coalition control. Since 2003, roughly 3,400 MEK members have been encamped at Ashraf in Iraq.

In 2003, French authorities arrested 160 MEK members at operational bases they believed the MEK was using to coordinate financing and planning for terrorist attacks. Upon the arrest of MEK leader Maryam Rajavi, MEK members took to Paris' streets and engaged in self-immolation. French authorities eventually released Rajavi. Although currently in hiding, Rajavi has made "motivational" appearances via video-satellite to MEK-sponsored conferences across the globe.

According to evidence which became available after the fall of Saddam Hussein, the MEK received millions of dollars in Oil-for-Food program subsidies from Saddam Hussein from 1999 through 2003. In addition to discovering 13 lists of recipients of such vouchers on which the MEK appeared, evidence linking the MEK to the former Iraqi regime includes lists, as well as video footage of both Saddam Hussein handing over suitcases of money to known MEK leaders, and of MEK operatives receiving training from the Iraqi military.

Strength

Estimates place MEK's worldwide membership at between 5,000 and 10,000 members, with large pockets in Paris and other major European capitals. In Iraq, roughly 3,400 MEK members are gathered at Camp Ashraf, the MEK's main compound north of Baghdad. As a condition of the 2003 cease-fire agreement, the MEK relinquished more than 2,000 tanks, armored personnel carriers, and heavy artillery. Between 2003–2006, a significant number of MEK personnel have voluntarily left Ashraf, and an additional several hundred individuals have renounced ties to the MEK and been voluntarily repatriated to Iran.

Location/Area of Operation

The MEK maintains its main headquarters in Paris and has concentrations of members across Europe, in addition to the large concentration of MEK located at Camp Ashraf in Iraq. The MEK's global support structure remains in place, with associates and supporters scattered throughout Europe and North America. Operations target Iranian government elements across the globe, including in Europe and Iran. MEK's political arm, the National Council of Resistance of Iran (NCRI), has a global support network with active lobbying and propaganda efforts in major Western capitals. NCRI also has a well-developed media communications strategy.

External Aid

Before Operation Iraqi Freedom began in 2003, the MEK received all of its military assistance and most of its financial support from Saddam Hussein. The fall of Saddam's regime has led MEK increasingly to rely on front organizations to solicit contributions from expatriate Iranian communities.

NATIONAL LIBERATION ARMY (ELN)

a.k.a. Ejercito de Liberacion Nacional

Description

The National Liberation Army (ELN) was designated as a Foreign Terrorist Organization on October 8, 1997. The National Liberation Army (ELN) is a Colombian Marxist-Leninist terrorist group formed in 1964 by urban intellectuals inspired by Fidel Castro and Che Guevara. It is primarily rural-based, although it also has several urban units. Peace talks between the ELN and the Colombian government began in Cuba in December 2005 and continued as recently as August 2007. To date, Bogota and the ELN have yet to agree on a formal framework for peace negotiations and talks have been indefinitely suspended. Suspensions have occurred before with talks subsequently resuming.

Activities

The ELN engages in kidnappings, hijackings, bombings, drug trafficking, and extortion activities. It has minimal conventional military capabilities. The group conducts kidnappings for ransom, often targeting foreign employees of large corporations, especially in the petroleum industry. On February 17, 2008, ELN rebels kidnapped a Radio Delfin journalist near Dibuya. It attacks energy infrastructure and has inflicted major damage on oil and natural gas pipelines and the electrical distribution network, but has lost much of its capacity to carry out these types of attacks in recent years. The ELN derives some revenue from taxation of the illegal narcotics industry, and its involvement may be increasing.

Strength

Approximately 2,000 armed combatants and an unknown number of active supporters.

Location/Area of Operation

Mostly in rural and mountainous areas of northern, northeastern, and southwestern Colombia, as well as Venezuelan border regions.

External Aid

Cuba provides some medical care and political consultation. In spite of this, Cuba appears to encourage the Colombian government and the ELN to reach an agreement.

NEW RED BRIGADES/COMMUNIST COMBATANT PARTY (BR/PCC)

a.k.a. Brigate Rosse/Partito Comunista Combattente

Description

This Marxist-Leninist group is a successor to the Red Brigades, active in the 1970s and 1980s. In addition to ideology, both groups share the same symbol, a five-pointed star inside a circle. The group is opposed to Italy's foreign and labor policies and to NATO.

Activities

In 2003, Italian authorities captured at least seven members of the BR/PCC, dealing the terrorist group a severe blow to its operational effectiveness, and the group continued to suffer setbacks in 2005 and 2006, with its leadership in prison, key suspects convicted and sentenced, and additional arrests made. In June 2005, a Rome court sentenced five BR/PCC members to life in prison for the 2002 assassination of Labor Ministry external adviser Marco Biagi. One month later, three of the five also were found guilty of the assassination of Labor Ministry external adviser Massimo D'Antona in 1999, again incurring a life sentence. An additional nine BR/PCC suspects were sentenced to between four and nine years, and some convicted members provided valuable information to Italian authorities, leading to additional arrests. In December 2005, an Italian judge refused to pardon Adriano Sofri, leader of Continuous Struggle (Lotta Continua), a precursor movement to the Red Brigades, whose life sentence was suspended for health reasons. Italian authorities in early December 2006 arrested Fabio Matteini, suspected of trying to recruit new members in an effort to revive the group. The BR/PCC in recent years has financed its activities in part through armed robberies.

Strength

Fewer than 20.

Location/Area of Operation

Italy.

External Aid

Has obtained weapons from abroad.

PALESTINE LIBERATION FRONT—
ABU ABBAS FACTION (PLF)

a.k.a. PLF-Abu Abbas; Palestine Liberation Front

Description

The Palestinian Liberation Front—Abu Abbas Faction (PLF) was designated as a Foreign Terrorist Organization on October 8, 1997. In the late 1970s the Palestine Liberation Front (PLF) splintered from the Popular Front for the Liberation of Palestine—General Command (PFLP-GC), and later split into pro-PLO, pro-Syrian, and pro-Libyan factions. The pro-PLO faction was led by Muhammad Zaydan (a.k.a. Abu Abbas) and was based in Baghdad prior to Operation Iraqi Freedom.

Activities

Abbas's group was responsible for the 1985 attack on the Italian cruise ship *Achille Lauro* and the murder of U.S. citizen Leon Klinghoffer. In 1993, the PLF officially renounced terrorism when it acknowledged the Oslo accords, although it was suspected of supporting terrorism against Israel by other Palestinian groups into the 1990s. In April 2004, Abu Abbas died of natural causes while in U.S. custody in Iraq. Current leadership and membership of the relatively small PLF appears to be based in Lebanon and the Palestinian territories. The PLF took part in the 2006 Palestinian parliamentarian elections but did not win a seat. In 2008, as part of a prisoner exchange between Israel and Hezbollah, Samir Kantar, a PLF member and purportedly the longest serving Arab prisoner in Israeli custody, was released from an Israeli prison. After going approximately 16 years without claiming responsibility for an attack, PLF claimed responsibility for two attacks against Israeli targets on March 14, 2008, according to media reports. One attack was against an Israeli military bus in Huwarah, West Bank, and the other involved a PLF "brigade" firing at an Israeli settler south of the Hebron Mountain, seriously wounding him. On March 28, 2008, shortly after the attacks, a PLF Central Committee member reaffirmed PLF's commitment to using "all possible means to restore" its previous glory and to adhering to its role in the Palestinian "struggle" and "resistance," through its military.

Strength

Estimates have placed membership between 50 and 500.

Location/Area of Operation

Based in Iraq from 1990 until 2003. The group currently is based in Lebanon and Syria.

External Aid

Unknown.

PALESTINIAN ISLAMIC JIHAD—SHAQAQI FACTION

a.k.a. PIJ; Palestine Islamic Jihad; PIJ—Shaqaqi Faction; PIJ—Shallah Faction; Islamic Jihad of Palestine; Islamic Jihad in Palestine; Abu Ghunaym Squad of the

Hizballah Bayt Al-Maqdis; Al-Quds Squads; Al-Quds Brigades; Saraya Al-Quds; Al-Awdah Brigades

Description

The Palestine Islamic Jihad (PIJ) was designated as a Foreign Terrorist Organization on October 8, 1997. Formed by militant Palestinians in Gaza during the 1970s, PIJ is committed to both the creation of an Islamic state in all of historic Palestine, including present day Israel, and the destruction of Israel through attacks against Israeli military and civilian targets.

Activities

PIJ terrorists have conducted numerous attacks, including large-scale suicide bombings against Israeli civilian and military targets. PIJ continues to plan and direct attacks against Israelis both inside Israel and in the Palestinian territories. Although U.S. citizens have died in PIJ mounted attacks, the group has not directly targeted U.S. interests. PIJ attacks in 2008 have primarily been rocket attacks aimed at southern Israeli cities. In April 2008 alone, PIJ fired 216 rockets and mortar shells at various Israeli towns. In March 2008, two IDF soldiers died as a result of an explosive device detonated near their jeep while patrolling the security fence in the central Gaza Strip, near Kissufim. Hamas and PIJ claimed responsibility for the attack.

Strength

Unknown.

Location/Area of Operation

Primarily Israel, the West Bank, and Gaza. The group's senior leadership resides in Syria. Other leadership elements reside in Lebanon and official representatives are scattered throughout the Middle East.

External Aid

Receives financial assistance and training primarily from Iran. Syria provides the group with safe haven.

PEOPLE AGAINST GANGSTERISM AND DRUGS (PAGAD)

a.k.a. Muslims against Global Oppression; Muslims against Illegitimate Leaders

Description

People against Gangsterism and Drugs (PAGAD) and its ally Qibla (an Islamic fundamentalist group that favors political Islam and takes an anti-U.S. and anti-Israel stance), view the South African government as a threat to Islamic values. The two groups work to promote a greater political voice for South African Muslims. PAGAD has used front names such as Muslims against Global Oppression and Muslims against Illegitimate Leaders when launching anti-Western protests and campaigns.

Activities

PAGAD formed in November 1995 as a vigilante group in reaction to crime in some neighborhoods of Cape Town. In September 1996, a change in the group's leadership resulted in a change in the group's goal, and it began to support violent jihad to establish an Islamic state. Between 1996 and 2000, PAGAD conducted a total of 189 bomb attacks, including nine bombings in the western Cape that caused serious injuries. PAGAD's targets included South African authorities, moderate Muslims, synagogues, gay nightclubs, tourist attractions, and Western-associated restaurants. PAGAD is believed to have masterminded the bombing on August 1998 of the Cape Town Planet Hollywood and the 2000 attack on a New York Bagel restaurant in Cape Town. Since 2001, PAGAD's violent activities have been severely curtailed by law enforcement and prosecutorial efforts against leading members of the organization. Qibla leadership has organized demonstrations against visiting U.S. dignitaries and other protests, but the extent of PAGAD's involvement is uncertain.

Strength

Early estimates were several hundred members. Current operational strength is unknown, but probably vastly diminished.

Location/Area of Operation

Operates mainly in the Cape Town area.

External Aid

May have ties to international Islamic extremists.

POPULAR FRONT FOR THE
LIBERATION OF PALESTINE (PFLP)

a.k.a. Halhul Gang; Halhul Squad; Palestinian Popular Resistance Forces; PPRF; Red Eagle Gang; Red Eagle Group; Red Eagles; Martyr Abu-Ali Mustafa Battalion

Description

The Popular Front for the Liberation of Palestine (PFLP) was designated as a Foreign Terrorist Organization on October 8, 1997. The PFLP, a Marxist-Leninist group founded by George Habash, broke away from the Arab Nationalist Movement in 1967. The PFLP views the Palestinian struggle not as religious, but as a broader revolution against Western imperialism. The group earned a reputation for spectacular international attacks in the 1960s and 1970s, including airline hijackings that killed at least 20 U.S. citizens. A leading faction within the PLO, the PFLP has long accepted the concept of a two-state solution but has opposed specific provisions of various peace initiatives.

Activities

The PFLP stepped up its operational activity during the al-Aqsa intifada. This was highlighted by at least two suicide bombings since 2003, multiple joint operations with other Palestinian terrorist groups, and the assassination of Israeli Tourism Minister Rehavam Ze'evi in 2001 to avenge Israel's killing of the PFLP Secretary General earlier that year. In March 2006, the PFLP's current Secretary General, Ahmed Sa'adat, then imprisoned by the Palestinian Authority for his involvement in the Ze'evi assassination, was seized from the Jericho prison compound by Israeli forces and sentenced to 30 years in prison by an Israeli military court in December 2008. The PFLP was involved in several rocket attacks against Israel in 2008.

Strength

Unknown.

Location/Area of Operation

Syria, Lebanon, Israel, the West Bank, and Gaza.

External Aid

Receives safe haven and some logistical assistance from Syria.

POPULAR FRONT FOR THE LIBERATION
OF PALESTINE—GENERAL COMMAND (PFLP-GC)

Description

The Popular Front for the Liberation of Palestine—General Command (PFLP-GC) was designated as a Foreign Terrorist Organization on October 8, 1997.

The PFLP-GC split from the PFLP in 1968, claiming it wanted to focus more on resistance and less on politics. Originally, the group was violently opposed to the Arafat-led PLO. Ahmad Jibril, a former captain in the Syrian Army whose son, Jihad, was killed by a car bomb in May 2002, has led the PFLP-GC since its founding. The PFLP-GC is closely tied to both Syria and Iran.

Activities

The PFLP-GC carried out dozens of attacks in Europe and the Middle East during the 1970s and 1980s. The organization was known for cross-border terrorist attacks into Israel using unusual means, such as hot-air balloons and motorized hang gliders. The group's primary focus is now on supporting Hezbollah's attacks against Israel, training members of other Palestinian terrorist groups, and smuggling weapons. The PFLP-GC maintains an armed presence in several Palestinian refugee camps and at its own military bases in Lebanon and along the Lebanon-Syria border. The PFLP-GC has been implicated by Lebanese security officials in several rocket attacks against Israel in 2008. In May 2008, the PFLP-GC claimed responsibility for a rocket attack on a shopping center in Ashkelon, wounding at least ten people. A health clinic took the brunt of the attack.

Strength

Several hundred to several thousand.

Location/Area of Operation

Headquartered in Damascus with bases in southern Lebanon and a presence in the Palestinian refugee camps in Lebanon and Syria.

External Aid

Receives logistical and military support from Syria and financial support from Iran.

AL-QAEDA

Translation "The Base"; Qa'idat al-Jihad (The Base for Jihad); formerly Qa'idat Ansar Allah (The Base of the Supporters of God)

a.k.a. the Islamic Army; Islamic Salvation Foundation; the Base; the Group for the Preservation of the Holy Sites; the Islamic Army for the Liberation of the Holy Places; the World Islamic Front for Jihad against Jews and Crusaders; the

Osama bin Laden Network; the Osama bin Laden Organization; al-Jihad; the Jihad Group; Egyptian al-Jihad; Egyptian Islamic Jihad; New Jihad

Description

Al-Qaeda was established by Osama bin Laden in 1988 with Arabs who fought in Afghanistan against the Soviet Union. The group helped finance, recruit, transport, and train Sunni Islamic extremists for the Afghan resistance. Al-Qaeda's near-term goal is uniting Muslims to fight the United States and its allies, overthrowing regimes it deems "non-Islamic," and expelling Westerners and non-Muslims from Muslim countries. Its ultimate goal is the establishment of a pan-Islamic caliphate throughout the world. Al-Qaeda leaders issued a statement in February 1998 under the banner of "The World Islamic Front for Jihad against the Jews and Crusaders" saying it was the duty of all Muslims to kill U.S. citizens, civilian and military, and their allies everywhere. Al-Qaeda merged with al-Jihad (Egyptian Islamic Jihad) in June 2001, renaming itself Qa'idat al-Jihad.

The Rise of bin Laden

On March 24, 2004, George Tenet, Director of Central Intelligence, said in his *Statement to the National Commission on Terrorist Attacks upon the United States* (www.au.af.mil/au/awc/awcgate/cia/tenet_testimony_03242004 .htm#early):

Bin Laden gained prominence during the Soviet-Afghan war for his role in financing the recruitment, transportation, and training of ethnic Arabs who fought alongside the Afghan mujahedin against the Soviets during the 1980s. At age 22, bin Laden dropped out of school in Saudi Arabia and joined the Afghan resistance almost immediately following the Soviet invasion in December 1979. . . . The Afghan experience provided bin Laden with an opportunity to make and strengthen contacts with a wide variety of Islamic extremists of various nationalities. Many of the men who became key members of al-Qaeda had met him in Afghanistan.

It was at this time in the mid- to late-1980s that bin Laden began perverting the teachings of Islam and the Prophet Mohammed for his own violent purposes. In addition, he began to exploit underlying social, political, and economic discontent and widespread resentment of the West in many parts of the Muslim world.

- In a 1988 press interview, he claimed that when a mortar shell that landed a few feet away from him did not explode, he felt it a sign from God to battle all opponents of Islam.
- Urged on by fervent Islamic radicals, he began using his personal fortune to shelter and employ hundreds of militant, stateless, "Afghan Arabs" and to train them for jihad, or holy war, around the world.

Although bin Laden returned to Saudi Arabia to work in his family's construction business after the Soviets left Afghanistan in early 1989, he continued to support militant Islamic causes and radicals who by then had begun redirecting their efforts against secular and moderate Islamic governments in the region. He began publicly criticizing the Saudi Government and condemned the Gulf War and the presence of U.S. and other Western forces in the Arabian Peninsula.

- Saudi officials seized bin Laden's passport in 1989 in an apparent try to prevent him from solidifying contacts with like-minded extremists he had befriended during the Afghan-Soviet war.
- The Saudis subsequently in 1994 stripped bin Laden of his citizenship while he was in Khartoum.

Bin Laden came to the attention of the CIA as an emerging terrorist threat during his stay in Sudan from 1991 to 1996.

- We saw him as a prominent financial backer of Islamic terrorist movements who was funding the paramilitary training of Arab religious militants operating in, or supporting fellow Muslims in, Bosnia, Egypt, Kashmir, Jordan, Tunisia, Algeria, and Yemen.
- While in Sudan, bin Laden and al-Qaeda financed Islamic extremists who opposed secular and moderate Islamic governments and who despised the West.
- We characterized him in January 1996 as among the most active financial sponsors of Islamic extremist and terrorist activity in the world.

During his five-year residence in Sudan, bin Laden combined business with jihad under the umbrella of the al-Qaeda organization. In association with powerful members of the ruling Sudanese National Islamic Front, he embarked on several business ventures. His workforce in Sudan included militant Afghan war veterans who were wanted by the authorities in their own countries because of their subversive or terrorist activities.

While in Sudan, bin Laden apparently paid particular attention to the turmoil in neighboring Somalia. We believe his perception of events in Somalia played a significant role in molding his views of the United States. He publicly said the U.S. withdrawal from Somalia demonstrated that Americans were soft and the United States a paper tiger that could be more easily defeated than the Soviets had been in Afghanistan.

CIA's assessment of bin Laden during the early 1990s continued to be that he was a major terrorist financier.

- We did not yet see him as the center of a significant organization or network focused on carrying out terrorist attacks on the United States.

- Moreover, he was only one of a number of potential terrorist threats. As such, the bin Laden and al-Qaeda targets competed for intelligence resources with other dangerous targets such as Hezbollah, then considered more threatening to U.S. interests.

Nevertheless, as bin Laden's prominence grew during the latter part of his residence in Sudan, our awareness of the threat he represented also grew significantly. In early 1996 we singled him out as a major target for our counterterrorism operations.

In fact, what began in early 1996 as an effort designed to penetrate and destroy bin Laden's financial network soon provided intelligence revealing a broader and more pernicious terrorist capability that reached well beyond financial activity.

By the time bin Laden left Sudan in 1996 and relocated himself and his terror network to Afghanistan, the Intelligence Community had gained a substantial appreciation of the significance of his threat and was taking strong action to try to stop him.

- For example, in January 1996 CIA focused more of its resources on him by creating a dedicated component in the Counterterrorist Center—the Bin Laden Issue Station—staffed by CIA, NSA, FBI, and other officers. The group's mission was to track him, collect intelligence on him, run operations against him, disrupt his finances, and warn policymakers about his activities and intentions.
- We monitored his whereabouts and increased our knowledge about him and his organization by using every available intelligence means.

It is important to remember that during this mid-1990s period, bin Laden was only one of several areas of terrorism concern that we were following. The others included Lebanon's Hezbollah, the Egyptian Islamic Jihad, the Sendoro Luminoso in Peru, Abu Sayyaf in the Philippines, and Sri Lanka's Tamil Tigers, just to name a few.

The Taliban Sanctuary Years: Evolving into a Strategic Threat

Tenet's 2004 *Statement to the National Commission on Terrorist Attacks upon the United States* continues:

If any doubts remain about the emerging threat bin Laden and al-Qaeda represented to the United States, they were gradually dispelled by a series of declarations he issued from his refuge in Afghanistan during the 1996–1998 timeframe.

- In an undated interview in Afghanistan published in July 1996 in the London daily *The Independent*, bin Laden declared that the killing of Americans in the

PROFILE: OSAMA BIN LADEN

The following profile appears on the website of the Foreign Policy Association (see www.fpa.org/newsletter_info2478/newsletter_info_sub_list.htm?section=Pro file%3AOsama%20bin%20Laden).

Osama bin Laden (also Usama, Ussamah) was born in Saudi Arabia in 1957. Osama's father, Muhammad bin Laden, is said to have been an illiterate bricklayer from southern Yemen who walked to Saudi Arabia as a young man in 1925. Having caught the attention of the founder of the Saudi kingdom while working on a palace construction project, Bin Laden senior established a modest bricklaying business which, using his royal connections, he later turned into a $5 billion construction empire, the largest and the richest in Saudi Arabia. The royal family awarded bin Laden's company major contracts for construction on the royal palace and, later, ambitious renovations of the holy cities of Mecca and Medina. Muhammad bin Laden died in a plane crash in 1967.

It is estimated that the value of Osama bin Laden's share of the family construction firm may be as great as $300 million. These assets have been frozen since 1994.

The young Osama attended a private school in Jidda where he learned English. Later, he studied civil engineering in nearby King Abdul Aziz University. He is never known to have traveled to the United States. Previous to the September 11 attacks, four of his brothers and at least 17 nieces and nephews were in the United States. The family has strong links with Boston and Osama's brother, Abdullah, studied at Harvard. In the 1990s, the family company endowed $1 million fellowships in both the design and law schools there.

When the Soviet Union invaded Afghanistan in 1979, Osama bin Laden immediately joined the mujahedin. By the late 1980s, he was a full-time holy warrior. A strict Sunni Muslim, he founded al-Qaeda, using his inherited millions, in order to recruit other young Muslim militants for jihad. In 1991, bin Laden moved the headquarters of his al-Qaeda network to Sudan having been expelled from Saudi Arabia as a result of his anti-government activities. Expelled from Sudan under American pressure, he returned to Afghanistan in 1996. Bin Laden's Saudi citizenship was revoked in 1994. Shortly afterwards his family convened an emergency meeting at which it was agreed to officially sever relations with him. . . .

Muhammad, Osama's father, had eleven wives and fifty-four children. Osama, the seventeenth of twenty-four sons, is said to have four wives and at least fifteen children. At least ten of his children reside with him in Afghanistan including a daughter who is married to Taliban head Mullah Omar; his 20-year-old son, Mohammad, who was married in February [2005] to the daughter of Mohammad Atef, al-Qaeda's military commander; and a 10-year-old son, Ali, who has appeared in propaganda footage. However, five of his children, including his eldest son, Abdullah (22), live in Saudi with their mother, who left Osama in the mid-1990s.

Bin Laden is described as 6-foot-6, thin, with brown hair and eyes, and an olive complexion. He is known to have a number of aliases and code names including the Emir, the Director, and Hajj. Bin Laden is suspected of involvement in the 1993 World Trade Center bombing, the bombing of the U.S. embassies in Nairobi, Kenya, and Dar es Salaam, Tanzania, in August 1998, the 2000 attack on the USS *Cole* in Yemen, and the events of September 11 in New York and Washington DC. He has a $25 million bounty on his head.

Khobar Towers bombing in Saudi Arabia in June 1996 marked the beginning of the war between Muslims and the United States.

- One month later, in August 1996, bin Laden, in collaboration with radical Muslim clerics associated with his group, issued a religious edict or fatwa in which he proclaimed a "Declaration of War," authorizing attacks against Western military targets on the Arabian Peninsula.
- In February 1998, six months prior to the August U.S. Embassy bombings in East Africa, bin Laden issued another fatwa under the banner of the "World Islamic Front for Jihad against Jews and Crusaders." This fatwa stated ominously that all Muslims have a religious duty "to kill Americans and their allies, both civilian and military" worldwide.
- During a subsequent media interview, bin Laden explained that all U.S. citizens were legitimate targets because they pay taxes to the U.S. Government.

By the time of the 1998 East Africa bombings, al-Qaeda had established its modus operandi, emphasizing careful planning and exhaustive field preparations toward a goal of inflicting high casualties. For example, bin Laden was asked in a November 1996 interview why his organization had not yet conducted attacks in response to its August fatwa. He replied, "If we wanted to carry out small operations, it would have been easy to do so after the statements, but the nature of the battle requires qualitative operations that affect the adversary, which obviously requires good preparation."

By early 1998, CIA knew that the United States was dealing with a sophisticated terrorist organization bent on causing large numbers of American casualties. The East Africa bombings in August 1998 and the attack on the USS *Cole* in October 2000 succeeded because of al-Qaeda's meticulous preparation and effective security practices.

- Al-Qaeda targeting studies and training materials captured around the time of the East Africa and USS *Cole* attacks revealed that much of the terrorists' advance planning involved careful, patient, and meticulous preparation.
- This included extensive surveillance and casing studies that detailed the vulnerabilities of potential targets. The terrorists' casing study of the U.S. Embassy in Nairobi, for example, was prepared in 1993, five years before the attack. It included information about the building's physical structure, security posture, and business hours, as well as the layout of the reception area inside the Embassy.
- The analysts also pointed out that the intelligence data indicated the terrorists were very much conscious of operational security.

We were also becoming increasingly concerned—and therefore we warned about—al-Qaeda's interest in acquiring chemical and biological weapons and nuclear materials.

- In a December 1998 interview, bin Laden called the acquisition of these weapons a religious duty.
- As early as July 1993, in testimony to the House Foreign Affairs Committee, DCI Woolsey warned of the Intelligence Community's heightened sensitivity to the prospect that a terrorist incident could involve weapons of mass destruction. In February 1996, in testimony to the Senate Select Committee on Intelligence, DCI Deutsch expressed his concern about the growing lethality, sophistication, and wide-ranging nature of the terrorist threat. He observed that terrorists would push this trend to its most awful extreme by using weapons of mass destruction. I made similar warnings to these committees as early as 1998, when I pointed to bin Laden's attempts to purchase or manufacture biological and chemical weapons for an attack against U.S. facilities.

Afghanistan Key to Terrorists' Development

Tenet's 2004 *Statement to the National Commission on Terrorist Attacks upon the United States* further states:

None of bin Laden's and al-Qaeda's extensive terrorist plotting, planning, recruiting, and training in the late 1990s would have been possible without the Taliban sanctuary in Afghanistan.

- The Taliban aided bin Laden by assigning him security guards, establishing communications facilities for him and al-Qaeda, spreading disinformation on his behalf, and permitting him to build and maintain terrorist camps. The Taliban refused to cooperate with efforts by the international community to extradite bin Laden after the United States indicted him in 1998 on 319 criminal counts, including conspiracy to murder U.S. citizens.
- In return, bin Laden invested money in Taliban projects and provided hundreds of well-trained fighters to help the Taliban consolidate and expand its control of the country. We often talk of two trends in terrorism: state supported and people working on their own. In bin Laden's case with the Taliban, what we had was something completely new—a terrorist sponsoring a state.

Afghanistan had served as a place of refuge for international terrorists since the 1980s. Since the Soviet invasion and its aftermath, Afghanistan had become a country with a vast infrastructure of camps and facilities for the refuge, training, indoctrination, arming, and financing of tens of thousands of Islamic extremists from all over the world.

- Afghanistan provided bin Laden an isolated and relatively safe operating environment to oversee his organization's worldwide terrorist activities.
- Militants who received training in Afghanistan were sent to fight in Kashmir, Chechnya, or Bosnia. When they returned to their homes to resume their

normal lives or migrate to other countries, they constituted a ready supply of manpower for terrorist operations.

The al-Qaeda/Taliban training camps formed the foundation of a worldwide network by sponsoring and encouraging Islamic extremists from diverse locations to forge longstanding ideological, logistical, and personal ties.

- Extremists in the larger camps received basic training in the use of small arms and guerrilla tactics. In the smaller camps, militants received advanced and specialized training in subjects such as explosives, poisons, and assassination techniques.
- Clandestine and counterintelligence tradecraft courses included basic instruction on how to establish secure, cell-based, clandestine organizations to support insurgencies or terrorist operations.
- Bin Laden emphasized indoctrination in extremist religious ideas. He included the constant repetition that the United States is evil and that the current regimes of Arab countries are not true believers in Islam and should be overthrown as a religious duty.
- Some of the Afghan camps—such as the Derunta camp—also provided the militants instruction in the production and use of toxic chemicals and biological toxins.

In summary, what bin Laden created in Afghanistan was a sophisticated adversary. To be sure, as CIA improved its understanding of the threat, it refocused and intensified its efforts to track, disrupt, and bring the terrorists to justice. We were handicapped, however, by the fact that we had no presence in or access to Afghanistan on a regular basis.

In February 1999, the CIA reported:

Americans increasingly are the favored targets. There is not the slightest doubt that bin Laden, his worldwide allies, and his sympathizers are planning further attacks against us. Despite progress against his networks, bin Laden's organization has contacts virtually worldwide, including in the United States. He has stated unequivocally that all Americans are targets. We have noted recent activity similar to what occurred prior to the African embassy bombings. We are concerned that one or more of bin Laden's attacks could occur at any time. Bin Laden's overarching aim is to get the United States out of the Persian Gulf, but he will strike wherever in the world he thinks we are vulnerable.

We all know how prophetic those words turned out to be.

Today, a lone terrorist is capable of wreaking horrendous damage by releasing a vial of anthrax spores into the air-conditioning system of a heavily populated office building, or exploding a biological bomb during the rush aboard a crowded subway train underground. The damage that could be caused by a small cell of highly committed, well funded, well equipped terrorists is even more terrifying. That is the threat we face with terrorism in the twenty-first century.

Activities

Even as al-Qaeda's top leaders continue to plot and direct terrorist attacks worldwide, terrorists affiliated with, but not necessarily controlled by al-Qaeda, have increasingly carried out high-profile attacks. Al-Qaeda, its affiliates, and those inspired by the group were involved in anti-U.S. and anti-Coalition attacks in Africa, Europe, the Middle East, Afghanistan, Pakistan, and Iraq, including suicide bombings and vehicle-borne improvised explosive devices. Although bin Laden remains the group's ideological figurehead, Zawahiri has emerged as al-Qaeda's strategic and operational planner.

Al-Qaeda is assessed to be the top terrorist threat to the United States and is developing stronger operational relationships with affiliates in the Middle East, North Africa, and Europe. Al-Qaeda remains committed to attacking the United States and focuses its planning on targets that would produce mass casualties, dramatic visual destruction, and economic dislocation.

In January 2008, militants attacked a convoy of Belgian tourists in Hadhramout, Yemen, killing two Belgian women and two Yemeni drivers. Al-Qaeda claimed responsibility for the attack. In June 2008, a suicide car bomber attacked the Danish Embassy in Islamabad, killing six people, including a Danish citizen. The blast was so powerful that it damaged windowpanes of buildings in a four-kilometer radius and left a three-foot crater at impact. In a press interview, an al-Qaeda commander in Afghanistan claimed responsibility for the attack, on behalf of al-Qaeda.

The Government of Pakistan accused al-Qaeda, along with the Taliban, of being responsible for the October 2007 suicide bombing attempt against former Pakistani Prime Minister Benazir Bhutto that killed at least 144 people in Karachi, Pakistan. On December 27, 2007, the Government of Pakistan stated that Baitullah Mahsud, a leading Pakistani Taliban commander with close ties to al-Qaeda, was responsible for the assassination of Benazir Bhutto.

Bin Laden's deputy Ayman al-Zawahiri claimed responsibility on behalf of al-Qaeda for multiple attacks on July 7, 2005, against the London public transportation system. The extent of senior leadership involvement in planning the July 2005 attacks was unclear. Some suspects in the attacks included homegrown UK-based extremists who were "inspired" by al-Qaeda.

In 2003 and 2004, Saudi-based al-Qaeda operatives and associated extremists launched more than a dozen attacks, killing at least 90 people, including 14 Americans in Saudi Arabia. Al-Qaeda may have been connected to the suicide bombers and planners of the November 2003 attacks in Istanbul that targeted two synagogues, the British Consulate, and the HSBC Bank, and resulted in the deaths of more than 60 people. Former Pakistani President Musharraf blamed al-Qaeda for two attempts on his life in December 2003.

In October 2002, al-Qaeda directed a suicide attack on the French tanker MV *Limburg* off the coast of Yemen that killed one and injured four. The group also carried out the November 2002 suicide bombing of a hotel in Mombasa, Kenya, that killed 15. Al-Qaeda probably provided financing for the October 2002 Bali bombings by Jemaah Islamiya that killed more than 200.

On September 11, 2001, 19 al-Qaeda members hijacked and crashed four U.S. commercial jets—two into the World Trade Center in New York City, one into the Pentagon near Washington, D.C., and a fourth into a field in Shanksville, Pennsylvania—leaving nearly 3,000 individuals dead or missing. In October 2000, al-Qaeda conducted a suicide attack on the USS *Cole* in the port of Aden, Yemen, with an explosive-laden boat, killing 17 U.S. Navy sailors and injuring 39. Al-Qaeda also carried out the August 1998 bombings of the U.S. embassies in Nairobi and Dar es Salaam, killing at least 301 individuals and injuring more than 5,000 others. Al-Qaeda and its supporters claim to have shot down U.S. helicopters and killed U.S. servicemen in Somalia in 1993, and to have conducted three bombings that targeted U.S. troops in Aden in December 1992.

Strength

Al-Qaeda's organizational strength is difficult to determine in the aftermath of extensive counterterrorist efforts since 9/11. The arrests and deaths of mid-level and senior al-Qaeda operatives have disrupted some communication, financial, and facilitation nodes and disrupted some terrorist plots. Additionally, supporters and associates worldwide who are "inspired" by the group's ideology may be operating without direction from al-Qaeda central leadership; it is impossible to estimate their numbers. Al-Qaeda serves as a focal point of "inspiration" for a worldwide network that is comprised of many Sunni Islamic extremist groups, including some members of the Gama'at al-Islamiyya, the Islamic Movement of Uzbekistan, the Islamic Jihad Group, Lashkar i Jhangvi, Harakat ul-Mujahadin, Ansar al-Sunnah, the Taliban, and Jemaah Islamiya.

Location/Area of Operation

Al-Qaeda worldwide networks are augmented by ties to local Sunni extremists. The group was based in Afghanistan until Coalition Forces removed the Taliban from power in late 2001. While the largest concentration of senior al-Qaeda members now resides in Pakistan's Federally Administered Tribal Areas (FATA), the network incorporates members of al-Qaeda in Iraq (AQI) and other associates throughout the Middle East, Southeast Asia, Africa, Europe, and Central Asia.

External Aid

Al-Qaeda primarily depends on donations from like-minded supporters and individuals who believe that their money is supporting a humanitarian or other cause. Some funds are diverted from Islamic charitable organizations. In addition, parts of the organization raise funds through criminal activities; for example, AQI raises funds through hostage-taking for ransom, and members in Europe have engaged in credit card fraud. U.S. and international efforts to block al-Qaeda funding have hampered the group's ability to raise money.

AL-QAEDA IN IRAQ (TANZIM QA'IDAT AL-JIHAD FI BILAD AL-RAFIDAYN)

a.k.a. al-Qaeda Group of Jihad in Iraq; al-Qaeda Group of Jihad in the Land of the Two Rivers; al-Qaeda in Mesopotamia; al-Qaeda in the Land of the Two Rivers; al-Qaeda of Jihad in Iraq; al-Qaeda of Jihad Organization in the Land of the Two Rivers; al-Qaeda of the Jihad in the Land of the Two Rivers; al-Tawhid; Jam'at al-Tawhid Wa'al-Jihad; Tanzeem Qa'idat al Jihad/Bilad al Raafidaini; Tanzim Qa'idat al-Jihad fi Bilad al-Rafidayn; the Monotheism and Jihad Group; the Organization Base of Jihad/Country of the Two Rivers; the Organization Base of Jihad/Mesopotamia; the Organization of al-Jihad's Base in Iraq; the Organization of al-Jihad's Base in the Land of the Two Rivers; the Organization of al-Jihad's Base of Operations in Iraq; the Organization of al-Jihad's Base of Operations in the Land of the Two Rivers; the Organization of Jihad's Base in the Country of the Two Rivers; al-Zarqawi Network

Description

In January 2006, in an attempt to unify Sunni extremists in Iraq, al-Qaeda in Iraq (AQI) created the Mujahedin Shura Council (MSC), an umbrella organization meant to encompass the various Sunni terrorist groups in Iraq. AQI claimed its attacks under the MSC until mid-October, when Abu Mus'ab al-Zarqawi's successor, Abu Ayyub al-Masri, took the first step toward al-Qaeda's goal of establishing a caliphate in the region by declaring the "Islamic State of Iraq," under which AQI now claims its attacks. Although Iraqis compose at least 90 percent of the group's membership, it is probable that the majority of the senior leadership of AQI is foreign-born. In an attempt to give AQI a more Iraqi persona, the Islamic State of Iraq (ISI), led by AQI, was created and headed by Abu Umar al-Baghdadi.

Abu Ayyub al-Masri, Zarqawi's successor, issued a statement pledging to continue what Zarqawi began, and AQI has continued its strategy of targeting Coalition Forces, Iraqi government groups, anti-AQI Sunni tribal and security elements, and Shia civilians to provoke violence and undermine perceptions that the Iraqi central government can effectively govern.

AQI has claimed joint attacks with both Ansar al-Islam and the Islamic Army in Iraq; however, ideological differences have prevented these groups from merging. More recently, Islamic Army in Iraq and the 1920 Revolution Brigades cooperated with Coalition Forces in targeting AQI.

Activities

The threat from AQI continued to diminish in 2008. AQI, although still dangerous, has experienced the defection of members, lost key mobilization areas, suffered disruption of support infrastructure and funding, and been forced to change targeting priorities. Indeed, the pace of suicide bombing countryside, which we consider one indicator of AQI's operational capability, fell significantly during last year. However, in April 2009, a radical Islamist group believed to be a front for AQI claimed responsibility for a suicide bombing that killed five U.S. soldiers in the northern city of Mosul. It was the single deadliest attack on Americans in more than a year.

High-profile attacks in 2007 included the suicide car-bombing attack of a mosque in Al Habbaniyah in February, the multiple suicide bombing attack of Shia pilgrims in Al Hillah in March, several chlorine gas canister bombings from January through June, an orchestrated bridge bombing campaign throughout Iraq aimed at isolating Baghdad Shia population concentrations and disrupting ground transportation from January through October, the suicide truck bombing of a market in Tall 'Afar in March, the suicide truck bombings of a market and Patriotic Union of Kurdistan (PUK) party offices in Amurli and Kirkuk in July, and the single deadliest attack of the Iraq war, the multiple suicide truck bombings of two Yazidi villages near Sinjar in August.

In August 2003, Zarqawi's group carried out major terrorist attacks in Iraq when it bombed the Jordanian Embassy in Baghdad, which was followed twelve days later by a suicide vehicle–borne improvised explosive device (VBIED) attack against the UN Headquarters in Baghdad that killed 23, including the Secretary-General's Special Representative for Iraq, Sergio Vieira de Mello. That same month the group conducted a VBIED attack against Shia worshippers outside the Imam Ali Mosque in al Najaf, killing 85, including the leader of the Supreme Council for the Islamic Revolution in Iraq. The group kept up its attack pace throughout 2003, striking numerous Iraqi, Coalition, and relief agency targets such as the Red Cross. Zarqawi's group conducted VBIED attacks against U.S. military personnel and Iraqi infrastructure throughout 2004, including suicide attacks inside the Green Zone perimeter in Baghdad. The group successfully penetrated the Green Zone in the October 2004 bombing of a popular café and market. It also claimed responsibility for the videotaped executions by beheading of Americans Nicholas Berg (May 11, 2004), Jack Armstrong (September 22, 2004), and Jack Hensley (September 21, 2004). AQI was likely involved in other hostage incidents as well. In 2005, AQI largely focused on conducting multiple high-profile, coordinated suicide attacks. AQI claimed numerous attacks primarily aimed against civilians, the Iraqi government, and security forces, such as the coordinated attacks against polling sites during the January elections and the coordinated VBIED attacks outside the Sheraton and

Palestine hotels in Baghdad on October 24. The group also continued assassinations against Shia leaders and members of the Shia militia groups Jaysh al-Mahdi and Badr Corps.

AQI increased its external operations in 2005 by claiming credit for three attacks: suicide bomber attacks against three hotels in Amman on November 9; a rocket attack against U.S. Navy ships in the port of Aqaba in August, which resulted in limited damage in Jordan and in Eilat, Israel; and the firing of several rockets into Israel from Lebanon in December. In August 2005, an AQI operative was arrested in Turkey while planning an operation targeting Israeli cruise ships. Prior to 2005, Zarqawi planned and conducted limited attacks in Jordan, including the assassination of USAID official Laurence Foley in 2002. In October 2006, AQI declared the ISI would become a platform from which AQI would launch terrorist attacks throughout the world. Following the announcement, AQI members marched through cities they considered to be part of their new state as a show of force. AQI attack claims, which the group released under the auspices of the MSC and now the ISI, increased in 2006 but decreased significantly starting in late 2007.

AQI was implicated in the February 2006 Samarra' al-Askari Mosque bombing that precipitated the escalation in sectarian violence.

AQI senior leaders in Iraq may have had advance knowledge of terrorist attacks in Iraq that incorporated chlorine into VBIEDs. However, the use of chlorine in suicide attacks probably represents an opportunistic evolution of conventional VBIED attacks.

Strength

Membership is estimated at 2,000 to 4,000, making it the largest, most potent Sunni extremist group in Iraq. AQI perpetrates the majority of suicide and mass casualty bombings in Iraq, using both foreign and Iraqi operatives. The selection of civilian targets, particularly in large urban areas, generates widespread media coverage, but garners public backlash against the group.

Location/Area of Operation

AQI's operations are predominately Iraq-based, but it has perpetrated attacks in Jordan. The group maintains an extensive logistical network throughout the Middle East, North Africa, Iran, South Asia, and Europe. AQI currently conducts the majority of its operations in Iraq in Ninawa, Diyala, Salah ad Din, and Baghdad provinces and to a lesser extent Al Anbar.

External Aid

AQI probably receives funds from donors in the Middle East and Europe, local sympathizers in Iraq, from a variety of businesses and criminal activities, and other international extremists throughout the world. In many cases, donors to AQI are probably motivated to support terrorism rather than an attachment to any specific terrorist group.

AL-QAEDA IN THE ISLAMIC MAGHREB

a.k.a. AQIM, formerly known as Group for Call and Combat; GSPC; le Groupe Salafiste pour la Predication et le Combat; Salafist Group for Preaching and Combat

Description

Al-Qaeda in the Islamic Maghreb (AQIM) was designated as a Foreign Terrorist Organization on March 27, 2002. The Salafist Group for Preaching and Combat (GSPC) officially merged with al-Qaeda in September 2006 and subsequently changed its name to al-Qaeda in the Islamic Maghreb. The GSPC formed in 1998 when its members left the Armed Islamic Group (AIG) over disagreements about leadership, tactics, and indiscriminant targeting of Algerian civilians. In contrast to the AIG, it has pledged to avoid attacks on civilians inside Algeria. Nevertheless, civilians have died in numerous GSPC/AQIM attacks. The GSPC retained the AIG's mission of overthrowing the Algerian government and installing an Islamic regime. AQIM is the most effective and largest armed group inside Algeria. AQIM and al-Qaeda have used the merger extensively in their propaganda.

Activities

AQIM employed sophisticated suicide tactics for the first time on April 11, 2007. The near-simultaneous bombings of multiple targets inside Algiers, including the office of Algeria's prime minister, claimed more than thirty lives. Shortly thereafter, AQIM vowed to continue to use suicide tactics, and proceeded to carry out five additional suicide attacks in Algeria in 2007. On December 11, AQIM carried out two near-simultaneous suicide vehicle–borne improvised explosive device (VBIED) attacks that struck two UN offices and the headquarters of Algeria's Constitutional Council, killing 41 people (including 17 UN employees) and wounding at least 170 others. AQIM had previously attacked vehicles belonging to foreign corporations several times during the year, beginning in December 2006 with an attack in Algiers on a bus belonging to a U.S.-Algeria joint venture and carrying several expatriate workers. There was a rise in terrorist attacks claimed by AQIM during the month of August 2008, with at least 79 people killed in various incidents across northeastern Algeria.

Outside Algeria, in December 2007, multiple AQIM-linked attacks in Mauritania were the first terrorist incidents since 2005, when the GSPC had claimed responsibility for an attack on a remote Mauritanian military outpost that killed 15; this appeared to indicate an AQIM shift towards a more regional terrorist campaign. Also during 2007, police in France, Italy, and Spain arrested several individuals from Algeria and other Maghreb countries suspected of providing support to AQIM. French officials announced that AQIM had issued an Internet call-to-action against France, declaring France "public enemy number one."

AQIM maintains a safe haven in northern Mali. This safe haven functions as a training area and logistics-facilitation hub for AQIM operations in Algeria and Mauritania. AQIM hostages are generally held in this area.

Strength

AQIM has an estimated several hundred fighters operating in Algeria with a smaller number in the Sahel. Abdelmalek Droukdel, a.k.a. Abu Mus'ab Abd al-Wadoud, is the leader of the group.

Location/Area of Operation

Algeria and the Sahel, with affiliates and logistics/fundraisers in western Europe.

External Aid

Algerian expatriates and AQIM members abroad, many residing in western Europe, provide financial and logistical support. AQIM members also engage in hostage-taking for ransom and criminal activity to finance their operations.

RAJAH SOLAIMAN MOVEMENT (RSM)

Description

The RSM is a Philippines-based Islamic extremist group comprising Christian converts to Islam, many of whom had embraced extremist Islamic ideology while working in the Middle East. RSM promotes the use of violence and terrorism against Philippine Christians and Westerners with the aim of turning the Philippines into an Islamic state. The group is named after Rajah Solaiman, the last indigenous Muslim ruler of Manila before Spanish rule began in the 16th century.

Activities

The RSM has assisted with the terrorist plots of the Abu Sayyaf Group (ASG) in Manila and other areas in the northern Philippines. It was involved in ASG's bombing of SuperFerry 14 in February 2004, and the February 2005 Valentine's

Day bombings, according to Philippine security officials. In 2005 the RSM suffered several major setbacks when in March, Philippine security forces seized more than 1,300 pounds of explosives from an RSM safe house in metropolitan Manila, and in October, Philippine intelligence agents arrested RSM leader Ahmad Santos in Zamboanga City and charged him with plotting to bomb high profile targets, including the U.S. Embassy in Manila. Two months later, Philippine security forces arrested another RSM leader in Zamboanga City. Philippine officials subsequently claimed that debriefing captives helped them thwart an alleged RSM plot to conduct attacks in Manila during the Christmas 2005 holiday season. In late 2006, another RSM leader, Feliciano de los Reyes, was arrested.

Strength

The exact number of members in the RSM is unknown, but the group likely has fewer than 50 members.

Location/Area of Operation

The RSM operates throughout the Philippines and maintains a significant presence in metropolitan Manila. Some RSM operatives trained alongside members of the Abu Sayyaf Group and other militants in the southern Philippines.

External Aid

The Abu Sayyaf Group and Jemaah Islamiya have provided training, funds, and operational assistance to the RSM. Some Middle East–based non-governmental organizations and other sympathizers also may provide funds to the RSM.

REAL IRA (RIRA)

a.k.a. Real Irish Republican Army; 32 County Sovereignty Committee; 32 County Sovereignty Movement; Irish Republican Prisoners Welfare Association; Real Oglaigh Na Heireann

Description

The Real IRA (RIRA) was designated as a Foreign Terrorist Organization on May 16, 2001. RIRA was formed in 1997 as the clandestine armed wing of the 32 County Sovereignty Movement, a "political pressure group" dedicated to removing British forces from Northern Ireland and unifying Ireland. RIRA also seeks to disrupt the Northern Ireland peace process and did not participate in the September 2005 weapons decommissioning. The 32 County Sovereignty Movement opposed Sinn Fein's adoption in September 1997 of the Mitchell principles of democracy and non-violence; it also opposed the amendment in December

1999 of Articles 2 and 3 of the Irish Constitution that laid claim to Northern Ireland. Despite internal rifts and calls by some jailed members, including the group's founder Michael "Mickey" McKevitt, for a cease-fire and disbandment, RIRA has pledged additional violence and continues to conduct attacks.

Activities

Many RIRA members are former Provisional Irish Republican Army members who left the organization after it renewed its cease-fire in 1997. These members brought a wealth of experience in terrorist tactics and bomb-making to RIRA. Targets have included civilians (most notoriously in the Omagh bombing in August 1998), British security forces, police in Northern Ireland, and local Protestant communities. RIRA's most recent fatal attack was in August 2002 at a London army base, killing a construction worker. The organization wants to improve its intelligence-gathering ability, engineering capacity, and access to weaponry; it also trains members in the use of guns and explosives. RIRA continued to attract new members, and its senior members were committed to launching attacks on security forces. Three suspected RIRA members that engaged in cigarette smuggling were arrested in Spain in 2006. From 2006 to November 2007, terrorist activity in the form of successful and attempted attacks by RIRA only slightly decreased. Notably, between August and November 2006, throughout Northern Ireland, RIRA targeted B&Q home-supply stores and other retail businesses in successful and attempted fire bombings, although a handful of these attacks were also claimed by the Continuity Irish Republican Army (CIRA). In November 2007, RIRA claimed two armed attacks that wounded two Police Service of Northern Ireland (PSNI) officers that same month. RIRA claimed responsibility for a May 2008 improvised explosive device that injured a PSNI officer in Belfast and the firebombing of two stores. The Independent Monitoring Commission, which was established to oversee the peace process, assesses that RIRA members were likely responsible for the majority of the shootings and assaults that occurred in Northern Ireland in 2008. In November 2008, Lithuania arrested a RIRA member for attempting to arrange a shipment of weapons to Northern Ireland.

Strength

According to the Irish government, RIRA has approximately 100 active members. The organization may receive limited support from IRA hardliners and Republican sympathizers who are dissatisfied with the IRA's continuing cease-fire and with Sinn Fein's involvement in the peace process. Approximately 40 RIRA members are in Irish jails.

Location/Area of Operation

Northern Ireland, Great Britain, and the Irish Republic.

External Aid

RIRA is suspected of receiving funds from sympathizers in the United States and of attempting to buy weapons from U.S. gun dealers. RIRA also is reported to have purchased sophisticated weapons from the Balkans.

RED HAND DEFENDERS (RHD)

Description

The RHD is a terrorist group formed in 1998 and composed largely of Protestant hardliners from Loyalist groups observing a cease-fire. RHD seeks to prevent a political settlement with Irish nationalists by attacking Catholic civilian interests in Northern Ireland. In January 2002, the group announced all staff at Catholic schools in Belfast and Catholic postal workers were legitimate targets. Despite calls in February 2002 by the Ulster Defense Association (UDA), Ulster Freedom Fighters (UFF), and Loyalist Volunteer Force (LVF) to announce its disbandment, RHD continued to make threats and issue claims of responsibility. RHD is a cover name often used by elements of the banned UDA and LVF. RHD was designated under E.O. 13224 in December 2001.

Activities

In early 2003, the RHD claimed responsibility for killing two UDA members as a result of what is described as Loyalist internecine warfare. It also claimed responsibility for a bomb that was left in the offices of Republican Sinn Fein in West Belfast, although the device was defused and no one was injured. In recent years, the group has carried out numerous pipe bombings and arson attacks against "soft" civilian targets such as homes, churches, and private businesses. In January 2002, the group bombed the home of a prison official in North Belfast. Twice in 2002 the group claimed responsibility for attacks—the murder of a Catholic postman and a Catholic teenager—that were later claimed by the UDA-UFF, further blurring distinctions between the groups. In 2001, RHD claimed responsibility for killing five persons.

Strength

Up to 20 members, some of whom have experience in terrorist tactics and bomb-making. Police arrested one member in June 2001 for making a hoax bomb threat.

Location/Area of Operation

Northern Ireland.

External Aid

None.

REVOLUTIONARY ARMED FORCES OF COLOMBIA (FARC)

a.k.a. Fuerzas Armadas Revolucionarias de Colombia

Description

The Revolutionary Armed Forces of Colombia (FARC) was designated as a Foreign Terrorist Organization on October 8, 1997. The Revolutionary Armed Forces of Colombia (FARC) is Latin America's oldest, largest, most capable, and best-equipped insurgency, and remains so in spite of recent losses at the hands of the Colombian government. It began in the early 1960s as an outgrowth of the Liberal Party–based peasant self-defense leagues, but took on Marxist ideology. Today, it only nominally fights in support of Marxist goals. The FARC is governed by a general secretariat led by new Supreme Commander Guillermo Leon Saenz (a.k.a. Alfonso Cano) and six others, including senior military commander Victor Suarez (a.k.a. Jorge Briceno or "Mono Jojoy"). The FARC is organized along military lines and includes some specialized urban fighting units.

In 2008, the FARC experienced several significant setbacks. A robust and continuing Colombian military offensive targeting key FARC units and leaders succeeded in capturing or killing a number of FARC senior and mid-level commanders. Colombian military operations on March 1 resulted in the death of Luis Devia Silva (a.k.a. Raul Reyes), the FARC's second-in-command at the time. In early March the FARC lost another secretariat member, Manuel Jesus Munoz Ortiz (a.k.a. Ivan Rios) when he was killed by one of his own security guards, and the FARC's co-founder and Supreme Leader Antonio Marin (a.k.a. Manuel Marulanda or "Tirofijo") died in late March, reportedly from heart failure. In July, the Colombian military pulled off a dramatic rescue of 15 high-value FARC hostages including three U.S. Department of Defense contractors and former Colombian presidential candidate Ingrid Betancourt.

Activities

The FARC has carried out bombings, murder, mortar attacks, kidnapping, extortion, and hijacking, as well as guerrilla and conventional military action against Colombian political, military, and economic targets. Foreign citizens were often targets of abductions that the FARC carried out to obtain ransom and political leverage. The FARC has well-documented ties to the full range of narcotics trafficking activities, including taxation, cultivation, and distribution.

Strength

Approximately 9,000 to 12,000 combatants and several thousand more supporters.

Location/Area of Operation

Primarily in Colombia with some activities, such as extortion, kidnapping, weapons sourcing, and logistics in neighboring countries.

External Aid

Cuba provided some medical care, safe haven, and political consultation. Venezuela supplied some logistical, financial, and lethal aid to the FARC, although this may be a result of individual corruption rather than official policy; available information is not conclusive. The FARC often used the Colombia/Venezuela, Colombia/Panama, and Colombia/Ecuador border areas for incursions into Colombia and also used Venezuelan and Ecuadorian territory for safe haven, although the degree of government acquiescence was not clear and may vary depending on localized cross-border relations.

REVOLUTIONARY NUCLEI

a.k.a. Revolutionary Cells; ELA; Epanastatiki Pirines; Epanastatikos Laikos Agonas; June 78; Liberation Struggle; Organization of Revolutionary Internationalist Solidarity; Popular Revolutionary Struggle; Revolutionary People's Struggle; Revolutionary Popular Struggle

Description

Revolutionary Nuclei (RN) was designated as a Foreign Terrorist Organization on October 8, 1997. RN emerged from a broad range of anti-establishment and anti-U.S./NATO/EU leftist groups active in Greece between 1995 and 1998. The group is believed to be the successor to or offshoot of Greece's most prolific terrorist group, Revolutionary People's Struggle (ELA), which has not claimed an attack since January 1995. Indeed, RN appeared to fill the void left by ELA, particularly as lesser groups faded from the scene. RN's few communiqués show strong similarities in rhetoric, tone, and theme to ELA proclamations.

Activities

Since it began operations in January 1995, the group has claimed responsibility for some two dozen arson attacks and low-level bombings against a range of U.S., Greek, and other European targets in Greece. In its most infamous and lethal attack to date, the group claimed responsibility for a bomb it detonated at the Intercontinental Hotel in April 1999 that resulted in the death of a Greek woman and injury of a Greek man. RN's modus operandi includes warning calls of impending attacks, attacks targeting property instead of individuals, use of rudimentary timing devices, and strikes during the late evening to early morning hours. RN's last confirmed attacks against U.S. interests in Greece occurred in November 2000, with two separate bombings against the Athens offices of Citigroup and the studio of a Greek-American sculptor. Greek targets have included judicial and other government office buildings, private vehicles, and the offices of Greek firms involved in NATO-related defense contracts in Greece. Similarly, the group has attacked European interests in Athens.

Strength

Group membership is unknown.

Location/Area of Operation

Unknown, but historically RN's area of operation was Athens.

External Aid

Unknown but believed to be self-sustaining.

REVOLUTIONARY ORGANIZATION 17 NOVEMBER

a.k.a. Epanastatiki Organosi 17 Noemvri; 17 November

Description

The Revolutionary Organization 17 November (17N) was designated as a Foreign Terrorist Organization on October 8, 1997. Revolutionary Organization 17 November (17N) is a radical leftist group established in 1975 and named for the student uprising in Greece in November 1973 that protested the ruling military junta. 17N is an anti-Greece, anti-U.S., anti-Turkey, and anti-NATO group that seeks the ouster of U.S. bases from Greece, the removal of Turkish military forces from Cyprus, and the severing of Greece's ties to NATO and the European Union (EU).

Activities

Initial attacks consisted of assassinations of senior U.S. officials and Greek public figures. Five U.S. Embassy employees have been murdered since 17N began its terrorist activities in 1975. The group began using bombings in the 1980s. In 1990, 17N expanded its targets to include Turkish diplomats, EU facilities, and foreign firms investing in Greece, and added improvised rocket attacks to its methods. The group supported itself largely through bank robberies. A failed 17N bombing attempt in June 2002 at the port of Piraeus in Athens, coupled with robust detective work, led to the arrest of 19 members, the first 17N operatives ever arrested, including a key leader of the organization. In December 2003, a Greek court convicted 15 members, five of whom were given multiple life terms. Four other alleged members were acquitted for lack of evidence. In May 2007, two of these 15 members were acquitted on appeal due to doubts surrounding the charges against them. The convictions of the other 13 were upheld on appeal.

Strength

Unknown but presumed to be small.

Location/Area of Operation

Athens, Greece.

External Aid

Unknown.

REVOLUTIONARY PEOPLE'S LIBERATION PARTY/FRONT

a.k.a. DHKP/C; Dev Sol; Dev Sol Armed Revolutionary Units; Dev Sol Silahli Devrimci Birlikleri; Dev Sol SDB; Devrimci Halk Kurtulus Partisi-Cephesi; Devrimci Sol; Revolutionary Left

Description

The Revolutionary People's Liberation Party/Front (DHKP/C) was designated as a Foreign Terrorist Organization on October 8, 1997. The DHKP/C originally formed in 1978 as Devrimci Sol, or Dev Sol, a splinter faction of Dev Genc (Revolutionary Youth). It was renamed in 1994, after factional infighting. "Party" refers to the group's political activities, while "Front" is a reference to the group's militant operations. The group espouses a Marxist-Leninist ideology and is vehemently an anti-U.S., anti-NATO, and anti-Turkey establishment. Its goals are the establishment of a socialist state and the abolition of F-type prisons, which contain one- to three-man prison cells. DHKP/C finances its activities chiefly through donations and extortion.

Activities

Since the late 1980s, the group has primarily targeted current and retired Turkish security and military officials. It began a new campaign against foreign interests in 1990, which included attacks against U.S. military and diplomatic personnel and facilities. In order to protest perceived U.S. imperialism during the Gulf War, Dev Sol assassinated two U.S. military contractors, wounded an Air Force officer, and bombed more than 20 U.S. and NATO military, commercial, and cultural facilities. In its first significant terrorist act as DHKP/C in 1996, the group assassinated a prominent Turkish businessman and two others; the perpetrators fled to Belgium, where legal cases continue. DHKP/C added suicide bombings to its repertoire in 2001, with successful attacks against Turkish police in January and September. Since the end of 2001, DHKP/C has typically used improvised explosive devices against official Turkish targets and soft U.S. targets of opportunity. Attacks against U.S. targets beginning in 2003 were probably a response to Operation Iraqi Freedom.

Operations and arrests against the group have weakened its capabilities. In late June 2004, the group was suspected of a bus bombing at Istanbul University, which killed four civilians and 21 other people. In July 2005, in Ankara, police intercepted and killed a suicide bomber who attempted to attack the Ministry of Justice. In June 2006, the group fired upon and killed a police officer in Istanbul; four members of the group were arrested the next month for the attack.

The DKHP/C was dealt a major ideological blow when Dursun Karatas, leader of the group, died in August 2008 in the Netherlands. Throughout 2008, several DHKP/C members were arrested in Turkey and Europe, and several members stood trial for previous terrorist activity. In early March, Turkish Authorities arrested three DHKP/C members preparing bombings. German authorities in late July indicted a DKHP/C senior leader, and in November German authorities arrested several individuals suspected of serving as high-ranking DHKP/C functionaries. In addition, Belgian authorities reviewed the acquittal of several DHKP/C members and began retrial to reach final judgment.

Strength

Probably several dozen terrorist operatives inside Turkey, with a limited support network throughout Europe.

Location/Area of Operation

Turkey, primarily Istanbul, Ankara, Izmir, and Adana.

External Aid

Widely believed to have training facilities or offices in Lebanon and Syria. DHKP/C raises funds in Europe.

REVOLUTIONARY PROLETARIAN
INITIATIVE NUCLEI (NIPR)

Description

The NIPR is a clandestine leftist extremist group that appeared in Rome in 2000. It adopted the logo of the Red Brigades of the 1970s and 1980s, an encircled five point star, for its declarations. NIPR opposes Italy's foreign and labor policies. The group has targeted property interests rather than personnel in its attacks.

Activities

The NIPR has not claimed responsibility for any attacks since an April 2001 bomb attack on a building housing a U.S.-Italian relations association and an international affairs institute in Rome's historic center. The NIPR claimed to have carried out a bombing in May 2000 in Rome at an oversight committee facility for implementation of the law on strikes in public services.

Strength

Fewer than 20 members.

Location/Area of Operation

Mainly in Rome, Milan, Lazio, and Tuscany.

External Aid

None evident.

REVOLUTIONARY STRUGGLE (RS)

Description

RS is a radical leftist group that is anti-Greek establishment and ideologically aligns itself with the Revolutionary Organization 17 November.

Activities

RS is widely regarded as the most dangerous indigenous Greek terrorist group still active and has been linked to attacks against Americans. RS first became known when the group conducted a bombing in 2003 against the courthouse where trials of alleged 17 November members were occurring. In 2004, the group detonated four improvised explosive devices at a police station in Athens. These two attacks were notable for their apparent attempts to target and kill first responders, the first time a Greek terrorist group had used this tactic. RS claimed responsibility for a large explosion in December 2005 in Constitution Square in the center of Athens, apparently targeting the Ministry of National Economy, injuring three and badly damaging the facade of a post office and other buildings. The group claimed responsibility for a bomb explosion in May 2006, near the residence of former Minister of Public Order Giorgos Voulgarakis. The remotely detonated bomb was placed next to a school along the minister's usual route to work and exploded just minutes before he was due to pass. The explosion wrecked several cars but caused no injuries. RS also claimed responsibility for a rocket-propelled-grenade (RPG) attack against the U.S. Embassy on January 12, 2007. The attack occurred early in the morning when few Embassy personnel were working and there were no injuries, but the RPG damaged a room at the front of the Embassy.

Strength

Likely less than 50 members.

Location/Area of Operation

Athens, Greece.

External Aid

Unknown.

RIYADUS-SALIKHIN RECONNAISSANCE AND SABOTAGE BATTALION OF CHECHEN MARTYRS (RSRSBCM)

Description

Riyadus-Salikhin Reconnaissance and Sabotage Battalion of Chechen Martyrs (RSRSBCM), led by Chechen extremist Shamil Basayev, uses terrorism as part of an effort to secure an independent Muslim state in the North Caucasus. Basayev claimed the group was responsible for the Beslan school hostage crisis of September 2004, which culminated in the deaths of about 330 people; simultaneous suicide bombings aboard two Russian civilian airliners in August 2004; and a third suicide bombing outside a Moscow subway that same month. The group has not mounted a terrorist attack since the Beslan operation. The RSRSBCM, whose name translates into English as "Requirements for Getting into Paradise," was not known to Western observers before October 2002, when it participated in the seizure of the Dubrovka Theater in Moscow. The group was designated under E.O. 13224 in February 2003. The group's viability is in question since its leader Shamil Basayev was killed by Russian forces in July 2006.

Activities

RSRSBCM has primarily engaged in terrorist and guerrilla operations against Russian forces, pro-Russian Chechen forces, and Russian and Chechen non-combatants.

Strength

Probably no more than 50 fighters at any given time.

Location/Area of Operation

Primarily Russia.

External Aid

May receive some external assistance from foreign mujahedin.

SHINING PATH (SL)

a.k.a. Sendero Luminoso; Ejercito Guerrillero Popular (People's Guerrilla Army); EGP; Ejercito Popular de Liberacion (People's Liberation Army); EPL; Partido Comunista del Peru (Communist Party of Peru); PCP; Partido Comunista del Peru en el Sendero Luminoso de Jose Carlos Mariategui (Communist Party of Peru on the Shining Path of Jose Carlos Mariategui); Socorro Popular del Peru (People's Aid of Peru); SPP

Description

Shining Path (SL) was designated as a Foreign Terrorist Organization on October 8, 1997. Former university professor Abimael Guzman formed the Shining Path (SL) in Peru in the late 1960s; his teachings created the foundation of SL's militant Maoist doctrine. In the 1980s, SL became one of the most ruthless terrorist groups in the Western Hemisphere. The Peruvian government made dramatic gains against SL during the 1990s, capturing Guzman in 1992 and killing a large number of militants. SL's stated goal is to destroy existing Peruvian institutions and replace them with a communist peasant revolutionary regime. It also opposes any influence by foreign governments. More recently, SL members have attempted to influence the local populace through indoctrination as opposed to violence.

Activities

In the past, SL has conducted indiscriminate bombing campaigns, ambushes, and selective assassinations. Remnants of SL now focus on drug-trafficking and production activities to obtain funds to carry out attacks.

A recent increase in SL attacks against Peruvian security forces and counternarcotics personnel during fall 2008 underscored that the SL remained a threat. In response to SL's bloody attacks, Peruvian authorities stepped up counterterrorism efforts against the group and have since kept the SL remnants largely on the defensive.

Strength

Unknown but estimated to be between 200 and 300 armed militants.

Location/Area of Operation

Peru, with most activity in rural areas, specifically the Huallaga Valley, the Ene River, and the Apurimac Valley of central Peru.

External Aid

None.

SIPAH-I-SAHABA/PAKISTAN (SSP)

a.k.a. Millat-I-Islami Pakistan

Description

The Sipah-I-Sahaba/Pakistan (SSP) is a Sunni sectarian group that follows the Deobandi school. Violently anti-Shia, the SSP emerged in central Punjab in the mid-1980s as a response to the Iranian revolution. Pakistani President Musharraf banned the SSP in January 2002. In August 2002, the SSP renamed itself Millat-i-Islami Pakistan, and Musharraf re-banned the group in November 2003. The SSP also has operated as a political party, winning seats in Pakistan's National Assembly.

Activities

The group's activities range from organizing political rallies calling for Shia to be declared non-Muslims to assassinating prominent Shia leaders. The group was responsible for attacks on Shia worshippers in May 2004, when at least 50 people were killed.

Strength

The SSP may have approximately 3,000 to 6,000 trained activists who carry out various kinds of sectarian activities.

Location/Area of Operation

The SSP has influence in all four provinces of Pakistan. It is considered to be one of the most powerful sectarian groups in the country.

External Aid

The SSP reportedly receives significant funding from Saudi Arabia and wealthy private donors in Pakistan. Funds also are acquired from other sources, including other Sunni extremist groups, madrassas, and contributions by political groups.

SPECIAL PURPOSE ISLAMIC REGIMENT (SPIR)

Description

The SPIR is one of three Chechen-affiliated terrorist groups that furnished personnel to carry out the seizure of the Dubrovka Theater in Moscow in October 2002. The SPIR has had at least seven commanders since it was founded in the late 1990s. Movsar Barayev, who led and was killed during the theater standoff, was the first publicly identified leader. The group continues to conduct guerrilla operations in Chechnya under its current leader, Amir Aslan, whose true identity is not known. SPIR was designated under E.O. 13224 in February 2003. In 2006, SPIR continued to target official Russian targets and Chechen elements it believes to be sympathetic to Russia.

Activities

SPIR has primarily engaged in guerrilla operations against Russian forces. Has also been involved in various hostage and ransom operations, including the execution of ethnic Chechens who have cooperated with Russian authorities.

Strength

Probably no more than 100 fighters at any given time.

Location/Area of Operation

Primarily Russia.

External Aid

May receive some external assistance from foreign mujahedin.

AL-TAWHID W'AL JIHAD (TWJ)

a.k.a. Tawhid Islamic Brigades; al-Tawhid Wa al-Jihad; Monotheism and Jihad Organization

Description

The TWJ is an Egypt-based Islamic extremist group motivated by Cairo's harsh treatment of the Bedouin community and difficult economic conditions in the Sinai. This group is comprised of radicalized Sinai Bedouin, criminals, and smugglers who use their knowledge of the rugged Sinai terrain and their compartmented cell structure to attack Western and Israeli tourist targets.

Activities

The TWJ has conducted bombings and suicide attacks, such as attacks at Taba in October 2004, Sharm ash Shaykh in July 2005, Dhahab in April 2006, and against the Multinational Force and Observers (MFO) in August 2005 and April 2006.

Strength

Unknown. Egyptian security services have killed or captured many high-ranking TWJ members during the past two years.

Location/Area of Operation

Sinai, Gaza.

External Aid

Unknown.

TEHRIK NEFAZ-I-SHARIAT MUHAMMAD (TNSM)

Description

Maulawi Sufi Muhammed (now imprisoned) established TNSM in May 1989 in the former Malakand District of the Northwest Frontier Province (NWFP) of Pakistan with the goal of instituting strict Islamic law in the region because they believe the government failed to institute Sharia law in the NWFP. The group held massive rallies in 1994 and effectively shut down the Malakand District. The uprising ended after the Pakistani government agreed to implement Sharia law in the Malakand District. Islamabad banned the group in 2002 in response to TNSM's deployment of fighters to Afghanistan to fight with the Taliban. Since Sufi Muhammad's arrest in early 2002, the leadership of the group has been in flux. Both Maulawi Faqir Muhammad and Maulawi Fazlullah-Sufi Muhammad's son-in-law have been mentioned as possible leaders of the group. Faqir Muhammad in November 2006 publicly pledged to continue the jihad in Afghanistan under Taliban leader Mullah Omar.

Activities

TNSM is a party to 2006 peace negotiations with Pakistan. Prior to the peace negotiations, the Pakistani government released nine prisoners associated with TNSM, to include Faqir Muhammad's brother and two senior clerics. On October 28, 2006, TNSM staged an anti-U.S. rally and vowed to continue to support the Taliban but agreed not to shelter foreigners. On October 30, 2006, a madrassa suspected of hosting a terrorist training camp was destroyed in a counter-terrorism operation and Pakistani forces killed Maulana Liaqat, the madrassa's director and deputy for the group. At a protest rally following the operation, Faqir Muhammad declared he would continue to wage jihad, but he renewed his pledge to abide by the peace accords and not attack the Pakistani government. Faqir also denied reports that al-Qaeda deputy leader Ayman al-Zawahiri was present at the madrassa. Press reports alleged TNSM was responsible for a suicide bombing on November 8 that killed 35 soldiers in Dargai, Pakistan, although the group did not claim responsibility. Pakistan security agencies have reopened investigations on members following this attack. Newspaper announcements requested certain members to appear in court and face charges filed against them under anti-terrorism laws.

Strength

Exact numbers are unknown; however, TNSM has recruited very high numbers of fighters in the past (in the thousands) and has also held demonstrations attended by several thousand people.

Location/Area of Operation

Eastern Afghanistan, Northern Pakistan—particularly Bajaur Agency and Malakand District.

External Aid

TNSM was founded to pursue the implementation of Sharia in the NWFP and strongly supports the Taliban. The group has also been linked to al-Qaeda, especially through Faqir Muhammad who has stated that he would welcome Ayman al-Zawahiri and Osama bin Laden if they were to come to his area.

TUNISIAN COMBATANT GROUP (TCG)

a.k.a. Jama'a Combattante Tunisienne

Description

The Tunisian Combatant Group (TCG), also known as the Jama'a Combattante Tunisienne, seeks to establish an Islamic regime in Tunisia and has targeted U.S. and Western interests. The group is an offshoot of the banned Tunisian Islamist movement, an-Nahda. Founded around 2000 by Tarek Maaroufi and Saifallah Ben Hassine, the TCG has drawn members from the Tunisian Diaspora in Europe and elsewhere. It has lost some of its leadership, but may still exist, particularly in western Europe. Belgian authorities arrested Maaroufi in late 2001 and sentenced him to six years in prison in 2003 for his role in the assassination of anti-Taliban commander Ahmed Shah Massoud two days before 9/11. The TCG was designated under E.O. 13224 in October 2002. Historically, the group has been associated with al-Qaeda as well. Members also have ties to other North African extremist groups. The TCG was designated for sanctions under UNSCR 1333 in December 2000.

Activities

Tunisians associated with the TCG are part of the support network of the broader international terrorist movement. According to European press reports, TCG members or affiliates in the past have engaged in trafficking falsified documents and recruiting for terror training camps in Afghanistan. Some TCG associates were suspected of planning an attack against the United States, Algerian, and Tunisian diplomatic missions in Rome in April 2001. Some members reportedly maintain ties to the Algerian Salafist Group for Preaching and Combat.

Strength

Unknown.

Location/Area of Operation

Western Europe and Afghanistan.

External Aid

Unknown.

TUPAC AMARU REVOLUTIONARY MOVEMENT (MRTA)

Description

MRTA is a traditional Marxist-Leninist revolutionary movement formed in 1983 from remnants of the Movement of the Revolutionary Left, a Peruvian insurgent group active in the 1960s. It aims to establish a Marxist regime and to rid Peru of all imperialist elements, primarily U.S. and Japanese influence. Peru's counter-terrorist program has diminished the group's ability to conduct terrorist attacks, and the MRTA has suffered from infighting, the imprisonment or deaths of senior leaders, and the loss of leftist support.

Activities

MRTA previously conducted bombings, kidnappings, ambushes, and assassinations, but recent activity has fallen drastically. In December 1996, 14 MRTA members occupied the Japanese Ambassador's residence in Lima and held 72 hostages for more than four months. Peruvian forces stormed the residence in April 1997, rescuing all but one of the remaining hostages and killing all 14 group members, including the remaining leaders. The group has not conducted a significant terrorist operation since and appears more focused on obtaining the release of imprisoned MRTA members, although there are reports of low-level rebuilding efforts.

Strength

Believed to be no more than 100 members, consisting largely of young fighters who lack leadership skills and experience.

Location/Area of Operation

Peru, with supporters throughout Latin America and western Europe. Many exiled members live in Bolivia.

External Aid

None.

TURKISH HEZBOLLAH

Description

Turkish Hezbollah is a Kurdish Sunni Islamic terrorist organization that arose in the early 1980s in response to the Kurdistan Workers' Party (PKK)'s secularist approach of establishing an independent Kurdistan. Turkish Hezbollah spent its first 10 years fighting the PKK, accusing the group of atrocities against Muslims in southeastern Turkey, where Turkish Hezbollah seeks to establish an independent Islamic state.

Activities

Beginning in the mid-1990s, Turkish Hezbollah, which is unrelated to Lebanese Hezbollah, expanded its target base and modus operandi from killing PKK militants to conducting low-level bombings against liquor stores, bordellos, and other establishments the organization considered "anti-Islamic." In January 2000, Turkish security forces killed Huseyin Velioglu, the leader of Turkish Hezbollah, in a shootout at a safe house in Istanbul. The incident sparked a year-long series of counterterrorist operations against the group that resulted in the detention of some 2,000 individuals; authorities arrested several hundred of them on criminal charges. At the same time, police recovered nearly 70 bodies of Turkish and Kurdish businessmen and journalists whom Turkish Hezbollah had tortured and brutally murdered during the mid-to-late 1990s. The group began targeting official Turkish interests in January 2001, when its operatives assassinated the Diyarbakir police chief in the group's most sophisticated operation to date. Turkish Hezbollah has not conducted a major operation since 2001, and probably is focusing at present on recruitment, fundraising, and reorganization.

Strength

Possibly a few hundred members and several thousand supporters.

Location/Area of Operation

Primarily the Diyarbakir region of southeastern Turkey.

External Aid

It is widely believed that Turkey's security apparatus originally backed Turkish Hezbollah to help the Turkish government combat the PKK. Alternative views are that the Turkish government ignored Turkish Hezbollah activities because its primary targets were PKK members and supporters, or that the government simply had to prioritize scarce resources and was unable to wage war on both groups simultaneously. Allegations of collusion have never been laid to rest, and the Government of Turkey continues to issue denials. Turkish Hezbollah also is suspected of having ties with Iran, although there is not sufficient evidence to establish a link.

ULSTER DEFENSE ASSOCIATION/ULSTER FREEDOM FIGHTERS (UDA/UFF)

Description

The Ulster Defense Association (UDA), the largest Loyalist paramilitary group in Northern Ireland, was formed in 1971 as an umbrella organization for Loyalist paramilitary groups such as the Ulster Freedom Fighters (UFF). Today, the UFF constitutes almost the entire UDA membership. The UDA/UFF declared a series of cease-fires between 1994 and 1998. In September 2001, the UDA/UFF's Inner Council withdrew its support for Northern Ireland's Good Friday Agreement. The following month, after a series of murders, bombings, and street violence, the British government ruled the UDA/UFF's cease-fire defunct. The dissolution of the organization's political wing, the Ulster Democratic Party, soon followed. In January 2002, however, the UDA created the Ulster Political Research Group to serve in a similar capacity. In October 2006, a splinter group of the UDA, calling itself Beyond Conflict, publicly announced its mission to assist former UDA members to disengage from the conflict and develop dialogue with local neighborhoods. Designated under E.O. 13224 in December 2001.

Activities

The UDA/UFF has evolved into a criminal organization deeply involved in drug trafficking and other moneymaking criminal activities through six largely independent "brigades." It also has been involved in murder, shootings, arson, assaults, and exiling. According to the Independent Monitoring Commission (IMC), "the UDA has the capacity to launch serious, if crude, attacks." Some UDA activities of a sectarian nature directed at the Catholic community are aimed at so-called "soft" targets, and often have taken place at the interface between the Protestant and Catholic communities, especially in Belfast.

Strength

Estimates vary from 2,000 to 5,000 members, with several hundred active in paramilitary operations.

Location/Area of Operation

Northern Ireland.

External Aid

Probably obtains weapons from abroad.

ULSTER VOLUNTEER FORCE (UVF)

Description

The UVF is a Loyalist terrorist group formed in 1966 to oppose liberal reforms in Northern Ireland that members feared would lead to unification of Ireland. The group adopted the name of an earlier organization formed in 1912 to combat Home Rule for Ireland. The UVF's goal is to maintain Northern Ireland's status as part of the United Kingdom; to that end, it has killed some 550 persons since 1966. The UVF and its offshoots have been responsible for some of the most vicious attacks of "The Troubles," including horrific sectarian killings like those perpetrated in the 1970s by the UVF-affiliated "Shankill Butchers." In October 1994, the Combined Loyalist Military Command, which included the UVF, declared a cease-fire, and the UVF's political wing, the Progressive Unionist Party, has played an active role in the peace process. Despite the cease-fire, the organization has been involved in a series of bloody feuds with other Loyalist paramilitary organizations, although the UVF is considering a stand-down similar to that of the Irish Republican Army. The Red Hand Defenders is linked to the UVF.

Activities

The UVF has been active in Belfast and the border areas of Northern Ireland, where it has carried out bombings, assassinations, kidnappings, hijackings, extortion, and robberies. UVF members have been linked to recent racial attacks on minorities; however, the UVF leadership reportedly did not authorize these assaults. On occasion, it has provided advance warning to police of its attacks. Targets include nationalist civilians, Republican paramilitary groups, and, on occasion, rival Loyalist paramilitary groups. The UVF is a relatively disciplined organization with a centralized command. The Independent Monitoring Commission has said that UVF members were responsible for the attempted murder in 2006 of Mark Haddock, a former UVF member turned police informant, and main suspect in the 1997 murder of Raymond McCord. Additionally, UVF members are suspected of murdering one individual and attempting to murder another, but the IMC assesses these actions were not sanctioned by UVF leadership.

Strength

Unclear, but probably several hundred supporters, with a smaller number of hard-core activists. Police counterterrorist operations and internal feuding have reduced the group's strength and capabilities.

Location/Area of Operation

Northern Ireland. Some support on the UK mainland.

External Aid

Suspected in the past of receiving funds and arms from sympathizers overseas.

UNITED LIBERATION FRONT OF ASSAM (ULFA)

Description

Northeast India's most prominent insurgent group, ULFA, an ethnic secessionist organization in the Indian state of Assam, which borders Bangladesh and Bhutan, was founded in 1979 at Rang Ghar, during anti-foreigner agitation organized by the state's powerful students' union. The group's objective is an independent Assam. ULFA enjoyed widespread support in upper Assam in its initial years, especially from 1985 to 1992. ULFA's kidnappings, killings, and extortion led New Delhi to ban the group and start a military offensive against it in 1990, which forced it to go underground. ULFA began to lose popularity in the late 1990s after it increasingly targeted civilians, including a prominent NGO activist. It lost further support for its anti-Indian stand during the 1999 Kargil conflict. In recent years, the group has been in decline, losing popular support and suffering from aggressive counterinsurgency operations by Indian security forces. The Royal Bhutan Army's attack on ULFA camps in Bhutan in 2003, and the suspension of operations by Bodo tribal insurgent groups in Assam, also contributed to the group's decline. Despite the ban on the group, New Delhi held official talks with ULFA's representative Peace Consultative Group in October 2005, which apparently have had little effect on dampening ULFA's operations against business and government targets in 2006.

Activities

ULFA trains, finances, and equips its cadres for a "liberation struggle," while extortion helps finance military training and weapons purchases. ULFA conducts hit-and-run operations on security forces in Assam, selective assassinations, and explosions in public places. During the 1980s and 1990s, ULFA undertook a series of abductions and murders, particularly of businessmen. In 2000, ULFA assassinated an Assam state minister. In 2003, ULFA killed more than 60 "outsiders" in Assam, mainly residents of the bordering state of Bihar. Some important ULFA functionaries surrendered in Assam, but incidents of violence continue, although of a lesser magnitude than in the past. In 2004, ULFA started targeting civilians and killed some 14 people in August that year.

Strength

ULFA's earlier strength of more than 3,000 dropped following the December 2003 attack on its camps in Bhutan. Total cadre strength now is estimated at several hundred, plus supporters providing safe houses and logistical and intelligence assistance.

Location/Area of Operation

ULFA is active in the state of Assam, and members transit and periodically conduct operations in parts of the neighboring states of Arunachal Pradesh, Meghalaya, and Nagaland. All ULFA camps in Bhutan are reportedly demolished.

External Aid

ULFA reportedly procures and trades in arms with other Northeast Indian groups.

UNITED SELF-DEFENSE FORCES/GROUP OF COLOMBIA

a.k.a. AUC; Autodefensas Unidas de Colombia

Description

The United Self-Defense Forces of Colombia (AUC) was designated as a Foreign Terrorist Organization on September 10, 2001. The United Self-Defense

Forces of Colombia (AUC), commonly referred to as the paramilitaries, was an umbrella group formed in April 1997 to organize loosely affiliated illegal paramilitary groups that had emerged to retaliate against leftist guerrillas fighting the Colombian government and the landed establishment. The AUC increasingly discarded its counter-guerrilla activities, electing instead to involve itself in the illegal drug trade. By 2007, as the result of a large demobilization process, most of the AUC's centralized military structure had been dismantled, and all of the top paramilitary chiefs had stepped down with the majority being held in a maximum security facility. More than 31,000 paramilitary members and support personnel demobilized bloc by bloc from 2003 to 2006. Colombia now faces criminal gangs composed of some demobilized paramilitaries and other individuals, and one minor paramilitary group that refused to disarm. Unlike the AUC, the new criminal groups make little claim of fighting insurgents. They are more clearly criminal enterprises focused primarily on drug trafficking, other lucrative illicit activities, and influencing local politics to facilitate their criminal ventures. These new criminal groups are not a reconstituted AUC, but they recruit from the pool of former AUC members. Some of the various groups' leadership appears to be former mid-level paramilitary commanders who did not participate in demobilization.

Activities

Prior to the 2006 demobilization, the AUC engaged in terrorist activity through a variety of activities including political killings and kidnappings of human rights workers, journalists, teachers, and trade unionists, among others. As much as 70 percent of the paramilitary operational costs were financed with drug-related earnings. The emerging criminal groups include some remnants of the AUC, and their members continued to engage heavily in criminal activities.

Strength

With the exception of a few paramilitary fronts who refused to participate in the demobilization process, the AUC's organizational structure no longer exists. According to Colombian government figures, approximately 10 to 15 percent of the 3,000 to 4,000 members of these criminal groups are former members of paramilitary groups, including the AUC.

Location/Area of Operation

Paramilitary forces were strongest in northwest Colombia in Antioquia, Cordoba, Sucre, Atlantico, Magdelena, Cesar, La Guajira, and Bolivar Departments, with affiliate groups in the coffee region, Valle del Cauca, and Meta Department.

External Aid

None.

Part II

A HISTORY OF TERRORISM

Chapter Five

America's Birth:
A Heritage of Conflict and Terror

The cacique received the trumpeter kindly, and sent an invitation to De Gourges to come on shore and hold a conference. He did so, and his young countryman acted as interpreter. The cacique, painted and bedecked, was seated on a log in a beautiful grove, with several allied chiefs sitting in a semicircle around him. He placed De Gourges on another log, and then opened the conference with bitter complaints against the Spaniards, because of their cruelties. They had driven the Indians from their homes, murdered their children, and desolated their fields because they had treated the Frenchmen kindly. . . . "Do you intend to make war upon them?" quickly asked the cacique. "I do," as quickly answered De Gourges. "We will join you!" said the cacique.

—*Our Country*, published in 1800

There seems to be a popular myth in America that "terrorism" is something new. But anyone familiar with the history of the New World, as America was once known, must know that the confluence of European and Native American cultures spawned a heritage of conflict and terror from the start.

THE NORTHMEN

Early in the summer of 1002, Leif Ericson fitted a stout ship with a crew of twenty-six men and sailed southwestward from his home in Greenland. The son of Eric the Red—who had discovered and colonized Greenland—Leif sought to follow his father's example and seek out unknown lands himself.

The dauntless crew braved rough seas, icebergs, and strong winds as they sailed on southward. They found a land that was "charmed by a soft climate,"

171

where they sought a harbor, finding one at the mouth of a river where the vessel was swept by the tide into a bay. The waters were filled with salmon, and herds of wild deer roamed the woods.

A young German who was Leif's servant was missing one day. They searched for him in all directions. They found him deep in the forest where he was "full of joy" because he had discovered grapes, delicious and abundant, such as grew in his own country—so Leif named the country Vineland. Shortly after Leif returned home to Brattahlid his father died, and Leif assumed the leadership of the Greenland colony.

Thorwald, Leif's younger brother, then bought the good ship and, with thirty companions, sailed for Vineland. They passed two winters there, occupying the huts built by Leif and his companions and subsisting, as they had done, upon fish. During the spring and summers, they explored. They sailed into a large inlet during the early autumn of the third year. They saw thick wooded highlands on each side.

"Here," said Thorwald, "is a goodly place—here I will make my abode." They found there some Natives—dark-skinned people, of small stature, like the Eskimos of Greenland. They were in canoes and appeared timid and harmless. The Northmen caught them and cruelly put them to death, excepting one who escaped to the hills and aroused his tribesmen. The angry Natives returned silently in their canoes and surprised Thorwald and his company. A sharp fight ensued. Arrows flew thick and fast. Thorwald was mortally wounded, but his companions escaped unhurt. The Natives fled to the wooded hills, and Thorwald's companions buried the body of their chief on the promontory where he intended to settle, with a cross at its head and another at its feet. The survivors passed the winter in Vineland, in mortal fear of the enraged Natives, and in the spring they returned to Greenland.

And so began an episode that would play out time and time again in America. The Native peoples would more often than not welcome the explorers with warm smiles and hospitality. Too often they would be repaid with enslavement, abuse, illness, and death. And their memories of mistreatment were passed from generation to generation.

THE SPANIARDS

Impelled by his own religious zeal and prompted by the priests in his train, Cortez at once proceeded to further humiliate, horrify, and exasperate the subdued people, by making a clean sweep, with the besom of destruction, over the idols and temples of the empire. In the great square in Mexico, the conqueror and his followers, with their garments stained with the blood of

their fellow-creatures, devoutly sang the Te Deum, and prostrating themselves before the image of the Blessed Virgin which they had set up, they
reverently thanked God for permitting them to be the humble instruments
in annihilating image-worship and in staying the horrid rites of human
sacrifice. Such was the spirit and temper of the age in which they lived.
So was introduced Christianity into Mexico.

—*Our Country*, published in 1800

Pedro Menéndez de Avilés commanded a great treasure-fleet of galleons on
their voyage from Mexico to Spain in 1561. One of the vessels containing
his son and several relatives and friends disappeared during the voyage. After Menéndez delivered the fleet to the Spanish crown, he asked permission
to go back in search of the lost vessel but was refused. Finally, after two or
three years delay, his request was finally granted, but only on condition that
he explore and colonize Florida. He fitted out an expedition for the purpose
at his own expense.

When Menéndez was about to sail, orders came to him from King Philip
that he was to exterminate all Protestants he might find there. Philip had heard
that French Huguenots fleeing persecution in France were hiding in the for-
ests beyond the Atlantic. The king's zeal to please the Catholic Church was
such that he gave the order to Menéndez to slaughter the "heretics" wherever
they were found. To refuse would mean torture and death in the dungeons of
the Spanish Inquisition for Menéndez.

Because the king regarded the voyage as a holy enterprise, he added ships
and treasure to support the venture. Soldiers and seamen flocked to the
standard of Menéndez in great numbers, and he sailed with a fleet of eleven
ships (one of them a galleon of nine hundred tons) with over twenty-six hundred persons, consisting, besides the soldiers and sailors, of adventurers and
priests. Only five of the ships survived the crossing.

Stopping briefly at present-day St. Augustine, Menéndez went ashore with
great pomp and circumstance to plant the Spanish flag, claiming Florida for
God and king. He then set sail to strike at the feeble French Fort Caroline near
the mouth of the St. Johns River.

The Huguenot fort was defended by only a handful of soldiers. The Spaniards closed with the fort before their presence was suspected. They attacked
without mercy. No person was spared. They were slaughtered in their beds,
screaming prayers for mercy, and in terrified flight. A few escaped to the
woods, but without food and with scanty clothing. Many later perished. A few
survivors made their way to two small French ships, in which they sailed for
Europe. According to Chaplain Mendoza, 142 Huguenots were slain, while
the Spaniards suffered no losses. The women and children were butchered. A

few men were hanged upon trees with a sign posted above inscribed: "Not as Frenchmen, but as Lutherans."

Chevalier Dominic de Gourges, a gentleman of Gascony, a member of an eminent family and a devoted Roman Catholic, was outraged. His hatred of the Spanish fueled by his experience as a prisoner of war enslaved aboard a Spanish galleon was further stoked by the slaughter of his countrymen and the indifference expressed by his French king. De Gourges sold his property, borrowed money from his friends, and fitted out three small vessels, manned by one hundred soldiers (many of them gentlemen volunteers), and eighty mariners prepared with crossbows and picks to act as soldiers.

Arriving at a small river north of the St. Johns in 1568, de Gourges met with a leader whose tribe had suffered terrible punishment by the Spaniards because of the tribe's friendly relations with the French. The *cacique* formed an alliance with the French nobleman to war on the Spanish. Over the next few days the allies attacked two Spanish forts south of Fort Caroline (Matheo), then turned north and slaughtered everyone they found except for a few prisoners that they reserved for a special event. Almost four hundred Spaniards perished during the conflict. Those few remaining were lined up beneath the same trees upon which the French Huguenots had been hanged. De Gourges addressed them as they were strung up, then he posted a wooden sign with an inscription reading: "Not as Spaniards and mariners, but as traitors, robbers, and murderers."

So much for the Golden Rule. Outrage was expressed throughout Europe—but it would be centuries before the sins committed in the name of Christianity would be resolved.

Menéndez remained undaunted. He ordered a fort and a settlement be established at the tip of Port Royal in 1566, where René Ribaut's Charlesfort lay in ruins. It was dubbed Santa Elena. The settlers found the local Yamassee tribe to be friendly and supportive, supplying corn, fish, and wild game.

Pedro Menéndez de Avilés, *adelantado* of Florida, died in 1574 while on a mission to Spain. During Menéndez's absence, Don Diego de Velasco, one of Pedro Menéndez's two sons-in-law and lieutenant governor, served as interim governor. Don Diego continued in that position following Menéndez's death. Menéndez's daughter, Catalina, then inherited the title of *adelantado* of Florida, and ultimately her husband, Hernando de Miranda, was appointed governor. Miranda, however, did not actually arrive at Santa Elena until February 1576.

During the years that Don Diego served as interim governor, he had several run-ins with settlers and mistreated the Natives residing in the vicinity now known as Parris Island, South Carolina. This poor relationship with the Natives led to a series of attacks on Santa Elena. The loss of thirty soldiers in these attacks ultimately forced the temporary abandonment of both the fort and the town at Santa Elena in late summer of 1576. One story has it that the soldiers' wives revolted, took the Spanish ship's captain prisoner and forced him to set sail for Spain. This early instance of women's suffrage occurred as the once-friendly Yamassees rained fire arrows down on the Spaniards' thatched huts. As the soldiers and settlers waited to cross the bar to depart Port Royal Sound, they were able to see the town and fort burning to the ground.

THE ENGLISH

On Roanoke Island the Englishmen were entertained, with a refined hospitality, by the mother of King Wingina (who was absent); and wherever they went, friendship was the rule. To the feelings of the strangers, everything on the islands and on the main was charming. Nature was then garnished in all her summer wealth, and to the eyes of the Englishmen her beauties there were marvelous. Magnificent trees were draped with luxuriant vines clustered with growing grapes, and the forest swarmed with birds of sweetest songs and beautiful plumage. After gathering what information they could about the neighboring country, Barlow and Amidas departed for England (August 1585), with their company, attended by Manteo and Wanchese, two dusky lords of the woods and waters.

—*Our Country*, published in 1800

When the first English settlers ventured to America's shores, there were an estimated 1 million Natives living throughout what is now the United States. In general, they were peaceable and religious within their own communities and hospitable to strangers. However, they were capable of being very vicious when crossed or threatened. Their culture of stoicism and their ability to live in harmony with nature made them excellent warriors, despite their limited resources—and they were vicious enemies.

By the time that Queen Elizabeth I acted upon Sir Walter Raleigh's advice to colonize the New World, atrocities inflicted against the Native people by earlier exploring parties and settlers had infused hostility and distrust among the tribes. Realizing that they were no match for soldiers in armor and breastplates with "firing sticks" capable of killing from great distances, the Natives relied on cunning and guile to gain advantage. Fearing the inevitable of these foreigners permanently settling on their lands and destroying their hunting grounds, the tribes formed alliances to resist the Europeans.

The conflict between the Native and European cultures seemed inevitable, given the choices made for leadership of the new colonies. Too few were enlightened men such as Thomas Harriot, a man of keen observation who was Sir Walter Raleigh's accountant and mathematical mentor, who looked upon everything with the eye of a Christian philosopher. He perceived that the best way to establish viable colonies was to treat the Natives kindly as friends and neighbors. He deprecated the conduct of Sir Richard Grenville, whom Raleigh put in charge of the Roanoke colonization venture, and tried to quench the fires of revenge that Grenville's cruelty kindled.

Harriot befriended Chief Wingina, sharing his Bible and his religion with the chief. When the chief became ill, he dismissed his medicine men and conjurers and called for Harriot to attend to him and pray for him. When Wingina recovered, many of his tribe embraced Christianity.

Grenville, however, responded with terror and intimidation. Upon returning with supplies for the small band of settlers at Roanoke, he sent Manteo, one of the Natives who served as interpreter, to precede the party to the mainland to announce their arrival. Grenville soon followed him with Harriot and others. For eight days they explored the country and were hospitably entertained everywhere. While they were being hosted at one Native village, however, a silver cup was stolen from the English. When it was not immediately restored on demand, Grenville ordered the whole town to be burned and the standing corn around it destroyed. A flame of indignation, furious and destructive, was kindled in the Native mind, which could not be quenched. Unaware of the consequences of his act, Grenville left the colonists and returned to England with his ships.

No one knows for sure what happened to the ill-fated colony. But many believe that no sooner had Grenville's sails disappeared over the horizon than the Roanoke settlement was raided. As survivors fled northward they apparently were met by Powhatan's warriors, who dispatched all who remained.

> The reason why worry kills more people than work is that more people worry than work.
>
> —Robert Frost

Many early attempts at setting up colonies failed simply because the settlers lacked the skills needed to ensure survival in the raw environment of this virgin land. Ironically, had the Natives not been so compassionate and sensitive to the newcomers' needs, most of the settlements would have failed because the colonists were more interested in finding gold and silver than in working the land.

Early Jamestown was no exception. Captain John Smith was a strong, intelligent leader, but half of the settlers who arrived in 1607 were described as "gentlemen" who considered themselves too refined for common work—the

other half of the settlers were artisans, craftsmen, soldiers, and laborers, including a tailor, a barber, and two surgeons among them. Smith ordered them
all to work a minimum of six hours per day. But while Smith was absent,
the gentlemen not only refused to work, they also failed to take care of basic
health needs. After eight months, only 38 of the original 120 pioneers were
still alive. New settlers arrived, who were no better equipped than the first.
Many died of starvation during the "starving time" of 1608–1609. Yet all
about them lay fertile ground that only lacked planting of seed and its tilling
and harvesting to sustain their needs.

When Smith first met Wahunsunacock—more commonly known as "Powhatan," leader of the Powhatan Confederation of Algonquian tribes number-
ing over fourteen thousand—he told him that the English did not plan on
staying in Virginia. As more settlers arrived, however, the chief considered
wiping out the small colony. He led an assault against the Jamestown settlers
shortly after Smith departed for England to treat severe burns resulting from
an explosion. Smith returned and made peace with Powhatan and the settlers
began to thrive.

When his favorite daughter, Pocahontas, embraced Christianity, changed
her name to Rebecca, and married John Rolfe, Powhatan pledged that his
confederation would let the settlers live in peace—but he remained suspicious. When his daughter and her son Tom sailed to England with John Rolfe
in 1617, Powhatan sent his adviser, Tomocome, along to count how many
Englishmen there were in the far land. The population of London was about
three hundred thousand. When Tomocome returned with his report, Powhatan
became despondent at the loss of his daughter, who died of disease, and the
realization that he and his people would never be able to stop the steady emi-
gration of the English into their lands.

Chief Powhatan died in 1618 and leadership passed to his younger brother,
Opechancanough, who believed that the English intended to seize the lands
of his empire and exterminate his race. Opechancanough planned an attack
on all English settlements throughout Virginia. The settlers lived primarily
on farms spread around the countryside. They were lulled into believing that
the Powhatans were not a threat—even to the point of inviting them into their
homes for meals and teaching them how to hunt with firearms, which was
strictly forbidden by the Jamestown Council.

Many Powhatans visited their English "friends" the evening of March
30, 1622. The settlers invited them to spend the night and share a meal with
them the next day. At noon the next day, thousands of Natives painted for
war rushed out from the dense woods to attack the remote settlements. Those
Natives sharing a meal suddenly drew tomahawks and knives to slaughter
their hosts and all their families. In the space of an hour 350 men, women,

and children were slain. Only the settlers living in Jamestown escaped the mayhem, thanks to Chanco, a Christian Native who heard of the conspiracy the evening before the massacre. He hastened to Jamestown to warn a friend of impending danger. The alarm spread, but far too late to reach the more remote settlements. The people at Jamestown repulsed their assailants and so averted the blow that might have extinguished the colony. Those at a distance who survived the carnage beat back the attacks and then fled to Jamestown. In the course of a few days, eighty inhabited plantations were reduced to eight. But a large part of the colony was saved.

The settlers retaliated quickly, waging all-out war on the Powhatan people. After the Indian uprising in 1622, the colonists gave up attempts to Christianize and live peacefully with the Powhatans. For over a decade, the English systematically razed villages, seizing or destroying crops, killing men and women, and capturing children. The English presence expanded rapidly as the Powhatan empire declined. In 1644, Opechancanough rallied his people for one final attempt to force the English off their land. Hundreds of colonists were killed, but the English captured and shot Opechancanough. Treaties were made with his successor, severely restricting the Powhatan people's territory and confining them to small reservations. By 1669, the Powhatan population in the area dropped to about eighteen hundred—almost one-tenth of its size just sixty years before. By 1722, many of the tribes comprising Chief Powhatan's former empire were reported extinct.

A QUEST FOR INDEPENDENCE

Government is not reason. Government is not eloquence. It is force. And, like fire, it is a dangerous servant and a fearful master.

—George Washington

As new settlers poured into the Atlantic seaboard colonies, the Native Americans were pushed beyond the Allegheny Mountains. The French employed them as allies during the French and Indian War. In fact, throughout the war, both the British and the French provided their Native allies with steel scalping knives specifically designed for that purpose. In frustration, the British became desperate and applied such horrible tactics as inflicting biological warfare on the Natives.

Toward the end of the war, Sir Jeffrey Amherst, commander in chief of the British forces in America, wrote to one of his underlings, a colonel who was then struggling against a particularly volatile Native American revolt on the western frontier, "Could it not be contrived to send smallpox among these disaffected tribes of Indians? We must use every stratagem in our power to reduce them." Evidently the colonel complied, as evidence shows the offending tribes suffered from the ravages of smallpox after the colonel presented the Natives with gifts of infected blankets.

Eventually, diplomacy won out and the British signed the Treaty of Easton with the Ohio River Valley Native Americans, which promised that if the Natives chose not to fight for the French, the British would not settle the lands west of the Allegheny Mountains after the war.

However, conflicts between the colonists and the Natives continued, at great expense to the British Crown. King George II wanted the colonists to pay some of that expense with higher taxes. He issued the Proclamation of 1763 prohibiting colonists from moving westward over the Appalachian Mountains.

Not only did this and other proclamations anger the colonists, but it frustrated their hopes of gaining new fertile land beyond the mountains and gave unfair advantage to Crown hunters and traders who monopolized the fur trade with the Native Americans.

Many colonial leaders fought with the British during the French and Indian War. They witnessed the raw beauty and bounty of the western lands beyond the mountains. They saw it as their birthright and resented being restrained by a king thousands of miles away. The colonies declared their independence and prepared for war.

> In the beginning of a change, the patriot is a scarce man, brave, hated, and scorned. When his cause succeeds, however, the timid join him, for then it costs nothing to be a patriot.
>
> —Mark Twain

Terror permeated every aspect of the American Revolution. This was civil war at its most intimate . . . neighbor against neighbor . . . family against family. In the beginning the Loyalists (also called Tories) outnumbered the "Rebels." In fact, by 1779, there were more Americans fighting with the British than with Washington! There were no less than twenty-one regiments of Loyalists (estimated to total 6,500 to 8,000 men each, or between 150,000 and 160,000 men) serving in the British army. Washington reported his field army numbered 3,468. About a third of Americans opposed the Revolution.

Back in July 1776, there were an estimated 2.5 million people living in the colonies. English farmers settled in New England villages; Dutch, German, Swedish, Scotch-Irish, and English farmers settled on isolated Middle Colony farms; English and some French farmers settled on plantations in tidewater and isolated Southern Colony farms in the Piedmont; Spanish immigrants, mostly lower-middle-class and indentured servants, settled the Southwest and California.

The Loyalist majorities were primarily located in Pennsylvania, New York, and the southern colonies of South Carolina and Georgia. Throughout the colonies, they represented a large minority of the elites in their respective communities.

On October 6, 1775, Congress passed a resolution calling for the arrest of all Loyalists who are dangerous to "the liberties of America." Many of the Loyalists fled north to other British colonies in what would become Canada. Patriots arrested some of those who remained behind. Some were tarred and feathered, others whipped, beaten, and abused by mobs of angry revolutionists. Lynchings occurred on both sides of the conflict.

Even before the first shots of rebellion were fired at Concord Bridge, "long hunters" were blazing trails into the wilderness to the West. Many of these adventurers were Scots and Irish immigrants with little love for the British. Many married Native American women—some of their offspring became leaders within their tribes. Others served as scouts and soldiers in the revolutionary militia that engaged the British and their Native allies operating in the frontier. Still others, such as Daniel Boone and Simon Kenton, began to lead settlers into this "dark and bloody ground" called Kentucky to settle.

The Native tribes resisted this incursion into what they considered to be their hunting grounds. Tecumseh, a minor Shawnee war chief, became the leading architect of a plan to unite all Native American tribes against inevitable domination by the whites flooding into their lands from the east. To this end, Tecumseh aligned his warriors with the British and launched a wave of terror throughout what would become known as Ohio, Kentucky, Indiana, and Tennessee. No pioneer settlement was safe. Captives were routinely scalped, burned at the stake, and their bodies mutilated.

Daniel Boone gained the respect of the Native tribes because of his courage. But even that failed to save his family from the horror of their oldest son, James, being skinned alive, nor his younger brother Israel of being slaughtered at the battle of Blue Licks (the last battle of the Revolution) and having his body chopped to bits.

Following the Revolution, thousands more settlers flooded across the mountains. Revolutionary War veterans were granted land in lieu of pay for serving. These grants were sold or given to younger sons and sometimes exchanged to satisfy debts.

As settlers cleared timber for farms and slaughtered buffalo wholesale for their valuable fur, the wildlife so central to Native American subsistence disappeared. In less than two generations huge herds were decimated. The tribes had no choice but to enter reservations or move west.

AMERICA'S FIRST WAR ON TERROR

Millions for defense, not a penny for tribute.

—Thomas Jefferson, 1800

As far back as the mid-1600s, marauding pirates were sponsored by a loose confederation of North African states tied together by a tacit fealty to the Turkish sultan in Constantinople. For almost two hundred years, they robbed, raped, ransomed, and sent countless thousands of souls into slavery or worse with impunity. Victims reported being fed near-starvation rations, beaten regularly, and put to work breaking rocks on chain gangs or scraping barnacles off ship hulls. Some of them were imprisoned for twelve years or more, waiting for their countrymen to save them—which at times came too late for those who died in captivity. Even the fledgling United States knuckled under following the Revolution by paying $80,000 annually in tribute—despite the objections of then U.S. Minister to France Thomas Jefferson.

In his autobiography, Jefferson wrote that in 1785 and 1786 he unsuccessfully "endeavored to form an association of the powers subject to habitual depredation from them. I accordingly prepared, and proposed to their ministers at Paris, for consultation with their governments, articles of a special confederation." Jefferson argued that "the object of the convention shall be to compel the piratical States to perpetual peace." Jefferson prepared a detailed plan for the interested states. "Portugal, Naples, the two Sicilies, Venice, Malta, Denmark, and Sweden were favorably disposed to such an association," Jefferson remembered, but there were "apprehensions" that England and France would follow their own paths, "and so it fell through."

So much for Jefferson's efforts at forming the first coalition to oppose terror!

It's not surprising then, that when Jefferson became president in 1801, he was prepared to go it alone against the "barbarians." He refused to accede to Tripoli's demands for an immediate payment of $225,000 and an annual payment of $25,000.

The pasha of Tripoli then declared war on the United States. Although as secretary of state and vice president Jefferson opposed developing an American navy capable of anything more than coastal defense, he then dispatched a squadron of naval vessels to the Mediterranean. As he declared in his first annual message to Congress:

> To this state of general peace with which we have been blessed, one only exception exists. [Tripoli], the least considerable of the Barbary States, came forward with demands unfounded either in right or in compact, and permitted

itself to announce war on our failure to comply before a given day. The style of the demand admitted but one answer. I sent a small squadron of frigates into the Mediterranean.

The American show of force quickly awed Tunis and Algiers into breaking their alliance with Tripoli. The humiliating loss of the frigate *Philadelphia* and the capture of her captain and crew in Tripoli in 1803, criticism from his political opponents, and even opposition within his own cabinet did not deter Jefferson from his chosen course during four years of war. The aggressive action of Commodore Edward Preble (1803–1804) forced Morocco out of the fight, and his five bombardments of Tripoli restored some order to the Mediterranean.

However, it was not until 1805 that a treaty brought an end to hostilities following a successful attack on Derna, Tripoli, by U.S. Navy Captain William Eaton, commanding a ragtag force of about fifty Christian and about five hundred Muslim mercenaries. The attack, spearheaded by Marine First Lieutenant Presely O'Bannon, commanding a detachment of seven Marines, supported by the American naval fleet under Commodore John Rogers, threatened to capture Tripoli and install the brother of Tripoli's pasha on the throne. Negotiated by Tobias Lear, former secretary to President Washington and now consul general in Algiers, the treaty of 1805 still required the United States to pay a ransom of $60,000 for each of the sailors held by the dey of Algiers, and so it went without Senatorial consent until April 1806.

Nevertheless, Jefferson was able to report in his sixth annual message to Congress in December 1806 that in addition to the successful completion of the Lewis and Clark expedition, "the states on the coast of Barbary seem generally disposed at present to respect our peace and friendship."

In fact, it was not until the second war with Algiers, in 1815, that naval victories by commodores William Bainbridge and Stephen Decatur led to treaties ending all tribute payments by the United States. However, European nations continued annual payments until the 1830s.

THE AMERICAN CIVIL WAR: SCORCHED-EARTH TACTICS AND BROTHER AGAINST BROTHER

I myself have seen in Missouri, Kentucky, Tennessee, and Mississippi, hundreds and thousands of women and children fleeing from your armies and desperadoes, hungry and with bleeding feet. . . . Now that war comes to you, you feel very different. You deprecate its horrors. . . . But these comparisons are idle. I want peace, and believe it can only be reached through union and war, and I will ever conduct war with a view to perfect an early success.

—General William Tecumseh Sherman,
Letter to the mayor and councilmen of Atlanta,
September 1864

On November 6, 1860, Abraham Lincoln, after declaring that "government cannot endure permanently half slave, half free," was elected president—the first Republican—receiving 180 of 303 possible electoral votes and 40 percent of the popular vote. Southern Americans were outraged, and on December 20, 1860, South Carolina seceded from the Union, followed within two months by Mississippi, Florida, Alabama, Georgia, Louisiana, and Texas. The fabric of our great democracy was rent apart.

The Confederate States of America was formed, with Kentuckian Jefferson Davis, a West Point graduate and former U.S. Army officer and senator from Mississippi, as president. Earlier, Davis had sought to find a compromise, declaring himself opposed to secession "as long as the hope of a peaceable remedy remained."

Abraham Lincoln was sworn in as the sixteenth president of the United States of America on March 4, 1861. At 4:30 a.m. on April 12, 1861, Confederates under General Pierre Beauregard opened fire on Fort Sumter in Charleston, South Carolina, with fifty cannons. The Civil War had begun.

The war was savage. Some of America's best and brightest military men—many classmates at West Point and sons of distinguished patriots who fought in the American Revolution—ended up on opposite sides of the conflict. Slavery certainly was a prominent issue, but for many, loyalties remained stronger to their home states than to the Republic.

Without doubt, the war must be considered as one of the most horrific episodes of our history. Families were rent apart—physically, psychologically, politically, and spiritually. Civilians suffered greatly as they were caught between the onslaughts of two great, determined armies. *This was terror to the nth degree!*

Although the Confederacy fought valiantly, they were outnumbered and outsupplied by the industrialized North. Gettysburg, Pennsylvania, became the South's high water mark. Thousands of Southern men were mowed down like sheaves of grain as they charged across open fields to attack fortified Union positions. Retreat became their only option.

General Ulysses S. Grant, determined to break the Confederacy's back, began an aggressive strategy of "total war." He launched aggressive attacks on the South's infrastructure in 1864. Blockades restricted resupply. Railheads were captured and rails destroyed. General William T. Sherman's relentless string of battles from Shiloh to Nashville, Stone River, Chattanooga, Rocky Face Ridge, and Resaca forced the Southern armies backward until they finally were almost eyeball to eyeball on the ridges surrounding Atlanta. On July 20, 1864, the battle of Atlanta was engaged.

The two armies maneuvered against each other. Both sides lost general officers to sharpshooters. For a time, it appeared that the Confederates might win the day—but Sherman's quick initiative to train an artillery barrage against a breech in his lines forced General John Bell Hood to withdraw. Casualties were a total of 12,140—3,641 for the Union and 8,499 for the Confederate States of America.

Sherman then imposed a siege on the city until August 25. He entered the city on September 2. Two days later, Sherman issued an order for the inhabitants to leave the town within five days so the city might be prepared for military purposes. He deemed the measure humane, under the circumstances, for he expected the Confederates to attack him. When Hood pleaded with Sherman to withdraw his order, he replied, "God will judge me in good time, and He will pronounce whether it be more humane to fight with a town full of women and the families of a brave people at our backs, or to remove them in time to places of safety among their own friends." In a few days Atlanta was thoroughly evacuated of civilians.

After setting fire to Atlanta's warehouses and railroad facilities, General Sherman began his "March to the Sea" with sixty-two thousand men on November 15, 1864. President Lincoln on advice from Grant approved the idea. "I can make Georgia howl!" Sherman boasted. He was determined to destroy the South's will to further prosecute the war.

Hood's Rebel Army of twenty-three thousand was crushed on December 15–16, 1864, at Nashville by fifty-five thousand federals, including black troops under General George H. Thomas. The Confederate Army of Tennessee ceased as an effective fighting force.

Sherman reached Savannah, Georgia, on December 21, 1864, leaving behind a three-hundred-mile-long path of destruction sixty miles wide, all the way from Atlanta. Sherman then telegraphed President Lincoln, offering him Savannah as a Christmas present. Meanwhile, Grant pressed the attacks in Virginia, forcing General Robert E. Lee to withdraw from Richmond. Lee's nine-day retreat ended at Appomattox Court House, where he surrendered his army on April 9, 1865.

More American soldiers died during the Civil War than in all the other wars Americans have fought in, combined. Three million uniformed men entered the four-year struggle. A total of more than six hundred thousand soldiers died (20 percent). Slightly more Union soldiers than Confederates made the supreme sacrifice—with more than four hundred thousand deaths resulting from disease, many of them while suffering inhumane conditions in military prison camps. More than four hundred thousand were wounded—resulting in one in three of every man engaged becoming a casualty.

Slash-and-burn tactics on both sides deprived civilians of their homes, and forced them to suffer the loss of their crops, livestock, and any means of livelihood. But the real terror came later.

Union soldiers assigned to protect the innocent too often exceeded their orders as they sought revenge of their own. The federal government was forced to pass the Posse Comitatus Act, which restrained federal troops from being used for law enforcement duties.

But the terror was not one-sided. As slaves were freed and the vanquished Southerners returned to what was left of their homes, self-proclaimed vigilantes organized as night riders in silk sheets who sought to right perceived wrongs with beatings, torching of homes, and the lynching of innocents. Domestic terrorism would plague Americans for generations to come.

Chapter Six

Domestic Terrorism

Our adversaries will keep evolving, national security and criminal threats will further converge, and old jurisdictional boundaries will become less and less relevant. If we are to address these trends successfully, we must be willing and able to evolve ourselves. The FBI must continue to build our intelligence capabilities, including a strong intelligence workforce. We must continue hiring and training personnel with technical expertise and foreign language skills. We must continue to seek new ways to share information and collaborate with partners in the Intelligence and Law Enforcement Communities. Above all, we must be agile, and encourage creativity, innovation, and strategic thinking. If we do all of these things, I am confident that we will out-network, out-think, and ultimately defeat our adversaries.

—Robert S. Mueller III,
Director, Federal Bureau of Investigation,
before the Senate Committee on Intelligence,
February 16, 2005

There have always been—and probably always will be—those individuals who feel disenfranchised and powerless. They just don't seem to fit in well on a social level. They immerse themselves in conspiracy theories and search for others to blame for their failures and disappointments. Sometimes they see themselves as ultra-religious or ultra-patriotic, and ready to sacrifice for what they believe. Too often, these people strike out with outrageous behavior, verbal abuse, twisted rhetoric—and sometimes violence.

For example, on October 15, 2005, about forty neo-Nazis associated with the National Socialist Movement in Roanoke, Virginia, planned to demonstrate in a neighborhood on the north side of Toledo, Ohio. They purported to be interested in demonstrating their support for residents who they say were being subjected to local black gang racial violence. Before the group began their march, however, they were confronted by protesters from the International Socialist Organization (the ISO), Anti-Racist Action (the ARA), and various members of the community, who counterdemonstrated against the Nazis.

Libertarian socialist news editor Bill White, in a press release posted on the neo-Nazi web page www.overthrow.com, said:

> We identified local communist leaders who have engaged in violent rhetoric several days ago and have had them under surveillance at the University of Toledo and elsewhere. We know who these people are, we have given extensive information on them and their activities to the police, and we feel confident that if they try to match their walk to their talk they will be arrested long before they have a chance to start a riot in the streets of North Toledo.

Police escorting the Nazis out of the neighborhood were pelted by rocks. The crowd of protesters and onlookers swelled to several hundred. The police fired tear gas and rubber and foam bullets to help disperse groups of rock-throwing gang members, without much effect. The raging gangs of youths eventually targeted a small neighborhood bar, which they broke into to steal liquor and then set afire. Several fire trucks that responded were pelted by rocks as the bar burned to the ground.

The police reported the arrest of 114 people on Sunday. Toledo declared a state of emergency and established an 8 p.m. to dawn curfew. The police announced that they would maintain a strong presence in the predominantly black community for the next few days.

To someone born during the Depression who grew up during World War II and who experienced the horrors inflicted on the world under the leadership of Germany's Adolph Hitler, Italy's Benito Mussolini, and Japanese Sh wa Emperor Hirohito, it is unbelievable that such an event could happen in an all-American city like Toledo.

Moreover, it's appalling that a march by a handful of radical outcasts and misfits should draw enough interest to be of concern, let alone be the subject of national and international news. But so it is in this global world of 24/7 news, which inundates the radio and television airwaves with hours of minutiae punctuated with tidbits of useful information.

Most shocking is that these are primarily American-born citizens pitted against other American-born citizens. Somehow, they have come to reject the basic tenets of equality and justice upon which "the land of the free and the home of the brave" was founded.

HOW SAFE IS AMERICA?

The FBI's Crime Clock for 2007 (www.fbi.gov/ucr/cius2007/about/crime
_clock.html) reported that there was an average of one murder committed
every 31.0 minutes, one forcible rape every 5.8 minutes, one robbery every
1.2 minutes, and one aggravated assault every 36.8 seconds.

According to the FBI's latest statistics, there were 7,624 hate crimes in 2007,
involving 9,006 offenses. Racial bias motivates more than half the single-bias
hate crime offenses reported; 66 percent were perpetrated because of an anti-
black bias, and 21.2 percent were due to an anti-white bias. Religious bias and
sexual-orientation bias each account for almost a fifth of all reported single-
bias hate crimes reported. Ethnicity or national origin bias prompted almost 15
percent of offenses, and disability bias spurred 0.5 percent of bias-motivated
offenses. Law enforcement reports that 1,400 single-bias hate crime offenses
resulted from a religious bias: 69.2 percent were an anti-Jewish bias, 10.9
percent were an anti-Islamic bias, 8.3 percent were an anti–other (unspecified)
religion bias, 5.5 percent were an anti-Catholic bias, 3.5 percent were an anti-
Protestant bias, and 0.9 percent were an anti-atheism/agnosticism bias. Nearly
2 percent (1.8 percent) of anti-religious hate crime offenses in 2007 were due
to a bias against groups of individuals of varying religions.

Within the 1,265 single-bias hate crime offenses perpetrated due to a
sexual-orientation bias, law enforcement identified 61.6 percent as having
an anti-male homosexual bias. In addition, 21.3 percent were due to an anti-
homosexual bias, 15.4 percent were committed because of an anti-female
homosexual bias, 1 percent were driven by an anti-heterosexual bias, and 0.6
percent involved an anti-bisexual bias.

HOW SAFE IS YOUR HOME?

An analysis of bias-motivated offenses with regard to location showed that
of the 3,844 incidents sparked by racial prejudice, 30.5 percent occurred at a
home or residence. Almost 19 percent (18.9 percent) occurred on a highway,
road, alley, or street, and 11.3 percent happened at a school or college.

Of the 1,343 incidents caused by religious intolerance, 29.8 percent occurred at a home or residence, and 16.9 percent took place at a church, synagogue, or temple. A school or college was the setting for 12.3 percent of the
total incidents attributed to a religious bias.

Incidents involving bias against a sexual orientation also occurred most
often in homes or residences—30.3 percent of the 1,239 incidents reported in
2003. Highways, roads, alleys, or streets were the location of 25.0 percent of

the incidents motivated by a sexual-orientation bias, and schools or colleges were the location for 11.9 percent of those incidents.

The Southern Poverty Law Center's website (www.tolerance.org/10_ways/index.html) points out:

> Somewhere in America . . . every hour, someone commits a hate crime. Every day at least eight blacks, three whites, three gays, three Jews, and one Latino become hate crime victims. Every week a cross is burned.
>
> Hate in America is a dreadful, daily constant. The dragging death of a black man in Jasper, Texas; the crucifixion of a gay man in Laramie, Wyo.; and post-9.11 hate crimes against hundreds of Arab Americans, Muslim Americans, and Sikhs are not "isolated incidents." They are eruptions of a nation's intolerance.
>
> Bias is a human condition, and American history is rife with prejudice against groups and individuals because of their race, religion, disability, sexual orientation, or other differences. The 20th century saw major progress in outlawing discrimination, and most Americans today support integrated schools and neighborhoods. But stereotypes and unequal treatment persist, an atmosphere often exploited by hate groups.

DEALING WITH A HERITAGE OF HATE

Is America unique in having this legacy of prejudice and hate? No—but it is our diversity and our openness that permit bias, prejudice, and hate to flourish for a time. We unknowingly welcome bigots and fanatics to our shores as we welcome downtrodden and oppressed immigrants from the world to share in our freedoms and opportunities.

Ironically, some ethnic groups who suffered from prejudice elsewhere choose to inflict prejudice on others when they arrive in America. Biases of every kind arrived with our early settlers, pioneers, and émigrés. Each new wave seems to suffer in their own way until they are assimilated or accepted—the latest being Muslims who suffer the negative fallout generated by the actions of militant Islamists bent on murder and mayhem to advance their twisted view of how the world should be.

America encourages tolerance and understanding of all religious and political views. But tolerance is a two-edged sword. It may encourage diversity—but it may also permit racism, prejudice, and bias to thrive for a season.

"BLEEDING KANSAS" AND THE KU KLUX KLAN

May 30, 1854, dawned as a pivotal point in our nation's history. The tide of national will was moving against the concept of slavery. Dozens of countries, including the possessions of the British and French empires, decided to abolish slavery.

President Franklin Pierce's signature on the Kansas-Nebraska Act permitted the citizens of newly formed territories to vote themselves into the Union as either slave or free. Political and moral passions exploded upon the Kansas frontier, as Southern settlers preached the principle of "popular sovereignty," which they believed would support their cause. By upholding their beliefs, 4 million Americans and their offspring could have been enslaved forever. But Northern settlers were equally fervent to bring their own prejudices and persuasions. The Northern alternative brought Kansas into the Union as a free state.

The United States prohibited slavery in the Northern states. The Missouri Compromise of 1820 provided that all land east of the Rockies located north of the southern border of Missouri would be organized as free territories. This compromise originally allowed Missouri to enter the union as a slave state. But the Kansas-Nebraska Act nullified the Missouri Compromise. Rev. Henry Ward Beecher raised funds to arm antislavery forces, in the belief that guns would be a stronger "moral" argument against proslavery men than the Bible. Abolitionist John Brown also took up arms, using the rifle and sword to press his beliefs that all men should be free.

Passions raged on both sides of the issue—and blood began to flow. With the election of Abraham Lincoln, the die was cast. The Union was torn apart as America's destiny was determined on the battlefields of the Civil War—and paid with the blood and sacrifice of 1 million of our youngest and bravest men.

After the war ended and Southerners were paroled back to their homes, emotions continued to run high. Some men who served honorably in war as raiding cavalry found it hard to settle down to the mundane occupations they worked before. Some, such as Quantrill's Raiders, the James brothers, and the Younger brothers continued their wild rides, holding up banks and escaping capture for years with the help of Confederate sympathizers.

Six middle-aged college students who were former Confederate officers founded the Ku Klux Klan (KKK) between December 1865 and a boring summer of 1866 in the town of Pulaski, Tennessee. The Civil War veterans, Captain John C. Lester, Major James R. Crowe, John D. Kennedy, Calvin Jones, Richard R. Reed, and Frank O. McCord, originally organized the KKK as a social club or fraternity. The name was constructed by combining the Greek "kyklos" (meaning "circle," which they transformed into "kuklux") with "clan." It was at first intended to be a humorous social club centering on practical jokes and hazing rituals.The men spent their leisure time in horseplay of various types, including wearing disguises to appear as ghosts of Confederate cavalrymen as they galloped about town after dark. They were amused to learn that their nightly appearances sometimes caused fear—particularly among former slaves in the area. They quickly took advantage of this effect, and the group began a rapid expansion aimed at resisting Reconstruction while attempting to restrict blacks from education, economic advancement, voting rights, and the right to bear arms.

Various factions formed in different towns, which led to a meeting in April 1867 to codify rules and organizational structure. Confederate General Nathan Bedford Forrest—declared by General Robert E. Lee as the best general on either side in the Civil War—was elected the KKK's first Grand Wizard and the Klan's national leader. But the Klan was an unruly bunch with many fringe groups who, though not Klan members, cloaked themselves in Klan costumes while they committed crimes against others with impunity. Forrest ordered the Klan to disband in 1869, stating that it was "being perverted from its original honorable and patriotic purposes, becoming injurious instead of subservient to the public peace."

Several states enacted anti-Klan laws, eventually leading to President Ulysses S. Grant's signing the Ku Klux Klan Act in 1971. That, coupled with the 1870 Force Act, was used to enforce the civil rights provisions of the Constitution in the 1964 murders of Chaney, Goodman, and Schwernethe; the 1965 murder of Viola Liuzzo; and the 1991 case *Bray v. Alexandria Women's Health Clinic*, which became an issue in the 2005 debate on the confirmation of John G. Roberts Jr.'s nomination to the Supreme Court.

These legal actions and their aggressive enforcement decimated the KKK—for a while. Other local organizations such as the White League, Red Shirts, saber clubs, and rifle clubs rose up to take its place. But none ever reached the strength and power of the KKK.

THE KKK'S REBIRTH

Thanks to the emerging popularity of a new entertainment medium, interest in the KKK was revived in 1915. D. W. Griffith's *Birth of a Nation* was an adaptation on the book and play *The Clansman* and the book *The Leopard's Spots*, both by Thomas Dixon. Both works glorified the original Klan. Dixon declared that his purpose in writing the book and the play was "to revolutionize northern sentiment by a presentation of history that would transform every man in my audience into a good Democrat!"

When the film premiered in Los Angeles, actors dressed as Klansmen were hired to ride by as a promotional stunt, and members of the newly reorganized Klan rode up and down the street at its later official premiere in Atlanta.

Unfortunately, the film created an unprecedented nationwide interest in the Klan. Unfortunate as well was Griffith's use of a quote from President Woodrow Wilson's *History of the American People*: "The white men were roused by a mere instinct of self-preservation . . . until at last there had sprung into existence a great Ku Klux Klan, a veritable empire of the South, to protect the Southern country."

That same year a factory worker named Mary Phagan was sexually assaulted and murdered. Leo Frank, the Jewish factory manager, was accused of the crime, which was sensationalized in newspaper accounts. He was convicted of murder. But the trial was very questionable because the Georgia judge asked that Frank and his counsel not be present when the verdict was announced due to the violent mob of people surrounding the courthouse. Frank's appeals failed, though Supreme Court Justice Oliver Wendell Holmes dissented, condemning the intimidation of the jury as failing to provide due process of law. The governor commuted Frank's sentence to life imprisonment. Then a mob calling itself the Knights of Mary Phagan kidnapped Frank from the prison farm and lynched him.

Georgia politician and publisher Thomas E. Watson, the editor for *The Jeffersonian* magazine at the time of Frank's trial and later a leader in the reorganization of the Klan, was elected to the U.S. Senate. Throughout the 1920s, the Klan gathered strength in numbers and political clout. Membership peaked at 4 million in 1920, but then began to drop precipitously due to scandals of some of its leaders—especially Indiana veterinarian James Colescott's association with Nazi-sympathizer organizations just prior to World War II. He was forced to disband the Klan in 1944—yet independent remnants remain, although membership dwindled to less than 2,000 by 1970.

VICTIMS FIGHT BACK

In 1958, a group of Klansmen decided to intimidate two Lumbee Native Americans whose "crime" was associating with white people. They placed burning crosses on their lawns and then attended a nearby nighttime rally. Suddenly the Klansmen were surrounded by over a hundred armed Lumbees. Gunfire was exchanged and the Klan retreated.

As the Klan focused on resisting civil rights during the '60s, they committed a number of outrages, including church bombings and murders. The FBI infiltrated the Klan's ranks and others began to bring million-dollar lawsuits against the Klan. Blacks, no longer intimidated by the Klan, began to ridicule them and taunt them. Membership was estimated to be about three thousand in 2005.

Many of the Klan's prospective members are now drawn to other hate groups such as the skinhead racist subgroups, Christian Identity and neo-Nazis.

RISE OF THE MILITIAS

> Who are the militia? Are they not ourselves? Is it feared, then, that we shall turn our arms each man against his own bosom? Congress shall have no power to disarm the militia. Their swords, and every other terrible implement of the soldier, are the birth-right of an American. . . . The un-limited power of the sword is not in the hands of either the federal or state governments, but where I trust in God it will ever remain, in the hands of the People.
>
> —Tench Coxe, political economist, 1788

Say the word "militia" today and you might either get a blank stare, or some-one might say, "Oh, yeah—those weirdos in Montana." Or they might think that you're referring to the Minuteman Project, headed by Jim Gilchrist, to monitor the Mexican border.

Unfortunately, the term "militia" no longer has the patriotic connotation it once enjoyed, because of several groups that wrap their organizations in the protection of the Second Amendment to the Constitution but pursue agendas of hate and racism. Even legitimate militias come under attack from gun control advocates who want to impose registration and government control on all firearms.

The current rhetoric enjoined by both sides of the so-called "gun control is-sue" beclouds the Founding Fathers' original intent in ensuring the individual right to bear arms as defined by the Second Amendment to the Constitution: "A well regulated Militia being necessary to the security of a free State, the right of the people to keep and bear arms shall not be infringed."

Key to understanding the full intent, one must review amplifying remarks by the contemporaries of those who drafted the Amendment. Virginia's Pat-rick Henry probably defined it in the most succinct manner when he said: "The great object is that every man be armed. . . . Everyone who is able may have a gun."

The American colonies first authorized militia in 1687. The charters of every American colony included the authority to create militia units separate and distinguishable from "troops." In general, all white "able-bodied free males" were ordered to maintain personal arms and to train with their local militias. Their model was the Massachusetts Minute Men, whose shots were "heard round the world" at Lexington when they ambushed the British army as it marched on Concord.

These early citizen-soldiers were needed to defend their communities from hostile Natives, marauding bands of bandits, and foreign invaders. Their guns were also needed to provide wild game for the dinner table. But the right—indeed, the responsibility—to bear arms as envisioned by the Constitution's framers was actually directly aimed at the threat of any tyrannical government—foreign or domestic—that might be tempted to unduly limit the personal freedoms so dearly preserved by the American Revolution.

Militias by and large evolved from mandatory service to volunteer units. The 1792 Uniform Militia Act, enacted by Congress to organize, arm, and discipline the militia, specified that militiamen purchase and maintain their own weapons. With little federal or state support—and with no penalties placed on states refusing to maintain their militias—official militia units almost died out.

The federal government called out the militia in 1805, 1807, 1812, 1814–1815, 1817, 1826, and 1840. But efforts to train and reform the units were in vain. Most states officially abolished compulsory militia duty during the 1840s. Those remaining volunteer units later evolved into the National Guard. But there is little comparison between the National Guard and today's militia.

The U.S. Code details federal law concerning employment of militia:

311. Militia: Composition and Classes

(a) The militia of the United States consists of all able-bodied males at least 17 years of age and, except as provided in section 313 of title 32, under 45 years of age [which deals with membership in the National Guard] who are, or who have made a declaration of intention to become, citizens of the United States and of female citizens of the United States who are members of the National Guard.

(b) The classes of the militia are—

(1) the organized militia, which consists of the National Guard and the Naval Militia; and

(2) the unorganized militia, which consists of the members of the militia who are not members of the National Guard or the Naval Militia.

It's the unorganized militia that is being targeted by left-wing anti–gun control proponents and others who are concerned with the rise of racist and hate groups who attempt to cloak their militant programs within the Second Amendment.

The Southern Poverty Law Center began tracking white supremacists and hate groups in 1971. They used litigation to thwart the activities of these groups and sponsored education programs to encourage tolerance. Despite their efforts and those of others, the rise of an antigovernment "patriot" movement and the militia groups it spawned caused concern in the 1990s. In 1994, a letter by Morris Dees addressed the Center's concerns about extremists in the militia movement to then attorney general Janet Reno and attorneys general of six states. Dees warned that the "mixture of armed groups and those who hate" was a "recipe for disaster."

One model of these hate groups was the Posse Comitatus—an antigovernment movement active in the 1970s and 1980s. Because the Posse was convinced that the federal government is controlled by "enemies" (usually Jews), Posse adherents resisted paying taxes as well as other duties of law-abiding citizens.

In the 1970s, Posses attracted Klan members and other anti-Semites (among them David Duke), and in 1983, these groups gained nationwide attention when active Posse member Gordon Kahl murdered two federal marshals in North Dakota and became a fugitive. When Kahl died in a shoot-out with Arkansas law enforcement officers, Posses and other Christian Identity groups made him a martyr.

Aspects of the Posse's ideology, most notably its fierce hostility to federal authority, reverberate among today's militia and common law court activists. Many of its leaders are Christian Identity adherents, whose ideology formed the basis of later groups such as the Montana Freemen. The Posse died away in the late 1980s, but former Posse leader James Wickstrom restarted it in the 1990s solely as a white supremacist group, shedding most of the group's pseudo-legal theories.

MILITANT ACTIVISTS AND THE OKLAHOMA CITY BOMBING

Timothy McVeigh

Timothy James McVeigh no doubt saw himself as a patriot. The twenty-seven-year-old certainly looked the part of the all-American boy—lean, close-cropped brush-cut hair, conservative yet casual dress. He received his first sidearm in 1987 and worked for a while as a security guard. He reportedly was passionate about the right to bear arms and drew his inspiration from the 1984 Patrick Swayze epic *Red Dawn* and a survivalist book titled *The Turner Diaries*. The hero of the latter—Earl Turner—responds to gun control by making a truck bomb and blowing up the Washington FBI Building.

McVeigh was a decorated veteran of the U.S. Army, having served in the Gulf War, where he was awarded a Bronze Star. He was an expert gunner

Oklahoma City, Oklahoma, April 26, 1995. The devastated Murrah Building following the Oklahoma City bombing that killed 168 people, injured more than 500, and damaged more than 300 buildings. FEMA News Photo

with the 25 mm cannon on the lightly armored Bradley fighting vehicle that he served in during the Gulf War. No doubt he was convinced that he acted to defend the Constitution when he blew up the Alfred P. Murrah Federal Building in Oklahoma City on April 19, 1995, killing 168 men, women, and little children. He chose as his WMD a two-ton load of ammonium nitrate agricultural fertilizer with nitromethane racing fuel as an accelerant. He apparently saw himself as a crusader—an avenging warrior and a self-styled American hero. But did he really act alone?

McVeigh's partner in crime, Terry Nichols, frequently visited the Philippines, where his wife was working on a degree in physical therapy. He sometimes traveled to the Philippines alone, while she remained in Kansas. Her home, Cebu City, was reputed to be a base for several militant organizations, including Liberation Army of the Philippines, the Communist Huk, and the al-Qaeda affiliate Abu Sayyaf. Stephen Jones, the trial attorney who first represented McVeigh, cited evidence of a meeting in Davao City in Mindanao in 1992 or 1993, when Ramzi Yousef, Abdul Hakim Murad, Wali Khan Amin Shah, and a "farmer" met to discuss the Oklahoma bombing. Jones said the FBI was aware of the meeting.

Ted Kaczynski

Theodore John Kaczynski, PhD, also known as the Unabomber, briefly shared time with McVeigh in prison, describing him as very intelligent. Kaczynski has been described as a Polish-American terrorist who felt a need to fight against what he perceived as the evils of technological progress by sending mail bombs to various people over almost eighteen years, killing three and wounding twenty-nine. He was the target of the FBI's most expensive manhunt ever.

Eric Rudolph

During the 1996 Summer Olympics in Atlanta, Georgia, a bomb hidden in a backpack at the park sent nails and screws through a crowd, killing one woman and wounding 111 other people. Shortly thereafter, two bombs exploded at an Alabama clinic—a smaller one to attract police to the scene, then a larger one that killed an officer. Six people were wounded. The following year a bomb at a gay nightclub in Atlanta wounded five people.

After hiding out for five years in the Appalachian Mountains in North Carolina, Eric Rudolph, a thirty-eight-year-old man who admitted to the triple string of deadly blasts, was finally captured by police. At his trial, Rudolph said his bombings were motivated by his hatred of abortion and of a federal government that lets it continue. Authorities suspect that some residents near where he hid may have provided clandestine support to the fugitive because they support his actions. After negotiating a plea bargain to save his own life, Rudolph was sentenced to three life sentences.

Animal Rights Activists

Hardest for some to comprehend are those who express compassion for the use of animals in medical research, yet seem to have no qualms about killing fellow human beings. ActivistCash.com, which traces where the money to support militant activist groups comes from, characterizes Dr. Jerry Vlasak as "a physician with an odd interpretation of the Hippocratic Oath's dictum that doctors should 'do no harm'":

> As a representative of the misnamed Physicians Committee for Responsible Medicine (PCRM), Vlasak told the "Animal Rights 2003" convention that he would endorse the murder of physicians whose research work requires the use of lab rats and other animals.

"I don't think you'd have to kill—assassinate—too many vivisectors," Vlasak said, "before you would see a marked decrease in the amount of vivisection going on. And I think for 5 lives, 10 lives, 15 human lives, we could save a million, 2 million, 10 million non-human lives." When one woman in the audience disagreed, saying that Vlasak's approach was no different from that of abortion-clinic bombers, Vlasak was undeterred. "Absolutely," he countered. "I think they had a great strategy going."

On April 21, 2009, for the first time an accused domestic terrorist was added to the FBI's list of "Most Wanted" terror suspects. Animal rights activist Daniel Andreas San Diego, a thirty-one-year-old computer specialist from Berkeley, California, is wanted for the bombing of two offices in California in 2003. No one was injured in the attacks, but officials have offered a $250,000 reward for his capture. He has a tattoo on his abdomen with the words "It only takes a spark" and pictures of burning and collapsed buildings tattooed. He is believed to be in Costa Rica. He is the twenty-fourth person on the list and the only domestic terrorist.

Unfortunately, America is not safe—from enemies either foreign or domestic!

Chapter Seven

International Terrorism

Terrorism in the modern sense emerged around the mid-nineteenth century. During the French Revolution in the 1780s and 1790s, the harshest period of the rule of the Committee of Public Safety was known as "The Terror." This is the first known use of the term "terrorism," although this is not strictly applicable to the modern use of the word.

Ironically, the word "assassin" is more than a thousand years old and comes from a Shi'ite Muslim sect called the Nizari Isma'ilis, who were also known as the hashashin because they used hashish when going out to kill. They were fighting on two fronts—against the Sunni Muslims and against the armies of the Christian Crusaders.

The Hashashin, or "Brotherhood of the Assassins," as they became known, launched a reign of terror, including the slaughter of women and children. How little has changed!

In 1867 the Irish Republican Brotherhood, a revolutionary nationalist group supported by Irish-Americans, carried out a number of attacks in England. These were the first acts of "republican terrorism," which were to become a feature of British history for the next 120 years. These Fenians were the forerunners of the Irish Republican Army. The ideology of the group was Irish nationalism, and their continued aim was to drive the British out of Ireland.

About the same time the intelligentsia in Russia, impatient with the slow pace of czarist reforms, worked to transform peasant discontent into open revolution. Anarchists like Mikhail Bakunin argued that progress was impossible without destruction. Their objective was the complete destruction of the state. Anything that contributed to this goal was regarded as moral. As explosives become more available, the anarchists had a powerful weapon to challenge those charged with protecting the state—the military and the police. Organized into secret societies like The People's Will, Russian revolutionaries launched a campaign of terror against the state that climaxed in 1881 when Czar Alexander II was killed in a bomb attack. The authorities' response was swift and ruthless and led to more than twenty years of state-sponsored terrorism. However, rather than stamping out dissent, the repression fueled the revolutionaries, and in 1918 they overthrew the Czarists and set up their own communist government.

In 1893 the Internal Macedonian Revolutionary Organization (IMRO) was founded in Thessaloniki, now in Greece but then part of the Ottoman Empire. Driven by Slavic nationalism, the organization acquired a reputation for ferocious attacks, including the 1934 assassination of Alexander I of Yugoslavia during a state visit to France.

The Fenians and the IMRO were the prototypes of today's terrorism. Both were fighting for what they believed in—national freedom. Ironically, neither was totally successful. While an independent Irish Republic was created, the six northern counties (Ulster) continue to be part of the British Isles; Macedonia was absorbed into Yugoslavia and didn't achieve its independence until 1991.

One problem with the term "terrorist" is that it depends which side you are on. It is ironic that many people once branded as terrorists are now called freedom fighters and considered heroes by their own people. These include Israeli statesman Yitzhak Shamir, Palestine Liberation Organization leader Yasser Arafat, and former South African President Nelson Mandela. All at one time were hunted men with prices on their head.

Three major events in the first half of the twentieth century—the Russian Revolution and the two World Wars—helped fuel nationalist sentiments. The Russian Revolution showed that an armed populist movement could topple an authoritarian, repressive regime. And peace treaties signed after the two World Wars inflamed many populations, as they saw their countries disappearing or being annexed.

As a result, many groups emerged in the twentieth century. They had different goals and different methods for achieving them. For some the goal was politics, for others it was religion—and some were simply groups of anarchists out to destroy the established order.

The most striking difference between terrorism in the first half and the second half of the twentieth century was tactics. In the first five decades, targets were singled out; by and large, care was taken to minimize innocent casualties. The last five decades of the century were marked by a crescendo in violence, with the aim being to cause maximum damage and destruction. The perpetrators wanted to cause maximum economic damage and truly cause terror.

State-sponsored terrorism became a feature of the Cold War. Different countries supported different terrorist groups, providing bases, funding, arms, and training, with the aim that these groups would destablilize rival governments.

An important date that can be attributed to the internationalizing of terrorism is 1966. That year Cuba hosted the Tri-Continental Conference, although the Soviet Union laid down the agenda. Terrorist groups from Europe, the Middle East, Asia, Africa, and Latin America attended and many started to build alliances. This collaboration included sharing finances, resources, and intelligence and led to a number of joint operations. It also launched a decade-long wave of terror in Europe and the Middle East.

In Germany, the Red Army Faction (German) allied itself with Black September (Palestinian); in France, Action Direct (French) allied with the Red Army Faction and the Red Army Brigade (Italian); in Japan, the Japanese Red Army allied with the Popular Front for the Liberation of Palestine.

The late '60s also saw the rapid rise of religious-based terrorism and the expansion of radical Islam in the Middle East. After the 1967 war in which Israel defeated Jordan, Egypt, and Syria and took control of the Golan Heights (from Syria), East Jerusalem and the West Bank (from Jordan), and the Gaza Strip and the Sinai Peninsula (from Egypt), the use of conventional war as a means to destroy Israel ended and the use of terror to focus attention on Israel and the Palestinians in the occupied territories began. This was accompanied by an increase in the use of suicide bombers.

Suicide bombing was a widely used tactic by the Japanese military during World War II. Kamikaze pilots caused massive damage by crashing their explosives-packed aircraft into targets, especially ships at sea. Following World War II, Viet Minh "death volunteers" were used against the French colonial army. In 1972 three Japanese used grenades and automatic rifles at Lod airport in Tel-Aviv, killing twenty-six people and wounding more than a hundred. The attackers were members of the Japanese Red Army (JRA), a terrorist organization created in 1969 and allied to the Popular Front for the Liberation of Palestine. It was the first suicide operation conducted in Israel.

Suicide bombing, however, is not a product of the twentieth century. It is a tactic that has been used by extremely committed groups for more than a thousand years.

It emerged again in the 1980s as a highly effective, highly lethal weapon, particularly among extreme militant groups whose members were willing to die as martyrs for the cause. It was a tactic used extensively by the Tamil Tigers in Sri Lanka and by the Kurdistan Workers Party and later adopted by Hamas, Hezbollah, al-Qaeda, and other extremist Islamic terrorist groups.

It is also a very cost-effective weapon if you have enough volunteers. A walking bomb can gain access to crowded places that a vehicle cannot. The bomber is usually wearing a specially constructed vest designed to carry up to forty pounds of explosives and shrapnel—usually nails, screws, and ball bearings—to inflict maximum damage. The vest is worn under everyday clothing and when it is detonated, the blast fans out in all directions. Shrapnel is responsible for about 90 percent of all casualties.

As terrorism increased globally, a nunber of states actively supported particular groups. Iran supported Hezbollah; Libya supported Abu Nidal; and Iraq, Cuba, Sudan, and Algeria provided training camps, economic support, and political support to other terrorist groups.

If the 1960s was the decade of the internationalization of terrorism, the 1970s was the decade of air terrorism, with more than a score of American and European passenger aircraft hijacked. The rise to power of Ayatollah Khomeini in 1979 further inflamed the situation, as militant Islamic groups increased their attacks in the Middle East.

The 1980s was the decade of hostage taking, and this was also a significant period because for the first time the United States became a principal target. Americans overseas were taken hostage, and U.S. embassies and interests were bombed.

Another major change in terrorist tactics between the 1960s–1980s and the 1980s to the end of the century was communications. Terrorist acts are committed to draw attention to a cause as part of the struggle to achieve their stated objectives. From the 1960s to the 1980s, terrorist acts were almost always followed by a statement from one group or another claiming responsibility. The rationale was to (a) commit a terrorist attack to get publicity and (b) claim responsibility to get further publicity and hopefully to encourage people to think about the merits of your cause. Toward the end of the century, the aim switched to getting maximum publicity courtesy of satellite television, cable news, and round-the-clock coverage of events.

A major downside of terrorism, however, is that the more horrific the atrocity, the more coverage it generates, so terrorists have a vested interest in planning and staging ever bigger events. When the first U.S. soldier was killed in Iraq, it was a major news story. Subsequent deaths, as tragic as they were, got pushed farther and farther down the page until they no longer even merited a place on the front page. In order to get back on the front pages, the terrorists have to carry out ever more horrific attacks. And in the process, the publicity also attracts more recruits and sympathizers to their cause.

TYPES OF TERRORISM

Security experts have identified four main types of terrorism:

- Nationalist-Separatist Terrorism (N): acts of violence undertaken by those seeking to establish a separate state for their own national or ethnic

group—e.g., the Irish Republican Army, Basque Homeland and Liberty, and the Kurdish Workers Party.
- Religious Terrorism (R): the use of violence by those seeking to further what they see as divinely commanded purposes, often targeting broad categories of "enemies" in an attempt to bring about sweeping changes—e.g., al-Qaeda, Hezbollah, and Hamas.
- Left-Wing Terrorism (L): violence undertaken by those seeking to destroy capitalism and replace it with a communist or socialist regime—e.g., Red Army Faction, German Red Brigades, Prima Linea, and the Symbionese Liberation Army.
- Right-Wing Terrorism (RW): The use of violence by those seeking to dispense with liberal democratic governments—e.g., Combat 18, the KKK, and Timothy McVeigh.

SOME PROMINENT GROUPS IN THE LATE TWENTIETH CENTURY

Action Directe (L) was a French left-wing urban terrorist group that committed a series of assassinations and violent attacks in France in the 1980s. It was founded in 1977 as a merger by two extreme left-wing groups, GARI (Groupes d'Action Révolutionnaire Internationalistes) and NAPAP (Noyaux Armés pour l'Autonomie Populaire). It carried out more than fifty assassinations and attacks, including a machine gun assault on the headquarters of the French Employers Federation. The group was outlawed by the French government in 1982 and in 1984 it allied with the German Red Army Faction. The three leaders were captured in 1987 and sentenced to life imprisonment. One was released on health grounds in 2004, but the other two remain incarcerated.

Angry Brigade (L) was a British communist urban guerrilla group founded in 1967 and responsible for around twenty-five bombings in the early 1970s targeting banks, embassies, and the homes of politicians. While property damage was caused, only one person was slightly injured in all the attacks. The group's leaders were arrested in 1972 and following a lengthy, highly publicized trial they were each sentenced to ten years' imprisonment.

Armed Islamic Group (N, R) was an Algerian Islamist extremist group committed to overthrowing the secular Algerian regime and replacing it with an Islamic state. The GIA began its violent activities in early 1992 after Algiers voided the victory of the Islamic Salvation Front (FIS)—the largest Islamic party—in the first round of legislative elections in December 1991. The GIA engaged in frequent attacks against civilians, journalists, and foreign residents. It used assassinations and bombings, including car bombs, and favored kidnapping victims and slitting their throats. The GIA hijacked an Air France flight to Algiers in December 1994, and suspicions centered on the group for a series of bombings in France in 1995.

Baader-Meinhof (L), also known as the Red Army Faction (RAF), was a German group with roots in the student riots of the late 1960s. Calling themselves urban guerrillas, the RAF was responsible for killing scores of prominent Germans during its twenty-year terror campaign. In 1968 four activists, including Gudrun Ensslin and Andreas Baader, decided to firebomb a number of German department stores. They were arrested and during the trial, journalist Ulrike Meinhof published a number of sympathetic articles. Baader went into hiding after the trial but was captured in April 1970. The next month, in a violent shoot-out, he was sprung from jail by Meinhof and his lawyer, Horst Mahler. Baader, Ensslin, Mahler, and Meinhof fled to the Middle East but were expelled from a Palestinian guerrilla training camp because they refused to follow the rules. They returned to Germany and robbed banks to fund their operation. They also carried out a number of arson attacks before being captured in 1972. While in prison their RAF supporters carried out kidnappings and took hostages to try to force the authorities to release their jailed colleagues, including a deadly attack on the German embassy in Sweden. Their trial started in 1975, and RAF attacks continued against government figures and prosecutors. In 1976 Meinhof committed suicide in her cell. The trial continued until April 28, when all the defendants were found guilty of murder and terrorist acts and sentenced to life imprisonment. RAF attacks, including kidnappings, continued in an attempt to get the leaders released. In October 1977 a Lufthansa plane was hijacked by four Arab sympathizers and eventually flown to Mogadishu, Somalia, where an elite German police unit stormed the plane, killing three of the four hijackers and releasing all the hostages. That night Baader was found dead in his cell from a gunshot wound and Ensslin was found hanged in her cell. A third jailed member died the next day in the prison hospital from wounds. The authorities claimed they had all committed suicide using weapons smuggled in by their lawyers. In the early 1980s RAF survivors allied with Action Directe and the group continued to murder industrialists. They claimed responsibility for bombing the U.S. Air Force base at Ramstein, killing three people. After German unification, evidence was discovered that the group had received financial and logistical support from the Stasi, East Germany's secret police. The group's last major attack was in 1993 when it bombed a prison. In 1998 it published a memorandum declaring the group dissolved.

Combat 18 (C18, RW) was a neo-Nazi organization founded in Britain in 1991 between far-right groups and football hooligans. The "18" in the name comes from Adolf Hitler's initials, the first and eighth letters of the alphabet.

The group claimed it had been set up to defend far-right groups from attacks by anti-fascist organizations. It encouraged and participated in violence against immigrants and left-wing groups. In a nationwide police operation between 1998 and 2000, scores of C18 members were arrested and charged and many sent to prison. In 1999, a one-time member of C18 conducted a brief nail bomb campaign against black, Asian, and gay communities in London. One bomb killed three people, including a pregnant woman, and injured a hundred others. The group was widely discredited by the end of the 1990s because of suggestions that it had been infiltrated by undercover MI5 agents.

Contras (N, L), short for *contrarrevolucionarios* (counterevolutionaries), were the armed opponents of Nicaragua's Sandinista regime, which in 1979 overthrew Anastasio Somoza Debayle and ended the family's forty-three-year rule. The Contras received support from both the Argentinian government and the CIA, and carried out a series of indiscrimate attacks over an eight-year period. A cease-fire negotiated in 1988 led to the Contras disarming. In 1990 elections an anti-Sandinista coalition was voted in. A small group of disaffected Contras briefly took up arms again in the 1990s before being persuaded to disarm permanently.

EOKA (Ethniki Organosis Kyprion Agoniston/National Organisation of Cypriot Fighters) (N), was a Greek Cypriot organization set up in the 1950s to end British sovereignty on the island and to form a union with Greece. EOKA mostly targeted British troops and military bases on the island; during their four-year campaign, more than a hundred British soldiers were killed. The British had more than thirty thousand troops on the island, but the EOKA had popular support. In 1959 agreement was reached to establish an independent republic of Cyprus, although the settlement specifically rules out union (*enosis*) with Greece. EOKA-B was formed in 1971 as a Greek Cypriot fascist paramilitary organization, with the aim of overthrowing the Greek Cypriot government and achieving enosis. This terrorist group had little public support and was further estranged when it murdered a government minister and tried to assassinate the island's president, Makarios. In 1974, backed by the Greek junta and the National Guard, EOKA-B overthrew the government and ousted Makarios. Rather than bringing about union with Greece, the coup prompted Turkey to invade the island; Turkish troops still control one-third of Cyprus.

FALN (N). From the late 1970s to the mid-1980s the Fuerzas Armadas Liberacion Nacional Puertoriquena (Armed Forces of Puerto Rican National Liberation) and the Ejercito Popular Boricua (Popular Boricua Army), known as the Macheteros, claimed responsibility for a wave of bombings and robberies in both the United States and Puerto Rico. The FALN operated in the continental United States, and the Macheteros were active mostly in Puerto Rico.

In October 1974, FALN claimed responsibility for five bombings in New York. Over the next decade, FALN was responsible for more than seventy bombings and forty incendiary attacks resulting in five deaths, eighty-three injuries, and more than $3 million in property damage. The Macheteros, who wanted complete autonomy for Puerto Rico, focused their attacks on the military and the police. In 1981 they infiltrated a Puerto Rican Air National Guard base and blew up eleven planes. The number of attacks steadily decreased, as more members were caught and imprisoned. In 1999 clemency was offered to sixteen terrorists still in federal prisons.

The **Japanese Red Army (L)** was founded by Fusako Shigenobu in 1971 after she broke with the Japanese Communist League's Red Army Faction. Although it never numbered more than forty or so members, it carried out numerous terrorist attacks around the world. Its aim was to overthrow the Japanese government, but by the early 1980s it was no longer active in Japan and was strongly linked with the Popular Front for the Liberation of Palestine, which it relied on for funding and weapons. During the 1970s and 1980s it carried out a series of attacks, including bombings and several hijackings. It was responsible for the machine gun and grenade attack at Tel Aviv's Lod airport that killed seventeen and injured eighty others. In several instances, the group took hostages who were freed only after jailed members of the JRA were released. In 1987 it bombed British and U.S. embassies in Rome, and in 1988 it bombed a USO club in Naples, killing five people. At the same time another member of the group was arrested with a large quantity of explosives on the New Jersey Turnpike; he remains in prison in the United States.

Khmer Rouge (L) was a Communist organization that ruled Cambodia from 1975 to 1979 and was one of the most ruthless and violent regimes of the twentieth century. The Cambodian Communist Party was formed in the 1950s and in the mid-1960s started to attack U.S. troops across the border in Vietnam. When the military took control of Cambodia in a coup in 1970, the Khmer Rouge turned its attention to them and by 1973 controlled much of the country. In April 1975, the government collapsed and the Khmer Rouge took over. Over the next three years it was responsible for the deaths of between 1.7 million and 3 million people as it closed schools, hospitals, factories, and churches; tried to wipe out intellectuals and the middle classes; and forced people out of cities and towns and into forced labor camps in the country-side. Although it changed its name to the Communist Party of Kampuchea in the 1970s and then to the Party of Democratic Kampuchea in the 1980s, it was universally referred to as the Khmer Rouge. Pol Pot led the group and its leadership changed little between the 1960s and 1990s. The group was funded by Vietnam and then by China.

At the end of 1978 Vietnam invaded Cambodia and in January 1979 ousted the Khmer Rouge regime. For the next ten years, the remnants of the Khmer Rouge waged a guerrilla war in an area close to the Thai border that they controlled. They were funded and armed by sections within the Thai army and China. A peace treaty signed in 1991 was shattered when the Khmer Rouge resumed hostilities, but by the mid-1990s they were fighting among themselves. In 1997 Pol Pot was tried and imprisoned by the Khmer Rouge itself; he died in 1998. Later that year, the remaining leaders of the Khmer Rouge apologized for the deaths in the 1970s and the Khmer Rouge effectively ceased to exist.

Red Brigade (L) was a Marxist group formed in 1969 to establish an independent revolutionary state of Italy. Claiming to be defending workers and trade unions, they conducted a campaign of kidnappings and attacks against factories, with occasional bombings in Greece and elsewhere. In 1974, with most of the original membership dead or in prison, a new leadership took over with a more violent agenda of attacks against the police, the army, and prominent businessmen and politicians. In 1978 they kidnapped and murdered former prime minister Aldo Moro. In the early 1980s the group split into two groups, the Communist Combatant Party and the Union of Combatant Communists. Both continued the campaign of high-profile political murders until 1988, when a massive crackdown by the Italian police led to the arrest of most of the leaders of the two factions. There have been sporadic incidents of violence since and the police continue to track down and arrest surviving members.

The **Symbionese Liberation Army (L)** was an American revolutionary organization that in the early 1970s carried out a series of assassinations, murders, bank robberies, and acts of violence. It was formed in 1973 by African American Donald DeFreeze after he escaped from prison. It is best known for the kidnapping of Patty Hearst, the newspaper heiress, who was initially snatched in a bid to get two of the SLA's leaders released from prison. The swap never took place and Hearst, who became known as Tania, took part in a bank robbery after her kidnapping. She was later found guilty of bank robbery but pardoned after serving twenty-one months. She was brutally treated during her captivity and was thought to be suffering from Stockholm Syndrome when she took part in the robbery. The group never had more than thirteen members. Many were killed in a shoot-out with the police in Los Angeles in May 1974, and the remaining members hid out in the Bay area carrying out minor bomb attacks and bank robberies. All have subsequently been captured and convicted for their crimes.

Tonton Macoutes (RW) was founded in Haiti in 1959 under the control of Papa Doc Duvalier, who came to power in 1957. He modeled it on the fascist

These are photographs of the twenty-two people on the FBI's "Most Wanted Terrorists" list, issued October 10, 2001.

Blackshirts of Italy and used it to brutally suppress all political opposition. He even rewrote the constitution to give an automatic amnesty to any Tonton Macoutes member who committed any crime while on "official business." Members were noted for wearing sunglasses and wielding machetes; they had a virtual license to torture and kill, and they would frequently hang their victims and leave the bodies in public places as a warning to others. Jean Claude Duvalier (Baby Doc) took over on his father's death in 1971 and changed the name to the National Security Volunteers, although they were still as brutal as ever. The Tonton Macoutes were responsible for hundreds if not thousands of deaths before they were officially disbanded when Baby Doc was overthrown in 1986. Bands of former members of the organization, however, continued to terrorize the population.

The **Weathermen (L)** was a group of militant left-wing revolutionaries who believed violence could overthrow the government. Founded in the late 1960s, the group collapsed following the U.S. withdrawal from Vietnam. During that time their tactics were mainly bombings, jail breaks, and causing riots. In 1970 they "declared war" on the United States, but their first mission—to plant a bomb at a dance at Fort Dix—failed when three of the group were killed while they were building the bomb in their Greenwich Village safe house. Subsequent bombings targeted the U.S. Capitol, the Pentagon, and police and prison buildings, but warnings were given to prevent casualties. The group also broke LSD guru Timothy Leary out of prison and escorted him to Algeria. The group started to dissolve in the late 1970s. Some members joined other militant groups, while many surrendered to the police. Few served prison time because of their activities in the organization.

Chapter Eight

The Spread of Global Terrorism

Every nation in every region now has a decision to make. Either you are with us, or you are with the terrorists.

—President George W. Bush

We share the common goal of denying al-Qaeda a safe haven in Pakistan or Afghanistan. The world has come too far to let this region backslide, and to let al-Qaeda terrorists plot further attacks. That's why we are committed to a more focused effort to disrupt, dismantle, and defeat al-Qaeda. That is why we are increasing our efforts to train Afghans to sustain their own security, and to reconcile former adversaries. That's why we are increasing our support for the people of Afghanistan and Pakistan, so that we stand on the side not only of security, but also of opportunity and the promise of a better life.

—President Barack Obama

The fact remains, America is awash in desirable targets—those that are symbolic like the U.S. Capitol and the White House, as well as the many infrastructure targets, like nuclear power plants, mass transit systems, bridges and tunnels, shipping and port facilities, financial centers, and airports, that if successfully hit, would cause both mass casualties and a crippling effect on our economy.

It remains the FBI's overriding priority to predict and prevent terrorist attacks. The threat posed by international terrorism, and in particular from al-Qaeda and related groups, continues to be the gravest we face.

—Robert S. Mueller III,
Director, Federal Bureau of Investigation,
before the Senate Committee on Intelligence,
February 16, 2005

Although there were indications during the last two decades of the twentieth century that terrorism was crossing borders and continents, it wasn't until the start of the twenty-first century that the spread of terrorism had become truly global.

Leading this terror assault were extremist Islamic groups in the Middle East, Far East, and North Africa, with breakaway and wannabe cells in Europe and possibly North America. How much cooperation there is between these groups is subject to speculation, but there is no doubt that alliances have been forged between them, that their numbers have grown, and that the United States is their main target.

The 2005 London bombings proved for the first time that there were al-Qaeda cells in western Europe whose members were prepared to give their lives for their cause. More troubling still was that these bombers were British citizens, born and bred in the U.K., and as far as everyone else was concerned, were leading ordinary, law-abiding lives.

Intelligence sources estimate that there could be up to seven hundred British-born extremist Muslims, with thousands more in all the major western European countries. There could be many thousands in the United States and Canada.

Further evidence of the global spread of the Islamic insurgency comes from attacks in the Russian town of Nalchik by Chechen rebels. Shamil Basayev, the most ruthless Chechen warlord, acknowledged that he ordered the storming of a southern Russian town in October 2005, which left 137 militants and officials dead. Basayev admitted that a local Islamic cell, not ethnic Chechens, carried out the assault. This is the first concrete evidence that there has been a fundamental shift in the fighting in the Caucasus. The issue is no longer simply independence for Chechnya but the formation of an Islamic republic that would take in several Russian provinces, including Chechnya, Dagestan, Ingushetia, and Kabardino-Balkaria. Russian officials confirmed that the dead terrorists were locals, not Chechen fighters.

Today, terrorism remains a global threat to which no nation is immune. Despite ongoing improvements in U.S. homeland security, military campaigns against insurgents and terrorists in Iraq and Afghanistan, and deepening counterterrorism cooperation among the nations of the world, international terrorism continues to pose a significant threat to the United States and its partners.

GLOBAL JIHAD

The U.S. State Department's *Country Reports on Terrorism 2004*, published on April 27, 2005, included the following assessment in chapter 3, "Global Jihad: Evolving and Adapting" (www.state.gov/documents/organization/45313.pdf):

The global jihadist movement—including its most prominent component, al-Qaeda—remains the preeminent terrorist threat to the United States, U.S. interests, and U.S. allies. While the core of al-Qaeda has suffered damage to its leadership, organization, and capabilities, the group remains intent on striking U.S. interests in the homeland and overseas. During the past year, concerted antiterrorist coalition measures have degraded al-Qaeda's central command infrastructure, decreasing its ability to conduct massive attacks. At the same time, however, al-Qaeda has spread its anti-U.S., anti-Western ideology to other groups and geographical areas. It is therefore no longer al-Qaeda itself, but increasingly groups affiliated with al-Qaeda or independent groups adhering to al-Qaeda's ideology, that present the greatest threat of terrorist attacks against U.S. and allied interests globally.

U.S. and Coalition successes against al-Qaeda have forced these jihadist groups to compensate by showing a greater willingness to act on their own and exercising greater local control over their strategic and tactical decisions. As a result of this growing dispersion and local decision making, there is an increasing commingling of groups, personnel, resources, and ad hoc operational and logistical coordination. These groups affiliated with al-Qaeda or indoctrinated with al-Qaeda's ideology are now carrying out most of the terrorist attacks against U.S. and allied interests. Their decreased power projection and limited resources mean that an increasing percentage of jihadist attacks are more local, less sophisticated, but still lethal. Some groups, however, are seeking to replicate al-Qaeda's global reach and expertise for mass casualty attacks. This trend underscores that America's partners in the global war on terror require the capabilities to identify and eliminate terrorist threats in their countries for their own security and ultimately to stop terrorists abroad before they can gain the ability to attack the U.S. homeland. . . .

The Global Jihadist Movement

The global jihadist movement predates al-Qaeda's founding and was reinforced and developed by successive conflicts in Afghanistan, Bosnia, Chechnya, and elsewhere during the 1990s. As a result, it spawned several groups and operating nodes and developed a resiliency that ensured that destruction of any one group or node did not destroy the larger movement. Since 2001, extremists, including members of al-Qaeda and affiliated groups, have sought to exploit perceptions of the U.S.-led global war on terrorism and, in particular, the war in Iraq to attract converts to their movement. Many of these recruits come from a large and growing pool of disaffected youth who are sympathetic to radical, anti-Western militant ideology. At the same time, these extremists have branched out to establish jihadist cells in other parts of the Middle East, South Asia, and Europe, from which they seek to prepare operations and facilitate funding and communications.

Foreign fighters appear to be working to make the insurgency in Iraq what [the resistance movement to the Soviet occupation of]Afghanistan was to the earlier generation of jihadists—a melting pot for jihadists from around the world, a training ground, and an indoctrination center. In the months and years ahead, a significant number of fighters who have traveled to Iraq will return to their home countries, exacerbating domestic conflicts or augmenting with new skills and experience existing extremist networks in the communities to which they return. . . .

The Spread of Al-Qaeda's Ideology

Al-Qaeda's ideology resonates with other Sunni extremist circles. Some affiliated groups—including Jemaah Islamiyah in Southeast Asia—look to their own spiritual leaders, yet historically have shared close ideological and operational ties to al-Qaeda. In recent years, however, the resonance of al-Qaeda's message has contributed to the formation of an assortment of grassroots networks and cells among persons that previously have had no observable links to bin Laden or al-Qaeda, aside from general ideological and religious affinity.

Examples of this trend include Salafiya Jihadia, a loosely organized Moroccan movement that carried out the bombings in May 2003 in Casablanca, and the terrorists who executed the March 2004 attack in Madrid. Although these cells do not appear to have been acting directly on al-Qaeda orders, their attacks supported al-Qaeda's ideology and reflected al-Qaeda's targeting strategy.

Terrorist capabilities for attacks will remain uneven, given the varying degrees of expertise and increasing decentralization within the movement. Most groups will be capable only of relatively unsophisticated but still deadly attacks. Others, however, may seek to acquire or replicate al-Qaeda's expertise and material support for mass-casualty attacks. The explosive growth of media and the Internet, as well as the ease of travel and communication around the world, have made possible the rapid movement of operatives, expertise, money, and explosives. Terrorists increasingly will use media and the Internet to advance key messages or rally support, share jihadist experiences and expertise, and spread fear.

Although the jihadist movement remains dangerous, it is not monolithic. Some groups are focused on attacking the United States or its allies, while others view governments and leaders in the Muslim world as their primary targets. The United States and its partners in the global war on terrorism will continue to use all the means available to identify, target, and prevent the spread of these jihadist groups and ideology.

AL-QAEDA

The U.S. State Department's *Country Reports on Terrorism 2008*, published on April 30, 2009, includes a strategic assessment highlighting terrorism trends and ongoing issues in 2008 (www.state.gov/s/ct/rls/crt/2008/122411.htm):

Al-Qaeda and associated networks continued to lose ground, both structurally and in the court of world public opinion, but remained the greatest terrorist threat to the United States and its partners in 2008. Al-Qaeda has reconstituted some of its pre-9/11 operational capabilities through the exploitation of Pakistan's Federally Administered Tribal Areas (FATA); the replacement of captured or killed operational lieutenants; and the restoration of some central control by its top leadership, in particular Ayman al-Zawahiri. Worldwide efforts to counter terrorist financing have resulted in al-Qaeda's appealing for money in its last few messages.

In the years since 9/11, al-Qaeda and its extremist allies have moved across the border to the remote areas of the Pakistani frontier, where they have used this terrain as a safe haven to hide, train terrorists, communicate with followers, plot attacks, and send fighters to support the insurgency in Afghanistan. Therefore, Pakistan's FATA provided al-Qaeda many of the benefits it once derived from its base across the border in Afghanistan.

The threat from al-Qaeda in Iraq (AQI) continued to diminish. While still dangerous, AQI experienced significant defections, lost key mobilization areas, suffered disruption of support infrastructure and funding, and was forced to change targeting priorities. Indeed, the pace of suicide bombings countrywide, a key indicator of AQI's operational capability, fell significantly during 2008. Initiatives to cooperate with tribal and local leaders in Iraq continued to encourage Sunni tribes and local citizens to reject AQI and its extremist ideology. The sustained growth and improved capabilities of the Iraqi forces increased their effectiveness in rooting out terrorist cells. In Baghdad, Anbar and Diyala provinces, and elsewhere, local populations turned against AQI and cooperated with the government of Iraq and Coalition forces to defeat it.

The late 2006 Ethiopian incursion into Somalia forced al-Qaeda on the run in East Africa but also served as a rallying point for anti-Ethiopian/anti-government militia and al-Shabaab. After Ethiopian forces drove the Islamic Courts Council (ICC) out of power, al-Shabaab (the militant wing of the former ICC) and disparate clan militias launched a violent insurgency targeting the Ethiopian presence in Somalia, the Transitional Federal Government of Somalia (TFG), and the African Union Mission in Somalia peacekeepers.

Attacks against the Ethiopian and TFG forces continued in 2008, following the early 2007 call to action by al-Qaeda's Ayman al-Zawahiri, who urged all mujahedin to extend support to Somali Muslims in a holy war against Ethiopian forces. The subsequent security vacuum in parts of central and southern Somalia has led divergent factions to oppose al-Shabaab and its extremist ideology. However, hardcore al-Shabaab fighters, foreign fighters, and allied militias continued to conduct brazen attacks in Mogadishu and outlying environs, primarily in South/Central Somalia. Al-Qaeda elements continued to benefit from safe haven in the regions of southern Somalia under al-Shabaab influence. After al-Shabaab's leaders publicly ordered their fighters to attack African Union peacekeeping troops based in Mogadishu, a suicide vehicle bomber detonated near an African Union base in the capital on January 24, 2008, killing an estimated 13 people.

Al-Qaeda in Yemen (AQY) carried out several attacks against tourism and U.S. and Yemeni government targets. The most notable was the September 17 attack against the U.S. Embassy in Sanaa, which killed 18 people. A half dozen other attacks occurred in Yemen in 2008, including a January attack that killed two Belgian tourists and two Yemeni drivers in the southern governorate of Hadramaut. Despite an August raid on an AQY cell that resulted in the death of its leader, the government of Yemen has been unable to disrupt other AQY cells. Yemen continued to increase its maritime security capabilities, but land border security along the extensive frontier with Saudi Arabia remained a problem, despite increased Yemeni-Saudi cooperation on bilateral security issues.

Al-Qaeda in the Islamic Maghreb (AQIM) maintained training camps and support networks in the isolated and remote areas of Algeria and the Sahel. AQIM continued to primarily target the Algerian government, but also made threats against what it termed "crusading" Westerners, particularly American and French citizens, although Russians, Danes, Austrians, Swiss, British, German, and Canadian citizens have been targeted as well, particularly in kidnappings for ransom. AQIM support cells have been discovered and/or dismantled in Spain, Italy, Morocco, Mauritania, Algeria, Tunisia, and Mali. In Algeria, there was a dramatic rise in terrorist attacks claimed by AQIM during August 2008, with at least 79 people killed in various incidents across the northeastern part of the country, many of them in suicide bombings.

Al-Qaeda continued its propaganda efforts seeking to inspire support in Muslim populations, undermine Western confidence, and enhance the perception of a powerful worldwide movement. Terrorists consider information operations a principal part of their effort. Their use of the Internet for propaganda, recruiting, fund-raising, and increasingly, training has made the Internet a "virtual safe haven." That said, bin Laden and al-Zawahiri appeared to be in the position of responding to events rather than driving them, particularly in the latter half of 2008.

Besides seeking to take advantage of international interventions in Iraq and Afghanistan as tools for radicalization and fund-raising, al-Qaeda also sought to use the Israeli/Palestinian conflict, but lacked credibility in this regard. The international community has yet to muster a coordinated and effectively resourced program to counter extremist propaganda.

THE TALIBAN

With regard to the Taliban, *Country Reports on Terrorism 2008* continues:

The Taliban and other insurgent groups and criminal gangs, some of whom were linked to al-Qaeda and terrorist sponsors outside the country, control parts of Afghanistan and Pakistan and threaten the stability of the region. Attacks against our troops, NATO allies, and the Afghan government have risen steadily. Taliban insurgents murdered local leaders and attacked Pakistani government outposts in the FATA of Pakistan. Ideological allies of the Taliban conducted frequent attacks in Pakistan's Northwest Frontier Province (NWFP), particularly in the Swat Valley, and have extended operations to the Punjab and the capital city of Islamabad. Suicide bombers are increasingly used to target Pakistanis, in addition to conducting cross-border raids on International Security Assistance Force (ISAF) forces.

The government of Afghanistan continued to strengthen its national institutions, and some polls indicated the majority of Afghans believed they were better off than they were under the Taliban. The terror-drug nexus and funding from the Gulf have increased the Taliban's ability to fight, and the Taliban's efforts to convince Afghanis that ISAF forces and corruption in the government of Afghanistan are the source of Afghani pain has fueled the insurgency and curtailed legitimate efforts to influence Afghanis to reject violent extremism. The international community's assistance to the Afghan government to build counterinsurgency capabilities, ensure legitimate and effective governance, and counter the surge in narcotics cultivation is essential to the effort to defeat the Taliban and other insurgent groups and criminal gangs.

A shaky peace agreement with the Pakistan government that would allow the Taliban to establish Islamic law in the Swat Valley broke down in May 2009, when armed Taliban forces tried to extend their area of influence approaching within sixty miles of Islamabad. The Pakistani army launched an all-out offensive against the Taliban and threatened to eradicate them.

STATE SPONSORS OF TERRORISM

According to the U.S. State Department's *Country Reports on Terrorism 2008*:

The terrorist groups of greatest concern—because of their global reach—share many of the characteristics of a global insurgency: propaganda campaigns, grassroots support, transnational ideology, and political and territorial ambitions. Responding requires a comprehensive response that focuses on recruiters and their networks, potential recruits, the local population, and the ideology. An holistic approach incorporates efforts aimed at protecting and securing the population, politically and physically marginalizing insurgents, winning the support and cooperation of at-risk populations by targeted political and development measures, and conducting precise intelligence-led special operations to eliminate critical enemy elements with minimal risk to innocent civilians.

Significant achievements in this area were made in 2008 against terrorist leadership targets, notably the capturing or killing of key terrorist leaders in Pakistan, Iraq, and Colombia. These efforts buy us time to carry out the nonlethal and longer-term elements of a comprehensive counterterrorist strategy: disrupting terrorist operations, communications, propaganda, subversion efforts, planning and fund-raising, and preventing radicalization before it takes root by addressing the grievances that terrorists exploit and discrediting the ideology that provides their legitimacy. Actions that advance these strategic objectives include building and strengthening networks among governments, multilateral cooperation, business organizations, and working within civil society. It is crucial to empower credible voices and provide alternatives to joining extremist organizations.

Working with allies and partners across the world, we have created a less permissive operating environment for terrorists, keeping terrorist leaders on the move or in hiding, and degrading their ability to plan and mount attacks. Canada, Australia, the United Kingdom, Germany, Spain, Jordan, the Philippines, Pakistan, Afghanistan, Iraq, and many other partners played major roles in this success. Dozens of countries have continued to pass counterterrorism legislation or strengthen preexisting laws that provide their law enforcement and judicial authorities with new tools to bring terrorists to justice. The United States has expanded the number of foreign partners with which it shares terrorist screening information. This information serves as an important tool for disrupting and tracking travel of known and suspected terrorists. Saudi Arabia has implemented one of the first rehabilitation programs for returning extremists to turn them against violent extremism and to reintegrate them as peaceful citizens.

Through the Regional Strategic Initiative, the State Department and other U.S. agencies are working with U.S. ambassadors overseas in key terrorist theaters of operation to assess threats and devise collaborative strategies, action plans, and policy recommendations. We have made progress in organizing regional responses to terrorists who operate in ungoverned spaces or across national borders. This initiative has produced better intragovernmental coordination among U.S. government agencies, greater cooperation with and between regional partners, and improved strategic planning and prioritization, allowing us to use all tools of statecraft to establish long-term measures to marginalize terrorists. . . .

Radicalization continued in immigrant populations, youth, and alienated minorities in Europe, the Middle East, and Africa. A special focus on new approaches in Europe has been productive and has informed the way we understand government's role in combating radicalization. It is increasingly clear that radicalization does not occur by accident, or because such populations are innately prone to extremism. Rather, we saw increasing evidence of terrorists and extremists manipulating the grievances of alienated youth or immigrant populations, and then cynically exploiting those grievances to subvert legitimate authority and create unrest. We also note a "self-radicalization" process, through which youths reach out to extremists in order to become involved in the broader al-Qaeda fight.

Efforts to manipulate grievances represent a "conveyor belt" through which terrorists seek to convert alienated or aggrieved populations, by stages, to increasingly radicalized and extremist viewpoints, turning them into sympathizers, supporters, and ultimately, in some cases, members of terrorist networks.

In some regions, this includes efforts by al-Qaeda and other terrorists to exploit insurgency and communal conflict as radicalization and recruitment tools, using the Internet to convey their message.

Counter-radicalization is a priority for the United States, particularly in Europe, given the potential for Europe-based violent extremism to threaten the United States and its key interests directly. The leaders of al-Qaeda and its affiliates are interested in recruiting terrorists from and deploying terrorists to Europe. They are especially interested in people familiar with Western cultures who can travel freely in the region and to the United States. However, countering such efforts requires that we treat immigrant and youth populations not as a threat to be defended against, but as a target of enemy subversion to be protected and supported. It requires that community leaders take responsibility for the actions of members within their communities and act to counteract extremist propaganda and subversion. It also requires governments to serve as facilitators, conveners, and intellectual partners to credible organizations/people who can do what governments cannot. Finally, bilateral, regional, and multilateral cooperation is essential.

Currently, there are four nations on the State Department's list of state sponsors of terrorism: Cuba, Iran, Syria, and Sudan. The following information on state sponsors of terrorism comes from the U.S. State Department's *Country Report on Terrorism 2008*, chapter 3 (www.state.gov/s/ct/rls/crt/2008/122436.htm):

State sponsors of terrorism provide critical support to nonstate terrorist groups. Without state sponsors, terrorist groups would have greater difficulty obtaining the funds, weapons, materials, and secure areas they require to plan and conduct operations. The United States will continue to insist that these countries end the support they give to terrorist groups.

Sudan continued to take significant steps towards better counterterrorism cooperation. Iran and Syria have not renounced terrorism or made efforts to act against Foreign Terrorist Organizations and routinely provided safe haven, substantial resources, and guidance to terrorist organizations. Cuba continued to publicly defend the FARC and provide safe haven to some members of terrorist organizations, though some were in Cuba in connection with peace negotiations with the Governments of Spain and Colombia.

On October 11, 2008, the United States rescinded the designation of the Democratic People's Republic of Korea (DPRK) as a state sponsor of terrorism in accordance with criteria set forth in U.S. law, including a certification that the Government of North Korea had not provided any support for international terrorism during the preceding six-month period and the provision by the government of assurances that it will not support acts of international terrorism in the future.

Cuba

Although Cuba no longer actively supports armed struggle in Latin America and other parts of the world, the Cuban government continued to provide safe haven to several terrorists. Members of ETA, the FARC, and the ELN remained in Cuba during 2008, some having arrived in Cuba in connection with peace negotiations with the governments of Spain and Colombia. Cuban authorities continued to publicly defend the FARC. However, on July 6, 2008, former Cuban President Fidel Castro called on the FARC to release the hostages they were holding without preconditions. He has also condemned the FARC's mistreatment of captives and of their abduction of civilian politicians who had no role in the armed conflict.

The United States has no evidence of terrorist-related money laundering or terrorist financing activities in Cuba, although Cuba has one of the world's most secretive and non-transparent national banking systems. Cuba has no financial intelligence unit. Cuba's Law 93 Against Acts of Terrorism provides the government authority to track, block, or seize terrorist assets.

The Cuban government continued to permit some U.S. fugitives—including members of U.S. militant groups such as the Boricua Popular, or *Macheteros*, and the Black Liberation Army to live legally in Cuba. In keeping with its public declaration, the government has not provided safe haven to any new U.S. fugitives wanted for terrorism since 2006.

Iran

Iran remained the most active state sponsor of terrorism. Iran's involvement in the planning and financial support of terrorist attacks throughout the Middle East, Europe, and Central Asia had a direct impact on international efforts to promote peace, threatened economic stability in the Gulf, and undermined the growth of democracy.

The Qods Force, an elite branch of the Islamic Revolutionary Guard Corps (IRGC), is the regime's primary mechanism for cultivating and supporting terrorists abroad. The Qods Force provided aid in the form of weapons, training, and funding to Hamas and other Palestinian terrorist groups, Lebanese Hezbollah, Iraq-based militants, and Taliban fighters in Afghanistan.

Iran remained a principal supporter of groups that are implacably opposed to the Middle East Peace Process. Iran provided weapons, training, and funding to Hamas and other Palestinian terrorist groups, including Palestine Islamic Jihad (PIJ) and the Popular Front for the Liberation of Palestine—General Command (PFLP-GC). Iran's provision of training, weapons, and money to Hamas since the 2006 Palestinian elections has bolstered the group's ability to strike Israel. In 2008, Iran provided more than $200 million in funding to Lebanese Hezbollah and trained over 3,000 Hezbollah fighters at camps in Iran. Since the end of the 2006 Israeli-Hezbollah conflict, Iran has assisted Hezbollah in rearming, in violation of UN Security Council Resolution 1701.

Iran's IRGC Qods Force provided assistance to the Taliban in Afghanistan. The Qods Force provided training to the Taliban on small unit tactics, small arms, explosives, and indirect fire weapons. Since at least 2006, Iran has arranged arms shipments including small arms and associated ammunition, rocket-propelled grenades, mortar rounds, 107 mm rockets, and plastic explosives to select Taliban members.

Despite its pledge to support the stabilization of Iraq, Iranian authorities continued to provide lethal support, including weapons, training, funding, and guidance, to Iraqi militant groups that targeted Coalition and Iraqi forces and killed innocent Iraqi civilians. Iran's Qods Force continued to provide Iraqi militants with Iranian-produced advanced rockets, sniper rifles, automatic weapons, and mortars that have killed Iraqi and Coalition Forces as well as civilians. Tehran was responsible for some of the lethality of anti-Coalition attacks by providing militants with the capability to assemble improvised explosive devices (IEDs) with explosively formed projectiles (EFPs) that were specially designed to defeat armored vehicles. The Qods Force, in concert with Lebanese Hezbollah, provided training both inside and outside of Iraq for Iraqi militants in the construction and use of sophisticated IED technology and other advanced weaponry.

Iran remained unwilling to bring to justice senior al-Qaeda members it has detained, and has refused to publicly identify those senior members in its custody. Iran has repeatedly resisted numerous calls to transfer custody of its al-Qaeda detainees to their countries of origin or third countries for trial. Iran also continued to fail to control the activities of some al-Qaeda members who fled to Iran following the fall of the Taliban regime in Afghanistan.

Senior IRGC and Qods Force officials were indicted by the Government of Argentina for their alleged roles in the 1994 terrorist bombing of the Argentine Israel Mutual Association which, according to the Argentine State Prosecutor's report, was initially proposed by the Qods Force.

Sudan

Sudan remained a cooperative partner in global counterterrorism efforts. During the past year, the Sudanese government continued to pursue terrorist operations directly involving threats to U.S. interests and personnel in Sudan. Sudanese officials have indicated that they view their continued cooperation with the United States as important and recognize the benefits of U.S. training and information-sharing. Though the counterterrorism relationship remained solid, some hard-line Sudanese officials continued to express resentment and distrust over actions by the U.S. government and questioned the benefits of the bilateral cooperation. Their assessment reflected disappointment that Sudan's counterterrorism cooperation has not resulted in its removal from the State Sponsors of Terrorism list. Nonetheless, there was no indication at year's end that the Sudanese government will curtail its counterterrorism cooperation with the United States.

Al-Qaeda-inspired terrorist elements, and elements of both Palestine Islamic Jihad (PIJ), and Hamas remained in Sudan. In light of the continuing hybrid UN-AU deployment to Darfur, various terrorist threats against this mission have emerged, and al-Qaeda leadership has called for "jihad" against UN forces in Darfur. In the early hours of January 1, 2008, attackers in Khartoum sympathetic to al-Qaeda shot and fatally wounded two U.S. Embassy staff members—an American and a Sudanese employee—both of whom worked for the U.S. Agency for International Development. Sudanese authorities cooperated closely with the U.S. government in investigating this terrorist crime. On February 1, five alleged conspirators were arrested and put on trial for murder on August 31. Their trial was ongoing at year's end. Other extremist groups also have threatened attacks against Western interests in Sudan. The July 14 request by International Criminal Court Chief Prosecutor Moreno-Ocampo for an arrest warrant against Sudanese President Omar al-Bashir on charges related to atrocities committed in Darfur has further inflamed tensions. Therefore, the terrorist threat level remained critical in Khartoum and Darfur, and potentially other parts of Sudan.

Elements of designated terrorist groups remained in Sudan. With the exception of Hamas, whose members the Sudanese government consider to be "freedom fighters" rather than terrorists, the government does not appear to openly support the presence of extremist elements. We note, however, that there have been open source reports that arms were purchased in Sudan's black market and allegedly smuggled northward to Hamas.

The Sudanese government has prevented foreign fighters from using Sudan as a logistics base and transit point for extremists going to Iraq. However, gaps remained in the Sudanese government's knowledge of and ability to identify and capture these individuals. There was evidence to suggest that individuals who were active participants in the Iraqi insurgency have returned to Sudan and were in a position to use their expertise to conduct attacks within Sudan or to pass on their knowledge. There was also evidence that Sudanese extremists continued to participate in terrorist activities in Somalia, which the Sudanese government has also attempted to disrupt.

Syria

Syria was designated in 1979 as a state sponsor of terrorism. Syria provided political and material support to Hezbollah and allowed Iran to use Syrian territory as a transit point for assistance to Hezbollah. Hamas, Palestine Islamic Jihad (PIJ), the Popular Front for the Liberation of Palestine (PLFP), and the Popular Front for the Liberation of Palestine-General Command (PFLP-GC), among others, based their external leadership within Syria's borders. The Syrian government insisted these groups were confined to political and informational activities, but groups with leaders in Syria have claimed responsibility for deadly anti-Israeli terrorist attacks.

Over the course of the year, Syria's public support for the Palestinian groups varied, depending on Syrian national interest and international pressure. President Bashar al-Asad continued to express public support for Palestinian terrorist groups. Hamas Politburo head and defacto leader Khalid Meshal and his deputies continued to reside in Syria. Syria provided a safe haven for Meshal and security escorts for his motorcades. Meshal's use of the Syrian Ministry of Information as the venue for press conferences this year could be taken as an endorsement of Hamas's message. Media reports indicated Hamas used Syrian soil to train its militant fighters. Though the Syrian government claimed periodically that it used its influence to restrain the rhetoric and activities of Palestinian groups, the Syrian government allowed a Palestinian conference organized by Hamas, PFLP-GC, and PIJ to occur in January, and another Hamas organized conference, reportedly funded by Iran, to take place in November.

Highlighting Syria's ties to the world's most notorious terrorists, Hezbollah Operations Chief Imad Mugniyah perished in a February 12 car bombing near Syrian Military Intelligence (SMI) headquarters in the Damascus neighborhood of Kafr Sousa. Among other atrocities, Mugniyah was wanted in connection with the 1983 bombings of the Marine barracks and the U.S. Embassy in Beirut, which killed over 350. Despite initial attempts to cover up the incident, the Syrian government reluctantly acknowledged some days later that one of the world's most wanted terrorists had been present and died on Syrian soil.

Syrian officials publicly condemned some acts of terrorism, while continuing to defend what they considered to be legitimate armed resistance by Palestinians and Hezbollah against Israeli occupation of Arab territory, and by the Iraqi opposition against the "occupation of Iraq." Syria has not been directly implicated in an act of terrorism since 1986, although an ongoing UN investigation into the February 2005 assassination of former Lebanese Prime Minister Rafiq Hariri continued to investigate Syrian involvement.

Syria itself was the location of at least one major attack. On September 27, the carbombing of a Syrian government facility reportedly injured 14 and killed at least 17 individuals, marking the first significant attack against regime institutions in nearly 20 years. Not since the Muslim Brotherhood uprising in the early 1980s had Syrian institutions been targeted by terrorists. Regional media reports indicated this bombing was directed at the Palestinian Branch of the Syrian Military Intelligence; the perpetrators remained unknown at year's end.

Throughout the year, Syria continued to strengthen ties with fellow state sponsor of terrorism, Iran. Syria's Minister of Defense visited Tehran in May and initiated a Memorandum of Understanding on defense cooperation. Syria also allowed leaders of Hamas and other Palestinian groups to visit Tehran. President Asad repaid a 2007 visit to Damascus by Iranian President Ahmadinejad with a visit of his own to Tehran in early August, his third visit since 2005. Asad continued to be a staunch defender of Iran's policies, including Iran's "civil" nuclear ambitions.

Syria increased border monitoring activities, instituted tighter screening practices on military-age Arab males entering its borders, hosted two Border Security
Working Group meetings with technical experts from the Iraqi Neighbors group,
and expressed a desire to increase security cooperation with Iraq. At the same
time, Syria remained a key hub for foreign fighters en route to Iraq.

The U.S. government designated several Iraqis residing in Syria and Iraqi-
owned entities, including Mishan Al-Jaburi and his satellite television channel
Al-Ra'y, under Executive Order 1348 for providing financial, material, and
technical support for acts of violence that threatened the peace and stability of
Iraq. The United States also designated known foreign fighter facilitators based
in Syria, including members of the Abu Ghadiyah network, that orchestrated the
flow of terrorists, weapons, and money from Syria to al-Qaeda in Iraq, under
Executive Order 13224.

Despite acknowledged reductions in foreign fighter flows, the scope and impact of the problem remained significant. Syria continued to allow former Iraqi
regime elements to operate in the country. Attacks against Coalition Forces and
Iraqi citizens continued to have a destabilizing effect on Iraq's internal security.
Though Syrian and Iraqi leaders met throughout the year both publicly and
privately to discuss border enhancements and other measures needed to combat foreign fighter flows, there were few tangible results. While Syria has taken
some positive steps, the Syrian government could do more to interdict known
terrorist networks and foreign fighter facilitators operating within its borders.

Syria remained a source of concern regarding terrorist financing. The Commercial Bank of Syria remained subject to U.S. sanctions. Industry experts reported that 70 percent of all business transactions were conducted in cash and
that nearly 90 percent of all Syrians did not use formal banking services. Despite
Syrian governmental legislation requiring money-changers to be licensed by the
end of 2007, many money-changers continued to operate illegally in Syria's
vast black market, estimated to be as large as Syria's formal economy. Regional
"hawala" networks remained intertwined with smuggling and trade-based
money laundering, facilitated by notoriously corrupt customs and immigration
officials, raising significant concerns that Syrian government and business elites
are, at the very least, complicit in illicit financing schemes.

Syria's government-controlled press continued to tout Syrian regime efforts to
combat terrorism. The Syrian government, using tightly-controlled press outlets,
was quick to blame a Lebanon-based, al-Qaeda-affiliated group, Fatah al-Islam,
for the September 27 attack against a prominent military intelligence installa-
tion. Syrian TV broadcasted a November 7 program featuring the confessions
of some 20 Fatah al-Islam members, including the daughter and son-in-law of
Fatah al-Islam leader Shakr al-Absy, of their involvement.

It remained unclear why Fatah al-Islam would have launched an attack
against Syrian security elements, but media reports suggested Absy's disap-
pearance inside of Syria as a possible motive. In response to the September 27
bombing, the Syrian security services conducted at least one reported raid on an

alleged terrorist cell residing in the Damascus area, killing and arresting several suspected militants and confiscating a cache of weapons and explosives.

CHEMICAL, BIOLOGICAL, RADIOLOGICAL, NUCLEAR (CBRN) TERRORISM

Production of weapons of mass destruction (WMD) and their delivery systems constitutes a major threat to international peace and security. The threat is compounded by the interests of terrorists in acquiring WMD. This would undermine the foundations of international order. We pledge to use all means available to avert WMD proliferation and the calamities that would follow.

—Joint statement by President George W. Bush, European Council President Konstandinos Simitis, and European Commission President Romano Prodi

According to the U.S. Department of State:

The September 11, 2001, attacks confirmed that terrorists will seek to produce mass casualties whenever they believe it serves their purposes. Although terrorists will probably continue to rely on traditional terrorist tactics, several groups—including al-Qaeda—increasingly look to chemical, biological, radiological, or nuclear (CBRN) materials as a means to cause mass casualties rivaling or exceeding those of September 11. Troublesome amounts of dangerous materials, and information about how to create and deliver CBRN weapons, remain available to terrorists.

Osama bin Laden has said he sees the acquisition of WMD as a "religious duty," and he has threatened to use such weapons. This rhetoric was underscored by reports that documents retrieved from al-Qaeda facilities in Afghanistan contain information on CBRN materials.

However, the threat is not limited to bin Laden and al-Qaeda. Information indicates that small but growing numbers of other terrorist groups are also interested in CBRN materials. In Europe, French police seized a chemical contamination suit and arrested a terrorist cell in December 2002 that allegedly was planning an attack using chemical agents.

CBRN terrorism events to date have generally involved crude and improvised delivery means that have been only marginally effective. With the exceptions of the 1995 Aum Shinrikyo attacks in Tokyo and the 2001 U.S. anthrax attacks, the materials employed in these events also have been crudely manufactured. Other events have involved dual-use materials that have legitimate civilian applications, such as industrial chemicals, poisons, pesticides, and radiological source materials embedded in legitimate measuring instruments. Although

Members of an area Emergency Medical Technician team undergo training required for certification as rescue and decontamination unit responders to hazardous material and toxic contamination situations. Photo by Win Henderson/FEMA

terrorist events involving these materials and improvised delivery systems can cause significant casualties, damage, and disruption, such events pale in comparison to the casualties and damage that could occur if terrorists acquired WMDs and the ability to deliver them effectively.

Preventing the proliferation of WMDs, their delivery systems, and related materials and technologies has long been a pillar of national security. Since September 11, the prevention of WMDs has become an even more urgent priority. President Bush made this urgency clear in his December 2002 National Strategy to Combat Weapons of Mass Destruction, in which he set out a comprehensive strategy to prevent WMD proliferation, including to terrorists.

The Proliferation Security Initiative (PSI) is a global multilateral arrangement to seize sensitive cargoes that may be in transit to and from states and nonstate actors of proliferation concern. PSI is an interdiction program. PSI participants jointly explore and train in how best to use counterproliferation tools—diplomatic, intelligence, and operational—to stop proliferation at sea, in the air, and on land.

The United States is working within multilateral nonproliferation regimes and other international forums. Bilaterally, the United States promotes more stringent nonproliferation policies and programs; strengthened export controls; and improved border security to prevent terrorists or their state sponsors from acquiring WMDs, their delivery systems, related materials, or technologies. As President Bush's National Strategy notes, however, should diplomatic efforts fall short, the United States will be prepared to deter and defend against the full range of WMD threats.

GLOBAL TERRORISM SITUATION

The following information is from the U.S. Department of State, Office of the Coordinator for Counterterrorism, *Country Reports on Terrorism 2008*, chapter 2 (www.state.gov/s/ct/rls/crt/2008/).

Africa Overview

A limited number of al-Qaeda operatives in East Africa and more numerous al-Shabaab militants in Somalia continued to pose the most serious threat to American and allied interests in the region. Somalia remained a permissive operating environment and emerged as a safe haven for both Somali and foreign terrorists. Its unsecured borders and continued political instability provided opportunities for terrorist transit and/or organization. Al-Shabaab and Islamic extremists in Somalia continue to disrupt peacemaking efforts, and desire to establish a harsh, abusive rule of law. A limited number of East Africa al-Qaeda operatives in Somalia will continue to represent a long-term threat to the international community. This threat has demonstrably increased; on October 29th, terrorists carried out five near-simultaneous suicide car bomb attacks against the United Nations Development Program and local government buildings across Puntland and Somaliland, killing at least 21. Al-Shabaab, which the United States designated as a terrorist group on March 19, 2008, has seized control of key parts of South and Central Somalia, including the port city of Kismayo and its environs.

In the North and West of the Continent, al-Qaeda in the Islamic Maghreb (AQIM) expanded the scope of its terrorist operations in the Sahel, conducting terrorist operations in Mauritania and Mali. On February 1, the Israeli Embassy in Nouackchott, Mauritania, and a nearby nightclub were attacked, which resulted in the wounding of one French civilian. In February, AQIM took two Austrian civilians hostage and released them eight months later after a ransom was paid. In September, AQIM murdered and beheaded eleven Mauritanian soldiers. According to Associated Press reports, AQIM kidnapped two Canadian UN diplomats on December 14, 2008, in Niger and held them hostage in Mali.

Many African governments improved their cooperation and strengthened their counterterrorism efforts. Both the African Union (AU) and African regional organizations continued initiatives to improve counterterrorism cooperation and information sharing. The Southern Africa Development Community (SADC) has publicly condemned all forms of terrorist activities and has expressed its readiness to work with the international community in the fight against terrorism. Despite its intentions, however, SADC's current capabilities and its efforts to date in fighting terrorism are limited.

The Financial Action Task Force (FATF), as the international standard-setting body to address threats of money laundering, terrorist financing, and other related crimes, established a network by which countries around the world can be included. These FATF-Style Regional Bodies (FSRBs) have the potential to serve both as a disciplinarian and as a resource. In sub-Saharan Africa, there are two such bodies recognized by the FATF: the Eastern and Southern Africa Anti-Money Laundering Group (ESAAMLG) and the Intergovernmental Action Group against Money Laundering and Terrorist Financing (GIABA). Like FATF and the other FSRBs, they conduct mutual evaluations, conduct typologies exercises, work on various issues with framework and implementation, and provide training for their members. Despite the existence and activities of these groups, Africa remains the single region in the world without FSRB coverage over wide swaths of its countries.

The Trans-Sahara Counterterrorism Partnership (TSCTP). The Trans-Sahara Counterterrorism Partnership (TSCTP) is a multi-faceted, multi-year strategy to combat violent extremism and defeat terrorist organizations by strengthening individual country and regional counterterrorism capabilities, enhancing and institutionalizing cooperation among the region's security and intelligence organizations, promoting democratic governance, and discrediting terrorist ideology. The overall goals are to enhance the indigenous capacities of governments in the pan-Sahel (Burkina Faso, Mauritania, Mali, Chad, and Niger, as well as

Nigeria, and Senegal), to confront the challenge posed by terrorist organizations in the trans-Sahara, and to facilitate cooperation between those countries and U.S. Maghreb partners (Morocco, Algeria, and Tunisia).

TSCTP was developed as a follow-on to the Pan-Sahel Initiative, which focused solely on the Sahel. Ongoing concern that extremists continued to seek to create safe havens and support networks in the Maghreb and Sahel, as well as recognition that al-Qaeda and others were seeking to impose radical ideologies on traditionally moderate Muslim populations in the region, highlighted the urgency of creating an integrated approach to addressing current threats and preventing conditions that could foster persistent threats in the future.

TSCTP's main elements include:

- Continued specialized Antiterrorism Assistance Training (ATA), Terrorist Interdiction Program (TIP), and Counterterrorist Finance (CTF) activities in the trans-Sahara region and possible regional expansion of those programs;
- Public diplomacy/countering violent extremism programs that expand outreach efforts in the trans-Sahara region and seek to develop regional programming embracing the vast and diverse region. Emphasis is on preserving the traditional tolerance and moderation displayed in most African Muslim communities and countering the development of extremism, particularly in youth and rural populations;
- Democratic governance programs that strive, in particular, to provide adequate levels of U.S. government support to build democratic institutions and address economic and social factors contributing to radicalism in the Maghreb and the Sahel, strengthening those states to withstand internal threats; and,
- Military programs intended to expand military-to-military cooperation, ensure adequate resources are available to train, advise, and assist regional forces, and establish institutions promoting better regional cooperation, communication, and intelligence sharing.

The African Union. The African Union (AU) has several counterterrorism legal instruments including a Convention on the Prevention and Combating of Terrorism (1999), a 2002 Protocol to the Convention, and a 2004 Plan of Action. The Addis Ababa–based AU Commission provided guidance to its 53 member states and coordinated limited technical assistance to cover member states' counterterrorism capability gaps.

The AU worked with member states to eliminate redundancies between the Algiers-based African Center for Study and Research in Terrorism (ACSRT) and the Committee on Intelligence and Security Services in Africa (CISSA), which was first established at the AU Summit in Abuja, Nigeria, in January 2005.

The Department of State and the Department of Defense's Africa Center for Strategic Studies (ACSS) have collaborated with the AU to run counterterrorism workshops. In December, ACSRT and ACSS jointly hosted an African Capacity Building Counterterrorism Workshop that focused on combating terrorist financing in North and West Africa. The workshop brought together approximately 50 African civilian and military officials from North and West African countries that are engaged in the Trans-Sahara Counterterrorism Partnership. ACSRT also held sub-regional counterterrorism seminars in Algeria in April, and in Congo in May, that examined the nature of terrorism threats in those regions, the capacity of countries in those regions to counter terrorism, and their needs for technical assistance to strengthen that capacity.

In 2005, with Danish funding, the AU hired a consultant to draft a counterterrorism Model Law to serve as a template to assist member states in drafting language to implement counterterrorism commitments. In December 2006, an AU-sponsored group of experts drafted counterterrorism language, which was in the process of being legislated. The group of experts decided to retain options for both broad and specific laws and determined that new legislation was needed to combat money laundering and other financial crimes. In August 2008, the AU Peace and Security Council requested that the AU Commission expedite the development of the African Counterterrorism Law.

Some AU member states maintained that Africa's colonial legacy made it difficult to accept a definition of terrorism that excluded an exception for "freedom fighters." Nonetheless, the AU is on record strongly condemning acts of terrorism. In August, the Peace and Security Council issued a statement condemning "unreservedly acts of terrorism, wherever they occur."

Although the AU Commission had the strong political will to act as an effective counterterrorism partner, AU staffing remained below requisite levels; consequently, capacity remained relatively weak. The AU created a counterterrorism unit at its Addis Ababa headquarters to coordinate and promote member state counterterrorism efforts more effectively. The AU welcomed technical and financial assistance from international partners and donors to bolster both AU headquarters and ACSRT activities approved by member states.

East Asia and Pacific Overview

Since 2001, the sustained commitment to counter terrorism by the governments in Southeast Asia and their citizens has significantly weakened Jemaah Islamiya (JI) and other regional terrorist groups. The efforts of law enforcement, intelligence, and prosecutors have been bolstered by increased regional security cooperation and committed support from the United States and other international partners. The interdiction of a small, semi-autonomous terrorist cell in Palembang, South Sumatra, by Indonesian security forces in July, however, demonstrated the possible reemergence of groups that espouse violent extremist ideologies. Six years after the 2002 Bali attacks, which killed over 200 people, elements of a seriously fractured JI and their adherents retained the intent to destabilize regional security and attack Western and U.S. interests in Southeast Asia. Additionally, the unresolved conflict in the Southern Philippines between the government of the Philippines and the Moro Islamic Liberation Front (MILF) boiled over late in the year when a carefully negotiated peace accord failed to win approval from the Philippine Supreme Court. This led to a renewal of violence in Mindanao as MILF insurgents perpetrated bombings, assassinations, and kidnappings aimed at government forces and in some cases the general civilian population.

In November, the government of Indonesia executed three of the 2002 Bali bombers: Amrozi bin Nurhasym, Imam Samudra, and Ali Gufron (aka Mukhlas). The executions provoked no serious security incidents despite calls by JI co-founder Abu Bakar Ba'asyir for retaliatory attacks. Additionally, in January, the government of Indonesia formally charged the ten suspected members of the Palembang Cell, who were arrested in July. Such trials of suspected violators of terrorism laws in Indonesia have demonstrated Indonesia's commitment to due process in all stages of the criminal justice process and have increased the credibility of Indonesia's counterterrorism policies.

The U.S. dual strategy of politically supporting the peace process between the government of the Philippines and the MILF while providing developmental assistance in areas at risk for terrorist recruitment continued to marginalize the few remaining ASG and JI terrorists in the southern Philippines. Philippine military and law enforcement agencies conducted intensive civil-military and internal security operations to eliminate terrorist safe havens in the Sulu Archipelago and central Mindanao. JI bomber Umar Patek and several ASG operatives remained on the run, probably on Jolo Island.

In February, Mas Selemat Kastari, the former leader of a JI cell in Singapore, escaped from Singaporean detention. Despite a massive manhunt, Singaporean authorities failed to locate and re-capture Kastari. Other prominent terrorists, such as key JI operatives Noordin Mohammad Top, Dulmatin, and Umar Patek, also remained at large in the region.

Malaysia continued to use the Internal Security Act (ISA) to detain terrorist suspects without bringing them to trial. At year's end, Malaysian authorities held 16 terrorist suspects linked to JI and 13 linked to Darul Islam—some of whom were undergoing a program of rehabilitation—under ISA detention. On average, the Malaysian government has held suspected terrorists and suspected terrorist supporters in ISA detention for two to six years. Over the past year, the government released 32 detainees, including 13 terrorist suspects linked to JI and six linked to Darul Islam.

Thai and U.S. government officials have long expressed concern that transnational terrorist groups could establish links with southern Thailand–based separatist groups. However, there were no indications that transnational terrorist groups were directly involved in the violence in the south, and there was no evidence of direct operational links between southern Thai separatist groups and regional terrorist networks.

Despite a series of violent incidents—none of which have been tied to terrorists—and threats leading up to the Beijing Olympics, the Games were held successfully without episodes of terrorism. Starting in June, representatives of a group calling itself the Turkistan Islamic Party (TIP) posted videos on the Internet taking credit for violent incidents in China and threatening to strike the Olympic Games. TIP is believed to be another name for the Eastern Turkistan Islamic Movement (ETIM), a UN-listed terrorist organization.

On October 11, the United States rescinded the designation of the Democratic People's Republic of Korea (DPRK) as a state sponsor of terrorism in accordance with criteria set forth in U.S. law, including a certification that the government of North Korea had not provided any support for international terrorism during the preceding six-month period and the provision by the government of assurances that it will not support acts of international terrorism in the future.

As in 2007, institutes like the United States–Thailand International Law Enforcement Academy (ILEA) in Bangkok, the Australian-Indonesian Jakarta Center for Law Enforcement Cooperation (JCLEC), and the Southeast Asia Regional Center for Counterterrorism (SEARCCT) in Malaysia sought to expand their efforts to provide effective counterterrorism training to law enforcement officers throughout the region. Multilateral forums, including the UN Security Council's Counterterrorism Committee (UNCTC), the G8's Roma-Lyon Group and Counterterrorism Action Group (CTAG), the Asia-Pacific Economic Cooperation (APEC) forum, the Association of Southeast Asian Nations (ASEAN), and the ASEAN Regional Forum (ARF), also promoted regional counterterrorism cooperation.

Australia maintained its position as a regional leader in the fight against terrorism and worked to strengthen the Asia-Pacific region's counterterrorism capacity through a range of bilateral and regional initiatives in forums such as APEC, ASEAN ARF, and the Pacific Island Forum. Japan also continued to assist counterterrorism capacity building in developing countries through seminars, workshops, and training. In October, the United States, Japan, and Australia convened for the fourth annual session of the Trilateral Strategic Dialogue Counterterrorism Consultations in Washington.

Europe and Eurasia Overview

European countries improved their capabilities to counter the terrorist threat, foiled several significant terrorist plots, and prosecuted and jailed terrorist suspects. European governments were increasingly concerned and sought greater understanding of the process of "radicalization" and how to prevent it. Toward that end, European governments continued their efforts at outreach to domestic Muslim communities and made attempts to gain support from those communities to counter the appeal of violent extremist ideology.

European nations continued to work in close partnership with the United States against a terrorist threat characterized by both external and, increasingly, internal components. The contributions of European countries in sharing intelligence, arresting members of terrorist cells, interdicting terrorist financing, and logistics were vital elements in the global effort to combat terrorism and violent extremism.

The United States and European Union continued to cooperate closely to counter terrorism. At the June 2004 U.S.-EU Summit, the sides agreed on a Declaration on Combating Terrorism that renewed the transatlantic commitment to develop measures to maximize capacities to detect, investigate, and prosecute terrorists; prevent terrorist attacks; prevent access by terrorists to financial and other economic resources; enhance information sharing and cooperation among law enforcement agencies; and improve the effectiveness of border information systems. These commitments were reaffirmed at the 2008 Summit, and work continued on the implementation and, in particular, the ratification of mutual legal assistance treaties intended to advance transatlantic cooperation.

European nations were active participants in a variety of multilateral organizations that contribute to counterterrorist efforts, including the G8, NATO, the Financial Action Task Force, the Global Initiative to Combat Nuclear Terrorism, the Organization for Security and Cooperation in Europe (OSCE), the International Maritime Organization, and the International Civil Aviation Organization. The United States worked with its international partners through multilateral organizations to establish and implement best practices, build the counterterrorism capabilities of "weak but willing" states, and help counter terrorism globally. OSCE members committed themselves to becoming parties to the 13 international terrorism conventions and protocols, to work together to modernize travel documents and shipping container security, to prevent and suppress the financing of terrorist organizations, and to implement UNSC Resolution 1540 to counter WMD (related materials and the means of delivery) proliferation.

Terrorist activity and the presence of terrorist support networks in Europe remained a source of serious concern. Efforts to combat the threat in Europe were sometimes slowed by legal protections that made it difficult to take firm judicial action against suspected terrorists, the absence of adequate legislation, or standards of evidence that limited the use of classified information in holding terrorist suspects. Terrorists also sought to take advantage of the ease of travel among Schengen countries. At times, some European states have not been able to prosecute successfully or hold some of the suspected terrorists brought before their courts—a product, in part, of insufficient measures to use intelligence information in judicial proceedings. The EU as a whole remained reluctant to take steps to block the assets of charities associated with Hamas and Hezbollah.

No major terrorist attacks took place in Europe in 2008, but arrests in Italy, Spain, France, Belgium, the UK, Turkey, and other countries brought home the scope of the challenge facing European governments and security forces. The level of threat in western Europe remained high, particularly in the Netherlands, Denmark, Germany, France, and Belgium. The deaths of Swedish extremists in Somalia and Iraq and the first-ever German-born suicide bomber in Afghanistan highlighted the global nature of the threat and the ease with which extremists can travel to conflict areas.

Cooperation with and among European law enforcement agencies remained vital for counterterrorism successes, and judicial proceedings in countries across Europe resulted in the successful convictions of several terrorist suspects. France and Spain continued to cooperate effectively against Basque Fatherland and Liberty (ETA), scoring major successes including the arrests of ETA alleged political and military chiefs. Germany and other European countries continued to maintain pressure on the militant Kurdish nationalist group Kurdistan Workers' Party (PKK), which raised funds, often through illicit activity, to support violence in Turkey. Cooperation between France and Belgium led in December to the arrests of 23 persons allegedly connected to al-Qaeda. German courts also convicted suspects for activities connected to organizations ranging from al-Qaeda and the Islamic Jihad Union, to the PKK. A Danish court convicted Hammad Khurshid, a Pakistani-born Danish citizen, and an accomplice for conspiring to commit terrorism. Italian authorities addressed similarly broad challenges, arresting, charging, and convicting suspects linked to Islamic extremism, the Tamil Tigers, and violent left- and right-wing fringe groups. Recent court decisions have called into question the European Council's regulations for implementing asset freezes against terrorists and supporters of terrorism, including those who have been designated by the UN. Trials in Belgium in the case of Bilal Soughir and five other men suspected of having recruited and trained terrorists for suicide attacks in Iraq resulted in convictions with sentences between ten and two years; all of the sentences were later reduced on appeal. There were also other appeals—an appeals court in The Netherlands acquitted the seven members of the Hofstad terrorist group of participating in a criminal and terrorist organization, though the convictions of three terrorists were upheld, and the prosecution appealed the acquittals to the Supreme Court. In Spain, the Supreme Court acquitted on appeal four of the 21 convicted defendants in the Madrid train bombings trial who had been sentenced in October 2007.

Middle East and North Africa Overview

Most governments in the region cooperated with the United States in counterterrorist activities and undertook efforts to strengthen their capabilities to counter terrorism effectively. These efforts included participation in U.S. Government–sponsored antiterrorism assistance (ATA) programs and taking steps to bolster banking and legal regimes to combat terrorist financing.

The Iraqi government, in coordination with the Coalition, made significant progress in combating al-Qaeda in Iraq (AQI) and affiliated terrorist organizations. There was a notable reduction in the number of security incidents throughout much of Iraq, including a decrease in civilian casualties, enemy attacks, and improvised explosive device (IED) attacks in the last quarter of the year. Terrorist organizations and insurgent groups continued their attacks on Coalition and Iraqi security forces using IEDs, vehicle-borne improvised explosive devices (VBIEDs), and suicide bombers. The Iraqi government continued to emphasize national reconciliation and made progress in passing key pieces of reconciliation-related legislation. There were also practical steps taken that helped to advance reconciliation at the provincial and local level. The United States continued its focused efforts to mitigate the threat posed by foreign fighters in Iraq. State sponsors of terrorism, Iran and Syria, continued to play destabilizing roles in the region.

The Expanded Neighbors Process continued to provide a forum for Iraq and its neighbors to address the political and security challenges facing Iraq and the region. In November, the Iraqi government sent representatives to Syria to participate in the second Neighbors Process working group on border security where the group sought new ways to limit the flow of foreign terrorists into Iraq.

Israel responded to the terrorist threat as it has in recent years, with operations targeted at terrorist leaders, terrorist infrastructure, and active terrorist activities such as rocket launching groups. Israel Defense Forces (IDF) and Israel Security Services (ISA) continued incursions into the West Bank to conduct roundups and other military operations designed to increase pressure on Palestinian terrorist organizations and their supporters. The Israeli security services also imposed strict and widespread closures and curfews in Palestinian areas. The regular and indiscriminate rocket attacks on Israel from Gaza were met by retaliatory fire by the IDF. Israel also maintained its targeted assassinations policy in Gaza. While there continued to be an overall decrease in the number of successfully perpetrated terrorist attacks in comparison to previous years, Israeli security officials maintained that the decrease was not for lack of terrorists' efforts, but because the security services were able to keep terrorist planners and operators off balance and foil acts before they were carried out. The Israeli Air Force increasingly launched airstrikes against launch teams in November and December following escalations in rocket and mortar attacks. Israel launched Operation Cast Lead in Gaza on December 27 in response to these rocket attacks.

In Lebanon, a campaign of domestic political intimidation continued, including several attacks against members of the Lebanese army and Internal Security Forces. In May, Lebanese Hezbollah initiated armed confrontations against Lebanese government and other Sunni and Christian elements in the country following the government's efforts to shut down Hezbollah's independent telecommunications network, in addition to the removal of the Hezbollah-affiliated head of airport security. A Hezbollah official suspected in several bombings against U.S. citizens, Imad Mughniyeh, was killed in Damascus, Syria, in February. No one has taken responsibility for his death.

Attacks in Algeria in August killed nearly 80 people. These attacks were indicative of the shifts in strategy made by al-Qaeda in the Islamic Maghreb (AQIM) towards attacks employing suicide tactics and improvised explosive devices (IEDs), and the targeting of Western interests as well as Algerian government officials and civilians.

On March 10, AQIM claimed responsibility for kidnapping two Austrian tourists near the Tunisia-Algeria border. The hostages were released on October 31 after a ransom was paid. In February, the Tunisian courts handed down guilty verdicts on eight of 30 Tunisians convicted in a December 2007/January 2008 plot targeting U.S. and UK interests in Tunisia.

The security situation in Yemen deteriorated significantly over the past year as al-Qaeda in Yemen increased its attacks against Western and Yemeni government institutions. On January 17, suspected al-Qaeda operatives ambushed a tourist convoy in the eastern Hadramout Governorate, killing two Belgians. The U.S. Embassy was attacked on September 17; fatalities included several Yemeni security personnel and citizens, as well as an American citizen.

South and Central Asia Overview

Already terrorism plagued, South and Central Asia experienced more tragedy in 2008 as terrorists expanded their operations and networks across the region and beyond. The impact of the region's terrorist problem on the United States and its citizens grew more severe as dozens of U.S. citizens were attacked, kidnapped, or killed by violent extremists. In response, the U.S. worked to increase counterterrorism cooperation with its partners in South Asia. However, continuing political unrest in the region, weak governments, and competing factions within various South Asia governments, combined with increased terrorist activities, resulted in limited progress and made South Asia even less safe for U.S. citizens and interests than it was in 2007.

Although hundreds of terrorist attacks were conducted throughout South Asia, the year was punctuated by several high-profile and immensely destructive acts of terrorism, including the July 7 bombing of the Indian embassy in Kabul, Afghanistan; the November 26 attacks in Mumbai, India; and the September 20 bombing of the Marriott Hotel in Islamabad, Pakistan.

The Taliban-led insurgency in Afghanistan remained strong and resilient in the south and east. Although the insurgency absorbed heavy combat and leadership losses, its ability to recruit foot soldiers from its core base of rural Pashtuns remained undiminished.

Pakistan continued to suffer from rising militancy and extremism. The United States remained concerned that the Federally Administered Tribal Areas (FATA) of Pakistan were being used as a safe haven for al-Qaeda terrorists, Afghan insurgents, and other extremists.

India ranked among the world's most terrorism-afflicted countries. It was the focus of numerous attacks from both externally-based terrorist organizations and internally-based separatist or terrorist entities. Several attacks inflicted large numbers of casualties, including the most devastating attack of the year on November 26 in Mumbai. Although clearly committed to combating violent extremism, the Indian government's counterterrorism efforts remained hampered by its outdated and overburdened law enforcement and legal systems. In the wake of the Mumbai terrorist attacks, India's Parliament has introduced bills to restructure its counterterrorism laws and has proposed a new agency, the National Investigative Agency, to create national-level capability to investigate and potentially prosecute acts of terrorism. Since the Mumbai attacks, India has also greatly increased counterterrorism cooperation with the United States.

Leading up to the national elections on December 29, Bangladesh's caretaker government attempted to crack down on those accused of terrorism and criminality. The Awami League won a landslide electoral victory, claiming 230 of the 299 seats in Parliament. It has pledged to focus serious attention on Bangladesh's counterterrorism needs and has championed the creation of a South Asia counterterrorism task force to enable countries to work together regionally to stamp out the rise of violent extremism.

In Sri Lanka, the government continued its military campaign against the Liberation Tigers of Tamil Eelam (LTTE), a U.S.-designated foreign terrorist organization. Both sides continued to engage in "any means necessary" tactics to fight the war. The LTTE used suicide bombings and other terrorist attacks, some of which caused serious civilian casualties. The government has been criticized for using paramilitary organizations that rely on abduction, extra-judicial killings, and other illegal tactics to combat the LTTE and their suspected sympathizers. At the end of the year, the military recaptured most of the LTTE-held territory, including Killinochchi, but the LTTE continued to fight, reverting to more asymmetrical tactics, including the continued use of suicide bombers in the capital Colombo.

In April, the Communist Party of Nepal (Maoists) won the national Constituent Assembly election, and took control of various government ministries as well as the Prime Minister's position. Despite their electoral victory, the Maoists remained a U.S.-designated terrorist entity under the Terrorism Exclusion List.

The Central Asian region's most significant terrorist organizations include the Islamic Movement of Uzbekistan (IMU) and a splinter group, the Islamic Jihad Group (IJG). However, radical extremist groups such as Hizb ut-Tahrir (HT) foment an anti-Semitic, anti-Western ideology that may indirectly generate support for terrorism. HT, an extremist political movement advocating the establishment of a borderless, theocratic Islamic state throughout the entire Muslim world, has followers in Kyrgyzstan, Kazakhstan, Tajikistan, Uzbekistan, and elsewhere. The United States has no evidence that HT has committed any acts of international terrorism, but the group's radical anti-American and anti-Semitic ideology is sympathetic to acts of violence against the United States and its allies. HT has publicly called on Muslims to travel to Iraq and Afghanistan to fight Coalition Forces.

Part III

BE PREPARED

Chapter Nine

Emergency Preparedness: Why Prepare?

The Federal Citizen Information Center in Pueblo, Colorado, offers the following information in its *Citizen Guide to Disaster Preparedness* (www .pueblo.gsa.gov/cic_text/family/disaster-guide):

Immediately after an emergency, essential services may be cut off and local disaster relief and government responders may not be able to reach you right away. Even if they can reach you, knowing what to do to protect yourself and your household is essential.

CREATING A DISASTER PLAN

One of the most important steps you can take in preparing for emergencies is to develop a household disaster plan.

1. Learn about the natural disasters that could occur in your community from your local emergency management office or American Red Cross chapter. Learn whether hazardous materials are produced, stored or transported near your area. Learn about possible consequences of deliberate acts of terror. Ask how to prepare for each potential emergency and how to respond.
2. Talk with employers and school officials about their emergency response plans.
3. Talk with your household about potential emergencies and how to respond to each. Talk about what you would need to do in an evacuation.
4. Plan how your household would stay in contact if you were separated. Identify two meeting places: the first should be near your home in case of fire, perhaps a tree or a telephone pole; the second should be away from your neighborhood in case you cannot return home.

5. Pick a friend or relative who lives out of the area, for household members to call to say they are okay.
6. Draw a floor plan of your home. Mark two escape routes from each room.
7. Post emergency telephone numbers by telephones. Teach children how and when to call 911.
8. Make sure everyone in your household knows how and when to shut off water, gas, and electricity at the main switches. Consult with your local utilities if you have questions.
9. Take a first aid and CPR class. Local American Red Cross chapters can provide information. Official certification by the American Red Cross provides "Good Samaritan" law protection for those giving first aid.
10. Reduce the economic impact of disaster on your property and your household's health and financial well-being.

   • Review property insurance policies before disaster strikes—make sure policies are current and be certain they meet your needs (type of coverage, amount of coverage, and hazard covered—flood, earthquake).
   • Protect your household's financial well-being before a disaster strikes— review life insurance policies and consider saving money in an "emergency" savings account that could be used in any crisis. It is advisable to keep a small amount of cash or traveler's checks at home in a safe place where you can quickly gain access to it in case of an evacuation.
   • Be certain that health insurance policies are current and meet the needs of your household.

11. Consider ways to help neighbors who may need special assistance, such as the elderly or the disabled.
12. Make arrangements for pets. Pets are not usually allowed in public shelters. Service animals, for those who depend on them, are allowed.

EMERGENCY PLANNING FOR PEOPLE WITH SPECIAL NEEDS

If you have a disability or special need, you may have to take additional steps to protect yourself and your household in an emergency. If you know of friends or neighbors with special needs, help them with these extra precautions. Examples include:

• Hearing impaired may need to make special arrangements to receive a warning.
• Mobility impaired may need assistance in getting to a shelter.
• Households with a single, working parent may need help from others both in planning for disasters and during an emergency.

- Non-English-speaking people may need assistance planning for and responding to emergencies. Community and cultural groups may be able to help keep these populations informed.
- People without vehicles may need to make arrangements for transportation.
- People with special dietary needs should have an adequate emergency food supply.

In addition, people with special needs should:

1. Find out about special assistance that may be available in your community. Register with the office of emergency services or fire department for assistance, so needed help can be provided quickly in an emergency.
2. Create a network of neighbors, relatives, friends, and co-workers to aid you in an emergency. Discuss your needs and make sure they know how to operate necessary equipment.
3. Discuss your needs with your employer.
4. If you are mobility impaired and live or work in a high-rise building, have an escape chair.
5. If you live in an apartment building, ask the management to mark accessible exits clearly and to make arrangements to help you evacuate the building.
6. Keep extra wheelchair batteries, oxygen, catheters, medication, food for seeing-eye or hearing-ear dogs, or other items you might need. Also, keep a list of the type and serial numbers of medical devices you need.
7. Those who are not disabled should learn who in their neighborhood or building is disabled, so that they may assist them during emergencies.
8. If you are a caregiver for a person with special needs, make sure you have a plan to communicate if an emergency occurs.

HOW TO PREPARE FOR A TERRORIST ATTACK

The American Red Cross offers the following information on how to prepare for a terrorist attack (www.redcross.org/portal/site/en/menuitem.86f46a 12f382290517a8f210b80f78a0/?vgnextoid=cbc95d795323b110VgnVCM 10000089f0870aRCRD&vgnextfmt=default):

What You Can Do to Prepare

Finding out what can happen is the first step. Once you have determined the events possible and their potential in your community, it is important that you discuss them with your family or household. Develop a disaster plan together.

1. Create an emergency communications plan. Choose an out-of-town contact your family or household will call or e-mail to check on each other should a disaster occur. Your selected contact should live far enough away that they would be unlikely to be directly affected by the same event, and they should know they are the chosen contact. Make sure every household member has that contact's, and each other's, e-mail addresses and telephone numbers (home, work, pager, and cell). Leave these contact numbers at your children's schools, if you have children, and at your workplace. Your family should know that if telephones are not working, they need to be patient and try again later or try e-mail. Many people flood the telephone lines when emergencies happen but e-mail can sometimes get through when calls don't.

2. Establish a meeting place. Having a predetermined meeting place away from your home will save time and minimize confusion should your home be affected or the area evacuated. You may even want to make arrangements to stay with a family member or friend in case of an emergency. Be sure to include any pets in these plans, since pets are not permitted in shelters and some hotels will not accept them.

3. Assemble a disaster supplies kit. If you need to evacuate your home or are asked to "shelter in place," having some essential supplies on hand will make you and your family more comfortable. Prepare a disaster supplies kit in an easy-to-carry container such as a duffel bag or small plastic trash can. Include "special needs" items for any member of your household (infant formula or items for people with disabilities or older people), first aid supplies (including prescription medications), a change of clothing for each household member, a sleeping bag or bedroll for each, a battery powered radio or television and extra batteries, food, bottled water, and tools. It is also a good idea to include some cash and copies of important family documents (birth certificates, passports, and licenses) in your kit.

Copies of essential documents—like powers of attorney, birth and marriage certificates, insurance policies, life insurance beneficiary designations, and a copy of your will—should also be kept in a safe location outside your home. A safe deposit box or the home of a friend or family member who lives out of town is a good choice.

4. Check on the school emergency plan of any school-age children you may have. You need to know if they will keep children at school until a parent or designated adult can pick them up or send them home on their own. Be sure that the school has updated information about how to reach parents and responsible caregivers to arrange for pickup. And, ask what type of authorization the school may require to release a child to someone you designate, if you are not able to pick up your child. During times of emergency the school telephones may be overwhelmed with calls.

For more information on putting together a disaster plan, request a copy of the brochure titled *Your Family Disaster Plan* (A4466) from your local American Red Cross chapter. You may also want to request a copy of *Before Disaster Strikes . . . How to Make Sure You're Financially Prepared* (A5075) for specific information on what you can do now to protect your assets.

If Disaster Strikes

- Remain calm and be patient.
- Follow the advice of local emergency officials.
- Listen to your radio or television for news and instructions.
- If the disaster occurs near you, check for injuries. Give first aid and get help for seriously injured people.
- If the disaster occurs near your home while you are there, check for damage using a flashlight. Do not light matches or candles or turn on electrical switches. Check for fires, fire hazards, and other household hazards. Sniff for gas leaks, starting at the water heater. If you smell gas or suspect a leak, turn off the main gas valve, open windows, and get everyone outside quickly.
- Shut off any other damaged utilities.
- Confine or secure your pets.
- Call your family contact—do not use the telephone again unless it is a life-threatening emergency.
- Check on your neighbors, especially those who are elderly or disabled.

A Word on What Could Happen

As we learned from the events of September 11, 2001, the following things can happen after a terrorist attack:

- There can be significant numbers of casualties and/or damage to buildings and the infrastructure. So employers need up-to-date information about any medical needs you may have and on how to contact your designated beneficiaries.
- Heavy law enforcement involvement at local, state, and federal levels follows a terrorist attack due to the event's criminal nature.
- Health and mental health resources in the affected communities can be strained to their limits, maybe even overwhelmed.
- Extensive media coverage, strong public fear, and international implications and consequences can continue for a prolonged period.
- Workplaces and schools may be closed, and there may be restrictions on domestic and international travel.
- You and your family or household may have to evacuate an area, avoiding roads blocked for your safety.
- Clean-up may take many months.

Evacuation

If local authorities ask you to leave your home, they have a good reason to make this request, and you should heed the advice immediately. Listen to your radio or television and follow the instructions of local emergency officials and keep these simple tips in mind:

- Wear long-sleeved shirts, long pants, and sturdy shoes so you can be protected as much as possible.
- Take your disaster supplies kit.
- Take your pets with you; do not leave them behind. Because pets are not permitted in public shelters, follow your plan to go to a relative's or friend's home, or find a "pet-friendly" hotel.
- Lock your home.
- Use travel routes specified by local authorities—don't use shortcuts, because certain areas may be impassable or dangerous.
- Stay away from downed power lines.
- Listen to local authorities. Your local authorities will provide you with the most accurate information specific to an event in your area. Staying tuned to local radio and television, and following their instructions is your safest choice.

If you're sure you have time:

- Call your family contact to tell them where you are going and when you expect to arrive.
- Shut off water and electricity before leaving, if instructed to do so. Leave natural gas service ON unless local officials advise you otherwise. You may need gas for heating and cooking, and only a professional can restore gas service in your home once it's been turned off. In a disaster situation it could take weeks for a professional to respond.

New Orleans, Louisiana, August 30, 2005. Coast Guard Petty Officer 2nd Class Scott D. Rady, 34, of Tampa, Florida, gives the signal to hoist a pregnant woman from her apartment. U.S. Coast Guard photograph by Petty Officer 2nd Class NyxoLyno Cangemi

New Orleans, Louisiana, August 29, 2005. Aerial of a flooded neighborhood with a rescue boat picking up victims. Jocelyn Augustino/FEMA Photo

South Florida, August 1992. FEMA worker helping an injured person. Bob Epstein/ FEMA Photo

New Orleans, Louisiana, March 13, 2006. Volunteers from the University of Alaska at Fairbanks and Rotaract shovel broken flood-soaked Sheetrock into a wheelbarrow. Marvin Nauman/FEMA Photo

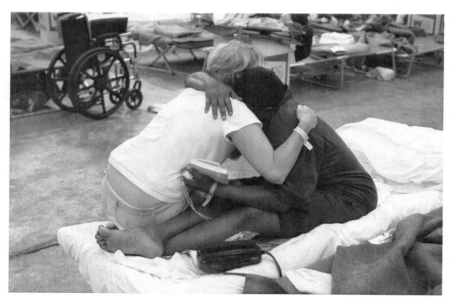

Houston, Texas, September 3, 2005. Counselors and volunteers help stressed and grief-stricken evacuees deal with the trauma of Hurricane Katrina in the Astrodome. Andrea Booher/FEMA Photo

Humans are not the only victims of natural disaster.

Sheltering-in-Place

If you are advised by local officials to "shelter in place," what they mean is for you to remain inside your home or office and protect yourself there. Close and lock all windows and exterior doors. Turn off all fans, heating and air-conditioning systems. Close the fireplace damper. Get your disaster supplies kit, and make sure the radio is working. Go to an interior room without windows that's above ground level. In the case of a chemical threat, an above-ground location is preferable because some chemicals are heavier than air, and may seep into basements even if the windows are closed. Using duct tape, seal all cracks around the door and any vents into the room. Keep listening to your radio or television until you are told all is safe or you are told to evacuate. Local officials may call for evacuation in specific areas at greatest risk in your community.

Additional Positive Steps You Can Take

Raw, unedited footage of terrorism events and people's reaction to those events can be very upsetting, especially to children. We do not recommend that children watch television news reports about such events, especially if the news reports show images over and over again about the same incident. Young children do not realize that it is repeated video footage, and think the event is happening again and again. Adults may also need to give themselves a break from watching disturbing footage. However, listening to local radio and television reports will provide you with the most accurate information from responsible governmental authorities on what's happening and what actions you will need to take. So you may want to make some arrangements to take turns listening to the news with other adult members of your household.

Another useful preparation includes learning some basic first aid. To enroll in a first aid and AED/CPR course, contact your local American Red Cross chapter. In an emergency situation, you need to tend to your own well-being first and then consider first aid for others immediately around you, including possibly assisting injured people to evacuate a building if necessary.

People who may have come into contact with a biological or chemical agent may need to go through a decontamination procedure and receive medical attention. Listen to the advice of local officials on the radio or television to determine what steps you will need to take to protect yourself and your family. As emergency services will likely be overwhelmed, only call 9-1-1 about life-threatening emergencies.

First Aid Primer

If you encounter someone who is injured, apply the emergency action steps: Check-Call-Care. **Check** the scene to make sure it is safe for you to approach. Then check the victim for unconsciousness and life-threatening conditions. Someone who has a life-threatening condition, such as not breathing or severe bleeding, requires immediate care by trained responders and may require treatment by medical professionals. **Call** out for help. There are some steps that you can take, however, to **care** for someone who is hurt, but whose injuries are not life threatening.

Control Bleeding

- Cover the wound with a dressing, and press firmly against the wound (direct pressure).
- Elevate the injured area above the level of the heart if you do not suspect that the victim has a broken bone.
- Cover the dressing with a roller bandage.
- If the bleeding does not stop:

  ○ Apply additional dressings and bandages.
  ○ Use a pressure point to squeeze the artery against the bone.

- Provide care for shock.

Care for Shock

- Keep the victim from getting chilled or overheated.
- Elevate the legs about 12 inches (if broken bones are not suspected).
- Do not give food or drink to the victim.

Tend Burns

- Stop the burning by cooling the burn with large amounts of water.
- Cover the burn with dry, clean dressings or cloth.

Care for Injuries to Muscles, Bones, and Joints

- Rest the injured part.
- Apply ice or a cold pack to control swelling and reduce pain.
- Avoid any movement or activity that causes pain.
- If you must move the victim because the scene is becoming unsafe, try to immobilize the injured part to keep it from moving.

Be Aware of Biological/Radiological Exposure

- Listen to local radio and television reports for the most accurate information from responsible governmental and medical authorities on what's happening and what actions you will need to take.

Reduce Any Care Risks

The risk of getting a disease while giving first aid is extremely rare. However, to reduce the risk even further:

- Avoid direct contact with blood and other body fluids.
- Use protective equipment, such as disposable gloves and breathing barriers.
- Thoroughly wash your hands with soap and water immediately after giving care.

It is important to be prepared for an emergency and to know how to give emergency care.

FOR MORE INFORMATION

All of these recommendations make good sense, regardless of the potential problem. For more information on how to get ready for disaster and be safe when disaster strikes, or to register for a first aid and AED/CPR course, contact your local American Red Cross chapter.

For information about your community's specific plans for response to disasters and other emergencies, contact your local office of emergency management.

For information on what a business can do to protect its employees and customers as well as develop business continuity plans, you may want to get a copy of the *Emergency Management Guide for Business and Industry* and/or

Biloxi, Mississippi, April 27, 2006. President George W. Bush meets with volunteers from Hands On Network at their base camp. White House Photo by Eric Draper

Preparing Your Business for the Unthinkable from your local American Red Cross chapter, or see www.redcross.org/services/disaster/beprepared.

For more information about the specific effects of chemical or biological agents, the following websites may be helpful:

- Centers for Disease Control and Prevention: www.bt.cdc.gov
- U.S. Department of Energy: www.energy.gov
- U.S. Department of Health and Human Services: www.hhs.gov
- Federal Emergency Management Agency: www.rris.fema.gov
- Environmental Protection Agency: www.epa.gov/swercepp

ARE YOU READY?

The Citizen Corps website (www.citizencorps.gov/ready) offers the following suggestions:

Here are some things you can do right now to be safer:

- Check and change the batteries in your smoke alarms and replace all alarms that are more than 10 years old.

- Make sure you know where your local fire department, police station, and hospital are and post a list of emergency phone numbers near all the telephones in your home.
- Organize and practice a family fire drill—make sure your children know what your smoke detector sounds like and what to do if it goes off when they are sleeping.
- Locate the utility mains for your home and be sure you know how to turn them off manually: gas, electricity, and water.
- Create an emergency plan for your household, including your pets. Decide where your family will meet if a disaster does happen: (1) right outside your home in case of a sudden emergency, like a fire; and (2) outside your neighborhood in case you can't return home—ask an out of town friend to be your "family contact" to relay messages.
- Prepare a 3-day disaster supply kit, complete with flashlights, batteries, blankets, and an emergency supply of water and food (and pet food!).
- Plan to hold a Neighborhood Watch meeting—your local Sheriffs' office or police station can help you get started or visit www.usaonwatch.org for more information.
- Check the expiration dates of all over-the-counter medications—discard all that are expired and replace any that are routinely needed.
- Make sure all cleaning products and dangerous objects are out of children's reach.
- Plan to sign up for a first aid training course. Call your local American Red Cross chapter, the National Safety Council, or American Safety & Health Institute to ask about courses in your area (www.redcross.org, www.nsc.org, or www.ashinstitute.org).
- Visit with your neighbors and discuss how you would handle a disaster in your area. Talk to neighbors with special needs and help them become safer too!

GENERAL INFORMATION ABOUT TERRORISM

FEMA's website includes the following information (www.fema.gov/hazard/terrorism/info.shtm):

Terrorism is the use of force or violence against persons or property in violation of the criminal laws of the United States for purposes of intimidation, coercion, or ransom.

Terrorists often use threats to:

- Create fear among the public.
- Try to convince citizens that their government is powerless to prevent terrorism.
- Get immediate publicity for their causes.

Acts of terrorism include threats of terrorism; assassinations; kidnappings; hijackings; bomb scares and bombings; cyber attacks (computer-based); and the use of chemical, biological, nuclear, and radiological weapons.

High-risk targets for acts of terrorism include military and civilian government facilities, international airports, large cities, and high-profile landmarks. Terrorists might also target large public gatherings, water and food supplies, utilities, and corporate centers. Further, terrorists are capable of spreading fear by sending explosives or chemical and biological agents through the mail.

Within the immediate area of a terrorist event, you would need to rely on police, fire, and other officials for instructions. However, you can prepare in much the same way you would prepare for other crisis events.

The following are general guidelines:

- Be aware of your surroundings.
- Move or leave if you feel uncomfortable or if something does not seem right.
- Take precautions when traveling. Be aware of conspicuous or unusual behavior. Do not accept packages from strangers. Do not leave luggage unattended. You should promptly report unusual behavior, suspicious or unattended packages, and strange devices to the police or security personnel.
- Learn where emergency exits are located in buildings you frequent. Plan how to get out in the event of an emergency.

Ninth Ward, New Orleans, Louisiana, March 6, 2006. New Orleans Department Fire Fighters Search and Recovery team probe for recovery of any bodies that may be in debris caused by Hurricane Katrina. Demolition and Search and Recovery workers ensure that human remains are not in houses being demolished. Marvin Nauman/FEMA Photo

- Be prepared to do without services you normally depend on—electricity, telephone, natural gas, gasoline pumps, cash registers, ATMs, and Internet transactions.
- Work with building owners to ensure the following items are located on each floor of the building:

  ○ Portable, battery-operated radio and extra batteries.
  ○ Several flashlights and extra batteries.
  ○ First aid kit and manual.
  ○ Hard hats and dust masks.
  ○ Fluorescent tape to rope off dangerous areas.

WHAT TO DO IN THE EVENT OF A TERRORIST ATTACK

The following information comes from FEMA's *Are You Ready? An In-Depth Guide to Citizen Preparedness* (IS-22), which is FEMA's most comprehensive source on individual, family, and community preparedness (www.fema.gov/areyouready):

Explosives

Terrorists have frequently used explosive devices as one of their most common weapons. Terrorists do not have to look far to find out how to make explosive devices; the information is readily available in books and other information sources. The materials needed for an explosive device can be found in many places including variety, hardware, and auto supply stores. Explosive devices are highly portable using vehicles and humans as a means of transport. They are easily detonated from remote locations or by suicide bombers.

Conventional bombs have been used to damage and destroy financial, political, social, and religious institutions. Attacks have occurred in public places and on city streets with thousands of people around the world injured and killed.

Parcels that should make you suspicious:

- Are unexpected or from someone unfamiliar to you.
- Have no return address, or have one that can't be verified as legitimate.
- Are marked with restrictive endorsements such as "Personal," "Confidential," or "Do not X-ray."
- Have protruding wires or aluminum foil, strange odors, or stains.
- Show a city or state in the postmark that doesn't match the return address.
- Are of unusual weight given their size, or are lopsided or oddly shaped.
- Are marked with threatening language.
- Have inappropriate or unusual labeling.
- Have excessive postage or packaging material, such as masking tape and string.

- Have misspellings of common words.
- Are addressed to someone no longer with your organization or are otherwise outdated.
- Have incorrect titles or titles without a name.
- Are not addressed to a specific person.
- Have handwritten or poorly typed addresses.

If you receive a telephoned bomb threat, you should do the following:

- Get as much information from the caller as possible.
- Keep the caller on the line and record everything that is said.
- Notify the police and the building management.

If there is an explosion, you should:

- Get under a sturdy table or desk if things are falling around you. When they stop falling, leave quickly, watching for obviously weakened floors and stairways. As you exit from the building, be especially watchful of falling debris.
- Leave the building as quickly as possible. Do not stop to retrieve personal possessions or make phone calls.
- Do not use elevators.

Once you are out:

- Do not stand in front of windows, glass doors, or other potentially hazardous areas.
- Move away from sidewalks or streets to be used by emergency officials or others still exiting the building.

If you are trapped in debris:

- If possible, use a flashlight to signal your location to rescuers.
- Avoid unnecessary movement so you don't kick up dust.
- Cover your nose and mouth with anything you have on hand. (Dense-weave cotton material can act as a good filter. Try to breathe through the material.)
- Tap on a pipe or wall so rescuers can hear where you are.
- If possible, use a whistle to signal rescuers.
- Shout only as a last resort. Shouting can cause a person to inhale dangerous amounts of dust.

Biological Threats

Biological agents are organisms or toxins that can kill or incapacitate people, livestock, and crops. The three basic groups of biological agents that would likely be used as weapons are bacteria, viruses, and toxins. Most biological agents are difficult to grow and maintain. Many break down quickly when exposed to sunlight and other environmental factors, while others, such as anthrax spores, are very long lived. Biological agents can be dispersed by spraying them into the air, by infecting animals that carry the disease to humans, and by contaminating food and water. Delivery methods include:

- Aerosols—biological agents are dispersed into the air, forming a fine mist that may drift for miles. Inhaling the agent may cause disease in people or animals.
- Animals—some diseases are spread by insects and animals, such as fleas, mice, flies, mosquitoes, and livestock.
- Food and water contamination—some pathogenic organisms and toxins may persist in food and water supplies. Most microbes can be killed, and toxins deactivated, by cooking food and boiling water. Most microbes are killed by boiling water for one minute, but some require longer. Follow official instructions.
- Person-to-person—spread of a few infectious agents is also possible. Humans have been the source of infection for smallpox, plague, and the Lassa viruses.

Specific information on biological agents is available at the Centers for Disease Control and Prevention's website, www.bt.cdc.gov.

Before a Biological Attack. The following are guidelines for what you should do to prepare for a biological threat:

- Check with your doctor to ensure all required or suggested immunizations are up to date. Children and older adults are particularly vulnerable to biological agents.
- Consider installing a High Efficiency Particulate Air (HEPA) filter in your furnace return duct. These filters remove particles in the 0.3 to 10 micron range and will filter out most biological agents that may enter your house. If you do not have a central heating or cooling system, a stand-alone portable HEPA filter can be used.

Filtration in Buildings. Building owners and managers should determine the type and level of filtration in their structures and the level of protection it provides against biological agents. The National Institute of Occupational Safety and Health (NIOSH) provides technical guidance on this topic in their publication *Guidance for Filtration and Air-Cleaning Systems to Protect Building Environments from Airborne Chemical, Biological, or Radiological Attacks*. To obtain a copy, call 1 (800) 35NIOSH or visit www.cdc.gov/NIOSH/publist .html and request or download NIOSH Publication 2003-136.

During a Biological Attack. In the event of a biological attack, public health officials may not immediately be able to provide information on what you should do. It will take time to determine what the illness is, how it should be treated, and who is in danger. Watch television, listen to radio, or check the Internet for official news and information including signs and symptoms of the disease, areas in danger, if medications or vaccinations are being distributed, and where you should seek medical attention if you become ill.

The first evidence of an attack may be when you notice symptoms of the disease caused by exposure to an agent. Be suspicious of any symptoms you notice, but do not assume that any illness is a result of the attack. Use common sense and practice good hygiene.

If you become aware of an unusual and suspicious substance nearby:

- Move away quickly.
- Wash with soap and water.
- Contact authorities.
- Listen to the media for official instructions.
- Seek medical attention if you become sick.

If you are exposed to a biological agent:

- Remove and bag your clothes and personal items. Follow official instructions for disposal of contaminated items.
- Wash yourself with soap and water and put on clean clothes.
- Seek medical assistance. You may be advised to stay away from others or even quarantined.

Using HEPA Filters. HEPA filters are useful in biological attacks. If you have a central heating and cooling system in your home with a HEPA filter, leave it on if it is running or turn the fan on if it is not running. Moving the air in the house through the filter will help remove the agents from the air. If you have a portable HEPA filter, take it with you to the internal room where you are seeking shelter and turn it on.

If you are in an apartment or office building that has a modern, central heating and cooling system, the system's filtration should provide a relatively safe level of protection from outside biological contaminants.

HEPA filters will not filter chemical agents.

After a Biological Attack. In some situations, such as the case of the anthrax letters sent in 2001, people may be alerted to potential exposure. If this is the case, pay close attention to all official warnings and instructions on how to proceed. The delivery of medical services for a biological event may be handled differently to respond to increased demand. The basic public health procedures and medical protocols for handling exposure to biological agents are the same as for any infectious disease. It is important for you to pay attention to official instructions via radio, television, and emergency alert systems.

Chemical Threats

Chemical agents are poisonous vapors, aerosols, liquids, and solids that have toxic effects on people, animals, or plants. They can be released by bombs or sprayed from aircraft, boats, and vehicles. They can be used as a liquid to create a hazard to people and the environment. Some chemical agents may be odorless and tasteless. They can have an immediate effect (a few seconds to a few minutes) or a delayed effect (2 to 48 hours). While potentially lethal, chemical agents are difficult to deliver in lethal concentrations. Outdoors, the agents often dissipate rapidly. Chemical agents also are difficult to produce.

A chemical attack could come without warning. Signs of a chemical release include people having difficulty breathing; experiencing eye irritation; losing coordination; becoming nauseated; or having a burning sensation in the nose, throat, and lungs. Also, the presence of many dead insects or birds may indicate a chemical agent release.

Before a Chemical Attack. Check your disaster supplies kit to make sure it includes:

- A roll of duct tape and scissors.
- Plastic for doors, windows, and vents for the room in which you will shelter in place. To save critical time during an emergency, pre-measure and cut the plastic sheeting for each opening.
- Choose an internal room to shelter, preferably one without windows and on the highest level.

During a Chemical Attack. If you are instructed to remain in your home or office building, you should:

- Close doors and windows and turn off all ventilation, including furnaces, air conditioners, vents, and fans.
- Seek shelter in an internal room and take your disaster supplies kit.
- Seal the room with duct tape and plastic sheeting.
- Listen to your radio for instructions from authorities.

If you are caught in or near a contaminated area, you should:

- Move away immediately in a direction upwind of the source.
- Find shelter as quickly as possible.

After a Chemical Attack. Decontamination is needed within minutes of exposure to minimize health consequences. Do not leave the safety of a shelter to go outdoors to help others until authorities announce it is safe to do so.

A person affected by a chemical agent requires immediate medical attention from a professional. If medical help is not immediately available, decontaminate yourself and assist in decontaminating others.

Decontamination guidelines are as follows:

- Use extreme caution when helping others who have been exposed to chemical agents.
- Remove all clothing and other items in contact with the body. Contaminated clothing normally removed over the head should be cut off to avoid contact with the eyes, nose, and mouth. Put contaminated clothing and items into a plastic bag and seal it. Decontaminate hands using soap and water. Remove eyeglasses or contact lenses. Put glasses in a pan of household bleach to decontaminate them, and then rinse and dry.
- Flush eyes with water.
- Gently wash face and hair with soap and water before thoroughly rinsing with water.
- Decontaminate other body areas likely to have been contaminated. Blot (do not swab or scrape) with a cloth soaked in soapy water and rinse with clear water.
- Change into uncontaminated clothes. Clothing stored in drawers or closets is likely to be uncontaminated.
- Proceed to a medical facility for screening and professional treatment.

Nuclear Blast

A nuclear blast is an explosion with intense light and heat, a damaging pressure wave, and widespread radioactive material that can contaminate the air, water, and ground surfaces for miles around. A nuclear device can range from a weapon carried by an intercontinental missile launched by a hostile nation or terrorist organization, to a small portable nuclear device transported by an individual. All nuclear devices cause deadly effects when exploded, including blinding light, intense heat (thermal radiation), initial nuclear radiation, blast, fires started by the heat pulse, and secondary fires caused by the destruction.

Hazards of Nuclear Devices. The extent, nature, and arrival time of these hazards are difficult to predict. The geographical dispersion of hazard effects will be defined by the following:

- Size of the device. A more powerful bomb will produce more distant effects.
- Height above the ground the device was detonated. This will determine the extent of blast effects.
- Nature of the surface beneath the explosion. Some materials are more likely to become radioactive and airborne than others. Flat areas are more susceptible to blast effects.
- Existing meteorological conditions. Wind speed and direction will affect arrival time of fallout; precipitation may wash fallout from the atmosphere.

Radioactive Fallout. Even if individuals are not close enough to the nuclear blast to be affected by the direct impacts, they may be affected by radioactive fallout. Any nuclear blast results in some fallout. Blasts that occur near the earth's surface create much greater amounts of fallout than blasts that occur at higher altitudes. This is because the tremendous heat produced from a nuclear blast causes an up-draft of air that forms the familiar mushroom cloud. When a blast occurs near the earth's surface, millions of vaporized dirt particles also are drawn into the cloud. As the heat diminishes, radioactive materials that have vaporized condense on the particles and fall back to the earth. The phenomenon is called radioactive fallout. This fallout material decays over a long period of time, and is the main source of residual nuclear radiation.

Fallout from a nuclear explosion may be carried by wind currents for hundreds of miles if the right conditions exist. Effects from even a small portable device exploded at ground level can be potentially deadly.

Nuclear radiation cannot be seen, smelled, or otherwise detected by normal senses. Radiation can only be detected by radiation monitoring devices. This makes radiological emergencies different from other types of emergencies, such as floods or hurricanes. Monitoring can project the fallout arrival times, which will be announced through official warning channels. However, any increase in surface build-up of gritty dust and dirt should be a warning for taking protective measures.

Radioactive Fallout. In addition to other effects, a nuclear weapon detonated in or above the earth's atmosphere can create an electromagnetic pulse (EMP), a high-density electrical field. An EMP acts like a stroke of lightning but is stronger, faster, and shorter. An EMP can seriously damage electronic devices connected to power sources or antennas. This includes communication systems, computers, electrical appliances, and automobile or aircraft ignition systems. The damage could range from a minor interruption to actual burnout of components. Most electronic equipment within 1,000 miles of a high-altitude nuclear detonation could be affected. Battery-powered radios with short antennas generally would not be affected. Although an EMP is unlikely to harm most people, it could harm those with pacemakers or other implanted electronic devices.

Protection from a Nuclear Blast. The danger of a massive strategic nuclear attack on the United States is predicted by experts to be less likely today. However, terrorism, by nature, is unpredictable.

If there were threat of an attack, people living near potential targets could be advised to evacuate or they could decide on their own to evacuate to an area not considered a likely target. Protection from radioactive fallout would require taking shelter in an underground area or in the middle of a large building.

In general, potential targets include:

- Strategic missile sites and military bases.
- Centers of government such as Washington, D.C., and state capitals.
- Important transportation and communication centers.
- Manufacturing, industrial, technology, and financial centers.

- Petroleum refineries, electrical power plants, and chemical plants.
- Major ports and airfields.

The three factors for protecting oneself from radiation and fallout are distance, shielding, and time.

- Distance—the more distance between you and the fallout particles, the better. An underground area such as a home or office building basement offers more protection than the first floor of a building. A floor near the middle of a high-rise may be better, depending on what is nearby at that level on which significant fallout particles would collect. Flat roofs collect fallout particles so the top floor is not a good choice, nor is a floor adjacent to a neighboring flat roof.
- Shielding—the heavier and denser the materials (thick walls, concrete, bricks, books and earth) between you and the fallout particles, the better.
- Time—fallout radiation loses its intensity fairly rapidly. In time, you will be able to leave the fallout shelter. Radioactive fallout poses the greatest threat to people during the first two weeks, by which time it has declined to about 1 percent of its initial radiation level.

Remember that any protection, however temporary, is better than none at all, and the more shielding, distance, and time you can take advantage of, the better.

Before a Nuclear Blast. To prepare for a nuclear blast, you should do the following:

- Find out from officials if any public buildings in your community have been designated as fallout shelters. If none have been designated, make your own list of potential shelters near your home, workplace, and school. These places would include basements or the windowless center area of middle floors in high-rise buildings, as well as subways and tunnels.
- If you live in an apartment building or high-rise, talk to the manager about the safest place in the building for sheltering and about providing for building occupants until it is safe to go out.
- During periods of increased threat increase your disaster supplies to be adequate for up to two weeks.

Taking shelter during a nuclear blast is absolutely necessary. There are two kinds of shelters: blast and fallout. The following describes the two kinds of shelters:

- Blast shelters are specifically constructed to offer some protection against blast pressure, initial radiation, heat, and fire. But even a blast shelter cannot withstand a direct hit from a nuclear explosion.

• Fallout shelters do not need to be specially constructed for protecting against fallout. They can be any protected space, provided that the walls and roof are thick and dense enough to absorb the radiation given off by fallout particles.

During a Nuclear Blast. If an attack warning is issued:

• Take cover as quickly as you can, below ground if possible, and stay there until instructed to do otherwise.
• Listen for official information and follow instructions.

If you are caught outside and unable to get inside immediately:

• Do not look at the flash or fireball—it can blind you.
• Take cover behind anything that might offer protection.
• Lie flat on the ground and cover your head. If the explosion is some distance away, it could take 30 seconds or more for the blast wave to hit.
• Take shelter as soon as you can, even if you are many miles from ground zero where the attack occurred—radioactive fallout can be carried by the winds for hundreds of miles. Remember the three protective factors: distance, shielding, and time.

After a Nuclear Blast. Decay rates of the radioactive fallout are the same for any size nuclear device. However, the amount of fallout will vary based on the size of the device and its proximity to the ground. Therefore, it might be necessary for those in the areas with highest radiation levels to shelter for up to a month.

The heaviest fallout would be limited to the area at or downwind from the explosion, and 80 percent of the fallout would occur during the first 24 hours.

People in most of the areas that would be affected could be allowed to come out of shelter within a few days and, if necessary, evacuate to unaffected areas.

Returning to Your Home. Remember the following:

• Keep listening to the radio and television for news about what to do, where to go, and places to avoid.
• Stay away from damaged areas. Stay away from areas marked "radiation hazard" or "HAZMAT." Remember that radiation cannot be seen, smelled, or otherwise detected by human senses.

Radiological Dispersion Device

Terrorist use of an Radiological Dispersion Device (RDD) — often called "dirty nuke" or "dirty bomb"—is considered far more likely than use of a nuclear explosive device. An RDD combines a conventional explosive device—such as a bomb—with radioactive material. It is designed to scatter dangerous and sub-lethal amounts of radioactive material over a general area. Such RDDs appeal to terrorists because they require limited technical knowledge to build and deploy compared to a nuclear device. Also, the radioactive materials in RDDs are widely used in medicine, agriculture, industry, and research, and are easier to obtain than weapons-grade uranium or plutonium.

The primary purpose of terrorist use of an RDD is to cause psychological fear and economic disruption. Some devices could cause fatalities from exposure to radioactive materials. Depending on the speed at which the area of the RDD detonation was evacuated or how successful people were at sheltering-in-place, the number of deaths and injuries from an RDD might not be substantially greater than from a conventional bomb explosion.

The size of the affected area and the level of destruction caused by an RDD would depend on the sophistication and size of the conventional bomb, the type of radioactive material used, the quality and quantity of the radioactive material, and the local meteorological conditions—primarily wind and precipitation. The area affected could be placed off-limits to the public for several months during cleanup efforts.

Before an RDD Event. There is no way of knowing how much warning time there will be before an attack by terrorists using an RDD, so being prepared in advance and knowing what to do and when is important. Take the same protective measures you would for fallout resulting from a nuclear blast.

During an RDD Event. While the explosive blast will be immediately obvious, the presence of radiation will not be known until trained personnel with specialized equipment are on the scene. Whether you are indoors or outdoors, home or at work, be extra cautious. It would be safer to assume radiological contamination has occurred—particularly in an urban setting or near other likely terrorist targets—and take the proper precautions. As with any radiation, you want to avoid or limit exposure. This is particularly true of inhaling radioactive dust that results from the explosion. As you seek shelter from any location (indoors or outdoors) and there is visual dust or other contaminants in the air, breathe through the cloth of your shirt or coat to limit your exposure. If you manage to avoid breathing radioactive dust, your proximity to the radioactive particles may still result in some radiation exposure.

If the explosion or radiological release occurs inside, get out immediately and seek safe shelter. Otherwise, if you are indoors:

- If you have time, turn off ventilation and heating systems, close windows, vents, fireplace dampers, exhaust fans, and clothes dryer vents. Retrieve your disaster supplies kit and a battery-powered radio and take them to your shelter room.
- Seek shelter immediately, preferably underground or in an interior room of a building, placing as much distance and dense shielding as possible between you and the outdoors where the radioactive material may be.

- Seal windows and external doors that do not fit snugly with duct tape to reduce infiltration of radioactive particles. Plastic sheeting will not provide shielding from radioactivity nor from blast effects of a nearby explosion.
- Listen for official instructions and follow directions.

  If you are outdoors:

- Seek shelter indoors immediately in the nearest undamaged building.
- If appropriate shelter is not available, move as rapidly as is safe upwind and away from the location of the explosive blast. Then, seek appropriate shelter as soon as possible.
- Listen for official instructions and follow directions.

After an RDD Event. After finding safe shelter, those who may have been exposed to radioactive material should decontaminate themselves. To do this, remove and bag your clothing (and isolate the bag away from you and others), and shower thoroughly with soap and water. Seek medical attention after officials indicate it is safe to leave shelter.

Contamination from an RDD event could affect a wide area, depending on the amount of conventional explosives used, the quantity and type of radioactive material released, and meteorological conditions. Thus, radiation dissipation rates vary, but radiation from an RDD will likely take longer to dissipate due to a potentially larger localized concentration of radioactive material.

Follow these additional guidelines after an RDD event:

- Continue listening to your radio or watch the television for instructions from local officials, whether you have evacuated or sheltered-in-place.
- Do not return to or visit an RDD incident location for any reason.

Terrorism Knowledge Check

Answer the following questions:

1. What would you do, if you were at work and . . .
   a. There was an explosion in the building?
   b. You received a package in the mail that you considered suspicious?
   c. You received a telephone call that was a bomb threat?
2. If caught outside during a nuclear blast, what should you do?
3. What are the three key factors for protection from nuclear blast and fallout?
4. If you take shelter in your own home, what kind of room would be safest during a chemical or biological attack?
5. In case of a chemical attack, what extra items should you have in your disaster supplies kit?

Homeland Security Advisory System

The Homeland Security Advisory System was designed to provide a national framework and comprehensive means to disseminate information regarding the risk of terrorist acts to the following:

- Federal, state, and local authorities
- The private sector
- The American people

This system provides warnings in the form of a set of graduated "threat conditions" that increase as the risk of the threat increases. Risk includes both the probability of an attack occurring and its potential gravity. Threat conditions may be assigned for the entire nation, or they may be set for a particular geographic area or industrial sector. At each threat condition, government entities and the private sector, including businesses and schools, would implement a corresponding set of "protective measures" to further reduce vulnerability or increase response capability during a period of heightened alert.

There are five threat conditions, each identified by a description and corresponding color. Assigned threat conditions will be reviewed at regular intervals to determine whether adjustments are warranted.

There is always a risk of a terrorist threat. Each threat condition assigns a level of alert appropriate to the increasing risk of terrorist attacks. Beneath each threat condition are some suggested protective measures that the government, the private sector, and the public can take.

In each case, as threat conditions escalate, protective measures are added to those already taken in lower threat conditions. The measures are cumulative.

Green: Low Risk

- Develop a family emergency plan. Share it with family and friends, and practice the plan. Visit www.Ready.gov for help creating a plan.
- Create an "Emergency Supply Kit" for your household.
- Be informed. Visit www.Ready.gov or obtain a copy of "Preparing Makes Sense, Get Ready Now" by calling 1-800-BE-READY.
- Know where to shelter and how to turn off utilities (power, gas, and water) to your home.
- Examine volunteer opportunities in your community, such as Citizen Corps, Volunteers in Police Service, Neighborhood Watch, or others, and donate your time. Consider completing an American Red Cross first aid or CPR course, or Community Emergency Response Team (CERT) course.

Blue: Guarded Risk

- Complete recommended steps at level green.
- Review stored disaster supplies and replace items that are outdated.
- Be alert to suspicious activity and report it to proper authorities.

Yellow: Elevated Risk

- Complete recommended steps at levels green and blue.
- Ensure disaster supplies are stocked and ready.
- Check telephone numbers in family emergency plan and update as necessary.
- Develop alternate routes to/from work or school and practice them.
- Continue to be alert for suspicious activity and report it to authorities.

Orange: High Risk

- Complete recommended steps at lower levels.
- Exercise caution when traveling, pay attention to travel advisories.
- Review your family emergency plan and make sure all family members know what to do.
- Be patient. Expect some delays, baggage searches and restrictions at public buildings.
- Check on neighbors or others that might need assistance in an emergency.

Red: Severe Risk

- Complete all recommended actions at lower levels.
- Listen to local emergency management officials.
- Stay tuned to TV or radio for current information/instructions.
- Be prepared to shelter or evacuate, as instructed.
- Expect traffic delays and restrictions.
- Provide volunteer services only as requested.
- Contact your school/business to determine status of work day.

DISASTER SUPPLY KITS

The following information is from the Federal Citizen Information Center's *Citizen Guide to Disaster Preparedness* (www.pueblo.gsa.gov/cic_text/family/disaster-guide):

You may need to survive on your own for three days or more. This means having your own water, food, and emergency supplies. Try using backpacks or duffel bags to keep the supplies together. Assembling the supplies you might need following a disaster is an important part of your disaster plan. You should prepare the following emergency supplies:

- Keep a disaster supply kit with essential food, water, and supplies for at least three days—this kit should be kept in a designated place and be ready to "grab and go" in case you have to leave your home quickly because of a disaster, such as a flash flood or major chemical emergency. Make sure all household members know where the kit is kept.

- Consider having additional supplies for use in shelters or home confinement for up to two weeks.
- You should also have a disaster supply kit at work. This should be in one container, ready to "grab and go" in case you have to evacuate the building.
- Keep a car kit of emergency supplies, including food and water, stored in your vehicle at all times. This kit would also include flares, jumper cables, and seasonal supplies.

The following checklists will help you assemble disaster supply kits that meet the needs of your household. The basic items that should be in a disaster supply kit are water, food, first-aid supplies, tools and emergency supplies, clothing and bedding, and specialty items. You will need to change the stored water and food supplies every six months, so be sure to write the date you store it on all containers. You should also re-think your needs every year and update your kit as your household changes. Keep items in airtight plastic bags and put your entire disaster supply kit in one or two easy-to-carry containers such as an unused trashcan, camping backpack or duffel bag.

Water: The Absolute Necessity

1. Stocking water reserves should be a top priority. Drinking water in emergency situations should not be rationed. Therefore, it is critical to store adequate amounts of water for your household.

- Individual needs vary, depending on age, physical condition, activity, diet, and climate. A normally active person needs at least two quarts of water daily just for drinking. Children, nursing mothers, and ill people need more. Very hot temperatures can double the amount of water needed.
- Because you will also need water for sanitary purposes and, possibly, for cooking, you should store at least one gallon of water per person per day.

2. Store water in thoroughly washed plastic, fiberglass, or enamel-lined metal containers. Don't use containers that can break, such as glass bottles. Never use a container that has held toxic substances. Sound plastic containers, such as soft drinks bottles, are best. You can also purchase food-grade plastic buckets or drums.

- Containers for water should be rinsed with a diluted bleach solution (one part bleach to 10 parts water) before use. Previously used bottles or other containers may be contaminated with microbes or chemicals. Do not rely on untested devices for decontaminating water.
- If your water is treated commercially by a water utility, you do not need to treat water before storing it. Additional treatments of treated public water will not increase storage life.

- If you have a well or public water that has not been treated, follow the treatment instructions provided by your public health service or water provider.
- If you suspect that your well may be contaminated, contact your local or state health department or agriculture extension agent for specific advice.
- Seal your water containers tightly, label them and store them in a cool, dark place.
- It is important to change stored water every six months.

Water Treatment

Treat all water of uncertain purity before using it for drinking, food washing or preparation, washing dishes, brushing teeth, or making ice. In addition to having a bad odor and taste, contaminated water can contain microorganisms that cause diseases such as dysentery, cholera, typhoid, and hepatitis.

There are many ways to treat water. None is perfect. Often the best solution is a combination of methods. Before treating, let any suspended particles settle to the bottom, or strain them through layers of clean cloth.

Following are four treatment methods. The first three methods—boiling, chlorination, and water treatment tablets—will kill microbes but will not remove other contaminants such as heavy metals, salts, most other chemicals, and radioactive fallout. The final method—distillation—will remove microbes as well as most other contaminants, including radioactive fallout.

Boiling is the safest method of treating water.

- Boiling water kills harmful bacteria and parasites. Bringing water to a rolling boil for 1 minute will kill most organisms. Let the water cool before drinking.
- Boiled water will taste better if you put oxygen back into it by pouring it back and forth between two containers. This will also improve the taste of stored water.

Chlorination uses liquid chlorine bleach to kill microorganisms such as bacteria.

- Use regular household liquid bleach that contains no soap or scent. Some containers warn, "Not for Personal Use." You can disregard these warnings if the label states sodium hypochlorite as the only active ingredient and if you use only the small quantities mentioned in these instructions.
- Add six drops (1/8 teaspoon) of unscented bleach per gallon of water; stir and let stand for 30 minutes. If the water does not taste and smell of chlorine at that point, add another dose and let stand for another 15 minutes. This treatment will not kill parasitic organisms.
- If you do not have a dropper, use a spoon and a square-ended strip of paper or thin cloth about 1/4 inch by 2 inches. Put the strip in the spoon with an end

hanging down about 1/2 inch below the scoop of the spoon. Place bleach in the spoon and carefully tip it. Drops the size of those from a medicine dropper will drip off the end of the strip.

Water treatment "purification" tablets release chlorine or iodine. They are inexpensive and available at most sporting goods stores and some drugstores. Follow the package directions carefully. NOTE: People with hidden or chronic liver or kidney disease may be adversely affected by iodized tablets and may experience worsened health problems as a result of ingestion. Iodized tablets are safe for healthy, physically fit adults and should be used only if you lack the supplies for boiling, chlorination, and distillation.

Distillation involves boiling water and collecting the vapor that condenses back to water. The condensed vapor may include salt or other impurities.

- Fill a pot halfway with water.
- Tie a cup to the handle on the pot's lid, so that the cup hangs right-side up when the lid is upside-down (make sure the cup is not dangling into the water).
- Boil for 20 minutes. The water that drips from the lid into the cup is distilled.

Food: Preparing an Emergency Supply

1. If activity is reduced, healthy people can survive on half their usual food intake for an extended period or without any food for many days. Food, unlike water, may be rationed safely, except for children and pregnant women.
2. You don't need to go out and buy unfamiliar foods to prepare an emergency food supply. You can use the canned goods, dry mixes, and other staples on your cupboard shelves. Canned goods do not require cooking, water, or special preparation. Be sure to include a manual can opener.
3. Keep canned goods in a dry place where the temperature is fairly cool. To protect boxed foods from pests and to extend their shelf life, store the food in tightly closed plastic or metal containers.
4. Replace items in your food supply every six months. Throw out any canned good that becomes swollen, dented, or corroded. Use foods before they go bad, and replace them with fresh supplies. Date each food item with a marker. Place new items at the back of the storage area and older ones in front.
5. Food items that you might consider including in your disaster supply kit include: ready-to-eat meats, fruits, and vegetables; canned or boxed juices, milk, and soup; high-energy foods like peanut butter, jelly, low-sodium crackers, granola bars, and trail mix; vitamins; foods for infants or people on special diets; cookies and hard candy; instant coffee, cereals, and powdered milk.

You may need to survive on your own after a disaster. Local officials and relief workers will be on the scene after a disaster, but they cannot reach everyone immediately. You could get help in hours, or it may take days. Basic services, such as electricity, gas, water, sewage treatment, and telephones, may be cut off for days, even a week or longer. Or you may have to evacuate at a moment's notice and take essentials with you. You probably won't have the opportunity to shop or search for the supplies you'll need. Your household will cope best by preparing for disaster before it strikes.

Managing Food Supplies

1. It is important to be sanitary when storing, handling, and eating food:

   - Keep food in covered containers.
   - Keep cooking and eating utensils clean.
   - Keep garbage in closed containers and dispose outside. Bury garbage, if necessary. Avoid letting garbage accumulate inside, both for fire and sanitation reasons.
   - Keep hands clean. Wash frequently with soap and water that has been boiled or disinfected. Be sure to wash:
     - Before preparing or eating food
     - After toilet use
     - After participating in flood cleanup activities
     - After handling articles contaminated with floodwater or sewage

2. Carefully ration food for everyone except children and pregnant women. Most people can remain relatively healthy with about half as much food as usual and can survive without any food for several days.
3. Try to avoid foods high in fat and protein, since they will make you thirsty. Try to eat salt-free crackers, whole-grain cereals, and canned foods with high liquid content.
4. For emergency cooking, heat food with candle warmers, chafing dishes, and fondue pots, or use a fireplace. Charcoal grills and camp stoves are for outdoor use only.
5. Commercially canned food can be eaten out of the can without warming. Before heating food in a can, remove the label, thoroughly wash the can, and then disinfect it with a solution consisting of one cup of bleach in five gallons of water, and open before heating. Re-label your cans, including expiration date, with a marker.

   - Do not eat foods from cans that are swollen, dented, or corroded even though the product may look OK to eat.
   - Do not eat any food that looks or smells abnormal, even if the can looks normal.
   - Discard any food not in a waterproof container if there is any chance that it has come into contact with contaminated floodwater.
   - Food containers with screw-caps, snap-lids, crimped caps (soda pop bottles), twist caps, flip tops, snap-open, and home canned foods should

be discarded if they have come into contact with floodwater because they cannot be disinfected. For infants, use only pre-prepared canned baby formula. Do not use powdered formulas with treated water.

6. Your refrigerator will keep foods cool for about four hours without power if it is left unopened. Add block or dry ice to your refrigerator if the electricity will be off longer than four hours. Thawed food usually can be eaten if it is still "refrigerator cold," or re-frozen if it still contains ice crystals. To be safe, remember, "When in doubt, throw it out." Discard any food that has been at room temperature for two hours or more, and any food that has an unusual odor, color, or texture.

If you are without power for a long period:

- If friends have electricity, ask them to store your frozen foods in their freezers.
- Inquire if freezer space is available in a store, church, school, or commercial freezer that has electrical service.
- Use dry ice, if available. Twenty-five pounds of dry ice will keep a 10-cubic-foot freezer below freezing for 3–4 days. Use care when handling dry ice, and wear dry, heavy gloves to avoid injury.

First Aid Supplies

Assemble a first aid kit for your home and for each vehicle. The basics for your first aid kit should include:

- First aid manual
- Sterile adhesive bandages in assorted sizes
- Assorted sizes of safety pins
- Cleansing agents (isopropyl alcohol, hydrogen peroxide)/soap/germicide
- Antibiotic ointment
- Latex gloves (2 pairs)
- Petroleum jelly
- 2-inch and 4-inch sterile gauze pads (4–6 each size)
- Triangular bandages (3)
- 2-inch and 3-inch sterile roller bandages (3 rolls each)
- Cotton balls
- Scissors
- Tweezers
- Needle
- Moistened towelettes
- Antiseptic
- Thermometer
- Tongue depressor blades (2)

- Tube of petroleum jelly or other lubricant
- Sunscreen

It may be difficult to obtain prescription medications during a disaster because stores may be closed or supplies may be limited. Ask your physician or pharmacist about storing prescription medications. Be sure they are stored to meet instructions on the label and be mindful of expiration dates—be sure to keep your stored medication up to date. Have an extra pair of prescription glasses or contact lens.

Have the following nonprescription drugs in your disaster supply kit:

- Aspirin and non-aspirin pain reliever
- Antidiarrhea medication
- Antacid (for stomach upset)
- Syrup of ipecac (use to induce vomiting if advised by the poison control center)
- Laxatives
- Vitamins

Tools and Emergency Supplies

It will be important to assemble these items in a disaster supply kit, in case you have to leave your home quickly. Even if you don't have to leave your home, if you lose power it will be easier to have these item already assembled and in one place.

- Tools and other items:
  - A portable, battery-powered radio or television and extra batteries (also have a NOAA weather radio, if appropriate for your area)
  - Flashlight and extra batteries
  - Signal flare
  - Matches in a waterproof container (or waterproof matches)
  - Shut-off wrench, pliers, shovel, and other tools
  - Duct tape and scissors
  - Plastic sheeting
  - Whistle
  - Small canister, A-B-C-type fire extinguisher
  - Tube tent
  - Compass
  - Work gloves
  - Paper, pens, and pencils
  - Needles and thread
  - Battery-operated travel alarm clock

- Kitchen items:

  ○ Manual can opener
  ○ Mess kits or paper cups, plates, and plastic utensils
  ○ All-purpose knife
  ○ Household liquid bleach to treat drinking water
  ○ Sugar, salt, and pepper
  ○ Aluminum foil and plastic wrap
  ○ Re-sealing plastic bags
  ○ If food must be cooked, small cooking stove and a can of cooking fuel

- Sanitation and hygiene items:

  ○ Washcloth and towel
  ○ Towelettes, soap, hand sanitizer, and liquid detergent
  ○ Toothpaste, toothbrushes, shampoo, deodorants, comb and brush, razor, shaving cream, lip balm, sunscreen, insect repellent, contact lens solutions, mirror, and feminine supplies
  ○ Heavy-duty plastic garbage bags and ties, for personal sanitation use
  ○ Toilet paper
  ○ Medium-sized plastic bucket with tight lid
  ○ Disinfectant and household chlorine bleach
  ○ Consider including a small shovel for digging a latrine

- Household documents and contact numbers:

  ○ Personal identification, cash (including change) or traveler's checks, and a credit card
  ○ Copies of important documents: birth certificate, marriage certificate, driver's license, Social Security cards, passport, wills, deeds, inventory of household goods, insurance papers, immunization records, bank and credit card account numbers, stocks and bonds (be sure to store these in a watertight container)
  ○ Emergency contact list and phone numbers
  ○ Map of the area and phone numbers of places you could go
  ○ An extra set of car keys and house keys

Clothes and Bedding

- One complete change of clothing and footwear for each household member. Shoes should be sturdy work shoes or boots. Rain gear, hat and gloves, extra socks, extra underwear, thermal underwear, and sunglasses.
- Blankets or a sleeping bag for each household member; pillows

Specialty Items

Remember to consider the needs of infants, elderly people, disabled people, and pets, and to include entertainment and comfort items for children.

- For baby
- For the elderly
- For pets
- Entertainment: books, games, quiet toys, and stuffed animals

It is important for you to be ready, wherever you may be, when disaster strikes. With the checklists above you can now put together appropriate disaster supply kits for your household:

- A disaster supply kit kept in the home with supplies for at least three days.
- Although it is unlikely that food supplies would be cut off for as long as two weeks, consider storing additional water, food, clothing, bedding, and other supplies to expand your supply kit to last up to two weeks.
- A workplace disaster supply kit. (It is important to store a personal supply of water and food at work; you will not be able to rely on water fountains or coolers. Women who wear high-heels should be sure to have comfortable flat shoes at their workplace in case an evacuation requires walking long distances.)
- A car disaster supply kit. Keep a smaller disaster supply kit in the trunk of your car. If you become stranded or are not able to return home, having these items will help you be more comfortable until help arrives. Add items for severe winter weather during months when heavy snow or icy roads are possible— salt, sand, shovels, and extra winter clothing, including hats and gloves.

EVACUATION

Evacuations are more common than many people realize. Hundreds of times each year, transportation and industrial accidents release harmful substances, forcing thousands of people to leave their homes. Fires and floods cause evacuations even more frequently. And almost every year, people along the Gulf and Atlantic coasts evacuate in the face of approaching hurricanes.

When community evacuations become necessary, local officials provide information to the public through the media. In some circumstances other warning methods, such as sirens or telephone calls, are also used. Government agencies, the American Red Cross, Salvation Army, and other disaster relief organizations provide emergency shelter and supplies. To be prepared for an emergency, you should have enough water, food, clothing, and emergency supplies to last at least three days. In a catastrophic emergency, you might need to be self-sufficient for even longer.

The amount of time you have to evacuate will depend on the disaster. If the event can be monitored, like a hurricane, you might have a day or two to get ready. However, many disasters allow no time for people to gather even the most basic necessities. This is why you should prepare now.

Planning for Evacuation

1. Ask your local emergency management office about community evacuation plans. Learn evacuation routes. If you do not own a car, make transportation arrangements with friends or your local government.
2. Talk with your household about the possibility of evacuation. Plan where you would go if you had to leave the community. Determine how you would get there. In your planning, consider different scales of evacuations. In a hurricane, for example, entire counties would evacuate, while a much smaller area would be affected by a chemical release.
3. Plan a place to meet your household in case you are separated from one another in a disaster. Ask a friend outside your town to be the "checkpoint" so that everyone in the household can call that person to say they are safe.
4. Find out where children will be sent if schools are evacuated.
5. Assemble a disaster supplies kit. Include a battery-powered radio, flashlight, extra batteries, food, water, and clothing.
6. Keep fuel in your car if an evacuation seems likely. Gas stations may be closed during emergencies and unable to pump gas during power outages.
7. Know how to shut off your home's electricity, gas, and water supplies at main switches and valves. Have the tools you would need to do this (usually adjustable pipe and crescent wrenches).

What to Do When You Are Told to Evacuate

Listen to a battery-powered radio and follow local instructions. If the danger is a chemical release and you are instructed to evacuate immediately, gather your household members and go. Take one car per household when evacuating. This will keep your household together and reduce traffic congestion and delay. In other cases, you may have time to follow these steps:

1. Gather water, food, clothing, emergency supplies, and insurance and financial records.
2. Wear sturdy shoes and clothing that provides some protection, such as long pants, long-sleeved shirts, and a cap.
3. Secure your home. Close and lock doors and windows. Unplug appliances. If a hard freeze is likely during your absence, take actions needed to prevent damage to water pipes by freezing weather, such as:

   • Turn off the water main.
   • Drain faucets.
   • Turn off inside valves for external faucets and open the outside faucets to drain.

4. Turn off the main water valve and electricity, if instructed to do so.
5. Let others know where you are going.
6. Leave early enough to avoid being trapped by severe weather.

7. Follow recommended evacuation routes. Do not take shortcuts. They may be blocked. Be alert for washed-out roads and bridges. Do not drive into flooded areas. Stay away from downed power lines.

Disaster situations can be intense, stressful, and confusing. Should an evacuation be necessary, local authorities will do their best to notify the public, but do not depend entirely on this. Often, a disaster can strike with little or no warning, providing local authorities scant time to issue an evacuation order. Also, it is possible that you may not hear of an evacuation order due to communications or power failure or not listening to your battery-powered radio. Local authorities and meteorologists could also make mistakes, including underestimating an emergency or disaster situation. In the absence of evacuation instructions from local authorities, you should evacuate if you feel you and your household are threatened or endangered. Use pre-designated evacuation routes and let others know what you are doing and your destination.

Appendix: Pandemic Flu: How Safe Are We?

For the past ten years the World Health Organization (WHO) and other international agencies have warned that an influenza (flu) pandemic is both "inevitable" and "imminent."

The warnings were originally issued because of concerns over avian (bird) flu, which emerged in Hong Kong in 1997. Over the next few years it spread throughout Asia, the Middle East, and Europe; over half (56 percent) of the people affected died. In the past few months this highly virulent strain of bird flu has reemerged in the Middle East, Africa, and Europe.

In April 2009, WHO officials traveled to Indonesia to investigate the largest cluster to date of confirmed human cases of avian flu, which could indicate that the disease has mutated enabling human-to-human transmission.

Also in April, the first cases of what was initially called "swine flu"—later correctly identified as novel H1N1 flu—were reported in Mexico.

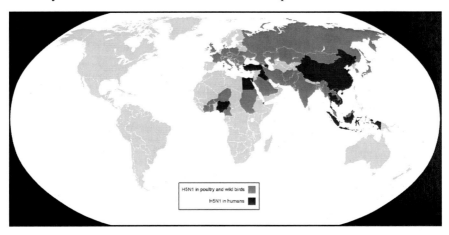

H5N1 in poultry and wild birds
H5N1 in humans

By the end of April, Mexican authorities reported almost 3,000 confirmed or suspected cases and 168 deaths. Thousands of cases were also reported in the United States, Canada, Europe, the Middle East, and the Far East.

As a result, the World Health Organization recently raised the worldwide pandemic alert level to Phase 5—a strong signal that a pandemic is imminent and that the time to finalize the organization, communication, and implementation of planned mitigation measures is short. (Phase 6 is a full-blown pandemic.)

The United States declared a public health emergency and the Centers for Disease Control and Prevention dispatched antiviral drugs, personal protective equipment, and respiratory protection devices to all fifty states. In addition, the federal government and manufacturers began the process of developing a vaccine against this new virus.

WHO stated that although this flu is highly contagious, the symptoms may be less severe than seasonal flu symptoms and older people exposed to earlier flu strains may have some immunity. This would explain why so many young, healthy adults are affected by the new H1N1 flu outbreak.

Scientists and health experts are monitoring both the bird flu and H1N1 flu outbreaks. If the deadly bird flu virus were to mutate with the highly contagious H1N1 virus, the world could be facing the worst pandemic ever.

Influenza pandemics are not new. Three flu pandemics caused public health emergencies during the last century, and experts knew that another was due. The current epidemic of highly pathogenic avian (bird) flu (A/H5N1), now widespread among poultry in Asia, is generally believed to have increased the likelihood of such an event occurring in the near future.

The consequences of an influenza pandemic would be serious, with the numbers of people falling ill and dying being far higher than with "ordinary" winter flu outbreaks.

Being prepared is not only necessary but prudent in today's globalized environment. The global expansion in tourism and the vast increase in air travel can accelerate the spread of infectious diseases, allowing little time to prepare. The rapid international spread of Severe Acute Respiratory Syndrome (SARS) in 2003, for example, provided some valuable lessons in emergency public health protection. This, together with an outbreak of avian flu in Hong Kong in 1997, highlighted the need for countries to develop or improve existing contingency plans.

PANDEMIC INFLUENZA: KEY FACTS

The Disease

Pandemic flu is a type of influenza that spreads rapidly to affect most countries and regions around the world.

Unlike the "ordinary" flu that occurs every winter, pandemic flu can occur at any time of year. Pandemics of influenza have occurred sporadically throughout history—three times in the last hundred years—resulting in many deaths. Pandemics often come in two or more waves several months apart. Each wave may last two to three months.

Pandemic flu is more serious than "ordinary" flu. As much as a quarter of the population may be affected—sometimes more. Pandemic flu is likely to cause the same symptoms as "ordinary" flu but the symptoms may be more severe because nobody has immunity or protection against a new virus.

A serious pandemic causes many deaths, disrupts the daily life of many people, and causes intense pressure on health and other services. Each pandemic is different, and until the virus starts circulating, it is impossible to predict its full effects.

What Causes It?

Pandemics of flu are due to the emergence of a new flu virus that is markedly different from recently circulating strains. Few—if any—people will have any immunity to this new virus. This allows it to spread widely and easily and to cause more serious illness.

Who's at Risk?

Once a pandemic of influenza starts, everybody is at risk of catching it. Certain groups may be at greater risk than others; until the virus starts circulating we will not know for sure who the risk groups are.

Is There a Vaccine to Protect against Pandemic Flu?

Medicines called antivirals can be used to treat influenza. They have been shown to be very helpful in the treatment of "ordinary" flu, and it is likely that they will also be effective in the treatment of pandemic flu, but their effectiveness won't be known until the pandemic virus is circulating. Antivirals do not stop the flu from developing but they do subdue the symptoms and reduce the time people are sick.

There is no vaccine ready to protect against pandemic flu. A vaccine to protect against pandemic flu cannot be made until the new virus has been identified. Before a pandemic starts it is difficult to predict what strain will cause it and even then, predictions may prove wrong. Also, the new virus may have changed enough for a pre-prepared vaccine to be ineffective.

"Ordinary" flu vaccines will not protect against pandemic flu. But "ordinary" flu can be serious, so it is very important that everyone who is due an "ordinary" flu vaccine has one.

What Is Being Done to Prepare for a Flu Pandemic?

The government has prepared a pandemic contingency plan that will be put into action in the event of a pandemic. The plan includes initiatives to improve our preparedness now, before another pandemic occurs.

The government is building up its stocks of antiviral drugs. They will be used in the most effective way to treat those most at risk of serious illness based on how the disease develops.

The government is taking steps to be in the best possible position for a vaccine to be manufactured as rapidly as possible when a pandemic virus is identified. Manufacture is still likely to take several months and vaccine will not be available at the start of a new pandemic.

What Can I Do?

You can reduce, but not eliminate, the risk of catching or spreading influenza during a pandemic by:

- Covering your nose and mouth when coughing or sneezing, using a tissue when possible
- Disposing of dirty tissues promptly and carefully
- Avoiding nonessential travel and large crowds whenever possible
- Maintaining good basic hygiene, for example washing your hands frequently with soap and water to reduce the spread of the virus from your hands to your face, or to other people
- Cleaning hard surfaces (e.g., kitchen counters, door handles) frequently using a normal cleaning product
- Making sure your children follow this advice

If you do catch flu:

- Stay at home and rest.
- Take medicines such as aspirin, ibuprofen, or paracetamol to relieve the symptoms (following the instructions with the medicines).
- Children under sixteen must not be given aspirin or ready-made flu remedies containing aspirin.
- Drink plenty of fluids.

WHAT IS PANDEMIC FLU?

Flu pandemics are global epidemics of a newly emerged strain of flu to which most people have little or no immunity. Much of our understanding of pandemic flu comes from the experience of three major flu pandemics last century, the first and worst of which killed an estimated 20 to 50 million people worldwide—more lives lost than during World War I. As history has shown, pandemic flu differs from "ordinary" flu in important ways. For example, "ordinary" flu occurs seasonally, allowing us time to identify the virus and administer a vaccine in advance, whereas pandemic flu can occur at any time, allowing no time for a vaccine to be prepared because the virus is completely new. "Ordinary" flu most seriously affects the elderly and vulnerable groups, while pandemic flu can affect people of any age. These differences strongly influence the way in which we respond to pandemic flu.

Being Prepared

Immunization—having the flu vaccine—is the principal countermeasure in protecting people from influenza. However, a vaccine for pandemic flu is unlikely to be available in the early stages of the pandemic since its development can only begin once the virus has been identified. Antiviral drugs, the second major tool in pandemic flu control, are likely to be effective in reducing the seriousness of the illness. However, it is impossible to measure their efficacy until the virus is circulating, and there is some concern that the virus could develop resistance. Antivirals are also costly and have a limited shelf life of five years.

Why should we worry about avian (bird) and the novel H1N1 flu? Evidence suggests that recent pandemic flu viruses originated in birds. During the last few years, the world has faced several threats with pandemic potential—principally from outbreaks of avian flu. Many experts believe that the outbreak of highly pathogenic avian flu (A/H5N1) in Hong Kong in 1997 in which eighteen people were infected, six of whom died, could have led to a pandemic, if it weren't for the prompt destruction of Hong Kong's entire poultry population—almost 1.5 million chickens. The current outbreak of highly pathogenic avian flu (A/H5N1), which has affected poultry in numerous countries in Asia, the Middle East, Africa, and Europe, and has to date infected 207 people, of whom 115 have died, has brought the threat of pandemic flu close again. The less virulent novel H1N1 flu has already shown it has pandemic potential.

While it is unlikely that a pandemic flu virus will originate in the United States, no country is exempt from risk. Once a pandemic virus emerges, we will probably not be able to prevent its global spread; but by being prepared we can significantly reduce its impact. How severe the next pandemic will be, who will be most at risk, and how many people will be affected cannot be predicted with any certainty. The scale and severity of illness associated with previous pandemics have varied; we can assume, however, that they will be of greater magnitude than even the most severe epidemic of "ordinary" flu. Experts predict anything between 2 million and 50 million deaths globally.

What we do know is that pandemic viruses spread rapidly. During the pandemics of 1957 and 1968, the viruses took only three to four months to spread from southeast Asia—where they were first identified—to Europe and North America. The intercontinental spread of Severe Acute Respiratory Syndrome (SARS) in 2003 was even faster. Within four months of the global alert, more than eight thousand people had been affected in thirty countries across six continents, and nine hundred people had died. The expansion of international air travel is likely to make the spread of pandemic flu just as rapid. All these experiences indicate that once a pandemic flu strain has been identified as causing illness in one country, it will be too late to begin planning.

The old adage "forewarned is forearmed" has particular resonance as we face this potential risk to global public health. The timing and the precise impact of another flu pandemic may not be clear but by preparing for every eventuality now, before it occurs, we stand the best chance of reducing its impact. Even with good planning and preparation though, the consequences of pandemic flu would still be very serious.

What Is Influenza or Flu?

Flu is an illness resulting from infection by an influenza virus. It is highly infectious and can spread easily from person to person. Because the flu virus constantly changes there are many different strains of flu. Some are more infectious and cause more severe illness than others.

Symptoms. People are affected by flu with varying degrees of severity, ranging from minor symptoms to pneumonia and death. Symptoms are generally of sudden onset and include:

- Fever
- Cough
- Headache
- Severe weakness and fatigue
- Aching muscles and joints
- Sore throat
- Runny nose

The symptoms of pandemic flu are similar to "ordinary" seasonal flu. However, in the case of pandemic flu, these symptoms are likely to be worse, resulting in more severe illness and possibly death.

How Flu Spreads. Influenza viruses are easily passed from person to person when an infected person talks, coughs, or sneezes and expels the virus into the air. You can also catch it through touching an infected person or surface contaminated with the virus, and then touching your, or another person's, face.

Flu viruses have an incubation period—the time a person is infected with flu before showing symptoms—of one to three days.

Adults are likely to be infectious from just before symptoms develop until four to five days after the onset of symptoms. Children, however, tend to be infectious for longer (typically up to seven days).

Different Types of Flu Virus. Flu viruses are divided into three main groups: influenza A, B, and C. Type A viruses are the source of most "ordinary" flu epidemics and have caused all previous pandemics. Whereas influenza B and C viruses infect humans only, influenza A viruses also infect birds and other animals such as pigs. This unique ability to jump the species barrier enables influenza A viruses to cause pandemics.

What Causes Pandemic Flu?

Some of the commonest infections have a particular ability to change, influenza viruses being the chameleons of the microbial world.

Flu viruses have a particular characteristic that enables them to cause annual epidemics and even pandemics: change. Type A viruses undergo frequent changes in their surface antigens or proteins. These changes can be minor (known as antigenic drift) or major (known as antigenic shift).

Antigenic Drift: "Ordinary" Flu. Antigenic drift occurs constantly among influenza A viruses, resulting in the emergence of new strains every year. These new strains cause the annual flu epidemics we experience each winter. Some annual flu epidemics are worse than others. This happens when the new strains are significantly different from previous strains. The more a strain differs from previous ones, the less immunity a population will have to it.

Antigenic Shift: Pandemic Flu. Occasionally major changes occur in the surface antigens (proteins) of influenza A viruses. These changes are much more significant than those associated with antigenic drift. Such changes can lead to the emergence of a pandemic strain by creating a virus that is different from recently circulating strains. The population would have very little or no immunity to it—since they will not have been infected with it or vaccinated against it before. This lack of immunity allows the virus to spread more rapidly and more widely than an "ordinary" flu virus.

Antigenic shift usually occurs in two ways: either as a sudden "adaptive" change during replication of a normal virus, or from an exchange of genes between a human strain of an influenza A virus and an animal strain. This genetic exchange or "reassortment" produces a new virus capable of causing a pandemic in humans. Genetic exchange occurs when an animal becomes infected with a human and an animal flu virus at the same time—so-called "coinfection." The animal in which this genetic exchange takes place is often described as a "mixing vessel." The domestic pig is a likely "mixing vessel" because it is susceptible to both human and avian (bird) flu. However, more recently experts fear that people may also serve as "mixing vessels."

This possibility that people could act as "mixing vessels" has caused particular concern in the context of the highly pathogenic avian flu (A/H5N1) currently circulating in Asia. This strain of avian flu has demonstrated the ability to infect people. Experts fear that people infected with avian flu could also become infected with a human flu strain at the same time, allowing the exchange of genes that could lead to the emergence of a pandemic strain. Alternatively, the avian flu strain could evolve into a pandemic strain simply by readapting to the human body, thereby acquiring the ability to pass easily from person to person.

The Differences between "Ordinary" Flu and Pandemic Flu

There are important differences between "ordinary" flu and pandemic flu. These differences explain why we regard pandemic flu as such a serious threat. Epidemics of "ordinary" flu occur every year around the world. An epidemic is a widespread outbreak of disease in a single community, population, or region. A pandemic, on the other hand, spreads around the world affecting many hundreds of thousands of people across many countries. The word pandemic comes from the Greek words *pan*, meaning "all," and *demos*, meaning "people." Other diseases of pandemic proportions include HIV/AIDS and tuberculosis.

Key Characteristics of Pandemic Flu

There are a number of key characteristics that experts look for when deciding whether or not a particular flu virus is a potentially pandemic strain.

For an influenza virus to be capable of causing a pandemic, it must be able to:

- Infect people (not just other mammals and birds)
- Cause illness in a high proportion of those infected
- Spread easily from person to person
- Spread widely because the virus is significantly different from previously circulating strains and most people will have little or no immunity to it

All previous flu pandemics exhibited these characteristics.

"Ordinary" Flu

"Ordinary" flu occurs every year during the winter months in the United States. It affects 5 percent to 20 percent of the population, causing around thirty-six thousand deaths every year. Globally, epidemics of "ordinary" flu are thought to kill between five hundred thousand and 1 million people every year. Most people recover from "ordinary" flu within one or two weeks without requiring medical treatment. Deaths are generally confined to "at risk" groups, including elderly people over sixty-five years of age; people with existing medical conditions such as lung diseases, diabetes, cancer, and kidney or heart problems; people whose immune systems are compromised due to HIV/AIDS or because they have a transplant; and for example the very young.

The vaccine against "ordinary" flu is effective because the virus strain in circulation each winter can be fairly reliably predicted. Annual vaccination, when the correct virus strain is fairly reliably predicted, and antiviral drugs are available for those at risk of becoming seriously ill.

Pandemic Flu

Pandemics have occurred sporadically throughout history and can take place in any season. They affect many more people than "ordinary" flu—a quarter or more of the population—and are associated with much higher rates of illness and death. For example, the worst flu pandemic in the last century—the 1918 "Spanish flu"—caused around 40 million deaths worldwide.

Pandemic flu, usually associated with a higher severity of illness and consequently a higher risk of death, represents a much more serious infection than "ordinary" flu. People of all age groups may be at risk of infection with pandemic flu, not just "at risk" groups.

A vaccine against pandemic flu will not be available at the start of a pandemic. This is because the virus strain will be completely new. It will be different from the viruses that circulated the previous winter, and not predictable in the same way.

Antiviral drugs may be in limited supply, their use depending on evidence of their efficacy, which will only emerge once the pandemic is under way.

Previous Flu Pandemics

Three times in the last century, influenza A viruses have undergone antigenic shift resulting in pandemics with large tolls in terms of both disease and deaths.

Influenza Pandemics

	Spanish Flu	Asian Flu	Hong Kong Flu
Strain	A(H1N1)	A(H2N2)	A(H3N2)
Years	1918–1919	1957–1958	1968–1969
Estimated deaths (global)	20–40 million	1 million	14 million

Using past pandemics to estimate the impact of future pandemics. Most estimates of the impact of a future pandemic are based on extrapolations from previous pandemics. However, it is important to remember that significant details of these events are still disputed, in particular the true number of deaths. Secondly, predictions based on previous pandemics need to take into account the fact that the modern world is very different from 1918, for example: since then there have been considerable improvements in nutrition, health care, and opportunities for interventions. It is, therefore, important to understand that all impact predictions are estimates and that the actual impact of the next pandemic may turn out to be very different.

THE NATURE OF AVIAN FLU

> WHO and influenza experts worldwide are concerned that the recent appearance and widespread distribution of an avian influenza virus, influenza A/H5N1, has the potential to ignite the next pandemic.

> —World Health Organization, December 8, 2004

Avian influenza or "bird" flu is a contagious disease of birds caused by influenza A viruses. All bird species are thought to be susceptible to infection, but domestic poultry flocks are especially vulnerable. In the latter, these viruses can cause epidemics associated with severe illness and high death rates.

There are different types of avian flu, some of which are more serious than others. The "highly pathogenic" form is extremely contagious and rapidly fatal with a death rate approaching 100 percent. Birds may die on the same day that symptoms first appear.

Avian flu occurs worldwide. The current outbreak of highly pathogenic avian flu (A/H5N1), which began in mid-December 2003 in Korea, has to date affected poultry in many countries in Asia and Europe. An up-to-date list of countries with A/H5N1 infections in poultry can be found at the website of the World Organisation for Animal Health (www.oie.int).

> Never before have we seen so many countries so widely affected by this disease, and with such devastating economic consequences, for rural farms and households as well as for the poultry industry.
>
> —Dr. Anarfi Asamoa-Baah, Assistant Director-General,
> Department of Communicable Diseases, World Health Organization

Avian Flu in People

Avian flu viruses do not normally infect species other than birds or pigs. Historically, human infections with avian influenza viruses have been rare and usually mild. However, when the first documented infection of people with an H5N1 avian flu virus occurred in Hong Kong in 1997, causing severe respiratory disease in eighteen people, six of them died. Investigation into this outbreak showed that close contact with live infected poultry was the source of human infection. A/H5N1 emerged again in February 2003 in Hong Kong, infecting two people and killing one. The current outbreak of A/H5N1 began in mid-December 2003 and has so far infected 112 people, killing 57 of them.

Two other avian flu viruses have recently caused illness in people but not on the same scale as that caused by A/H5N1: A/H7N7 emerged in the Netherlands in February 2003, causing mild illness in 83 people, and one death. A/H9N2 also caused mild cases of flu in two children in Hong Kong in 1999 and one child in mid-December 2003.

How Does Avian Flu Spread?

Avian flu viruses spread through poultry flocks either via respiratory secretions or contact with contaminated feces (droppings). A single gram of contaminated feces can contain enough virus to infect 1 million birds. Droppings can also contaminate dust, soil, water, feed, equipment, and clothing. People are usually infected through close contact with infected birds or their feces. Person-to-person spread, if it has occurred, has done so only with difficulty and has not so far resulted in onward transmission of the infection. However, following a meeting hosted by the WHO in Manila in May 2005, experts have expressed concern that human H5N1 viruses are continuing to evolve in a manner consistent with the possible development of human-to-human transmission. At the time of writing, there remains no conclusive evidence that human-to-human transmission has occurred.

Symptoms

The symptoms of avian flu in people range from conjunctivitis to typical flu-like symptoms, which can lead to pneumonia, acute respiratory distress, viral pneumonia, and other severe and life-threatening complications.

How Avian Flu Could Lead to a Pandemic

> WHO believes the appearance of H5N1, which is now widely entrenched in Asia, signals that the world has moved closer to the next pandemic.

> —World Health Organization, December 8, 2004

The current outbreak of highly pathogenic avian flu in Asia known as A/H5N1—unprecedented in its scale and rate of spread—is thought to have significantly heightened the risk of another flu pandemic. Since its emergence in poultry in Korea in mid-December 2003, this strain has infected poultry in countries in Asia and Eastern Europe. Although A/H5N1 has appeared before, the current epidemic of this strain represents a more serious threat to public health. This time it has caused outbreaks at the same time in several countries and is proving difficult to eliminate.

Transmission to people remains relatively rare and in most cases, investigation has identified contact with infected poultry as the principal cause of infection. Although human infections have been documented in only four countries, it seems likely that additional cases have occurred in other countries but have remained unrecognized because of a lack of clinical awareness or diagnostic facilities.

How Could A/H5N1 Cause a Pandemic in People?

Experts fear that A/H5N1 could trigger the next pandemic for several reasons. First, it has already demonstrated an ability to infect people and cause severe disease—one of the key characteristics of a pandemic strain. Second, this particular virus has a documented ability to mutate and to acquire genes from viruses infecting other species. Experts fear that the virus could either adapt, giving it greater affinity for humans, or exchange genes with a human flu virus, thereby producing a completely novel virus capable of spreading easily between people, and causing a pandemic.

The continued spread of A/H5N1 in birds increases the opportunities for direct infection of people. If more people become infected over time, the likelihood also increases that, if they are concurrently infected with human and avian influenza strains, they could serve as the "mixing vessel" for the emergence of a novel subtype virus with sufficient human genes to be easily transmitted from person to person. Such an event could mark the start of an influenza pandemic. However, the likelihood of this mutation occurring is not easy to predict.

Person-to-Person Transmission

Human infection with A/H5N1 has been rare up to now. The virus has not acquired the ability to pass easily from person to person. Should it acquire this characteristic, it would meet all the criteria of a pandemic flu strain.

While there have been instances of possible person-to-person transmission, so far these have been isolated occurrences. Person-to-person transmission must be efficient and sustainable if the virus is to become capable of causing a pandemic. In other words, there must be a sustained chain of transmission causing communitywide outbreaks.

To date, investigators have not been able to prove the occurrence of person-to-person transmission. However, the pattern of disease appears to have changed in a way that makes the development of person-to-person transmission possible. At the WHO inter-country consultation in Manila in May 2005, experts concluded that the viruses are "continuing to evolve and pose a continuing and potentially growing pandemic threat."

Why Is A/H5N1 Difficult to Eradicate in Poultry?

The eradication of A/H5N1 in domestic birds is of major importance in pandemic influenza prevention. However, despite international efforts, A/H5N1 has so far escaped elimination. There are several reasons for this:

- *High proportion of poultry in backyard farms.* The internationally recommended measures for controlling infection in poultry (culling, quarantining, and disinfection, for example) are difficult to apply to small rural and backyard farms. Yet in several of the countries experiencing outbreaks, 80 percent of poultry are contained in such situations. In China alone, 60 percent of its estimated 13.2 billion chickens are raised on small farms in close proximity to people and domestic animals, including pigs.

- *Economic significance of poultry production.* Because so many people in the region are so dependent on poultry, important measures such as culling are difficult to implement.
- *Lack of experience.* Since the disease is new to most countries in the region, very little experience exists at national and international levels to guide the best control measures at the country level.
- *Lack of resources.* Several countries with very widespread outbreaks lack adequate infrastructure and resources, including funds to compensate farmers in order to encourage compliance with government recommendations.
- *Scale of spread.* With so many adjacent countries affected, one country's gains in control may be compromised by inadequate control in another.

For these reasons, elimination of highly pathogenic avian flu in Asia is expected to take several years (and may not even be achievable), during which time the possibility that the virus could mutate into a pandemic strain remains.

Is There a Vaccine against Avian Flu?

There are several potential vaccines for protecting humans from infection with avian flu. They are currently at various stages of testing and production. Vaccine manufacturers and institutions working to develop and produce avian flu vaccines are using candidate virus strains made available by WHO for the development of vaccine against A/H5N1. The U.K.'s National Institute for Biological Standards and Control (NIBSC) is one of several organizations worldwide participating in the development of an H5N1 vaccine. Whether these will be suitable for use against a pandemic flu strain derived from A/H5N1 depends on how much the pandemic strain has "drifted" from the A/H5N1 virus currently in circulation in poultry.

What Drugs Are Available against A/H5N1?

There is evidence that recent A/H5N1 viruses respond to an antiviral drug called oseltamivir ("Tamiflu"). This has led experts to conclude that it may also be effective against a pandemic flu strain. However, the efficacy of antiviral drugs in a pandemic situation cannot be known with any certainty until the pandemic is under way.

WHAT CAN WE DO TO PREVENT
OR CONTAIN A FLU PANDEMIC?

It is unlikely that the global spread of a pandemic flu virus could be prevented once it emerges. The emphasis in pandemic flu control is, therefore, on reducing its impact. Several tools help achieve this aim:

• Year-round global surveillance
• Effective and accurate methods of diagnosis
• Vaccines (once they become available)
• Antiviral drugs
• Social interventions

Surveillance

Surveillance is a year-round global activity. Its objective is to monitor the evolution of flu viruses and associated illness to inform recommendations for the annual vaccine, but also to detect the emergence of "unusual" viruses (that may have pandemic potential) as soon as they emerge. The sooner a potential pandemic virus is detected, the sooner control measures can be put in place and the sooner the development of a vaccine can begin. Effective surveillance is vital, not only in detecting the first virus, but also for example, in detecting the first signs of person-to-person transmission. The United States is an integral part of an international network of flu surveillance to which it contributes, and from which it receives, data.

The World Health Organization Global Influenza Surveillance Network. This is an international network of laboratories that provides a mechanism for monitoring flu viruses and detecting the emergence of new viruses with pandemic potential. The World Health Organization network consists of four WHO Collaborating Centers (in Australia, Japan, the United States, and the U.K.), which perform genetic analyses of around two thousand flu viruses each year, and 112 contributing national influenza laboratories in eighty-three countries.

Diagnosis

Doctors usually diagnose flu from a person's symptoms without sending samples for laboratory tests. However, laboratory testing is vital for detecting the emergence of new flu strains, assessing their risk to public health, and monitoring and containing the spread of disease. It can be difficult to distinguish flu from illnesses caused by other respiratory viruses or even bacteria by symptoms alone. There are two methods for confirming the presence of flu infection:

- Laboratory tests, the most common method for diagnosing flu. Samples from swabs taken from the nose and throat are sent to a laboratory for analysis.
- Rapid "near patient" tests, which have recently become available and can detect the presence of flu within thirty minutes. However, they cannot provide the information required to determine which specific virus is causing the infection—for example, whether it is a novel virus or whether human cases are caused by the same virus, indicating possible person-to-person transmission.

Vaccines

Vaccination is the mainstay of seasonal influenza control. However, vaccines may not be available during the early stages of a pandemic.

How do vaccines work? Vaccines are biological agents that stimulate the body to produce antibodies or other immunity. These antibodies are designed to protect the body from the strains of the virus contained in the vaccine. On exposure to the flu virus, the antibodies help prevent infection or reduce the severity of illness.

Generally, vaccines reduce infection by around 70 to 80 percent, hospitalizations in high-risk individuals by around 60 percent, and deaths by around 40 percent.

Vaccination against "ordinary" flu. Every year, a new vaccine must be developed to protect against the three most prevalent influenza virus strains likely to be circulating that winter. In the United States, vaccination is recommended for those most at risk of serious illness from flu. Vaccination is also offered to health care workers involved in direct patient care. The effectiveness of the vaccine depends on how well the vaccine strains match the circulating strains. The World Health Organization Global Influenza Surveillance Network decides which virus strains are likely to be circulating during the forthcoming flu season and should be covered by the vaccine. The strains in the vaccine are chosen to match as closely as possible the most virulent strains in circulation.

Vaccination during a pandemic. Vaccines also offer the best line of defense in reducing illness and deaths during a flu pandemic. However, currently available flu vaccines are likely to provide little or no immunity in a pandemic situation (although people who are due for their "ordinary" annual flu vaccine should still have one). A new vaccine must be developed to match the pandemic strain of virus. This work can only begin once that strain has been identified, although preparatory work can shorten the lead time in production.

This means that:

- Once a pandemic virus has been identified, even with the preparatory work under way, it will probably take around four to six months to produce a vaccine, possibly longer.
- Vaccines are unlikely to be available during the early stages of a pandemic and even then will not offer 100 percent protection.
- When a vaccine is available, the aim will be to immunize the whole population as quickly as possible as vaccine supplies increase.
- Manufacturers will not be able to produce enough vaccines to immunize everyone immediately. This means that vaccines will be given to some high-priority groups of people before others.

Why will there not be enough vaccines immediately? Another constraint to ensuring sufficient vaccine supply during a pandemic is current manufacturing capacity, which is based on the annual use of influenza vaccines for targeted population groups. A vaccine cannot be produced until the virus strain is known. It is likely to take four to six months before quantities of vaccine will become available, and then over a period of time. Discussions continue at the international and national level on how to boost vaccine production in the event of a pandemic.

Second, it is likely that in a pandemic situation two doses of the vaccine will be required rather than one.

Antiviral Drugs

Medicines known as antivirals active against flu are the only other major medical countermeasure available. They may be used in the absence of, or as an adjunct to, vaccination.

How do antiviral drugs work? Antiviral drugs work by preventing the flu virus from reproducing. For treatment, they must be taken within forty-eight hours of the onset of symptoms in order to be effective. Treatment at this stage can shorten illness by around a day and reduce hospitalizations by an estimated 50 percent. They must then be taken either before, or within forty-eight hours of, exposure.

Antiviral drugs are normally recommended to treat people more at risk of serious illness, but during a pandemic different criteria will almost certainly apply.

Antiviral drugs for pandemic flu. Antiviral drugs are likely to have an important role in the prevention and treatment of pandemic flu, especially when sufficient vaccine supplies are not available. However, it is important to note the following:

- The effectiveness of antiviral drugs in a pandemic and in particular in reducing mortality in cases of severe disease is not known.
- It is recommended that antiviral drugs should be given to treat those at risk of serious illness. However, until the pandemic is under way, we cannot say for certain who will benefit most. The pandemic flu virus may develop resistance to antiviral drugs.

Are there enough antiviral drugs available for everyone during a pandemic? Antiviral drugs are expensive, take time to manufacture, have a limited shelf life, and will be in high international demand at the time of a pandemic. As with other medicines, it will be necessary to use them in the most effective way.

Social Interventions

Nonmedical, "social" or "social distancing" interventions may be important in delaying or slowing the spread of pandemic flu to allow time for a vaccine to be produced.

These interventions are still under consideration and may be amended pending guidance from the World Health Organization and national advisory bodies, and based on evidence acquired during the pandemic.

Personal Interventions. Some basic measures can be taken at the individual level to reduce the risk of infection:

- Respiratory hygiene: covering the mouth and nose with a tissue when coughing or sneezing
- Disposing of dirty tissues promptly and carefully
- Avoiding nonessential travel and large crowds, where possible
- Washing hands frequently with soap and water: reduces acquiring the virus from contact with infected surfaces and from passing it on
- Cleaning hard surfaces (e.g., kitchen counters, door handles) frequently, using a normal cleaning product
- Making sure your children follow this advice

Populationwide Interventions. Other interventions at the national level may also be introduced at various stages during the pandemic:

- Restrictions of mass gatherings: This will probably only be effective early on and could include the prohibition of large international gatherings such as pop concerts and sporting events. It may also include local gatherings.
- Travel restrictions: Travel to or from infected areas may be restricted. However, this measure cannot be enforced. Recommendations on restricting national travel may also apply.
- School closure: Schools may be closed to prevent the spread of infection.
- Voluntary home isolation of cases.
- Voluntary quarantine of contacts of known cases.

Screening of People Entering U.S. Ports. This is unlikely to be effective because of the highly infectious nature of the flu virus. Screening can only detect people who are showing symptoms. Pandemic flu victims may be infectious even before they exhibit symptoms yet would not be detected by port screening systems.

Wearing of Masks. The widespread wearing of masks by the general public during a pandemic is unlikely to be effective in preventing people from becoming infected with the virus. However, they may have some limited use for those already infected with the virus in order to prevent them spreading it.

HOW WILL PANDEMIC FLU AFFECT THE UNITED STATES?

If a pandemic flu strain is causing outbreaks overseas, it will almost certainly reach the United States. Once it reaches our shores, it is expected to spread throughout the country in a matter of weeks, causing much more illness and higher death rates than those associated with "ordinary" flu. This will result in intense pressure on health care and other essential services and disruption to many aspects of daily life.

It is currently impossible to predict when the flu pandemic will begin. It is also difficult to predict its impact with any accuracy. A great deal of uncertainty is associated with estimating the scale of illness, death rates, and the identification of those likely to be most affected.

Scale and Severity of Illness

Experts predict that the global death toll could range from anything between 2 million to over 50 million deaths worldwide. Studies by the Centers for

Disease Control and Prevention reduce that range to between 2 million and 7.4 million deaths worldwide. However, narrowing down the range cannot be done with any confidence until the pandemic is under way. The level of preparedness in each country will also influence the final death toll.

While the precise figures are not known, the burden on health care systems is likely to be considerable. In high-income countries alone (including the United States), which represent 15 percent of the world's population, experts anticipate around 280,000 to 650,000 deaths, 134 million to 233 million hospital visits, and 1.55 million to 2 million hospital admissions. The impact is likely to be more severe in developing countries, whose health care systems are already overburdened.

For planning purposes the World Health Organization advises that national plans be based on a cumulative clinical attack rate of 25 percent, compared to the attack rate of 5 percent to 10 percent associated with "ordinary" flu. A clinical attack rate is the percentage of the total population who become infected and exhibit symptoms of the virus.

Experts predict that the next pandemic is likely to affect around a quarter of the U.S. population with up to 207,000 deaths occurring over one or more waves lasting around three months each. Of the total U.S. population (about 296 million), an estimated 40 million to 45 million people will become ill.

Estimated Deaths and Hospitalizations during an Influenza Pandemic

	Expected Deaths	*Expected Hospitalizations*
Global	250 million	6.4–28.1 million
High-income countries	280,000–650,000	1.55–2 million
United States	89,000–207,000	314,000–734,000

Impact on Health Services. As the above figures indicate, a flu pandemic will place great pressure on health and social services due to the increased burden of patients with flu requiring treatment and the depletion of the workforce due to illness and other disruption. This could mean delays in dealing with other medical conditions, as sometimes occurs during a particularly bad epidemic of "ordinary" flu. Non-urgent work will have to be prioritized during the peak weeks and some work canceled because of pressure on beds, staff, and resources.

Impact on Business. A flu pandemic is likely to affect all age groups, with more than 10 percent of the population likely to lose working days. The U.K. plan assumes that 25 percent of the U.K. workforce will take fifty-eight working days off over a three-month period.

During the peak of the pandemic, estimates suggest that absenteeism will double in the private sector and increase by two-thirds in the public sector.

Schools. Pandemic flu is likely to spread rapidly in schools and other closed communities, leading to potential closures. Schools could also be affected by staff absenteeism and disruption to transportation services.

Services. Pandemic flu will impact all services including police, fire, the military, fuel supply, food production, distribution and transportation, prisons, education, and businesses. All are likely to be affected by staff sickness, travel restrictions, and other potentially disruptive countermeasures.

The civil emergency response is covered by other contingency plans, which will come into effect should they be required. These will ensure the maintenance of essential services, transportation, food distribution, pharmaceutical supplies, utilities and communications, the maintenance of public order, and the role of the police and armed services.

U.S. PREPAREDNESS: THE NATIONAL STRATEGY FOR PANDEMIC INFLUENZA

Material found in the remainder of this appendix was originally presented by President George W. Bush on November 1, 2005, in response to the avian flu outbreak (see nationalepidemicplan.com).

The *National Strategy for Pandemic Influenza* guides our preparedness and response to an influenza pandemic, with the intent of (1) stopping, slowing or otherwise limiting the spread of a pandemic to the United States; (2) limiting the domestic spread of a pandemic, and mitigating disease, suffering and death; and (3) sustaining infrastructure and mitigating impact to the economy and the functioning of society. . . .

Our *Strategy* addresses the full spectrum of events that link a farmyard overseas to a living room in America. While the circumstances that connect these environments are very different, our strategic principles remain relevant. The pillars of our *Strategy* are:

- **Preparedness and Communication**: Activities that should be undertaken before a pandemic to ensure preparedness, and the communication of roles and responsibilities to all levels of government, segments of society and individuals.
- **Surveillance and Detection**: Domestic and international systems that provide continuous "situational awareness," to ensure the earliest warning possible to protect the population.
- **Response and Containment**: Actions to limit the spread of the outbreak and to mitigate the health, social and economic impacts of a pandemic.

This *Strategy* reflects the federal government's approach to the pandemic threat. While it provides strategic direction for the Departments and Agencies of the U.S. Government, it does not attempt to catalogue and assign all federal responsibilities. The implementation of this *Strategy* and specific responsibilities will be described separately.

Pillar One: Preparedness and Communication

Preparedness is the underpinning of the entire spectrum of activities, including surveillance, detection, containment and response efforts. We will support pandemic planning efforts, and clearly communicate expectations to individuals, communities and governments, whether overseas or in the United States, recognizing that all share the responsibility to limit the spread of infection in order to protect populations beyond their borders.

Planning for a Pandemic. To enhance preparedness, we will:

- Develop federal implementation plans to support this *Strategy*, to include all components of the U.S. government and to address the full range of consequences of a pandemic, including human and animal health, security, transportation, economic, trade and infrastructure considerations.
- Work through multilateral health organizations such as the World Health Organization (WHO), Food and Agriculture Organization (FAO), World Organization for Animal Health (OIE) and regional organizations such as the Asia-Pacific Economic Cooperation (APEC) forum, as well as through bilateral and multilateral contacts to:

  ○ Support the development and exercising of avian and pandemic response plans;
  ○ Expand in-country medical, veterinary and scientific capacity to respond to an outbreak; and
  ○ Educate populations at home and abroad about high-risk practices that increase the likelihood of virus transmission between species.

- Continue to work with states and localities to:

  ○ Establish and exercise pandemic response plans;
  ○ Develop medical and veterinary surge capacity plans; and
  ○ Integrate non-health sectors, including the private sector and critical infrastructure entities, in these planning efforts.

- Build upon existing domestic mechanisms to rapidly recruit and deploy large numbers of health, medical and veterinary providers within or across jurisdictions to match medical requirements with capabilities.

Communicating Expectations and Responsibilities. A critical element of pandemic planning is ensuring that people and entities not accustomed to responding to health crises understand the actions and priorities required to prepare for and respond to a pandemic. Those groups include political leadership at all levels of government, non-health components of government and members of the private sector. Essential planning also includes the coordination of efforts between human and animal health authorities. In order to accomplish this, we will:

- Work to ensure clear, effective and coordinated risk communication, domestically and internationally, before and during a pandemic. This includes identifying credible spokespersons at all levels of government to effectively coordinate and communicate helpful, informative messages in a timely manner.
- Provide guidance to the private sector and critical infrastructure entities on their role in the pandemic response, and considerations necessary to maintain essential services and operations despite significant and sustained worker absenteeism.
- Provide guidance to individuals on infection control behaviors they should adopt pre-pandemic, and the specific actions they will need to take during a severe influenza season or pandemic, such as self-isolation and protection of others if they themselves contract influenza.
- Provide guidance and support to poultry, swine and related industries on their role in responding to an outbreak of avian influenza, including ensuring the protection of animal workers and initiating or strengthening public education campaigns to minimize the risks of infection from animal products.

Producing and Stockpiling Vaccines, Antivirals and Medical Material. In combination with traditional public health measures, vaccines and antiviral drugs form the foundation of our infection control strategy. Vaccination is the most important element of this strategy, but we acknowledge that a two-pronged strategy incorporating both vaccines and antivirals is essential. To establish production capacity and stockpiles in support of our containment and response strategies, we will:

- Encourage nations to develop production capacity and stockpiles to support their response needs, to include pooling of efforts to create regional capacity.
- Encourage and subsidize the development of state-based antiviral stockpiles to support response activities.
- Ensure that our national stockpile and stockpiles based in states and communities are properly configured to respond to the diversity of medical requirements presented by a pandemic, including personal protective equipment, antibiotics and general supplies.
- Establish domestic production capacity and stockpiles of countermeasures to ensure:

  ○ Sufficient vaccine to vaccinate front-line personnel and at-risk populations, including military personnel;

- ◦ Sufficient vaccine to vaccinate the entire U.S. population within six months of the emergence of a virus with pandemic potential; and
- ◦ Antiviral treatment for those who contract a pandemic strain of influenza.

- Facilitate appropriate coordination of efforts across the vaccine manufacturing sector.
- Address regulatory and other legal barriers to the expansion of our domestic vaccine production capacity.
- Expand the public health recommendations for domestic seasonal influenza vaccination and encourage the same practice internationally.
- Expand the domestic supply of avian influenza vaccine to control a domestic outbreak of avian influenza in bird populations.

Establishing Distribution Plans for Vaccines and Antivirals. It is essential that we prioritize the allocation of countermeasures (vaccines and antivirals) that are in limited supply and define effective distribution modalities during a pandemic. We will:

- Develop credible countermeasure distribution mechanisms for vaccine and antiviral agents prior to and during a pandemic.
- Prioritize countermeasure allocation before an outbreak, and update this prioritization immediately after the outbreak begins based on the at-risk populations, available supplies and the characteristics of the virus.

Advancing Scientific Knowledge and Accelerating Development. Research and development of vaccines, antivirals, adjuvants and diagnostics represent our best defense against a pandemic. To realize our goal of next-generation countermeasures against influenza, we must make significant and targeted investments in promising technologies. We will:

- Ensure that there is maximal sharing of scientific information about influenza viruses between governments, scientific entities and the private sector.
- Work with our international partners to ensure that we are all leveraging the most advanced technological approaches available for vaccine production.
- Accelerate the development of cell culture technology for influenza vaccine production and establish a domestic production base to support vaccination demands.
- Use novel investment strategies to advance the development of next-generation influenza diagnostics and countermeasures, including new antivirals, vaccines, adjuvant technologies, and countermeasures that provide protection across multiple strains and seasons of the influenza virus.

Pillar Two: Surveillance and Detection

Early warning of a pandemic and our ability to closely track the spread of avian influenza outbreak is critical to being able to rapidly employ resources to contain the spread of the virus. An effective surveillance and detection system will save lives by allowing us to activate response plans before the arrival of a pandemic virus to the United States, activate additional surveillance systems and initiate vaccine production and administration.

Ensuring Rapid Reporting of Outbreaks. To support our need for "situational awareness," both domestically and internationally, we will:

- Work through the International Partnership on Avian and Pandemic Influenza, as well as through other political and diplomatic channels such as the United Nations and the Asia-Pacific Economic Cooperation forum, to ensure transparency, scientific cooperation and rapid reporting of avian and human influenza cases.
- Support the development of the proper scientific and epidemiologic expertise in affected regions to ensure early recognition of changes in the pattern of avian or human outbreaks.
- Support the development and sustainment of sufficient U.S. and host nation laboratory capacity and diagnostic reagents in affected regions and domestically, to provide rapid confirmation of cases in animals or humans.
- Advance mechanisms for "real-time" clinical surveillance in domestic acute care settings such as emergency departments, intensive care units and laboratories to provide local, state and federal public health officials with continuous awareness of the profile of illness in communities, and leverage all federal medical capabilities, both domestic and international, in support of this objective.
- Develop and deploy rapid diagnostics with greater sensitivity and reproducibility to allow onsite diagnosis of pandemic strains of influenza at home and abroad, in animals and humans, to facilitate early warning, outbreak control and targeting of antiviral therapy.
- Expand our domestic livestock and wildlife surveillance activities to ensure early warning of the spread of an outbreak to our shores.

Using Surveillance to Limit Spread. Although influenza does not respect geographic or political borders, entry to and egress from affected areas represent opportunities to control or at the very least slow the spread of infection. In parallel to our containment measures, we will:

- Develop mechanisms to rapidly share information on travelers who may be carrying or may have been exposed to a pandemic strain of influenza, for the purposes of contact tracing and outbreak investigation.
- Develop and exercise mechanisms to provide active and passive surveillance during an outbreak, both within and beyond our borders.
- Expand and enhance mechanisms for screening and monitoring animals that may harbor viruses with pandemic potential.
- Develop screening and monitoring mechanisms and agreements to appropriately control travel and shipping of potentially infected products to and from affected regions if necessary, and to protect unaffected populations.

Pillar Three: Response and Containment

We recognize that a virus with pandemic potential anywhere represents a risk to populations everywhere. Once health authorities have signaled sustained and efficient human-to-human spread of the virus has occurred, a cascade of response mechanisms will be initiated, from the site of the documented transmission to locations around the globe.

Containing Outbreaks. The most effective way to protect the American population is to contain an outbreak beyond the borders of the United States. While we work to prevent a pandemic from reaching our shores, it recognizes that slowing or limiting the spread of the outbreak is a more realistic outcome and can save many lives. In support of our containment strategy, we will:

- Work through the International Partnership to develop a coalition of strong partners to coordinate actions to limit the spread of a virus with pandemic potential beyond the location where it is first recognized in order to protect U.S. interests abroad.
- Where appropriate, offer and coordinate assistance from the United States and other members of the International Partnership.
- Encourage all levels of government, domestically and globally, to take appropriate and lawful action to contain an outbreak within the borders of their community, province, state or nation.
- Where appropriate, use governmental authorities to limit non-essential movement of people, goods and services into and out of areas where an outbreak occurs.
- Provide guidance to all levels of government on the range of options for infection-control and containment, including those circumstances where social distancing measures, limitations on gatherings, or quarantine authority may be an appropriate public health intervention.
- Emphasize the roles and responsibilities of the individual in preventing the spread of an outbreak, and the risk to others if infection-control practices are not followed.
- Provide guidance for states, localities and industry on best practices to prevent the spread of avian influenza in commercial, domestic and wild birds, and other animals.

Leveraging National Medical and Public Health Surge Capacity. Rather than generating a focal point of casualties, the medical burden of a pandemic is likely to be distributed in communities across the nation for an extended period of time. In order to save lives and limit suffering, we will:

- Implement state and local public health and medical surge plans, and leverage all federal medical facilities, personnel and response capabilities to support the national surge requirement.

- Activate plans to distribute medical countermeasures, including non-medical equipment and other material, from the Strategic National Stockpile and other distribution centers to federal, state and local authorities.
- Address barriers to the flow of public health, medical and veterinary personnel across state and local jurisdictions to meet local shortfalls in public health, medical and veterinary capacity.
- Determine the spectrum of public health, medical and veterinary surge capacity activities that the U.S. military and other government entities may be able to support during a pandemic, contingent upon primary mission requirements, and develop mechanisms to activate them.

Sustaining Infrastructure, Essential Services and the Economy. Movement of essential personnel, goods and services, and maintenance of critical infrastructure are necessary during an event that spans months in any given community. The private sector and critical infrastructure entities must respond in a manner that allows them to maintain the essential elements of their operations for a prolonged period of time, in order to prevent severe disruption of life in our communities. To ensure this, we will:

- Encourage the development of coordination mechanisms across American industries to support the above activities during a pandemic.
- Provide guidance to activate contingency plans to ensure that personnel are protected, that the delivery of essential goods and services is maintained, and that sectors remain functional despite significant and sustained worker absenteeism.
- Determine the spectrum of infrastructure-sustainment activities that the U.S. military and other government entities may be able to support during a pandemic, contingent upon primary mission requirements, and develop mechanisms to activate them.

Ensuring Effective Risk Communication. Effective risk communication is essential to inform the public and mitigate panic. We will:

- Ensure that timely, clear, coordinated messages are delivered to the American public from trained spokespersons at all levels of government and assist the governments of affected nations to do the same.
- Work with state and local governments to develop guidelines to assure the public of the safety of the food supply and mitigate the risk of exposure from wildlife.

Roles and Responsibilities

Because of its unique nature, responsibility for preparedness and response to a pandemic extends across all levels of government and all segments of society. No single entity alone can prevent or mitigate the impact of a pandemic.

The Federal Government. While the federal government plays a critical role in elements of preparedness and response to a pandemic, the success of these measures is predicated on actions taken at the individual level and in states and communities. Federal responsibilities include the following:

- Advancing international preparedness, surveillance, response and containment activities.
- Supporting the establishment of countermeasure stockpiles and production capacity by:

  ○ Facilitating the development of sufficient domestic production capacity for vaccines, antivirals, diagnostics and personal protective equipment to support domestic needs, and encouraging the development of production capacity around the world;
  ○ Advancing the science necessary to produce effective vaccines, therapeutics and diagnostics; and
  ○ Stockpiling and coordinating the distribution of necessary countermeasures, in concert with states and other entities.

- Ensuring that federal departments and agencies, including federal health care systems, have developed and exercised preparedness and response plans that take into account the potential impact of a pandemic on the federal workforce, and are configured to support state, local and private sector efforts as appropriate.
- Facilitating state and local planning through funding and guidance.
- Providing guidance to the private sector and public on preparedness and response planning, in conjunction with states and communities.

Lead departments have been identified for the medical response (Department of Health and Human Services), veterinary response (Department of Agriculture), international activities (Department of State) and the overall domestic incident management and federal coordination (Department of Homeland Security). Each department is responsible for coordination of all efforts within its authorized mission, and departments are responsible for developing plans to implement this *Strategy*.

States and Localities. Our communities are on the front lines of a pandemic and will face many challenges in maintaining continuity of society in the face of widespread illness and increased demand on most essential government services. State and local responsibilities include the following:

- Ensuring that all reasonable measures are taken to limit the spread of an outbreak within and beyond the community's borders.
- Establishing comprehensive and credible preparedness and response plans that are exercised on a regular basis.

- Integrating non-health entities in the planning for a pandemic, including law enforcement, utilities, city services and political leadership.
- Establishing state and community-based stockpiles and distribution systems to support a comprehensive pandemic response.
- Identifying key spokespersons for the community, ensuring that they are educated in risk communication, and have coordinated crisis communications plans.
- Providing public education campaigns on pandemic influenza and public and private interventions.

The Private Sector and Critical Infrastructure Entities. The private sector represents an essential pillar of our society because of the essential goods and services that it provides. Moreover, it touches the majority of our population on a daily basis, through an employer-employee or vendor-customer relationship. For these reasons, it is essential that the U.S. private sector be engaged in all preparedness and response activities for a pandemic.

Critical infrastructure entities also must be engaged in planning for a pandemic because of our society's dependence upon their services. Both the private sector and critical infrastructure entities represent essential underpinnings for the functioning of American society.

Responsibilities of the U.S. private sector and critical infrastructure entities include the following:

- Establishing an ethic of infection control in the workplace that is reinforced during the annual influenza season, to include, if possible, options for working offsite while ill, systems to reduce infection transmission, and worker education.
- Establishing contingency systems to maintain delivery of essential goods and services during times of significant and sustained worker absenteeism.
- Where possible, establishing mechanisms to allow workers to provide services from home if public health officials advise against non-essential travel outside the home.
- Establishing partnerships with other members of the sector to provide mutual support and maintenance of essential services during a pandemic.

Individuals and Families. The critical role of individuals and families in controlling a pandemic cannot be overstated. Modeling of the transmission of influenza vividly illustrates the impact of one individual's behavior on the spread of disease, by showing that an infection carried by one person can be transmitted to tens or hundreds of others. For this reason, individual action is perhaps the most important element of pandemic preparedness and response.

Education on pandemic preparedness for the population should begin before a pandemic, should be provided by all levels of government and the private sector, and should occur in the context of preventing the transmission of any infection, such as the annual influenza or the common cold. Responsibilities of the individual and families include:

- Taking precautions to prevent the spread of infection to others if an individual or a family member has symptoms of influenza.
- Being prepared to follow public health guidance that may include limitation of attendance at public gatherings and non-essential travel for several days or weeks.
- Keeping supplies of materials at home, as recommended by authorities, to support essential needs of the household for several days if necessary.

International Partners. We rely upon our international partnerships, with the United Nations, international organizations and private non-profit organizations, to amplify our efforts, and will engage them on a multilateral and bilateral basis. The international effort to contain and mitigate the effects of an outbreak of pandemic influenza is a central component of our overall strategy. In many ways, the character and quality of the U.S. response and that of our international partners may play a determining role in the severity of a pandemic.

The International Partnership on Avian and Pandemic Influenza stands in support of multinational organizations. Members of the Partnership have agreed that the following 10 principles will guide their efforts:

1. International cooperation to protect the lives and health of our people;
2. Timely and sustained high-level global political leadership to combat avian and pandemic influenza;
3. Transparency in reporting of influenza cases in humans and in animals caused by virus strains that have pandemic potential, to increase understanding and preparedness and especially to ensure rapid and timely response to potential outbreaks;
4. Immediate sharing of epidemiological data and samples with the World Health Organization (WHO) and the international community to detect and characterize the nature and evolution of any outbreaks as quickly as possible, by utilizing, where appropriate, existing networks and mechanisms;
5. Rapid reaction to address the first signs of accelerated transmission of H5N1 and other highly pathogenic influenza strains so that appropriate international and national resources can be brought to bear;
6. Prevent and contain an incipient epidemic through capacity building and in-country collaboration with international partners;
7. Work in a manner complementary to and supportive of expanded cooperation with and appropriate support of key multilateral organizations (including the WHO, Food and Agriculture Organization and World Organization for Animal Health);

8. Timely coordination of bilateral and multilateral resource allocations; dedication of domestic resources (human and financial); improvements in public awareness; and development of economic and trade contingency plans;
9. Increased coordination and harmonization of preparedness, prevention, response and containment activities among nations, complementing domestic and regional preparedness initiatives, and encouraging where appropriate the development of strategic regional initiatives; and
10. Actions based on the best available science.

Through the Partnership and other bilateral and multilateral initiatives, we will promote these principles and support the development of an international capacity to prepare, detect and respond to an influenza pandemic.

Hopefully, any outbreak can be contained before it reaches our shores. If not, the above measures should help us mitigate the impact. We all have a role to play and it is critical that you know what you have to do in order to protect yourself, your families, and your loved ones.

Bibliography

AMERICAN MEDICAL ASSOCIATION

Mallonee, S., S. Shariat, G. Stennies, R. Waxweiler, D. Hogan, and F. Jordan. "Physical Injuries and Fatalities Resulting from the Oklahoma City Bombing." *Journal of the American Medical Association* 276, no. 5 (1996): 382–387. Abstract available at jama.ama-assn.org/cgi/content/abstract/276/5/382.

CENTERS FOR DISEASE CONTROL AND PREVENTION/NATIONAL INSTITUTE FOR OCCUPATIONAL SAFETY AND HEALTH

Guidance for Filtration and Air Cleaning Systems to Protect Building Environments from Airborne Chemical, Biological, or Radiological Attacks. Publication No. 2003-136. April 2003. Available at www.cdc.gov/niosh/docs/2003-136/2003-136.html.

Guidance for Protecting Building Environments from Airborne Chemical, Biological, or Radiological Attacks. Publication No. 2002-139. May 2002. Available at www.cdc.gov/niosh/bldvent/2002-139.html.

CENTRAL INTELLIGENCE AGENCY

Chemical, Biological, Radiological Incident Handbook. October 1998. Available at www.cia.gov/cia/publications/cbr_handbook/cbrbook.htm.

FEDERAL EMERGENCY MANAGEMENT AGENCY

Risk Management Series. Primer to Design Safe School Projects in Case of Terrorist Attacks. FEMA 428. December 2003.

Risk Management Series. Reference Manual to Mitigate Potential Terrorist Attacks against Buildings. FEMA 426. December 2003.
Understanding Your Risks, Identifying Hazards, and Estimating Losses. FEMA 386-2. August 2001.

NATIONAL RESEARCH COUNCIL

Protecting Buildings and People from Terrorism: Technology Transfer for Blast-effects Mitigation. Washington, D.C.: National Academies Press, 2001.

USEFUL ORGANIZATIONS

The American Institute of Architects (AIA), Security Resource Center: www.aia.org/security
American Lifelines Alliance: www.americanlifelinesalliance.org
Applied Technology Council: www.atcouncil.org
Architectural Engineering Institute (AEI) of ASCE: www.asce.org/instfound/aei.cfm
Battelle Memorial Institute, National Security Program: www.battelle.org/natsecurity/default.stm
Center for Strategic and International Studies (CSIS): www.csis.org
Centers for Disease Control and Prevention (CDC)/National Institute for Occupational Safety and Health (NIOSH): www.cdc.gov/niosh
Central Intelligence Agency (CIA): www.cia.gov
Federal Aviation Administration (FAA): www.faa.gov
Federal Bureau of Investigation: www.fbi.gov/publications/terror/terroris.htm
Federal Emergency Management Agency (FEMA): www.fema.gov
Federal Facilities Council (FFC) Standing Committee on Physical Security and Hazard Mitigation: www7.nationalacademies.org/ffc/Physical_Security_ Hazard_Mitigation.html
The Infrastructure Security Partnership (TISP): www.tisp.org
International CPTED [Crime Prevention through Environmental Design] Association (ICA): new.cpted.net/home.amt
National Academy of Sciences: www4.nationalacademies.org/nas/nashome.nsf
National Defense Industrial Association (NDIA): www.ndia.org
National Institute of Justice (NIJ): www.ojp.usdoj.gov/nij
National Research Council: www.nationalacademies.org/nrc
Office of Domestic Preparedness (ODP): www.ojp.usdoj.gov/odp
Public Entity Risk Institute: www.riskinstitute.org
Security Industry Association (SIA): www.siaonline.org/
U.S. Army Corps of Engineers: www.usace.army.mil
U.S. Department of Justice: www.usdoj.gov
U.S. Marshals Service (USMS): www.usdoj.gov/marshals

Index

About the Authors

Robert T. Jordan teaches for the Public Affairs Leadership department, Defense Information School, Fort George G. Meade, Maryland. He is an award-winning writer, photographer, artist, and broadcaster. Jordan is an expert in mass communications and strategic planning. A retired Marine Corps major, he also served as a combat correspondent in Vietnam and distinguished himself as the Marine Corps/DoD spokesman in Beirut, Lebanon, in 1983. In that role, he reported the terrorist truck bomber attack on October 23, which took 241 lives. He appeared on *20/20*, *Nightline*, *Frontline*, and *CNN*, and was later the subject of a Bill Moyers special report.

Jordan was awarded the Navy Commendation Medal and the USMCCCA's special Distinguished Performance Award for his service in Beirut. During his other military service, Jordan also received the Bronze Star Medal with "V" for valor; the Air medal with two flight/strike awards; the Combat Action Ribbon with one bronze star; Combat Aircrew Wings; and numerous other personal, campaign, and service awards.

He is the founding president of the Beirut Veterans of America and a life member of the Veterans of Foreign Wars, the Marine Corps League, the Vietnam Veterans of America, and the U.S. Marine Corps Combat Correspondents Association.

Jordan is a former editor of *Homeland Defense Journal* and was a contributing author for *The American War Machine*. His other writing credits include *Flying Tiger* magazine, *Leatherneck* magazine, the *Marine Corps Gazette*, *Sea Power* magazine, *TechTrends*, *International*, *Police Magazine*, *World Market Perspective*, *Defense Electronics*, *Defense World*, *Homeland Defense Journal*, and various newspapers.

Don Philpott has been writing, reporting, and broadcasting about security, civil unrest, and terrorism for almost forty years. For twenty years he was a senior correspondent with Reuters–Press Association, the wire service, traveling the world reporting on major events and trouble spots including Northern Ireland, Lebanon, Israel, South Africa, and the Far East.

He is editor of *International Homeland Security* and former editor of *Homeland Defense Journal.* He writes for magazines and newspapers in the United States and Europe.

He is the author of more than ninety books and is a regular contributor to radio and television programs on security issues. His latest books include *The Wounded Warrior Handbook, Workplace Violence Prevention Handbook,* and the *Education Facilities Security Handbook,* all published by Rowman & Littlefield.

He has produced special reports on *Protecting the Athens Olympics, The Threat from Dirty Bombs, Anti-Terrorism Measures in the UK, The National Guard, Nanotechnology and the U.S. Military,* and *The Global Impact of the London Bombings,* published in August 2009, which resulted in a number of radio interviews in the United States and the U.K.